THE NEW ACTS *of* THE APOSTLES

OR

THE MARVELS OF MODERN MISSIONS

BY

ARTHUR T. PIERSON

SCRIPTURE TESTIMONY EDITION

WALKING TOGETHER PRESS

ESTES PARK · JENTA MANGORO

Published in 2024 by
Walking Together Press
Estes Park, Colorado USA
Jenta Mangoro, Jos, Plateau Nigeria
walkingtogether.press

ISBN: 978-1-961568-30-3

Cover design by D. Thaine Norris
Typeset in Adobe Garamond Pro by Peter Kurdor

1

ABOUT THE SCRIPTURE TESTIMONY EDITION

THROUGH CAPTIVATING tales of evangelism to unbelieving people groups, pioneering gospel work, medical missions, signs and wonders, women in ministry, and even martyrdom, Arthur T. Pierson in *The New Acts of the Apostles* chronicles the ongoing work of God's Spirit in "this modern missionary century" and the similarities to His work in the apostolic age. Most powerfully, this book proclaims the eternal, unchanging nature of Jesus Christ—that He remains the same, yesterday, today, and forever—and His unwavering commitment to building His kingdom and government upon the earth through the agency of imperfect men and women. As you read, you will be inspired and encouraged by these stories that illustrate how the message of salvation continues to spread to all nations, as the Holy Spirit empowers believers to boldly share the good news of Jesus Christ. Pierson makes the case that the same God who worked mightily through the original apostles is still actively working through His people today and is urging us all to take the all-important job of evangelism seriously.

Data science reveals trends and patterns in information. The Scripture Testimony Index is an extensive research project using artificial intelligence and data science to develop a New-Testament driven subject index across a large body of missionary biographies and personal narratives. As the story enthusiasts at Walking Together Press study these books programmatically; beautiful, bright threads emerge—threads of prayer, provision, deliverance, specific leading, healing, transformation, revival, and miraculous conversion. The end result is an index of thousands of short story excerpts organized by subject and Bible verse that empirically demonstrate the truth of the Scriptures, and which is freely available on our website at walkingtogether.life. Another result of this research was the discovery of dozens of great books that are long out of print and in danger of being forgotten. The Scripture Testimony Collection is a set of such books that we enthusiastically recommend, to the degree that we are making the effort to republish them.

Walking Together Press has enhanced this classic title, *The New Acts of the Apostles,* by identifying and marking forty-five portions of the narrative that illustrate specific Biblical topics and verses. An extensive *Scripture Testimony Index* has also been added containing short summaries of how each Scriptural topic is illustrated, making locating specific stories easy. Furthermore, this title is one of many in the *Scripture Testimony Collection.*

DEDICATION.

AS A GRATEFUL OFFERING TO THE MEMORY OF
THE REV. ALEXANDER DUFF, D.D., LL.D.
WHO, BEYOND MOST OTHER MEN OF THIS CENTURY OF MISSIONS,
CONTRIBUTED TO THE NEW CHAPTERS OF ITS MISSIONARY HISTORY;
AND WHO,
HAVING "SERVED HIS OWN GENERATION BY THE WILL OF GOD,"
"BEING DEAD, YET SPEAKETH"
AND, AS AN AFFECTIONATE TRIBUTE TO
THE REV. ANDREW THOMSON, D.D., F.R.S.E.,
OF EDINBURGH, SCOTLAND,
SENIOR MEMBER OF THE DIRECTORY OF THIS LECTURESHIP,
WHO, HAVING PASSED FOUR SCORE YEARS, AT HIS ADVANCED AGE
STILL HOLDS FORTH THE WORD OF LIFE,
PREACHING THE MESSAGE OF THE GOSPEL
AND URGING THE CHURCH OF CHRIST TO GREATER FIDELITY
IN HER MISSION TO MANKIND,
THIS VOLUME IS INSCRIBED
BY THE AUTHOR.

INTRODUCTION.
By Rev. Andrew Thomson, D.D., F.R.S.E.,
Edinburgh, Scotland.

THE DUFF MISSIONARY LECTURESHIP.

THE DUFF Missionary Lectureship was founded by William Pirie Duff, Esq., son of the Rev. Alexander Duff, D.D., LL.D. Dr. Duff was a man distinguished alike by his fine genius, his glowing eloquence, and his Christian zeal—a man whose name, familiar as a household word in many parts of India at the present day, stands in the front rank of those great missionaries who have been incalculable blessings to India during recent generations. When Dr. Duff died on the twelfth of February, 1878, leaving his son, his heir, Mr. Duff immediately proceeded to make arrangements for the establishment and endowment of a quadrennial course of lectures on some subject "within the range of foreign missions, and cognate subjects," as a suitable memorial of the venerable missionary. He was prompted to this at once by filial piety and by the fact that, during his later years, his father had repeatedly expressed a wish that, as a means of perpetuating his influence, a considerable portion of the bequest which he would leave behind him, should be consecrated to this end.

Trustees were appointed to arrange and administer the trust, and these, being selected from the various evangelical denominations, fitly represented Dr. Duff's catholicity of spirit. In the same spirit, it was provided that the lecturer should be a minister, professor, or godly layman of any evangelical church, and that he should hold the lectureship for four years. The course must consist of not fewer than six lectures on his chosen subject, and these must be delivered in Edinburgh and Glasgow during the second year of his tenure of the lectureship, on consecutive

Sabbath evenings in the months of January and February, and re-delivered at such other times and places as the Trustees might direct.

A further condition, binding on the lecturer, was that he should print and publish, at his own expense and hazard, at least one hundred copies of his lectures, which he should distribute free of cost among the Trustees and libraries of evangelical churches and missionary societies at home and abroad, it being understood that then he should be at liberty to publish as many further copies as he might see fit, and the profits of which should belong to himself. In 1880, the arrangements had been completed, and, between that year and the present, four courses of lectures have been delivered, showing an interesting and edifying variety in the particular branch of the great subject treated by the lecturers, but each and all making a valuable contribution to the literature of Christian Missions.

I.

The Rev. Thomas Smith, D.D., professor of Evangelistic Theology in the Free Church of Scotland, was chosen to deliver the first course of lectures in the Duff Missionary Lectureship. Being amply satisfied with his qualifications in other respects, it was felt by the Trustees, as well as by Dr. Duff's own family, that there would be a seemly gracefulness in Dr. Smith's being appointed to lead the van of lecturers, arising from the fact that he had been associated with Dr. Duff in mission work, first in Bengal and afterwards in Edinburgh, for the long period of forty years, during all which time the friendship of the two men had been most intimate and uninterrupted; while, to quote Dr. Smith's own words, "he shared with the universal Church the sentiment of admiration of his gifts and veneration of his graces."

Dr. Smith's lectures were delivered in Edinburgh and Glasgow in the spring of 1880, and were seven in number. His selected theme was Mediaeval Missions, and the lectures were mainly historical and biographical. But when we consider that the mediaeval ages extended over a period of a thousand years, namely, from the fifth century to the Reformation, and that the geographical range of the word included all Europe and even large portions of Asia and Africa, besides; it will be seen that the history of Christian missions, during so many ages and over so vast a space, could only be touched by the lecturer at certain points, and many of them not referred to at all. Nevertheless, Dr. Smith has done much within his narrow limits to increase our knowledge of those periods in which attempts were made to Christianize nations in the mass and at the point of the sword, and when the change effected was, of course, little more than nominal. In almost every page, we can discern evidence that the lecturer knew a great deal more on the subjects treated by him than he was able to compress within the compass of seven lectures. He has done good and permanent service in separating the fabulous from the real, in disentangling knots that had perplexed earlier writers, in shedding additional information at times upon the struggles of light with darkness, and in giving us good reasons for believing that, even in the midst of much error that was mingled on some occasions in what was written, there was sufficient truth to lead anxious hearts to Christ. At times men rise before us in the narrative who were not missionaries merely, but reformers, influencing extensive regions and transmitting their light to succeeding generations; and who, like St. Patrick in Ireland and St. Columba in Scotland, with the sea-girt island of Iona as his centre of action, sending forth his evangelists over wide districts of Scotland to found Culdee settlements and "houses of Christ," did almost Apostolic work, and helped to prepare the way for the glorious Reformation that was to come.

II.

The second of the Duff missionary lecturers was the Rev. William Fleming Stevenson, D.D., minister of Rathgar Presbyterian Church, Dublin, and convener of the Foreign Mission Committee of the Irish Presbyterian Church and Synod. He stood preeminent as a preacher among the ministers of his church, and his position as convener of its Foreign Mission Committee kept his mind in unbroken contact with missions and missionaries. Everything was looked at by him from this sacred centre, and was coloured by it. Nor was this his only qualification; for before the period of his being engaged to be one of the Duff lecturers, he had visited nearly all the great mission fields in the world, especially those scattered over India, and had brought back with him gathered stores of knowledge from many lands, and a heart glowing with zeal and full of hope for the great future which seemed to brighten before him, for India and the world.

He chose as the title of his course, "The Dawn of the modern Mission," his intention being to restrict his lectures to the ages which immediately followed the Reformation, when the Protestant Churches had not yet been fired by the missionary spirit, or become alive to the all-embracing authority of the great gospel commission which included in it every Christian disciple: "Go ye into all the world and preach the gospel to every creature." While individual men, such as Ziegenbalg and Zinzendorf and Schwartz, as if they had been born before their time, did noble work in their narrow spheres, and were as morning stars which foretold the rising of the sun, the Churches themselves were not yet awake. It is not unlikely that Dr. Stevenson hoped to have time and opportunity to record the later history of foreign missions, when the Churches should have awakened to their responsibility, and the dawn of the mission should have passed into the day. But this was not to be. Even his course of lectures on the Dawn of the Mission was never completed. In 1884, he delivered four lectures in the appointed places. And these, in so far as he had strength to give them a full revision, were worthy of himself, distinguished by vigorous thought, comprehensiveness of view, and literary beauty. His finely appreciative and living portraits of the great pioneers of missions whom we have named, and of many others, could scarcely have been surpassed in their rich colouring and felicitous touches by any writers of his day. But death came with its sad interdict, the effect of overwork, and "in the midtime of his days" he was summoned upward. His accomplished widow, who had been "of one heart and soul" with him in all his cares and toils, superintended the publication of the four lectures which he had delivered, under the felicitous title which he himself had chosen. In its incomplete form, the little volume is like a broken pillar, but the pillar is composed of the finest marble and it is chiselled with a master's hand.

III.

Sir Monier Monier Williams, the distinguished Oriental scholar, was the third lecturer appointed in connection with the Duff Missionary Lectureship. His chosen subject was Buddhism. And his first intention was to present in seven lectures a scholarly sketch of true Buddhism. But he very soon perceived that in order to do justice to this form of false religion, which was the faith of so large a portion of the human race, it was necessary that he should exhibit it in connection with Brahmanism and Hinduism, and even Jainism, and also in its contrast with Christianity. And as the subject expanded in his mind, he became more and more convinced that any endeavour to give an outline of the whole subject of Buddhism in seven lectures would be "like the effort of a foolish man trying to paint a panorama of London on a sheet of note-paper." The result of this conviction was that the seven lectures multiplied into eighteen, the greater number of these far exceeding in length the dimension of ordinary lectures which might be delivered in an hour. The literature of Buddhism has immensely gained by this expansion into a massive volume of 563 octavo pages; the parts which formed the lectures which were delivered in Edinburgh in 1888 having been absorbed into the volume.

In a modest and manly preface, the learned author claims for his elaborate treatise an individuality which separates it from those which have been written on the same vast subject by others,—an individuality which, as he says, may "commend it to thoughtful students of Buddhism as helping to clear a thorny road, and to introduce some order and coherence into the chaotic confusion of Buddhistic ideas." The unanimous favourable opinion of Oriental scholars, and the continuous and extensive sale of the book ever since its publication, far more than realized the hopes of the accomplished scholar; while its value and authority are greatly enhanced by the fact that, on three occasions, Sir Monier Monier Williams travelled through the "sacred land" of Buddhism, and carried on his investigations personally in the place of its origin, as well as in Ceylon and on the borders of Thibet.

IV.

The fourth and most recent Duff Lecturer was the Rev. Arthur T. Pierson, D.D., of Philadelphia, U.S.A., whose name is pleasantly familiar to the Churches of Christ on both sides of the Atlantic. The title of his lectures, which form the contents of the present volume, is, "The New Acts of the Apostles; or, The Marvels of modern Missions," and their design was to compare the Christian Church in the nineteenth century with the Church in the first century, especially in their missionary aspects, and to bring out the features of resemblance and of contrast between them. They were addressed in the early months of 1893, to crowded audiences, not only in Edinburgh and Glasgow, but in Aberdeen, Dundee and St. Andrew's, and some individual lectures were also delivered in other places, as in Arbroath. I had the pleasure of listening to some of them, and knowing as I did, that they had been composed by Dr. Pierson while he was occupying Mr. Spurgeon's place in the Metropolitan Tabernacle in London—a task, which of itself would have exhausted and even overstrained the energies of most men—I was astonished at their power, and freshness, and varied excellence. They were as new and fragrant as the flowers of spring. His vigour and originality of thought, his extraordinary knowledge of all subjects connected with Christian missions, his ingenuity and skill in the exposition of Scripture, and in extracting from familiar texts new and unexpected stores of instruction, his inexhaustible command of anecdotes which helped to enrich and enliven his addresses, his power of making external nature pay tribute to spiritual instruction, as well as the glowing fervour of his appeals—made multitudes listen unwearied for hours in hushed silence. I trust that the powerful impressions and healthful impulses, produced by his lectures when spoken, will be equalled in their influence and blessing when they are read, and I am sure that my honoured and beloved friend will own himself to have received in such results his richest reward.

ANDREW THOMSON.

Edinburgh, March, 1894.

x

AUTHOR'S PREFACE.

IN THE winter of 1890, while wandering among the ruins of the picturesque abbey at Arbroath, Scotland, my eye rested upon an old and much worn headstone which had marked the grave of some member of that large family whose name I bear. Along the side of this slab could be distinctly traced the letters, Pierson, and the ancestral "coat of arms" graven upon the stone had not been quite obliterated by the unsparing hand of Time. In presence of such a memorial of my forefathers, I felt like a lad visiting the old homestead where his ancestors had dwelt, and ready, in a filial spirit, to render to dear old Scotland any service asked of me.

One might well hesitate to attempt to fill the appointment to the "Duff Missionary Lectureship;" to follow such men as the heroic missionary, Rev. Thomas Smith, D.D., the seraphic advocate of missions, Rev. William Fleming Stevenson, D.D., and the accomplished scholar, Sir Monier Monier Williams; but, like Franklin at the Court of Versailles, I may say, I come, "not to *succeed* but only to *follow*" those who have gone before me.

To Dr. Alexander Duff, America owes a debt which can never be paid; and the visit of one of her sons to Scotland upon this errand was but a slight acknowledgment of that obligation, a tribute of the gratitude of my fellow-countrymen for that new impulse imparted to missions by that eloquent advocate, who, in the year 1854, visited our shores and set us all aflame with his holy enthusiasm.

By an undesigned coincidence, the opening lecture of this course fell, in Edinburgh, upon the exact anniversary of the death of Doctor Duff, February 12, 1893, fifteen years after the departure of that illustrious man, who was the Raimond Lull of our century.

One of the conditions of this trust is that each course of lectures shall, so far as practicable, be delivered in the various academic centres of Scotland. Hence, I undertook to give the full course in Edinburgh, Glasgow, Aberdeen and Dundee, and three lectures in St. Andrew's also.

Another condition of the lectureship is that the lectures shall, after delivery, appear in printed form. This made preparation with the pen necessary and proper, on a scale more extensive than was available for oral delivery, within the usual limits. In the lectures as given there was a fragmentary and perhaps disconnected character, which, it is hoped, may be relieved by that fuller and final form in which they now appear.

For many years my habit has been to speak not only without manuscript, but without much penwork in preparation. It was perhaps well that the necessity of furnishing material for the press compelled the writing of these lectures; for the theme became so absorbing that, but for this check upon my utterance, the treatment of it, like some of our American railways, might have lacked "solid foundations," "close connections," and "terminal facilities." Even in seeking finally to revise the manuscript for publication, Rousseau's remark seems forcibly verified, that "one half a man's life is too little to write a book—the other half too little to correct it when written."

To make this volume as far as possible complete, I have undertaken, at no little cost both of toil and money, to add to it a Map of the World, which may exhibit to the eye the prevailing religions of the world, with their comparative territory and area, and may also show the progress of the Protestant missions of the world toward permeating and penetrating the habitable globe. In this part of my work I owe especial thanks to my friend, Mr. William E. Blackstone, of Oak Park, Illinois, whose careful research largely forms the basis of this valuable addition to my published lectures.

It would be ungrateful to close this introductory word without acknowledging the many unselfish and untiring efforts of various friends who, in the several places of delivery, so largely contributed to whatever measure of success crowned my humble efforts to demonstrate and to illustrate the essential correspondence between the features of this missionary century and the age of the Apostles.

ARTHUR T. PIERSON.

2320 Spruce St., Philadelphia, May, 1894.

CONTENTS

PART I.

THE NEW LINKS OF MISSION HISTORY

I.

THE NEW CHAPTERS.

God's coin has the mark of His mint, and bears His image and super-scription. When His Son came to earth, though His divinity wore the disguise of our humanity, behind His robe of flesh there flashed upon His breast "the star of empire." And so, when the word of God came in the dress of human speech, it shone with the glory of God.

The manifold uses of the Holy Scripture grow clearer as we study the inspired book. It is the key that unlocks all perplexities. As Arthur Hallam said, it proves itself God's book, because it is man's book, fitting every turn and curve of the human heart. Bengel's motto was: "Apply thyself wholly to the scriptures, and apply the scriptures wholly to thyself." The Son of God Himself found in His Father's word, His sword in temptation, His stay in trial, His guide in teaching; its prophecies were the seals of His messiahship, its precepts the rule of His obedience, its promises the balm for His suffering; through life He had no grander theme, and in death no richer legacy. Modern critics often handle it with irreverent hands, but to Him it was sacred in every part; and Michel Angelo's romantic devotion to the famous torso of Hercules in the Vatican, seeking to feel through touch the thrill of delight no longer granted through his blind eyes, is but a faint image of the divine and holy rapture with which Jesus studied the inspired Scriptures.

World-wide missions present for solution a most perplexing practical problem. Where shall we come for guidance if not to these oracles of God? Over these "pillars of Hercules" is forevermore written, *ne plus ultra*. Beyond this word there is nothing satisfactory, nothing needful. God has magnified His word above all His name, and here are hid all the treasures of wisdom and knowledge.

This principle we seek now to apply to one book of the New Testament, which will be found to be both a history and a philosophy of missions in one. That book is the Acts of the Apostles. Here, what is found in the gospels in precept, is found in practice; gospel teaching as set forth by the Evangelists, applied actually and historically, by the coming of the Holy Spirit.

Luke, who, in the gospel, tells us what Jesus *"began,"* in the Acts tells us what He *"continued,* both to do and teach," by the Spirit, through disciples, as to the kingdom of God. Here, as in the very order of the gospels, the door of faith is successively opened to Hebrew, Roman, and Greek believers. Pentecost links Old Testament prophecy with New Testament history. This is the book of witness: both man's witness to God, and God's witness to man; the sequel of the gospels, the basis of the epistles; not so much the acts of the apostles, as the acts of the Holy Spirit and of the risen Redeemer in the person of the Paraclete.

Here the Spirit is seen, first applying the truth and the blood to penitent believers, then anointing believers for service, then sending them forth as heralds and witnesses to preach the kingdom, to make disciples, and to organize disciples into churches. What meaning is wrapt up in the fact that the period of time covered by this book is only about thirty-three years—the length of our Lord's human life, the average of one generation—as though plainly meant to teach us what may be and should be done in every successive generation, until the end of the world-age itself!

The Acts of the Apostles thus forms one great inspired book of missions: God's own commentary and cyclopedia for all ages, as to every question that touches the world's evangelization.

The opening verses of each gospel narrative show a fourfold completeness and comprehensiveness; and what Bernard calls "a progress of doctrine:"

MATTHEW:	MARK:	LUKE:	JOHN:
"The Book of the Generation of Jesus Christ, the Son of David," etc.	"The beginning of the Gospel of Jesus Christ, the Son of God," etc.	… "A declaration of those things which are most surely believed among us," etc.	"In the beginning was the Word, and the Word was with God and the Word was God," etc.

Thus Matthew links on messianic predictions of the Old Testament to the historic chain of New Testament events, tracing our Lord's human beginning as born of Mary but begotten of the Holy Spirit. Mark starts with His mature manhood, and shows the Divine messenger delivering his message. Luke sets forth an orderly statement of facts and truths held to be beyond dispute by primitive believers. John goes back beyond them all, to the eternity of the Divine Word.

So do the initial chapters of the Acts bear marks of design as the sequel not of Luke's former treatise only, but of all the four accounts which this book follows. It braids together into one their four strands of testimony. In the structure of the New Testament this is the entablature resting upon and uniting the four columns which support it and which it surmounts. Hence, to read this book aright, we must perceive its fourfold character or aspect. It is the book of the advent of the Holy Spirit, and of the generation of the Church of Christ, begotten of the Spirit in the womb of our humanity. It is the beginning of the gospel of the Holy Spirit, the third person of the Godhead. It is the orderly setting forth of the great fact and truth of the Spirit's outpouring, as most surely believed among those who were eye-witnesses of His majestic advent. And it is the first clear revelation of the person of Him who as the Spirit of God was in the beginning with God and was God.

In a word, just what the fourfold gospel is to Christ, the Acts of the Apostles is to the Spirit—the inspired account of His advent, and of the birth of the Bride of Christ; the beginning of the gospel of the Spirit's presence and power; the declaration in order of that supreme secret of all holy living and faithful service, His inward working; and finally, the unveiling of His eternal identity with, and procession from, the Godhead. Truly this book is the Acts of the Holy Spirit.

Thus the advent of the Spirit, and His activity in and through the Church, are the keys which open the doors to all the chambers in this House of the Interpreter. From the first chapter to the last, the theme is the same: the coming of the Spirit, to apply the truth, arouse the conscience, soften the heart, subdue the will, anoint the tongue, and hallow the lip—to take the place of the absent Lord—nay, to make real to believers the promise of His perpetual presence, by becoming to every renewed soul all that Christ would have been had He remained on earth.

Upon one grand fact we lay great stress, and shall recur to it from time to time, that by blow upon blow repetition may deepen impression. This book of the Acts, which is to the Church the *Principia* embodying the great laws and principles for our guidance in the work of missions; this book, which is the history of primitive missions, and like all history is "philosophy teaching by examples," illustrating the practical operation of these laws and principles during one whole generation—this book is manifestly and designedly incomplete, unfinished.

This unfinished character is shown both by its beginning and its close. That "former treatise of all that Jesus began both to do and teach until the day in which He was taken up," implies this *latter* treatise of all that He *continued* both to do and teach after that He was taken up. This introduction stamps this book as a continuance and sequel to a previous narrative, which is necessary to its full interpretation. Accordingly, we are prepared to see Christ in the Acts continuing

His words and works through the Spirit. He who for forty days after His resurrection gave in His personal presence many infallible proofs of the reality of that resurrection, here gives equally infallible proofs of His perpetual presence in the work of the Holy Spirit.

How long will He continue thus to do and teach? So long as He has a believing body of disciples who still go forth into all the world as witnesses bearing His message. The wondrous story opens with the enduement of power, and throughout exhibits its effect in qualifying witnesses for their work: nor is there any hint that this Power ever was, or will be, withdrawn. The narrative stops, but the history goes on. Wherever devout disciples claim in prayer and by faith their full share in that Pentecostal fulness, they may go forth endued with power from on High. Wherever, from that day to this, Christ's witnesses have gone forth in obedience to His word, the same essential marks as in the Apostolic age have attended their service and explained their success.

If now we turn to the conclusion of the Acts, we find a close so abrupt that it suggests yet again a continuance and sequel. The curtain of silence suddenly falls upon a scene of continued action. Paul, dwelling in his own hired house, is still seen receiving all who come unto him, preaching the Kingdom of God, and teaching those things which concern the Lord Jesus Christ. Not only the act, but even the scene, is incomplete. Paul's life is not brought to a close, and his work at Rome is yet going on. Surely this is an unfinished picture; the canvas awaits other touches and tints from the Divine Artist; new scenes in missionary history are to supply new material for suggestion. These last two verses furnish a formula for record for all true witnesses through all aftertime. Change but the name, and the number of the years, and each successive disciple may here find a brief epitome of his life and labour; for whoever, by fulfilling his mission, adds one more unpretending entry to this Apostolic record, belongs to the Apostolic succession. You may think of yourself as less than the least of all saints, yet if, in obedience to your Lord and dependence on His Spirit, you spread the good tidings, to you is this grace given to add and form one more link in that golden chain that reaches from the upper chamber of the Jewish capital to the bridal chamber of the New Jerusalem, and which unites in one glorious succession all in whom Jesus thus continues by the Spirit to speak and work.

We have therefore written intelligently and discriminatingly, in referring to the Acts of the Apostles, as closing rather than ending, for the story comes to no proper conclusion, and is designedly left incomplete. Here is the story of a generation; and no generation ever reaches completeness, but is linked and woven into the next, and its history merges into that of its successor as to-day melts into to-morrow. So, most of all is it in the work of missions. It is so far one work that no eye can trace the point where the mission of one of God's witnesses ends and that of another begins. Paul's preaching and teaching still form threads in the fabric of missionary history, and will unto the end.

But in a grander sense the Acts of the Apostles reaches no conclusion. When the late Bishop of Ripon characterized the thrilling story of the Apostle of the South Seas as the "Twenty-ninth chapter of the Acts of the Apostles," he was but partly right. To that striking remark history adds one criticism and correction: that was a new chapter, but not the *first* new chapter added since Apostolic days. Long before John Williams sailed upon his holy mission, many additions had been made to that unfinished book. Of some of these chapters we have no human memorial: they are written only by the Recording Angel in God's Book of Remembrance, to be unsealed when those other books are opened and read amid the flaming splendours of the Great White Throne. But it is sublimely true that the triumphant advance of that Tottenham lad who became the great witness for the gospel in the Pacific Polynesia, added a new and glorious chapter to the annals of Apostolic Missions. And so far and so fast as Apostolic working and witnessing have survived and revived, so far and so fast have new chapters in the Acts been enacted, if not written. Nor will the age of missions ever end, until this Divine Mission of witness to men is accomplished. And therefore is this book left incomplete, as it always will be while one believer is left to teach and preach those things which concern the Lord Jesus Christ and to fill up that which is behind of the afflictions of Christ in his own flesh for His body's sake,—which is the Church.

Our present purpose, then, is declared in advance. We shall treat the age of Modern Missions, and especially the century of organized missionary activity since Carey led the way, as an illustration of this continuation of the Acts of the Apostles. We shall note some points of comparison, and of contrast between the Apostolic age and our own. We shall look in this book for the clue to some of the intricate, complicated problems of missions, and carefully and prayerfully search to find the secrets of success in world-wide witness.

As both brevity and unity of treatment will be conserved by setting proper limits to this discussion, we shall consider, first, the new Pentecosts and the new openings of doors; then the calling and sending forth of the new apostles; then the new voices and visions; then the new converts and martyrs; then the new signs and wonders; and finally, the new hopes and incentives.

For such a study both the writer and reader may well invoke higher help. There is something unusually solemn in treating such a theme. We are to occupy our minds with the New Chapters in the Acts of the Apostles. Only a spiritual eye can read them: only a spiritual mind interpret them. With no careless hand would we venture to fill out the sacred outlines of missionary biography and history, and, peradventure, add another touch to God's unfinished book. But if that same Spirit who guided the pen of the Evangelist as he wrote this latter treatise, shall deign to open our eyes and direct our gaze, we shall be able to read the records which history has imperfectly written, and gather inspiration for such holy living and heroic serving as shall add yet other chapters in the days to come!

II.

The New Pentecosts.

Owen, in his *Pneumatologia*, affirms that every age has its own test of orthodoxy or apostasy, and that the criterion of a standing or falling Church in this age is found in its attitude toward the Spirit of God.

The gospel age is especially His dispensation. This divine person peculiarly fills the horizon as we study the Acts of the Apostles; and we cannot open the pages of this book of the Acts without starting an inquiry which is first in order and fundamental in importance. What is the actual place which Pentecost fills in Christian history? Was that outpouring both the first and the last, or only the foremost in a series of similar effusions? Was that revelation of the Spirit's power and presence full and final, or was it, like Christ's own advent, but the beginning of miracles and wonders with others to follow? and is that first advent of the Spirit to be succeeded by another, even more glorious, at the end of the age?

Christ's Incarnation was, in fact, a hiding of His true self behind a veil of flesh. His star in the East, seen by a few wise watchers, guided them to his cradle, and a few holy souls who waited for His salvation were not taken by surprise. A little band of disciples felt His charms and bowed to His claims: they saw His glory shine at times when, as in the Transfiguration and Ascension, His disguise was laid aside. In fact, His Baptism, Transfiguration, Resurrection, Ascension, were so many stages of revelation of His glory, which is to be fully disclosed when, at His second coming, the curtain is finally lifted, and the last act in this divine drama completes the marvellous manifestation.

There is a mystery of correspondence between Christ and the Paraclete. Possibly that upper chamber was but the cradle of the Spirit's revelation: other and higher unfoldings and unveilings of His grace and glory are yet to follow; more signal triumphs over Satan; louder and clearer voices and visions of God; new raptures and radiances when devout souls, transfigured in His presence, are changed from glory to glory by the Lord the Spirit, as they with open face behold His supernal beauty. That coming of the Spirit may have been, like the blush of the "conscious water" at Cana, only the beginning of miracles, wherein He showed forth His glory, a type and prophecy of things to come. This question is not one of idle curiosity, but of practical value; and is reverently raised at the vestibule of this theme, because upon our answer all that follows is dependent.

It has been commonly assumed, without Scriptural warrant, that on the day of Pentecost the Spirit was, once for all, poured out, thenceforth to dwell in the individual believer, and especially in the collective body of believers—the Church; and some hold that to pray for the outpouring of the Spirit, either upon saints or sinners, implies absurdity and contradiction, since He is already bestowed upon and abiding in the Church.

To this position exception may certainly be taken. First of all, there is in the way an exegetical difficulty. The inspired Scriptures are marked by an exactness in the use of words which shows that the Spirit guided in language as well as in thought. When Peter quotes that unique prediction of Joel, "I will pour out of my Spirit upon *all flesh*" his words are carefully chosen. He does not say: "Now is *fulfilled* that which was foretold by Joel;" but, "*this is that which was spoken by the prophet Joel.*"

Precision is one mark of perfection, and to perfection nothing is trivial. Matthew's uniform phrase, when he refers to the coincidences and convergences of prophecy and history is, "then was fulfilled," or "so that it was fulfilled which was spoken by the prophet"—often, naming the prophet. But, when referring to Christ's residence in Nazareth, he, for the first and only time uses the plural— "that it might be fulfilled which was spoken *by the prophets*: He shall be called a Nazarene;" because while no single prediction was thus accomplished, the trend of many prophecies is in this direction. So in the Gospel according to John, it is very noticeable with what accuracy of precision two prophecies are referred to in connected verses, yet in different terms. Christ's legs were not broken, but His side was pierced; and it is added, as to the former fact, "that the Scripture *should be fulfilled*, a bone of Him shall not be broken;"but, as to the latter, "and again *another Scripture* saith, they shall look on Him whom they pierced." In this latter case the prediction is yet to be *fulfilled**, and hence while the language of prediction is applied to the event by way of correspondence, how carefully is the record guarded so as not to exclude its true fulfilment hereafter.

---

*   Comp. Revelation 1. 7.

Peter might naturally have said, at Pentecost, "Now is fulfilled that which was spoken;" but Joel's prediction was not then fulfilled. The "great and terrible day of the Lord" is yet to come, and the wonders in heaven above and in the earth beneath have yet to be wrought. And another and greater effusion—the universal outpouring of the Spirit upon all flesh—is in the future. Joel's prophecy, though not fulfilled, furnished the true philosophy of Pentecost, explaining what was then seen and heard. Spectators said, "these men are full of new wine." Peter answered, that this was not spirituous intoxication but spiritual exhilaration; they were not drunk with wine wherein is excess, but were filled with the Spirit, the new wine from heaven's vineyards. Careful comparison of the second chapters of Joel and of the Acts must convince us that the cup of prediction has not yet been full to the brim, and waits for a more copious outpouring. Pentecost was the summer shower after long drought; the final outpouring will make springs gush forth and turn the desert into a garden, and a thousand rills, singing their song, shall blend in rivers of grace that roll like a liquid anthem to the sea.

There is also a grammatical reason for not limiting to the original Pentecost the Spirit's outpourings. Different prepositions are used to express the relations of the Spirit to the believer. A sharp line seems drawn between "in" or "within," and "on" or "upon." When the work of the Spirit in regenerating, renewing, sanctifying, is referred to, "in" and "within" represent His permanent work and abiding presence: for character must be perpetual. But when His office in qualifying for service by special enduement is referred to, "on" and "upon" are the prepositions commonly used to express that endowment or enduement which is not permanent but is for the period of such service.

This distinction is more than grammatical: it is philosophical. A renewed heart must neither lose its renewal nor let go its Renewer. But the anointed tongue needs its special unction only while it is used in witness for Christ. Charles G. Finney held that a true servant of God might have more than one enduement, and that he who, even in spiritual self-culture, forgets his call to service, may forfeit his enduement. It is possible to be so absorbed in the permanent ministry of the indwelling Spirit as to overlook the occasional ministry of the enduing Spirit.

Even if it be conceded that, on the day of outpouring, the Spirit was once for all given in saving and sanctifying power, it does not follow that He does not, from time to time, come anew to saints in gifts of power for witnessing and working. Some careful Bible students regard Pentecost as a baptism wherein the Spirit was outpoured as into a vast reservoir, and would now urge disciples to ask not for a baptism of the Spirit, but to be *filled* with the Spirit, like empty vessels dipped into this Divine fulness.

But our contention is not for a form of statement. The one practical question is, whether we are in faith and by prayer to seek for new effusions of power from on High, for tongues of fire to make our witness a Divine flame. Here lies the hope of world-wide missions. Without some new unction from the Spirit, we shall never feel that burning fire shut up in our bones which compels us to witness; nor will our witness without that be a power. If that lost art of Apostolic days may be recovered to the Church, it were worth while to learn it in the severe school of fasting and prayer. A Church halfasleep, a world wholly dead, wait for such a renaissance.

Yet a third argument is the historical. As a fact Pentecost was not the last, but only the first outpouring. It actually opened a series of such manifestations. This book of the Acts records repeated wonders similar in kind if not in degree.

When Philip preached in Samaria, and the rumour of his success reached Jerusalem, Peter and John were sent thither by the Apostles; and when they came down they prayed for the Samaritan converts that "they might receive the Holy Ghost; for as yet He was fallen upon none of them." And they also received the Spirit, similar signs following as at Jerusalem.

Again, at Cesarea, when Peter first preached to a representative Roman audience, as he began to speak the Holy Spirit fell on them, and, as he expressly adds, "as on us at the beginning." Here, once more, were the signs of the first Pentecost wrought, repeated even in the gift of tongues. The gathering of the kinsmen, friends and retainers of the Centurion in the palace of the Caesars is believed to have exceeded in number the original hundred and twenty at Jerusalem; certainly the results were proportionately larger, for the Holy Spirit fell on all those that heard the word, not only in advance of baptism but, apparently, of believing also. And here possibly we have a forecast of the final outpouring *upon all flesh*.

Yet again, at Ephesus, among the Greeks, Paul found certain disciples, probably adherents of Apollos, who, like him, had not got beyond John's preliminary baptism of repentance; and when Paul laid hands on them, the Holy Spirit came upon them also, and they spake with tongues and prophesied.

Thus, within the bounds of this book and the limits of one generation, three instances are on record subsequent to the day of Pentecost, when in each case, with language most explicit, the Spirit is said to have "come upon," "fallen upon," been "received," by disciples. If within forty years there were four distinct and separate outpourings in the Apostolic age, who is competent to say that in the centuries succeeding there have been no other Pentecostal effusions, and some of them scarcely less wonderful in some respects and aspects than that earliest enduement? May there not be modern saints upon whom the Spirit has not yet fallen in the Pentecostal sense, but would come in power in answer to believing prayer?

Recent history argues with the resistless logic of events that Pentecostal wonders may be repeated. This modern missionary century has been made both lustrous and illustrious by outpourings of the Spirit, in some respects surpassing any recorded in Apostolic days. Witness the story of Tahiti and all Western Polynesia; of the Hawaiian, Marquesan, Micronesian groups; of New Zealand, Madagascar and the Fiji Islands; of Nanumaga under Thomas Powell; of Sierra Leone under William Johnson; of the missions in the valley of the Nile, in Zululand, and on the Gaboon River; in Banza Manteke under Henry Richards, and Basutoland under Dr. Moffat. Read the memoirs of Dr. Grant and Fidelia Fiske in Oroomiah; of Mackay in Uganda and his namesake in Formosa. Follow the work of Judson in Burma, of Boardman among the Karens; of Cyrus Wheeler on the Euphrates, of Clough and Jewett at Ongole, of William Duncan in his Metlakahtla and Joseph Neesima in his Doshisha. What are these, and hundreds more that might be cited, but instances of mighty outpourings, in all essentials reproducing Pentecostal signs and wonders, often on a scale of majesty and magnificence scarcely paralleled.

If this preliminary question seem to have undue heed given to it, it is for a purpose. Our supreme aim is to offset the discouraging lack and need of spiritual life and power by the encouraging fact that from time to time, and in many cases, that original blessing of Pentecost has in its main features been repeated. The history of missions with uplifted finger points to the glowing and glorious records on her shining scroll, and solemnly attests the fact that, wherever the most consecrated witnesses have gone faithfully preaching the gospel, there God has exhibited His power and bestowed His new Pentecosts.

These divine marvels have been wrought especially in the following forms:

First, in the manifest calling and anointing of special messengers to bear the tidings.

Secondly, in the providential removal of the natural barriers of language, furnishing, for the rapid acquisition of strange tongues, facilities which were unknown in ancient times.

Thirdly, in the preparation for the universal diffusion of the gospel message, through numerous translations of the word of God and Christian literature.

Fourthly, in the sudden and strange subduing even of hostile communities and rulers, when human influences were wholly inadequate.

Fifthly, in marked and multiplied cases of conversion and the transformation of whole peoples.

Pentecost may have been repeated in modern times without reproducing its exact original features. Similar effects do not depend on uniform causes, nor do similar causes always produce uniform effects. Facts assume various forms, and are independent of them. God does not waste power, nor use the supernatural where the natural suffices. When human hands may as well take away the stone, He does not bid it move without hands or send angels to roll it away. The great Economist of the Universe works no needless miracles. He may choose not to bestow the gift of tongues, while He so stimulates philological research as that a hundred languages hitherto without written form have their alphabet and grammar, lexicon and literature; and the word of God is without a miracle both preached and translated in over three hundred vernaculars. In our day, within a space of time in which Paul could scarcely have found his way to strange peoples, our missionaries learn to preach in their tongues, and then teach them to read and write their own language and present them with the word of God as the first printed book in their own speech. So multiplied and marvellous are the facilities for the rapid acquisition of the great tongues of mankind that Bengali, Chinese, Japanese, Arabic, Sanskrit, may be learned in the Universities of England and America. This is something more than a triumph of human scholarship; it belongs to the Theology of Inventions, and is part of God's wonder workings. In these and many other ways He who bestowed miraculous blessing at the Pentecost in Jerusalem is giving in His own unique fashion New Pentecosts of privilege and power to a witnessing Church.

III.

THE NEW TIMES AND SEASONS.

T HE WORK of a master hand is seen in the mutual fitness of all its parts. There are a few phrases which God meant should be the watchwords of missions. They are trumpet tongued, they are fit signals for advance, whose clarion call should peal all along the lines; and when heard by obedient souls, they have an electrifying power to arouse to action. Among them this is worthy to ring out like the blast of Gabriel's trump:

THE FULNESS AND FITNESS OF TIMES.

Here is the hiding of a divine idea. In Abraham's day, judgment waited, because the iniquity of the Amorites was not yet full. The vividness of the metaphor is startling. We see the cup slowly filling, and then running over with the blood-red wine of sin. Judgment calmly waits until the scarlet flood reaches the brim and overflows the iron chalice, and then He who is patient because He is eternal, empties the phial of His righteous wrath, and war, pestilence, famine, earthquake, pour their woes upon the earth. So oftentimes in human history, retribution waited for the fit and full season of judgment.

For blessing, as well as cursing, there is a fitness and fulness of times. The advent of Messiah waited till the world was made ready, and the fit and full time had come for Christ to be born. The obelisks of prophecy had for hundreds of years stood unread, waiting for the Champollion of history to interpret their hieroglyphs, and give meaning to their mysteries. All false faiths, weighed in the balances, had been found wanting. Persian civilization with its sun adoration, Greek civilization with its wisdom and art, Roman civilization with its law and valor, Indian civilization with its philosophy of contemplation, Chinese civilization with its ancestral worship—all these had utterly and confessedly failed to arrest decay; and even Judaism was but a skeleton-leaf of forms, whence the sap of piety had fled. There was a felt need of some great religious reform.

There was preparation positive as well as negative. Roman roads had run a highway from the golden mile-stone in the Forum to the ends of the earth; and the Greek dialect had even in Syria forged swift wheels for the Gospel chariot to speed along the highway. Universal peace reigned, and war no longer set nations at variance, locking their gates and shutting their ports. The common and conscious want of a more satisfying faith was the prophecy of a new teacher and deliverer; and in every land there were seers who watched for the star that heralded the advent of "The Desire of All Nations."

Just at this time, the first and only point in the annals of the race where such converging lines met, while so many facts hinted one grand issue, and so many voices blended in one loud appeal, a virgin of Bethlehem felt in her womb the quickening of the Holy Spirit, and the greatest birth of the ages gave to man Jesus, the world's Saviour. When the fulness of time was come God sent forth His Son, to bring fulfilment to prediction and redemption to humanity. The advent of the long-promised seed of the woman had awaited its full hour. Both His cradle and His cross were ready; the believer and the betrayer were both at hand. Never before, as never since, had God's clock of the ages struck an hour so awfully meet for the crisis of history.

Here was another of what Dr. Croly, half a century ago, called "the birth hours" of the race. Man's advent was the first; the advent of Christ, another; and the period of the great Reformation was another. That religious revolution whose leaders were John de Wyclif and John Bunyan in England, John Knox in Scotland, John Huss in Bohemia, John Calvin in Switzerland, Luther in Germany, Savonarola in Italy, was, if not a new birth hour, at least a resurrection mom, to the long-buried Apostolic faith. After a thousand years in the sepulchre of the dark ages, rolling away the stone of sacerdotalism, bursting the cerements of formalism and traditionalism, breaking the scarlet seal of Papal infallibility and inviolability, behold, coming forth into new life, the imperial truth of justification by faith!

When, one hundred years ago, the hand of William Carey rung out from the belfry of the ages, the signal for a new crusade of missions, a fourth birth hour of history struck; and even yet we are but half awake to the full significance of this new signal. It may be well for us to stop and ask how we are to recognize God's plan in our generation, and fall into line with His majestic march—in other words, what are the signs that God's fitness and fulness of times has come?

Our Lord rebuked the Pharisees and Sadducees when they demanded a sign from heaven, because they were keener observers and safer interpreters of the weather signals than of the signs of the times. In the red and glowing sky of sunset, in the lurid and lowering sky of sunrise, they saw the forecast of the fair or foul day succeeding; but to God's signals that flame and flash on the prophetic and historic horizon, they were blind.

Behind this rebuke hides an indirect hint that to the devout watcher history becomes prophecy. The morning forecasts the evening; and to-day, tomorrow. God gives us premonitory and preparatory signs of His providential purpose, and we should be on the alert to detect them.

The undevout historian is mad. Only the fool says in his heart there is no God in history. Of the world of events as of the world of matter, it is true that "every house is builded by some builder; and He who built all is God." History is not a heap of "*disjecta membra,*" but an articulated body, made upon a plan, and with joints and bands compacted. In God's book all coming events were written, when as yet there was none of them, in continuance to be fashioned as His eternal purpose should be wrought into form. Weather forecasts may fail, but God's signs and signals are sure.

Because the present, rightly read, predicts the future, because God's fit, full time gives prophetic and providential indications of its approach, of what immense importance is it for us to get a proper point from which to view the horizon, and then to keep up our watch! The golden chalice which is filling is God's purpose; its flood is man's opportunity. And whenever God's full time comes, the angel whose stride spans sea and land declares: "There shall no longer be delay!" Then, or never, we fall into line with God's movement. His times and tides wait for no man. Swiftly His plan sweeps on to its goal, leaving behind the sluggard and the idler. Ye watchers, be ready, and when the full hour is come for the work and war of the ages, stand in your lot and be not found faithless!

How then are we to read God's signals, and what are the signs on our horizon?

To him who, in the study of current events would read the immediate future, God gives two guides: inspired prophecy and converging providence. When the two combine, practical certainty results; for when prediction nears fulfilment, and providential events converge toward the same centre, the true seer finds clear foretokens of what is at hand.

Let us apply these criteria to the great birth hours already noted. Christ's Incarnation did not surprise such devout seers as Simeon and Anna. They knew that the seventy heptades of years which were to elapse before the coming of Messiah the Prince, were about complete, and as students of the prophetic word, they were on the watch-tower looking toward Bethlehem. The universal exhaustion of man's resources, the wide prevalence of peace, the common expectation of a coming Deliverer, were fingers all pointing in the same direction, and so prophecy and providence confirmed each other's witness to the nearness of the Advent of Immanuel; and so that "just and devout man" who was "waiting for the consolation of Israel" was not found staggering in unbelief when the infant Jesus was laid in his arms; and that aged prophetess who came into the temple at that same instant, was prepared both to accept the Messiah in His swaddling clothes, and speak of Him to others who "looked for redemption, in Jerusalem." To God's watchers, like them, the Advent was the crown of expectation and anticipation.

The Reformation era came not without horizon signals. Long before, in parables, vivid as panoramic pictures, Christ had hinted the history and "mystery of the Kingdom of Heaven," the sowing of the seed and the growing of the plant; the tares of hypocrisy and the leaven of heresy; the period of apparent decay, when the precious treasure was buried in the field or sunk in the sea, to be dug up and dived after. Such figures seem meant to forecast the accession of Constantine, with the inroads of formalism, secularism and scepticism, and the thousand years of nightshade when evangelical truth was buried beneath the rubbish of forms and falsehood. The next two scenes in this parabolic series hint the finding of the hid treasure and the recovery of the priceless pearl.

But if the forecast of prophecy was dim, converging providences lit up the horizon with clearer rays that told of a new dawn after the dark ages. The marshalling of events was signally significant. In the middle of the fifteenth century the fall of Constantinople had started the revival of learning. Greek scholars, dispersed over Europe with their manuscripts of the New Testament, opened the door and paved the way for the translation of the Word into other tongues and its wide dissemination among the people. In the last decade of that century, a new route to the Indies linked Protestant Britain with the heart of Oriental heathenism; also a new world was unveiled toward the sunset. This was likewise the period of the fall of feudalism, and of the assertion of individualism with its doctrine of human rights and personal liberty.

The theology of inventions found grand illustration. The reformation in philosophy ushered in a revolution in science. The mariner's compass then first coming into common use, began to act as a pilot over unknown seas. The printing-press in 1450 issued its first book, and that, a Latin Bible. The steam engine, too, between the meridian hours of that century and the next, supplied man with a new motive power. And so, just as Luther's hammer was heard nailing his theses to "All Saints'" door, God was loudly calling all saints to rally about the reformed standard, give the Bible to the common folk, and vindicate their right to read and interpret it for themselves; and to go on swift keels and wheels to the very bounds of the globe with the message of the Reformed Faith.

We take one more illustration of the signs of the times, nearer to our day and pertinent to our duty.

That any of God's watchers could misread the signs of the times, in William Carey's day, is to us now a marvel. In all prophecy an age of world-wide evangelism is foretold; and in that prophetic panorama in the thirteenth of Matthew, the recovery of the treasure and the pearl is followed by the casting of the drag-net into the sea, and by great hauls of fish. All prediction treads toward one goal. Abram had the promise of a blessing to come through him to "all the families of the earth;" and all down the ages, with voices growing ever louder and clearer, prophets had told of a day of world-wide missions. Christ plainly taught that before the end of the age the Gospel must first be preached as a witness among all nations.

Many fingers pointed to the close of the last century as God's time for the new era of missions. While the former half of the century witnessed an awful decline which threatened complete apostasy, the latter half was the most remarkable era of revived piety and evangelistic preaching since the days of Paul. Jonathan Edwards, John Wesley and Charles Wesley, George Whitefield, Walker of Truro and Fletcher of Madeley, William Grimshaw and William Romaine, Daniel Rowlands and Rowland Hill, John Berridge and Henry Venn, James Hervey and William Toplady, and others like-minded, began as the evangelists of a new era to stir a half dead Church to proclaim the Gospel to the poor and outcast classes. The two Northamptons answered to each other across the sea, and Carey, whose cobbler's bench was a watch-tower, saw that for missions to the heathen God's fit and full time was come. For ten years he bore the brunt of sneer and taunt, and the worse hostility of inertia and indifference; felt the keen sting of Sydney Smith's wit and the sharp rebuke of John Ryland's hyper-calvinism. But when God lets loose a thinker and a seer—when a saint gets on his knees watching the dawn, and sees God's signals flashing—floods and flames cannot stay his progress. Between the Scylla of apathy and the Charybdis of antipathy, Carey boldly steered for India. While others slept he had been on the watch. He had seen God's signs and heard God's step, and he dared not falter or delay; he must move, though he moved alone.

Another birth hour of history has now come, and blessed are the sages who see the star that guides to the cradle of the new age of missions. Even yet, not every eye sees the vision of God or catches its full meaning. One of the wisest thinkers of the age says, that "nothing but deep initiation into the Spirit of the Bible can enable us to form the faintest idea as to what historical events belong most to the divine plan, or have most relation to the Kingdom of the Eternities." If there be any defect in these words, it is in lack, not excess, of emphasis.

There was One who was in the world, and the world was made by Him and the world knew Him not. He came to His own possessions and His own people received Him not. This is the one parable and paradox of all ages. There is One who is in history, and all history is His curious handiwork, and yet even historians recognize Him not. He comes to the age which is of His own framing and moves amid events which unfold His own eternal plan, and yet His own people too often receive Him not. But to as many as receive Him, recognize His majestic presence and beneficent providence, to them He gives authority to become co-workers with God, sharers in the glory of divine achievement.

The conviction grows upon us that the birth hour, now fully come, is in some aspects the most important crisis of all history. It marks the nativity of twin offspring. Time has brought forth two giants: Opportunity and Responsibility. And as might be expected, never before has there been such combination and concentration of world-wide signals. The whole horizon is aflame with aurora borealis lights— fingers of fire which reach toward the zenith as if to point man's gaze upward to God. Our risk is not so much that we shall not see these signs, as that we shall not feel their force and read their lesson. Marvels are so common that they cease to be startling. The blare of God's trumpets dulls our ears by its peal, and the flare and glare of His flash-lights dims our eyes by its glory.

This is no exaggeration of rhetoric or outburst of enthusiasm. The half of the wonders of this age have never been told, and their full meaning yet awaits an interpreter. Let any devout student of history, any sagacious seer of God who reads the signs of the times, tell us what is the forecast of the future. Behind the developments of our day is a divine directing power. A man's hand writes on the wall; but the writing is a decree of God, telling of world powers and of false faiths, weighed in the balances and found wanting; and of a Conqueror about to receive the Kingdom which human monarchs are unworthy to administer.

IV.

The New Open Doors.

That word *Opportunity* is a pictorial word. It suggests a ship, before the port, just sailing into harbour after the fight with wind and wave. True opportunity is always God-given: "Behold I have set before thee an open door, and no man can shut it." But doors unentered do not remain open, and if God once shuts no man can open, and we may knock in vain. Unused opportunity never returns: it is forfeited forever. One fact is plain: open doors now challenge us to enter every land. Before us stands the opportunity of the ages. The rapid and sudden multiplication and accumulation of these openings compel us to wonder and adore, for He who only doeth wondrous things is at work, and so the iron gates open of their own accord before His messengers and heralds.

A few familiar facts, which are leaders of a vast host, show that God is on the march, and summoning His Church to follow. Brevity compels classification: we must look at facts only in groups. And this age of wonders is but one century beyond that of Carey; yet within one hundred years what was local and exceptional has become cosmopolitan and universal. With the swift touch of God, He has opened the world, over which the Cobbler of Hackleton sighed, to the Gospel which he loved, and given to the Church the chance to occupy it for Christ.

Keeping in mind that our theme is missions, we select seven of the remarkable features of our own age, all of which are gigantic in character and cosmopolitan in extent, and which constitute in our day the seven wonders of the world.

1. World-wide *Exploration*.

If we are to preach the Gospel to every creature we must first go into all the world, and this has not been possible to any previous age as it is to ours, for all the world has not hitherto been accessible or even known. At last the trackless pathways of the ocean have been crossed and the penetralia of all the continents reached. Land and sea yield up the secrets of six thousand years. Navigation and exploration have been so thorough that we feel sure that no continent is unveiled, nor even one island undiscovered. The frozen poles have been forced to unbar the gates of their ice castles and the flag of the triumphant explorer is unfurled on their crystal battlements. For the first time since the world began man knows his own habitation and domain.

All this is full of meaning. When God set Canaan before His people, His word was: "Every place that the sole of your foot shall tread upon, that have I given unto you." That law is general. Every land of promise waits for possession, and possession hangs on appropriation. The first condition of a world's evangelization is its exploration; and, because the prows of our ships, ploughing furrows in every sea, have made the vast oceans harvest-fields of commerce; because the dauntless explorer has pierced Asiatic jungles and African forests, traced the rivers to their source, and scaled the mountains to their brow; because the exclusion and seclusion of hermit nations has been invaded and the veil rent in twain before their closely-guarded fanes and shrines; because the public sentiment of mankind forbids locked gates and sealed ports, the way is open as never before for the Gospel chariot.

2. World-wide *Communication*.

This naturally follows, but not of necessity, for doors, wrested or wrenched open by sheer force, are closed almost as soon as opened. In this case, however, the iron bars of resistance have been broken down, and the two-leaved gates have yielded to the gentler touch of diplomacy as well as to the harsher hand of war,—to the still small voice of commerce as well as the louder threat of compulsion. Bonds of union have been braided out of mutual treaties, and barriers that stood firm for ages have been razed to the ground, or fallen like Jericho's walls without a blow.

Facilities for mutual contact and communication are so multiplied and marvellous that we scarcely recognize our own world. Within the century steamships have diminished distance, by shortening time to less than one-tenth of the period required for ocean voyages. Steam carriages cross the continents so swiftly that the limited express needs but a continuous track to run round the globe in three weeks; and the black-horse not only climbs the steep mountain side but bores his way through its rocky heart, bridges river chasms, tramps down thickest forests, and dares alike Sahara sands and Siberian snows. The postal union bears letters and papers from the great centres to the remotest outskirts of the earth in six weeks; and the telegraph wire and ocean cable yoke God's lightning to human thought, flash news to the ends of the globe; and, threading the vast body politic with its mysterious system of sensor and motor nerves, electricity makes the whole world thrill with instantaneous intelligence.

Now, at last, there are no distant lands, no foreign peoples; the whole world is one neighborhood; those who were afar off are brought nigh. Once, to love one's neighbour meant to love him who lived next door: but now everybody lives next door—and by that law we must love the race of man. Communication such as this, making possible a contact so constant, so sympathetic, so universal, never entered into the wildest dreams of the ancients, and to our grandfathers would have seemed incredible. Had Carey foreseen and foretold what one century has made real, his prediction would have ranked him among madmen. The tales of the Arabian Nights are outdone in extravagance by actual facts. God has, through modern science, given to man the magic wand, the magic lamp. The genius of nature, with all his mighty forces waits to do our bidding, helping us to carry out the last command of our Lord.

3. World-wide *Civilization*.

This comprehensive term includes all that builds mankind into a compact state or civil society,—intelligence and industry, enterprise and education, manners and morals.

Barbarism is the burglar of history; its deeds of wrong, robbery, violence, are of the night, and cannot abide the day which dawns when civilization sheds its light. In the flush of the morning, blushing for shame, it seeks the cover of darkness. Such crimes against God and man as infanticide and cannibalism, such orgies of lust and blood as the rites of Juggemath and the Meriah groves; such cruelties as those of the torture rack and suttee pyre, are things of the past.

Education is a revolutionist, overturning intellectual errors and superstitious faith. Cuvier knew too much to fear the ghost with horns and hoofs that came to his bed and growled out, "I will eat you!" He coolly surveyed the sheeted form, and said to himself, " Horns and hoofs! Humph! Graminivorous, not carnivorous! that beast feeds on grass and grain, and won't eat me." And so the comparative anatomist went to sleep. Knowledge is power. It destroys even where it does not construct. The Hindu cannot study astronomy and geology without seeing his absurd cosmogony fall in ruins; yet that cosmogony is so built into his religious system that the two fall together, and he loses faith in the Vedas. The Chinese study geography and history, and learn that the Middle Kingdom must reconstruct its map of the world and its notions of the race of man; for the Celestial Empire is but one among many great nations, and Confucius but one among many great teachers. The Siamese cannot look into medical science without the uprooting of hoary superstitions; nor the degraded Hottentot learn common facts about earth, air and water, without finding that the witches he fears are not human beings nor demons, but miasma and malaria, to be exorcised by scientific drainage and sanitary conditions.

Civilization is in our day the forerunner of missions, not only in casting up a highway and gathering out the stones, but in putting into the hands of Christian and Protestant peoples the balance of power. That those nations where the most enlightened form of Protestant Christianity prevails hold the sceptre that sways the world, there is no doubt. Their sovereignty is a conceded fact. The pillars of the world's throne are wrought not of brute force but of brain force; the granite columns of character and culture, intelligence and integrity. Great Britain and the United States, the giant empire of the east and the great republic of the west, joined by Prussia, the Protestant kingdom of the continent of Europe, wield jointly an influence which Papal, Pagan and Moslem powers, combined, could not resist. Such a fact bears the stamp and seal of God's design, and its bearing on world-wide missions cannot be measured.

4. World-wide *Assimilation.*

Communication promotes actual contact and communion. The intercourse of travel and the interchange of trade have begotten new relations and suggest a new science which Lieber calls Catallactics— the exchange of thoughts. There has come to be a new trade in ideas, a commerce of sentiments. Hermit nations emerge from their cell and shell. From the sunrise kingdom young Japanese pour into western channels to absorb the secrets of occidental progress, and in their reflow, bear back the new ideas they have acquired. China sends her younger statesmen to study at the centres of Christendom the problems of human progress, and bring back their solution. The gods of the Celestial Empire actually ask questions of the foreign devils! Confucius, the Chinese Pope, no longer wears the tiara of infallibility. He who shook his own hand now shakes ours, respects the head that wears no queue, and the feet that are shod with elastic hide instead of unbending wood.

The barriers between peoples are down. Barriers of language once more impassable than mountains or oceans are silently crumbling. In Yokohama and Hong Kong, Cairo and Capetown, Calcutta and Constantinople, English is spoken: it is becoming the court-language of the world. Thousands in India and Japan flock to hear men like Julius Seelye and Joseph Cook, who use only their own mother tongue, and in some of the capitals of the Orient a translator or interpreter is becoming so far unnecessary.

Barriers of mutual misunderstanding and suspicion are falling. Acquaintance dissipates false impressions. The "foreign devils" are found to be brothers; there is no evil fascination in their eye, no curse in their speech, no fatality in their touch. Trust takes the place of distrust, and love the place of hate.

The era of universal peace seems to be at hand. Men are learning the divine lesson that war is based not only on a bad principle, but a bad policy, and that

O'Connell was not far wrong in stoutly maintaining that "no social revolution is worth one drop of human blood." Generous forbearance, mutual concession, fraternal conference and impartial arbitration, may settle any controversy without striking a blow. War is a serpent, with a crush in its coils, a fang in its jaws, and a sting in its tail. Its venom heats the blood for generations. France has never forgotten nor forgiven Waterloo, and the memory of conflicts more remote than the Crimean War, the Battle of Plassey, or even the fall of Constantinople, rankles still; for though men die, nations survive. Waste of treasure and of life are bad, but waste of good feeling and kindly relations is worse.

God sits at His loom. With many shuttles He weaves into one fabric the threads of national life; and in the woof and warp the blood-red threads are getting scarce. Peaceful compacts guard the rights and promote the concord of men. Trade and travel bring men together, and they come to know each other, and to feel that war must be no more. In 1884, in Berlin, fourteen nations sent representatives to the conference that gave a constitution to the Congo Free State. That conference marks perhaps the first parliament of man and forecasts the federation of the world; for Protestant, Catholic, Greek and even Mohammedan communities had delegates there. The various congresses and conferences connected with the Columbian Exposition would have been impossible half a century ago; so marked was their testimony to the assimilation going on among men, that there seems risk of losing sight even of some vital distinctions.

5. World-wide *Emancipation*.

This is another marvel of this age. From the fall of man until now, human slavery has been the fatal foe of the best good of the race; equally bad for master and slave. The nightingale will not sing in a cage until its eyes are put out. The light of man's intelligence must be quenched, the eyes of his intellect be blinded, before he will submissively wear his bonds. Hence the castle of human bondage has been built upon the base-blocks of ignorance and degradation, and buttressed with oppression and compulsion.

But, even when blinded, Samson was a safe victim of tyranny only while his hair was kept shorn; and so, close in the steps of human knowledge and enlightenment, has followed the uprising of man in behalf of his fellow-man; if the slave or serf did not burst his own bonds, civilization has broken them for him.

Great Britain could not further share this crime of the age without relapsing toward barbarism, and so British intelligence and integrity sounded the tocsin that on that memorable first day of August, 1838, pealed out liberty in Jamaica. It was not Clarkson and Wilberforce, but the "Magna Charta," and the Bible, that original charter of human rights, that put beneath the walls where human beings were imprisoned, a lever mightier than that of Archimedes. Even despotic Russia had to grant at least a nominal release to her serfs; and the late four years' conflict in America could not end while upon one slave there was left an unbroken fetter: those four millions of bondmen were God's "contraband of war."

Who but He has brought it about that not one enlightened nation dares openly to espouse slave traffic or maintain slave labour? The market for human bodies and souls has long been transferred from London and New York to Cairo and Constantinople. The voice of mankind is heard saying, "Away with fetters!" and appealing for a parliament of man in which there shall be no commons, but all shall sit as peers!

Emancipation means more than bodily freedom; it brings individualism. Knock from the body its shackles and the mind begins to be free. Men begin to learn and think, to reflect and reason. Speech bursts its bonds and the dumb tongue is loosed. Instead of a mass in which individuals are lost, each man learns that he is himself a born sovereign rather than subject, having a little empire of his own. He begins to assert himself and his inalienable right of self-rule. He learns the dignity and majesty of mind, and that no chain ever forged is strong enough to bind a thinker. He learns the grandeur of reason, and that truth is resistless like the waves of the sea, mighty enough to wreck the strongest bark of falsehood and grind to powder the age-long rocks of error. And so to-day we see intelligence, that great agitator, striding over the vast steppes of Asia and river highways of Africa, scattering the seeds of social revolution; and a bloodless warfare of ideas is going on, before which strongholds of error and injustice are falling.

When man begins to be free in body and mind he learns also the divinity of conscience. God has decreed that no human device of tyranny or torture shall suffice to kill or curb man's moral sense; and the cell, the rack, the axe, the stake, have proved powerless to change that decree. Though blinded and made the sport of foes, conscience is still a giant, that has but to get hold of the pillars of Dagon's temple, to lift them from their foundations and bring down to the dust the fabric of organized oppression and regal wrong. Dr. Francis W. Upham says: "The conscience is the servant only of God, and is not subject to the will of men. Through His words, this truth, which reaches to social as well as religious institutions, has an indestructible life. If it be crucified it will rise again. If buried in the sepulchre the stone will be rolled away, and the keepers become as dead men."*

Never before has liberty, both civil and religious, reigned among men so widely and wisely. The consequences are most significant touching the work of missions. For example: In most lands, persecution for religious opinion is already done

---

*   St. Matthew's Gospel, by F. W. Upham.

away, or if it still survives it is a relic of a barbarous age, hiding in the darkness and resorting to the secret weapons of the assassin. Enlightened civilization which shut the gates of the arena also put out the fires of the stake. Years since in China, the last of the missionary martyrs who died by government decree, was beheaded. Where in Spain the dungeons of the Inquisition stood, harvests for God are growing out of the ashes of saints. India may ostracise, but dare not execute, converts. All this forecasts that wider emancipation of the soul of man, when such self-conscious sovereign shall learn to be the willing subject of the Lord of all, and find his highest freedom in the service of a Higher Master. That will be the world's year of jubilee!

V.

The New Era.

Two of these seven wonders yet remain to be considered, and they serve to inaugurate a new era; for one of them puts multiplied facilities, implements, instruments or weapons into our hands, and the other organizes and mobilizes the forces available for the work and war of the ages.

The first of these is World-wide *Preparation*.

In one sense, all that has been said of other wonders implies preparation. But there is one aspect of the present condition of the world which implies a preparation in itself so peculiar that it needs extended reference; namely, the obvious and providential furnishing of facilities exactly adapted for, and preparatory to, a world-wide work of evangelization. These of themselves serve to introduce a new era.

There is a divine meaning in the fact that this century, most prolific of missions, has been also most fertile in invention, of all ages; the one great epoch of discovery, not only in political and social developments, but in general progress in art and science, leaving behind all other centuries. The leading statesman of Britain is credited with saying, that social advance has moved on such flying feet that in the first fifty years of the nineteenth century all previous history was outrun; that even this was surpassed by the next twenty-five, and this again by the rate of progress of the next ten. If Mr. Gladstone's estimate be correct, one decade of years from 1875 to 1885 witnessed a forward stride of the race more gigantic than all the previous ages of history!

This is doubtless no exaggeration. Certainly since the world began no such epoch of improvement has been known. We have seen huge strides, leaps forward which make all past advance seem like a snail's pace. During the years of this century the movement onward and upward seems, even to those who are borne on and up by it, incredible. Since Rome was founded the rate of progress has increased at least a thousandfold.

To appreciate this fact, we need to stop long enough to study comparative history. This is the world's golden age so far as invention and discovery, intelligence and material progress, can bring it. Measured by achievement each year is a century. This is the age of railway and steamship, photograph and phonograph, telescope and microscope, spectroscope and spectrum analysis; audiphone and microphone, petroleum and aniline dyes; steam printing press and machine typesetter; typewriter and sewing machine; of the discovery of forty new metals, and the revolution of chemical science; of the ocean cable and the signal service; of anaesthetics, and a score of new sciences and arts, of cheap postage and the universal postal union; of newspapers, magazines and popular literature; of machine work instead of handwork; of free schools and universities for the people; of giant explosives and gigantic enterprises. Most wonderful of all, this is the age of electricity, which already serves man as motor, messenger and illuminator, is to be applied to forging as well as plating metals, and no one knows to how many other uses.

In Robert Mackenzie's graphic sketch of "The Nineteenth Century," he calls this feature of our times "the great outbreak of human inventiveness which left no province of human affairs unvisited." With strange and startling suddenness men's eyes opened to see how rude and crude were previous methods and appliances, and at the same time those eyes became endowed with a scientific insight and foresight almost superhuman. Man became not only scientist but seer; before him limitless paths of possible progress stretched toward a goal so advanced, yet so entrancing, that the enchanting vision quickened the pace of the whole race, as though men had on the mythical "seven-league boots," or the winged sandals of Mercury.

Wherever a high civilization has shone, mankind has felt the thrill of a new passion for investigation and improvement. See the human form become practically transparent, as the speculum, stethoscope, laryngoscope, opthalmoscope, microscope, and electric lamp guide the physician and surgeon in searching the darkest hiding places of disease. Lithotomy gives place to lithotrity. Limbs, once amputated, are now straightened and strengthened. Since 1815, the treatment of the insane has undergone a revolution as radical and significant as the new era of conservative surgery. Machinery now works cotton and wool, metal and wood, and new motors do our planing and carving, hammering and rolling, sowing, mowing, ploughing, reaping, threshing and binding.

We do not appreciate all this glory of achievement, because the wonders of the age dazzle our eyes and dull our vision.

Let us glance once more at the electric telegraph. As the earth's rotation on its axis takes a full day, points on its surface at antipodes to each other are twelve hours apart, reckoning by the sun. But telegraphic signals flash instantaneously, and so far outrun the sun's apparent motion that an afternoon message, cabled from London, is read in San Francisco on the morning of the same day, and there are points further westward where we might have the paradox of publishing news of an event twenty-four hours before it takes place! This prompts Mackenzie to rank the telegraph as the first human invention which is obviously final. In the race of human improvement, steam may give place to some yet mightier power, as gas is already superseded by a better method of lighting; but, "no agency for conveying in telligence can ever excel that which is instantaneous. Here for the first time the human mind has reached the utmost limit of its progress."*

This unparalleled progress belongs mostly to the half century now nearing its close. During fifty years the more prominent achievements of the age have been reduced to practical form. Almost the entire system of railway is the product of this brief period. The first sun-picture dates back but sixty years, just before the death of Daguerre, from whom it took 'its name, and already we have a score of new applications of this principle. These inventions alone link the ages together, ushering in a new era of art and letters, making the sun himself the artist and sculptor of the coming era. Already the sun's ray has wedded the delicate lens, and given birth to microscopic photography; so that during the siege of Paris pages of the London Times, photographed upon a square inch of surface, were borne by carrier pigeons to the French capital, there to be magnified and reproduced. And it would seem that the sunbeam, already used for a pencil and chisel, is about to surpass the pigments of the painter, using sensitized paper in place of canvas and giving us colour as well as form.

The phonograph, at first a scientific toy, has become an automatic clerk, recording and repeating a message, and has begun to be used for that difficult art, the analysis and reproduction of animal sounds and utterances; and it makes possible for future generations to hear the words and voices of dead orators and statesmen, poets, and preachers. It is within this half century that the spectroscope has brought other orbs near enough to analyze their light and learn the substances burning in their photospheres; and the invaluable service of the spectroscope in refining and working metals, shows its possible utility in manufacture.

Anaesthetics, which renders medical and surgical treatment comparatively painless and so reduces human suffering to a minimum, is so recent a discovery that many yet living remember its well-nigh . tragic beginning in Edinburgh in 1847.

---

* The Nineteenth Century, 197.

The giant explosives—nitroglycerine, dynamite, giant powder, etc., have already displaced older and tedious methods of clearing the earth's surface of stumps and debris, and opening its veins of metal and mineral. Delicate photometers and micrometers, every form of monster machinery or delicate mechanism, belong to this age; while science teaches us drainage and irrigation, analysis and enrichment of the soil and secrets of fertility, turns deserts into gardens, and makes every spot available for building a habitation and earning a livelihood.

If such be the progress of this half century, nothing which men may imagine to do seems impossible in the new era just opening, when science promises to navigate air as well as sea and build ships to master winds as well as waves. Forms of force hitherto unknown are now undergoing experiment. Secrets, hidden even from this century, are yielding to human investigation, and a decade of years may witness a revolution greater than that which even in our day has turned the world upside down.

We have laid stress upon this march of human improvement, not so much because of the lightning pace of this advance, as because of its obvious connection with God's providential purpose. It is one great sign of the times. It marks this as the golden age of opportunity. A world's evangelization is not only possible but practicable, with a rapidity proportionate to progress in other directions. On the pages of history in large letters it is written that the periods of most marked progress exactly synchronize with the eras of most active missionary effort. Clear as the weather signals in the sky, is this glowing sign of God's plan in this generation, His mind is the vital spring of man's intellectual life. He is the fountain of life, and in His light do we see light. It was He who kept a continent veiled for five thousand years, rending the veil only when a reformed Church with an unchained Bible was ready to enter it and make it the theatre of new gospel triumphs. It was He who locked nature's secrets within her dark chambers, until a missionary Church was aroused to yoke to His chariot the new forces and appliances. God is surely speaking. To the reverent ear the still small voice is more impressive than peals of thunder. "Behold I have set before thee an open door." An open door to the nations— the world before us; an open door into Nature's Arcana, with all her machinery and forces to do our bidding. Opportunities are matched by facilities equally great. Never such a work to be done, never such tools to work with. What responsibility, if such opportunity be lost and such facilities lie unused!

The last of these seven modern wonders is world-wide *Organization*.

Organization is the watchword of the Age. Never before was there such a period of practical union among men for all the ends of material, intellectual and social improvement. Organization is rapidly extending and far-reaching; its triumphs are so multiplied and magnificent that they constitute the peril of the age, threatening to erect a despotism whose iron sceptre shall be resistless and remorseless. Already the Giant is on the throne; he lifts his finger, and great railway systems are locked in inaction; factory wheels stop, ships lie in the docks, buildings wait for workmen, mines remain unworked; labor's hundred hands are chained, and action is exchanged for petrifaction. Man has created a Frankenstein, and knows not how to manage the monster.

While we cannot deny the risks attending organization in reckless hands, we must confess both its widespread influence, and its great utility when under rational control. What master organizations the Church already commands as helpers! The Young Men's Christian Association is an example, the creation of the last half century, yet a huge banyan, whose original root was in British soil, but throwing out branches on all sides, across continents and oceans into new countries, bending down to take root in papal, pagan, moslem and heathen communities, until there remains scarce a land in any clime where this gigantic and beneficent growth has not reached.

The Young People's Society of Christian Endeavour is a yet younger giant, fourteen years old, yet in rapidity of growth, daring enterprise, boundless influence and burning enthusiasm, leaving already behind it any other organization ever known on this planet.

Let these illustrate the genius of the age when everybody organizes. Barristers and judges, physicians and surgeons, artists and artisans, underwriters and undertakers, cabmen and cartmen, shoeblacks and newsboys—every learned profession and every form of work resorts to organization. Were there some new trade to-day with only two engaged in it, they would begin by drawing up articles of association and forming a co-operative union.

The reason is plain. Men will dare attempt, and can together accomplish, what no one would try to do, or could do, alone; and so they resort to associated effort. Great and manifold advantages spring from co-operation. When hand joins hand, the weak and timid get strength and courage, and momentum is imparted to a movement in which individual forces are combined and concentrated. Great enterprises are possible only to an epoch of organization, and so we find business schemes pushing triumphantly to the very borders of civilization.

Compare present history with past records. Before the time of Christ, isolation was the law. Nations had little touch with each other. Universal empires were the aggregates of separate states, held together by those iron bands which conquest imposes and despotism rivets. The unity was that of frost, not of fire and fusion. To gather strange peoples under one sceptre, or conglomerate empires into one huge monarchy, insures no unity. Barriers are not broken down, and there is no sympathetic bond or brotherhood any more than between Jews and Samaritans.

How changed the whole aspect of affairs! We stand in the blazing focal centre of world-wide enterprise. Discovery sends its heralds to trumpet its triumph from rising to setting sun. Invention yokes to its car steam and lightning, and flies as on the wings of the morning to the uttermost parts of the earth and sea. Many run to and fro; and knowledge is increased. Material advance has its million messengers who haste to do its bidding. This is the world's Messiah, which bids disciples go into all the world and proclaim to every creature the good tidings of human improvement; and forthwith go the myriad missionaries of invention and discovery, needing no second summons. The swiftest ships and carriages are not fleet enough conveyances for the new apostles of science and art. They dare the sea with its tempest and tornado; defy forest and jungle, river and mountain, plague and famine, hot sands and frozen bergs. And all for what? To tell men of the oil-lamp and the sewing-machine, the timepiece and the parlor organ; to sell ribbons and calicoes, fire-arms and rum-jugs, soap and flour, at the earth's ends. Trade and traffic, agriculture and manufacture, push their conquests by organizing and co-operating; and so, in quarters most remote, in inland hamlets as well as populous cities, and on islands a half century ago unknown, you may find to-day all the appliances of enlightened society.

The theme loudly enforces its own lesson and appeal. To world-wide missions, organization and co-operation are essential. Shall the Church be slow to learn the lesson of the age? and her Master wait for willing feet to run on His errand of grace, His mission of mercy and salvation?

It is true the children of light have already resorted to organized effort in missions. William Carey was the pioneer, not of missions so much as of organization; and since his day, this has become so distinctive a feature of Church activity that the marked success attained since 1792 is traceable to associated work. By organization it has already come to pass that, although we have not absolutely reached every nation, still less every creature, our network of missions stretches round the globe and covers the earth.

And yet, in many quarters, how large are the meshes and how far apart the cords of that network. We have more than one hundred and seventy missionary boards and societies, and over one hundred and ten missionary organizations controlled by women; and these all, nearly three hundred, are the outcome of this century past, and most of them of the last fifty years. Yet what are even these among so many! We have but begun as yet our work of a world's evangelization.

The old command of Christ echoes down the long aisles of the ages, Evangelize! And the new voice of the Providence that speaks through events in this missionary era, peals out, Organize! Lengthen thy cords and strengthen thy stakes. A love that is like God's, must multiply and extend a thousandfold its lines of holy effort, and drive ten thousand times as many stakes deep down into the intelligent conviction and unselfish affection of Christ's disciples.

God leaves His Church without excuse or even pretext, if missions be not prosecuted as a world-wide enterprise. In a sense never thought of when that promise was spoken, the Lord is with us—with us, unlocking the gates of hermit nations, battering down the wall of China, unsealing the ports of Japan and Corea, cleaving a path to the heart of Africa—with us to unchain the human mind and reveal the secrets of nature. We may now go into all the world, and to every man in his own tongue give the word of God.

There was never such a work for the time, nor such a time for the work. The opportunities and facilities offered to us make even such a task easy and such a load light, turning weights into wings and burdens into pinions, to the willing soul. Knowing God's season, the fulness and fitness of His appointed time, it is also man's opportune hour, high time to awake out of sleep, and the world's critical hour of need and want. Dull and dead, indeed, must he be who sees not the signs of the times, hears not the voices that call and the signals that sound, and heeds not the approaching end of the age! The Captain of our Salvation is blowing a blast on His bugle—everything echoes His command, Forward! Why do we delay?

PART II.

THE NEW APOSTOLIC SUCCESSION

I.

THE CALLING OF THE NEW APOSTLES.

"THERE WERE giants in those days" is the terse record of the age before the flood.

Every age has its own giants; some great in physical stature, others mighty in mind, majestic in moral character, born to command and control. Even in earth's golden ages the giants are rare, for God does not make such gifts too common; but it is the few, always, whose words shake the world, whose deeds move and mould men, whose lives shape the history and destiny of the race. Carlyle calls history but the "lengthened shadows" of the world's great men. Is it not rather the lingering twilight, prolonging their influence, perpetuating their memory even when their sun has set, and long lighting up the evening sky? Is not the horizon still aflame from many a grand and noble life, long since withdrawn from among men?

The modern missionary era has given birth to a royal race of giants; in fact, so mighty have been these men and women, so herculean their labors, so heroic their achievements, that they seem rather to have made the age than the age them. Some of them were before our day, but we trace the path they trod, by their gigantic footprints. Others we have seen growing to great stature and mounting to thrones of power; and still others yet walk among men, and make the continents shake beneath their tread. They have made the priests of idol fanes tremble with fear; and as the God of this world sees them, like their Master, working the works and speaking the words of God, he knows that his time is short. They are not always recognized as great by the world, for their greatness is not of this world nor measured by its standards. God's giants have not always great heads, but they always have "great hearts." His captains are not the princes of this world that come to naught, not the

33

wise, mighty, noble in men's eyes; but those of great faith, holy love, who walk with God and work and war in His name, like those of old whose names are graven in that record in Hebrews—that "Westminster Abbey" of Old Testament worthies—"who through faith subdued kingdoms, wrought righteousness, obtained promises, out of weakness were made strong, waxed valiant in fight, turned to flight the armies of the aliens." Let us thank God for a type of gianthood to which all believers may both aspire and attain! Not only venerable "fathers," but "young men," in whom the word of God abideth, may be strong, and even "little children" may overcome the evil one; because greater is He that is in them than he that is in the world. The fable of Hercules is in Christian History become fact; for new-born babes while yet in the cradle of faith have laid hold of the serpent with a giant's grip.

The study of the missionary age is the story of the giants, and let us hope to read so well the lessons of their lives as to work wonders in the same Almighty name!

Every work must wait for workmen, trained to fitness in their work. And so this book of the Acts and facts of the Apostolic age, reveals the actors, the factors in this work for God. The history of primitive missions gives glimpses of the primitive missionaries.

Because history is the record of facts which demand the personal factor, the key of history is biography, that most suggestive and instructive of all studies. To portray the lives of men is, as Dionysius of Halicarnassus said, to "teach philosophy by examples." By the analysis of character we detect the elements of success and the causes of failure. Principles and precepts are abstract statements of truth, but virtue and vice teach best through concrete forms; and hence this, best of all books, is a gallery of portraits, where we may study the lives of men, following their faith and shunning their faults and follies; a gallery where the picture of one perfect life, so lustrous as to disdain even a frame of gold, forever challenges imitation.

Thus, then, our study of the Acts of the Apostles leads us to look at the actors who took part in missions to a lost world. First there was Peter, to whom it was given to open the door of faith to both Jew and Gentile, and whose figure stands out boldly in the opening scenes of this history. But a more significant point, both critical and pivotal, is reached further on, in the formal selection and separation of Barnabas and Saul, to a distinct and distinctive missionary career and service.

Let us place prominently before us the opening verses of the thirteenth chapter of the Acts:

Now there were in the church that was at Antioch certain prophets and teachers; as Barnabas, and Simeon that was called Niger, and Lucius of cyrene, and Manaen, which had been brought up with Herod the tetrarch, and Saul.

As they ministered to the Lord, and fasted, the Holy Ghost said, separate me Barnabas and Saul for the work whereunto I have called them. And when they had fasted and prayed, and laid their hands on them, they sent them away. So they, being sent forth by the Holy Ghost, departed.

The oversight of the Spirit of God is plainly seen in the very words here used. What precision of terms, not one useless phrase or needless adjective; no superfluous suggestion to divert the reader from the one lesson God would teach! How majestic the march of the narrative! How rapid and resolute the onward movement! What an impact of impression! A hundred words in the English, standing for but eighty in the terse Greek, put on eternal record one of the grandest lessons that God ever taught His people about the work of missions. Well may we ask for the open ear and the teachable spirit, that we may learn.

All the surroundings comport with the august solemnity of the occasion. It is Antioch, the Syrian capital, the first gentile centre of Christianity. It is a season of worship, with fasting and prayer. At least five of the early prophets and teachers were there, for they are mentioned by name. While this devout assembly draws near to the secret place where God dwells, the Holy Spirit, no doubt in an audible voice, through one or more of those prophet teachers, says:

"Separate Me Barnabas and Saul
For the work whereunto I have called them!"

That was the signal for the birth hour of foreign missions, the true nativity, of which Christ's Ascension message of ten years before was the annunciation. Every circumstance and detail is precious, for it is a presage of things to come, a forerunner to guide the Church to the end of the age. God says, "Write the vision and make it plain upon the tablets set up along the highway of missions, that even by a cursory glance he that runneth may read." All true missionaries, most of all pioneers in mission work, always have been and always will be, those whom the Holy Spirit has singularly separated unto His work. Seldom, if ever, has the Church led the way in setting them apart; in almost if not quite every case, the pioneers have led the Church, and have found sometimes their main hindrance in the apathy, if not antipathy, of those who should have been prompt to encourage and help. As at Antioch, it was not the Church but the Holy Spirit of God that took the lead in selecting and separating the first foreign missionaries, so, always, God by His providence and His Spirit has called out his servants, and the Church has sent away those whom the Spirit had already sent forth.

Thus it came to pass that in this earliest of gentile Churches, missions to the gentiles had their origin. The five prophet-teachers who there ministered before the Lord stand for gentile peoples. One a Cyrenian, one from Cyprus, one perhaps from Idumea, like Herod, another from the Cilician gates, and the last may have been a black man. When the Lord called his pioneers of missions, he went outside of the sacred circle of Jewish communities and turned from the mother Church to her first-born gentile daughter. And, even then, had not the Antiochan Church been fasting and praying, they might not have heard, or hearing they might not have heeded, the voice of God; they might not have sent away promptly, if at all, those whom the Spirit separated and called, and so would have forfeited that rich blessing that within two years returns to the bosom of the Church in that first missionary report!

In the New Acts of the Apostles, the Holy Spirit, if not as audibly, not less surely, has separated unto Himself and His work His select servants. By unmistakable signs He has set apart His pioneers. But instead of a Church praying, fasting, responsive, how often He has found a Church prayerless, feasting, secularized, corrupt. It is a sad chapter which records the separation of the New Apostles. Torpor and indifference, spiritual decay and death, ridicule and resistance often to the point of persecution, these holy men and women have found even within the "body of Christ!" Sometimes what should have been a sanctuary where the Spirit's voice was clearly heard and devoutly heeded, has been a sepulchre, where selfishness wound about God's messengers the cerements of inertia and would not loose them and let them go.

This lesson, so supremely taught in the inspired narrative, must have urgent emphasis. The one hope of missions is the faith that God's Spirit does select and separate unto Himself, call out from His Church and send forth into His work, His own divinely appointed and divinely anointed messengers.

Such only can be the apostles of missions. For what is an apostle, or missionary, but *one who is sent*! Apostle is missionary spelt Greek-wise, and missionary is apostle spelt Latin-wise. But both words mean one thing: *God-sent*. Take fast hold of this thought, let it not go, for it is the life of missions; and our daily risk is in losing sight of it and depending on human argument and appeal and the wisdom of man's selection, to furnish the force for the field. The new apostles, like the old, must be selected, separated, sent forth, by the Spirit.

Because this lesson is vital to success, let us linger yet longer to learn it fully. Two marked passages of Scripture stand confronting each other, like two pillars that hold up a grand arch: one gives us the theory, the other the practice—one the law, the other the example of God's methods. We set them side by side for comparison:

"Then saith Jesus unto His disciples:
The harvest truly is plenteous;
But the labourers are few:
PRAY YE THEREFORE THE LORD OF THE
HARVEST, THAT HE WILL THRUST FORTH
LABOURERS INTO HIS HARVEST."
—*Matt.* ix. 37,38.

"There were in the church that was at
Antioch certain prophets and teachers;
"As they ministered to the Lord and fasted,
THE HOLY GHOST SAID:
SEPARATE ME BARNABAS AND SAUL, FOR THE
WORK WHEREUNTO I HAVE CALLED THEM."
—*Acts,* xiii. 1-4.

The correspondence here shows one hand and design in both; they fit each other, like tenon and mortise, ball and socket. Our Lord, already foreseeing the harvest field waiting for seed and sickle, and the fewness of labourers ready to reap, also foretold us what was to be done. We are to resort from first to last, to Prayer.

We face a vast field of world-wide need. Where is the source of supplies, and who shall furnish workers? Do you answer, they are to be found in the Church, in her colleges and theological halls? But who shall choose and make them willing, send them forth and give them power? What if the Church, like Sarah, be barren of offspring, or having sons and daughters, be loath to give them up to God? What if those whom the Church may choose, have not the self-sacrifice to go, but cling to the easychair of home comfort and careless indulgence?

Hear the voice which spake as never man spake: "Pray ye therefore the Lord of the harvest, that He will send—thrust forth—labourers into His harvest!" Why are our eyes thus to be fixed on God alone? Because He only is the competent Judge of who are fit for His work—because He only can make them willing, can train them to greater competency and higher efficiency, and then thrust them forth into the actual field.

This is the law, and of this law the narrative before us is both example and illustration. The mother church at Jerusalem was the natural cradle of missionaries to the gentiles; yet God passes her by, and at the breast of her eldest gentle daughter suckles His first messengers to the heathen. The first two missionaries selected are neither of them from Palestine: one is a Levite from Cyprus, the other a converted persecutor and blasphemer from Cilicia.

The Holy Spirit is the one prominent personality in their appointment. He spake in an audible voice and named the very men—declared, "I have called them," and demanded that they should be separated unto Himself. All that the Church at Antioch had to do was to hear and heed this Voice from above. In laying hands upon them and sending them away, those disciples took no initiative step, but followed where the Spirit went before, ordaining and separating those whom He had first ordained and separated. Our last glimpse of them as they depart recalls not the action of the Church but of the Spirit: "So they being sent forth by the Holy Ghost, departed." Christ's words thus find an exact example. The Church prays the Lord of the Harvest, and takes no other step until He lays His hand on the very men He has chosen.

Not only this history, but all history, illustrates the same law. *We cannot raise up workmen.* We do not know God's chosen men and women. Our wisdom is folly; our steps will be missteps and mistakes. We must resort to prayer. At our peril we seek to multiply workmen by human means. God must call, select, separate and send forth, those whom He ordains—who hear His call and willingly offer themselves; those on whom He sets His seal in their conscious calling to His work and evident knowledge of Him, those who prove their fitness by their passion for souls and the fulness of the Spirit—upon such the Church may safely lay hands, commissioning them with such authority as she can confer. All other choice of labourers is premature, officious, unsafe.

This book of the Acts opens with the election of an Apostle to fill out the original number. Peter is here conspicuous, and not the Spirit of God. It was before the day of Pentecost had set this Divine Leader in the foreground of Church history. Of Matthias we hear nothing more; but, later on, God in His own marvellous way makes choice of Saul of Tarsus, and of his career the rest of the New Testament history is full. Hence many reverent students of the Word have been constrained to ask whether, in the supplying of Judas' place, Peter was not hasty, acting in advance of the Spirit's leading; whether Matthias be not an example of a man chosen of men but not called of the Spirit, owned of men rather than recognized of God.

Whatever may be thought of Peter's course on this occasion, no reader can compare the first and the thirteenth chapters of the Acts without feeling the marked contrast. In one case the leading steps are obviously human; in the other, as obviously superhuman; and while we must resort to doubtful tradition to follow Matthias further, Paul was the most active missionary of all history.

The New Acts of the Apostles adds emphasis to this lesson. The Potter sits at His wheel, with the clay in His hand. He needs the earthen vessel to bear His name to the gentiles, and He moulds it Himself, and sometimes out of material the most unpromising, and into shapes most strange. But He knows what He wants and can use. The Church has her faultless machinery of pulpit and pastor-ate, home-training and theological school. The State erects great universities, and sets running the golden wheels of scholarly culture, at which preside the skilful hands of great educators. But all these never yet moulded one apostle or turned out of human clay one true man. The shelves of man's great pottery stand to-day full of choice wares—polished porcelain, hand-painted with oriental designs and occidental art—brilliant and costly products of education, rated at the highest market-price, graceful and ornamental, the pride of nineteenth century scholarship. Yet, how often the Divine Potter passes them all by, and takes instead a rude, crude lump of earth from the slime pits, full of flaws and defects, and shapes it beneath His own hand as He wills. Then He puts it into His furnace, and in fires of hot trial bakes it into hardness and firmness, and glazes it with an unearthly lustre. Man's fine delicate wares cannot stand the fire, and crack with harsh handling. God's earthenware may be called common, but hard blows will not break it, and in fierce flames it only takes on a new glory like the face of Him whom John saw in apocalyptic vision.

As God only can choose, so He only can train missionary apostles. Human schools often spoil, puffing up with pride of learning and worldly wisdom, self-consciousness and carnal ambition. What an irreverent spirit is it, that under the guise of historical and literary criticism shamelessly and recklessly treads on holy ground, unawed by the burning bush of prophecy or the Shekinah glory of inspired history; that puts the word of God on a level with Homer and Hesiod and Herodotus, Sophocles and Socrates, Plato and Milton, forgetting that only the spiritual man illumined by the Spirit is competent to perceive or receive the revelation of the Spirit; And so it is that God finds humble, uneducated believers more ready to be taught the secrets of His word and will than many of the foremost scholars who lean to their own understanding and are wise in their own eyes.

Strange indeed are the theological schools wherein God trains His workmen. He sent Moses into the sheep pastures of Midian for forty years; Elijah into the caves of Carmel and Horeb; John the Baptist into the wilderness of Judea; Saul, for three years, into the solitudes of Arabia. When that superb Alexandrian orator, Apollos, the Apollo of the early Church, needed to get beyond the baptism of John and learn the way of God more perfectly, God chose two humble disciples, tent-makers at Corinth, and one of them a woman; and their dwelling became a theological school, and Apollos the solitary student. God has his own educators, but they would not be chosen of man; and His own armoury for His soldiers, but it is not stocked with carnal weapons.

As our studies in the New Acts of the Apostles thus compel us to become familiar with the new apostles, no fact is more conspicuous than this fact and law of a divine selection—all the great pioneers and leaders of modern missions have been eminently God-appointed and God-anointed. Again we put this fact boldly to the front—the Church has not led the way in their choice, but they have often, if not always, led the Church. Had the Church chosen, they would not have been selected, for some of them have been a century in advance of their own times, derided as fanatics and fools, apostates of the anvil, the plough and the loom. God has first trained them in His own secret schools, equipped them with weapons forged in the trial fires, then called them out from a reluctant and hostile body; and not a few of them have lived and wrought and died unrecognized as God's great ones.

This lesson can be learned only by examples, and it should be well learned, for it bears upon the coming age of missions. And here, again, we meet in our study of this grand theme an embarrassment of riches. The names of the consecrated men and women who belong to this new age of missions must be numbered by hundreds, by thousands. To pay even a passing tribute to all, we must use only the most general terms; and many of the most eminent yet survive, and delicacy if not decorum forbids that the story of their heroism should now be written; for there is an anointing which befits only burial, and the spices consecrated for embalming the dead are desecrated when used for anointing the living. It seems best therefore to choose a few representative examples from those who in some department have been pioneers and whose earthly record is complete.

The study of missionary biography reveals a true and remarkable "apostolic succession." Missions are so vital to Church life that probably should they wholly cease the Church itself would die. Never since the day of Pentecost has Christ been without witnesses. The dark ages were a millennium of death, yet the lamp of testimony, burning however faintly, never went out. No century or generation has been without its missionaries; and these lives have so been linked together, that, since the first link was forged amid the white-heat of Pentecostal fires, this grand succession has continued, without one break or missing link in the chain. Who can fail to see God's hand in all this? At the same time, in different lands, without knowledge of each other, messengers have been preparing to work side by side in the great harvest field; or at different times raised up so as to keep up the succession.

II.

The New Pioneers.

Raimundus Lullius—Pioneer To The Mohammedans.

1236-1315.

To find the pioneer missionary to the Moslem field, we must go back more than six and a half centuries before Keith Falconer fell at Aden, to that young noble of Majorca, born in Palma in 1236. He was trained as a soldier, and thirty years of his life were wasted, not in frivolity only but in sensuality, in scandalous excesses. Even his scholarly culture and philosophical mind, like those of Augustine before him, were only like polished bow and arrow without practical purpose or unselfish love to give them serviceableness.

But God had for this prodigal son a grander career. While writing a song for the siren of lust, he had a vision of the Crucified, which left upon his soul not only its impress but its image. The Captain of the Lord's Host laid hold of the trumpet that hung idle and useless on the walls of society, blew a blast upon it, waked it to music and turned it to a warrior's bugle. The grace that changed the poet of passion into a saint, made the saint a servant of Christ and a witness to a lost world. Born in 1236, he had from his cradle heard the story of the crusades. He conceived the noble purpose of beginning a new crusade against Saracen infidels, not by force of arms to rescue the Saviour's sepulchre from profane hands, but by prevailing prayer and preaching of good tidings to lead the followers of the false prophet to bow before Christ's cross and worship at His empty tomb.

He suddenly renounced the world and its pleasures, divided his estate among kinsmen and friends, took the Franciscan garb, and went into solitude to prepare for his sacred mission. He studied philosophy, theology and the ancient tongues. Learning Arabic from a slave, he made himself familiar with the works of Averroes—the Moorish Aristotle of Cordova—and other Moorish writers, and so derived the germ of that system of dialectics unfolded in his "*Ars Magna*" whereby he hoped to reform science and make converts to Christianity.

The rest of his life was one long and toilsome pilgrimage after the moving pillar. Old habits of sin, like Pharaoh's hosts in pursuit of Israel, would have drawn him back into bondage, but he dared a Red Sea of blood for the sake of following the "vision." Like the young Count at Halle, he had covenanted with God: "To thee, O Lord God, I offer myself, my wife, my children, and all that I possess;" and being free from all worldly hindrances he gave himself unreservedly to missionary service. Part of his plan for bringing unbelievers to accept the truth of Christianity was to establish missionary training colleges, where young men might be taught Arabic and other tongues; for his was no petty ambition; he aspired to nothing less than to surround and subjugate the whole Moslem territory in Christ's name. There is something sublime in this solitary man, moving the King of Aragon to establish at Palma a monastery to educate monks as missionaries, and spending years in fruitless but tireless endeavour to kindle in successive popes and kings an enthusiasm like unto his own. Then, nothing daunted, crowning all else by going himself into Moslem territory to preach Christ—he was the first of the missionary martyrs to die for the sake of the Dark Continent.

Those who doubt the romance of missions should read the story, more fascinating than any fiction, of this, the first and greatest of missionaries to the Mohammedans, and deservedly wearing the title of the "greatest missionary orator of history," whose work, on "Divine Contemplation," ranks with the Confessions of Augustine, the Meditations of Thomas A Kempis, or Bunyan's "Grace Abounding." Follow this Spaniard, pleading with kings to found training schools for Franciscan missionaries, and with the "Vicars of Christ" to decree missionary institutes and lead on the new crusade. Then see turn in 1292, just seven centuries before that famous meeting at Kettering when the first Baptist missionary society led the way, himself landing in Tunis, daring to go defenceless and alone to win converts where proselytism was a crime, and conversion was apostasy, and both punishable with death.

Scarcely had he broached his design, when he was cast into prison and then driven out of the country. He returned to Europe for aid, and again unsuccessful, went back to Africa in 1307, though threatened with stoning, and, at Bougiah, employed his "great art" in an argument with a learned Mohammedan under cover of an inquiry into the truth of Islamism. His real design was detected, and he escaped death only through his antagonist's intercession. Again in prison, he wrote there a defence of Christianity, and compelled even his foes to respect the fanatical philosopher who risked life itself for the sake of his faith and his mission.

He was a second time deported, and at seventy years of age we find him on a tour of the chief cities of Europe, like another Peter, the Hermit, preaching his crusade and declaring, "God wills it!" Once more unsuccessful, with a zeal that no discouragement could quench or even dampen, in 1314, at seventy-eight years of age, this grand old hero once more crossed the Mediterranean to Bougiah, and there, in his eightieth year, met death, like the first martyr, by stoning.

Whatever his faults or fanaticism, he had an iron resolution and chivalric ardor seldom equalled, and on the scroll of missionary history the name of this noble of Palma has a grand record. Dr. George Smith says of him; "No church, papal or reformed, has produced a missionary so original in plan, so ardent and persevering in execution, so varied in gifts, so inspired by the love of Christ, as this saint of seventy-nine, whom Mohammedans stoned to death on the 30th of June, 1315. In an age of violence and faithlessness, he was the apostle of heavenly love." Let this motto from his own great book be adopted by all his true successors:

> "He who loves not, lives not;
> He who lives by the Life, cannot die."

Francis Xavier—Romish Apostle to the Indies.

1506-1552.

Five centuries stretch between Lull and Carey, and few are the missionary names that history meanwhile records, but sufficient to preserve the succession unbroken and show that God always has true children to become the seed of the Kingdom.

The Reformation period was not one of missionary activity: from the days of the Bohemian martyr to those of the Florentine, the reformers did little more than purge the Church of false doctrine; but the Reformation moved the Romish Church to aggressive measures, and one of the most conspicuous fruits of mediaeval missions was Francis Xavier, the apostle to the Indies.

This remarkable and unique man, born in 1506, was in youth tainted by association with Protestant "heretics" but was, by Ignatius Loyola, founder of the Jesuit order, saved from these "deplorable dangers." At forty-six he died on the Island of Sancian, or St. John, off the coast of China, in 1552. But what an all-consuming flame burned in his bosom during those last ten years and set the Orient aglow!

He was misguided, no doubt; but no other life, since Paul's, has shown such ardour and fervour, such absorbing zeal for the greater glory of God, such self-forgetting, self-denying passion for the souls of men, as that of the young Saint of Navarre, whose withered relics are still adored in the Church of born Jesus at Goa.

It was not until 1542, ten years before his death, that the Jesuit missionary landed in Portuguese India. Yet what labors abundant crowded that decade! For three years he toiled in Southern India; for nearly three more, in the Chinese Archipelago; and the last four were given to India and Japan.

To the doctrine of free grace, unconsciously imbibed in boyhood, he owed his genuine experience of faith in Christ, his strong hold upon Him, and the inspiration of an unselfish purpose. To his Papal and Jesuit training we trace that admixture of confidence in outward rites and good works which alloyed and vitiated his otherwise superb service. To sprinkle holy water in baptism, to recite the creed and a few prayers, limited his methods and measured his success. His preaching practically knew nothing of the purging away of sin by intelligent faith in the atoning blood. He said, "*feci Christianos*"— "I make Christians"; and it is not strange if the disciples he made often shocked their "maker" by glaring vices and flagrant sins.

He mastered no oriental language, and was often without an interpreter; sometimes, as among the pearl fishers of Tuticorin, he was, as he himself felt, but an adept in a dumb show, an actor in a pantomime. His was the gospel of sacraments and ceremonies, preached in mute action, but with what lofty enthusiasm! To baptize a new-born babe would save a soul; to mumble a few prayers would deliver from purgatory; and so he went on with wild passion for numbers, carrying the counting of converts to the last extreme of error and absurdity. It was the lasting warning against that mechanical theory which gauges the success of missions by numerical results.

In one month, in Travancore, he baptized ten thousand natives, and at the close of his ten years' work reckoned his converts by the million. In fact, with an ambition that knew no pounds, he planned the conversion of the whole Empire of the Rising Sun, and wanted only time enough to Christianize the Orient.

Yet, notwithstanding all these drawbacks, this Jesuit fanatic puts to shame all who read the story of his life, by the utter self-abnegation he exhibited. The man who on ship-board could night and day devote himself to watching over and nursing a crew sick with the scurvy, himself bathing their disgusting bodies and washing their filthy clothes; who could suffer the pangs of hunger, famishing himself to feed the starving; who could, unresting, make journeys over thousands of miles without care or thought as to personal comfort; who could cheerfully forsake the paths of indulgence and scholarship for one perpetual pilgrimage amid the sickening sights and stifling air of oriental heathenism; who could, on God's altar lay himself, with his brilliant mind and prospects of preferment, with youth, wealth, worldly ambition, all tempting him to self-seeking—and know only the glory of God—such a man cannot be simply set aside as a fool or a fanatic. If his mistaken zeal for Papal supremacy caused Japan to seal her sea-gates to all foreign approach for two and a half centuries, on the other hand his consecrated earnestness has lit a flame of devotion to Christ in hundreds who have wept over the story of his heroism.

Xavier might have chosen any career however illustrious, and success would have had his crown ready. When at twenty-four, he was graduated at the college of St. Barbara in Paris as master of philosophy, and licensed to lecture upon Aristotle; when he taught with applause at the College of Beauvais, and in the Sorbonne gained the title of "doctor," he was like a new star rising on the firmament of European civilization, and men asked whereunto his fame might not reach. But on August 15, 1534, he with five others, led by Loyola, took their vows in the chapel of Montmartre, and from that time he never swerved nor looked back. After his ordination as priest, he went to Bologna, and there in his preaching and visits to hospitals and prisons, evinced such apostolic zeal and love, that he seemed a combination of Peter and Paul and John in one; and, when missionaries were in demand for Portuguese settlements in the Indies, he was one of the first two selected. Bell in hand, he went through the streets of Goa calling upon Christian inhabitants to send children and slaves to be taught the true faith; went to the coast of Cormorin and the island of Ceylon, and many other parts of the East, reviving the dead faith of nominal Christians, and gathering flourishing congregations which he left in the care of his disciples, himself pressing onward to the regions beyond. Intrepidly he met the intrigues and violence of Japanese priests, publicly disputed with the bonzes, and won many from the cultured classes; so that, on returning to Goa in 1551, he left three great princes of the empire as converts and vast numbers of baptized disciples from the humbler ranks. He meant to pierce the Chinese wall of exclusion; and when the fatal fever laid hold upon him he could only look toward the Walled Kingdom, and cry, "O rock! rock! when wilt thou open to my Master?" During these ten years this Romish "apostle" had planted the cross "in fifty-two different kingdoms, had preached through nine thousand miles of territory, and baptized over one million persons." In visions of the night when he saw the world conquered for Christ, he would spring up shouting, "Yet more, O my God, yet more!" and his whole life was a commentary on his own motto:

"Ad Majorem Dei Gloriam."

John Eliot—Apostle to the North American Indians. 1604-1690.

Like Ziegenbalg and Zinzendorf, properly belonging to the century before Carey, Eliot was one of those who formed the mould in which modern missions took shape. He was a pioneer of pioneers, and history has yet to give him his true niche in her Westminster. His period nearly spans the seventeenth century, and three features are conspicuous in his personality: first, a pious parentage with its rich legacy of character; secondly, his connection with the Puritan exile, Thomas Hooker, whom he followed to the New World; and thirdly, his absorbing passion for the souls of the red men. For sixty years he filled his sole pastorate at Roxbury, from this centre radiating influence over a wider sphere of effort.

A forecast of his work was seen in his early aptitude for language. At nineteen, graduated from Cambridge, he had already mastered the original languages of the Bible, and shown unusual skill as a grammarian and philologist. At thirty-five, the colonial leaders chose him to aid in the new version of the Psalter, and his "Bay Psalm Book" was the first book printed in America.

He had barely taken up his pastoral staff at Roxbury when his unselfish love was drawn out toward the Indians. Through a young Pequot, he got hold of their strange tongue, and in 1646, in Chief Waban's wigwam preached the first sermon in their language ever known on American soil. This memorable service in camp, near Brighton, lasted three hours. A new camp-fire was kindled, and the spirit of religious inquiry began to burn. Two weeks later, a second visit found an old warrior weeping lest it should be too late to find God; and a fortnight after, Waban himself was found talking to his followers of the strange story of the cross, in face of fierce opposition from the Indian priests.

What, two hundred years after him, William Duncan did in his "Metlakahtla," Eliot did in his "Nonantum," five miles west of Boston—building a model state for his "praying Indians," who as such became known in history, like Cromwell's "Ironsides." The Roxbury pastor, aflame with holy passion to civilize and Christianize these wild men of the forest, organized his converts into a commonwealth, with civil courts, social and industrial improvements and religious institutions.

No circle of ten miles diameter could fence in such a man. Neponset, Concord, Brookfield, Pawntucket, felt his power, and from all quarters came clamorous appeals for new law-codes, Bible institutions and Christian teachers. Chiefs and their sons became converts, and then leaders; and, when Eliot's visits involved risk to him, the sachem and his brave warriors became his escort; while fearless, if not heedless of danger, alone on horseback, he dared perils and bore privations for Christ's sake.

Not only were snares of death laid for him by hostile and treacherous chiefs, but his own countrymen, not content to withhold aid, pitilessly pelted him with the hail of ridicule, or hurled at him the mudclods of aspersion; they made him the butt of jest as a trader in fables, or charged him with selfish greed. But God "stepped in and helped." Before the century had reached its noon, his work had won a double victory; for it had both conquered the Indian and compelled recognition from Britain. Devout souls, across the sea, heard the fame of his deeds and felt the flame of his zeal; and so it came to pass that, more than half a century before the "Society for the Propagation of the Gospel," a similar organization was formed to propagate the gospel in New England, and sent fifty pounds a year to the Nonconformist exile at Roxbury.

Like Livingstone, Eliot was a missionary general and statesman. In 1650, he gathered most of his converted Indians into "Natick," a tract of six thousand acres on the Charles River, where each family had a house-lot, where large buildings were erected for church and school, and where distinguished visitors heard Eliot's praying Indians teach and preach. The evangelist and statesman now became also theological professor, training a native ministry—that secret of the perpetuity of all mission work. He who had toiled for thirty-eight years to gather about thirty-six hundred converted Indians into fourteen settlements in 1671, left twenty-four native preachers behind him when he died in 1690.

This versatile man was not only preacher and pastor, general and statesman, founder of model settlements and trainer of native evangelists; he was also a translator. In 1661 the New Testament, and two years later the Old Testament, were published in the native tongue; and so that famous Indian Bible, which has now not one living reader, was the first Bible printed west of the Atlantic. As Bayard Taylor said of Humboldt—it is "not a ruin but a pyramid," no mere lonely relic of the past for the curious antiquarian, but a grand structure from whose lofty apex the red man got a glimpse of the City of God; and it is still a pillar of witness, testifying to one of God's kings who, against such odds, builded this monument to the glory of God! Both as a memorial of holy zeal and as a testimony to fine scholarship, it merits what Edward Everett said of it, that "the history of the Christian Church contains no example of resolute, untiring labour superior to it." Eliot likewise created for his beloved children of the forest a new Christian literature, translating such practical guides as "Baxter's Call," and preparing catechism and psalter to follow grammar and primer. When age and weakness kept him at home, and he could not go to his Indians, he besought families to send to him their negro servants that he might teach them saving truth.

Southey pronounced John Eliot "one of the most extraordinary men of any country;"and Richard Baxter said there was "no other man whom he honoured above him." We claim for him a certain priority of pedigree in this apostolic succession. In a peculiar sense he was, on this side the sea, father and founder of modern missions; for it was his life and work that moved and moulded David Brainerd, James Brainerd Taylor, Jonathan Edwards, Adoniram Judson, as also William Carey and others who followed him. Yet this stream of holy influence which watered so many trees of life, Eliot himself traces to its spring in the home of Hooker. "When I came into this blessed family," said he, "I saw as never before the power of godliness in its lively vigour and efficiency." What a lesson in living! Eliot held for a time the position of usher in Hooker's grammar school, and the family piety he saw exhibited there led to his conversion and consecration. Thus do the streams whose fountains are beneath the Temple of God flow softly through their hidden channels, and come up to the surface, from time to time, in some Siloam basin or Bethesda pool. Hooker reappears in Eliot, Eliot in Edwards, Edwards in Carey, Carey in Judson, and so on without end.

The last words on John Eliot's lips were "Welcome, joy!" and were probably the response of the departing soul to the vision of bliss which glorified his dying moments. But there is a brief sentence written at the end of his Indian grammar which is the key to the lock of his life, furnishing at once the interpretation of the man and the revelation of his secret. As I stood, in 1893, by the simple slab of stone that in a Boston burial-ground bears his name, that sentence seemed a fit motto for all true missions:

"PRAYER AND PAINS

THROUGH FAITH IN JESUS CHRIST

WILL DO ANYTHING."

BARON JUSTINIAN ERNST VON WELZ

PIONEER TO DUTCH GUIANA.

The roots of modern missions reach back to the Reformation, and the plant that hangs with such abundant fruit is at least four centuries old. But much of this growth was below the surface; and a distinct and definite line marks the last hundred years as the period of *organized* missionary effort.

Luther, and his fellow reformers, revived primitive apostolic faith, which must be the precursor and prepare the way if apostolic life and work are to follow. The Church must always be evangelical before it is evangelistic. Soon after the reformed faith had laid hold upon the convictions of God's people, the debt of duty to a lost race began loudly to demand payment, and the Reformed Church felt the movings of a new impulse to spread the good tidings far and wide. But, after a thousand years of inaction, of spiritual sloth and sleep, apathy and lethargy loose their hold slowly, as the ice-bonds of an arctic winter yield to the summer sun. Here and there one man was reached and roused, his eyes opening to the fact that millions were dying without the gospel; his ears opening to the cry of want and woe which, like the moan and sob of waves on the sea-shore, tells of storm and wreck. Now and then a man went forth, while as yet the Church as a whole seemed locked in icy indifference and insensibility.

Von Welz, who belongs before Spener, Francke and Zinzendorf, is one of the precursors of the coming era of missions. About 1664 he issued his invitation for a society of Jesus, to promote Christianity and the conversion of heathendom; and the same year, another manifesto of like purport which, like Carey's Inquiry into the Obligations of Christians, a hundred years later, turned a powerful search-light upon the superficial piety of his day and laid bare its hollowness and shallowness.

There is something grand in this solitary man, blowing upon God's silver trumpet a solemn alarm to set in motion the camps. No such voice had before been heard in the Reformed Church, but it awakened no sympathetic responsive echo. Those "light words," which are the "Devil's keenest swords," pierced him again and again. Unsparing ridicule and contemptuous opposition swept over him, but only to fix deeper the roots of his holy purpose, as storms fasten the cedars to the rock-sides of Lebanon. Another manifesto still more searching succeeded: an appeal to court preachers and learned professors to establish a college for training missionaries. Von Welz joined to the capacity of a statesman and organizer, the enthusiasm of a zealot, the persistency of a born leader, and the courage of a warrior. Because he would not keep silence but kept blowing his bugle blast in men's ears, summoning the sleeping Church to propagate the faith among unbelieving peoples, he was laughed at as a dreamer and fanatic, and denounced as a hypocrite, heretic and blasphemer. Dr. Ursinus, severer in rebuke than Ryland was with Carey, prayed, concerning the proposed Jesus-Association, "protect us from it, dear Lord God," as though the proposed missionary society and training college were to be classed with those malicious and seditious schemes from which the litany implores, "Good Lord, deliver us." The famous doctor of Ratisbon regarded the heathen as dogs to whom we are not to give that which is holy, or swine that will wallow in the mire and trample under foot the pearls of the gospel, and he would have given them over to work all uncleanness with greediness.

When the proposal to send out artisans and laymen to evangelize the heathen met, like other appeals, only rebuff and ridicule, that heroic soul that could not move others to action found relief in selfoffering. Ordained an apostle to the gentiles by Breckling, a poor priest in Holland, Von Welz, like Zinzendorf after him, left behind his baronetcy and his baronial estate, and himself became the humble messenger to Dutch Guiana, where he laid down his life. Like other seers of God and prophets of humanity, he saw farther than his contemporaries; and, had the bold originality of his missionary schemes found earnest co-operation, organized missions might have found in the soil of Protestant Germany their germination at least a hundred years before Carey and his humble twelve sat down in widow Wallis' parlor at Kettering.

Von Welz was another of the examples of which history is full, of great and extraordinary minds endowed with a consciousness of strength, impelled by a Divine impulse which is their truest and best adviser. There is a "perspicacity of eye" which is the direct effect of that mystic anointing with God's own eye salve; and God's born prophets must not be disobedient to the heavenly vision, though others see not the form and hear not the voice. Baron Von Welz ' could say of his manifestos what Thucydides said of his histories, "I give these to the public as an everlasting possession, and not as a contentious instrument of temporary applause."

Such men are God's agitators, sent to marshal the conscience of the Church, to mould the law of its life and the methods of its work in conformity with His word and will. They are educators of the race, but too often they find dull pupils, that, ever learning, are never able to come to the full knowledge of the truth. To us it now seems incredible that the Austrian baron, who would found a new Jesus society—not a Jesuit order—to rally to itself those whom the love of Jesus constrained to bear His gospel to the lost, and who offered the capital of 30,000 thalers as a fund whose interest should support the missionaries in training,—should be met not only by the sneers of the worldly, but by the unsparing condemnation of leading Churchmen; that John Heinrich Ursinus, superintendent of Ratisbon, otherwise an excellent man, could so violently oppose a scheme which took all its inspiration from the New Testament! Yet, in so doing, he represented the general attitude of the Lutheran Church of his day.

The zeal of this first missionary martyr within the Lutheran Church, who found a grave at Surinam, may have flamed with excess of enthusiasm, but we cannot, with Plitt, dismiss him as a "missionary fanatic."His motives were too unselfish, his purpose too lofty, his self-sacrifice too sublime, his appeals too scriptural and too spiritual, to be thus classed with the outcome of a half-disordered brain. How true it is that the madness of one generation is the wisdom of the next, and the fanaticism of one decade becomes the heroism of the next! The men that are martyrs to the hatred and violence of one age, are the saints that a succeeding age canonizes. Would that we might not slay God's prophets, leaving a wiser generation to pay its too tardy tribute at their sepulchres!

BARTHOLOMEW ZIEGENBALG—PIONEER TO INDIA.

1683-1719.

If we seek the pioneer in the East Indies, we must go back beyond Duff and Carey to those devoted pietists of Denmark, Bartholomew Ziegenbalg and Henry Plütschau, who, in 1706, just one hundred years before Alexander Duff was born, landed at Tranquebar.

Ziegenbalg, born in Pulsnitz, Upper Lusatia, in 1683, and dying in India, of cholera, at thirty-six, crowded into twelve 'years of missionary life such abundant service as few of the most devoted men have ever offered to the Master on the altar of missions. Trained at Halle in theology and biblical literature, and ordained at Copenhagen in 1705, he arrived at Tranquebar after eight months at sea, only to be imprisoned by the Danish authorities. Unknown to him and his fellow-student, by the same vessel on which they sailed, secret instructions were despatched by the Danish East India Company, authorizing the governor at Tranquebar to block their way by every means and crush their mission in the bud. And the governor did his best to obey instructions.

These first Protestant missionaries that ever trod the soil of India, had gone over the wide seas to win a new empire for Christ, and as they stood, on the night after they landed, with no shelter

> **SCRIPTURE TESTIMONY**
>
> *Become all things to all people*
>
> I CORINTHIANS 9:19-23

but the sky and no companions but the stars, left by the governor to shift for themselves, a pathetic interest invests their loneliness. What a task before them, and what a welcome to their new field! One of the governor's suite took pity upon them and they found for the first few days a place of sojourn; then they were allowed to occupy a house upon the wall, close by the heathen quarters; and, all undaunted by difficulties, Ziegenbalg, six days after his landing, was busy at Tamil, though he had neither dictionary, grammar nor alphabet. He sat down with native children, writing with fingers on the sand to learn the strange language in which were locked up the secrets of access to the people and their religion.

By almost unparalleled industry and application, he could in eight months talk in Tamil. All day long busied with reading and writing, translating and reciting, he managed not only to master the intricate construction of the language, but to catch the inflection and tone in pronunciation, so that in 1709, Tamil was to him as his native German. He had now, however, made only a start, and applied himself to the making of a grammar and two lexicons, which together contained nearly 60,000 words. Before he had been in India two years, the translation of the

New Testament was in progress, and within a third year completed. Then, when serious illness hindered other work, he began the Old Testament.

Here was a young missionary of twenty-six, preaching in Tamil, and giving the people the New Testament in their own tongue. On the ship sailing from Copenhagen he had learned the broken Portuguese dialect that all along the coast was used by the half-breeds, and he turned this to good use, opening a school and preaching service for such as could be reached by this language; and the first fruits of his labour were five converted slaves of Danish masters within the first year after his arrival, and, four months later, nine adult Hindus.

Against the persistent opposition of the governor, and the failure of funds to carry on the mission, in 1708, Ziegenbalg made his pioneer preaching tour into the kingdom of Tanjore, and at Negapalam began his friendly conferences with the Brahmans. He not only first gave India a Tamil New Testament and vernacular dictionaries, but he set up the first press.

Left alone by Plütschau's return, he was himself driven home by sickness. In 1715 he suddenly appeared in Denmark; then hurried into Germany to Francke and Halle, preaching to crowds that no church could hold; then with his newly wedded wife, hurrying through Holland to London, he went back to Tranquebar, where he found the governor who had tyrannically fought him displaced by a warm friend of missions.

For two years more, as though he felt that death was approaching, with almost reckless enthusiasm he sped toward his goal—the winning of India for Christ. At Christmastide, 1718, he preached, but a week later his voice was so feeble that he could scarce be heard, and he never again spoke in public. On the last Sunday his bed was his pulpit, and from his pillow he exhorted his native converts to hold fast the faith. Soon after morning prayer, February 23, 1719, the chill of death was upon him.

Two scenes, one at the beginning, the other at the end of this singularly devoted life, should be placed side by side for the lessons they teach. When his mother died she left to her children as her last legacy, "a great treasure," which she bade them seek in the Bible. "There," said she, "you will find it; there is not a page that I have not wet with my tears."

Ziegenbalg was very young at the time, but he never forgot the impression of those words; and when he went to India, his mother's legacy to him was the treasure he sought to bequeath to his converts. And when about himself to depart, so intense was the glory that smote him, that he suddenly put his hands to his eyes, exclaiming, "How is it so bright, as if the sun shone full in my face!" Soon after, he asked that his favourite hymn might be sung, "Jesus, meine zuversicht"(my confidence), and on the wings of sacred song he took his flight, leaving behind over three hundred and fifty converts, catechumens and pupils, a missionary seminary and a Tamil lexicon, but best of all the Tamil Bible.

When, a hundred and thirty-four years later, Alexander Duff stood in the pulpit where Ziegenbalg, as well as Grundler and Schwartz, so often told of Jesus, his heart swelled with emotion. To him the Danish missionary was, among all that had gone to India, not only great, but "first, inferior to none, scarcely second to any that followed him." On the sides of a plain altar lay the dust of Ziegenbalg and Grundler, those two men of such "brief but brilliant and immortal careers in the mighty work of Indian evangelization," whose "lofty and indomitable spirit breathed the most fervid piety."*

As truly as Ignatius or Huss, Ziegenbalg was a martyr of Christ. But, as Shelley's heart was found unconsumed in the ashes of his pyre on Italy's shore, the heart of such a pioneer is still the inspiration of all later heroism. Whatever property Ziegenbalg had in himself was made over to God, unencumbered with mortgages; to him self-denial was a joy, and sacrifice was amply compensated by service. Like the Maid of Orleans, he would "rather have died than do anything which was known to be contrary to the will of God;" and, like Richard Knill, his contribution to missions was the offering of himself.

For courageous faith and patient faithfulness, for keen insight and practical wisdom, for untiring industry and deep devotion, few missionaries anywhere have equalled Bartholomew Ziegenbalg; and we cannot but see him repeated and reproduced in that most conspicuous figure in India during the eighteenth century, Christian Frederick Schwartz, who like him was a German, a student and translator in Tamil, ordained at Copenhagen, and who sailed to Tranquebar. These two men, though one life measured but half the other's in years, wielded a power in India that can be measured only at the last day.

HANS EGEDE—THE APOSTLE OF GREENLAND.

1686-1758.

We turn now toward that repellant clime, the frozen pole, to find another example of one whom God called and thrust forth to unfurl the flag of the cross upon the ice-castles of the north.

It was early in the last century that a

> **SCRIPTURE TESTIMONY**
>
> *Spiritual burden for a lost people group to be saved*
>
> ROMANS 9:1-3

humble Dane who was the village pastor in Vaagen, off the Norway coast, in the Lifoden Isles, felt oppressed with the woe and want of the heathen a thousand

---

* Smith's Short History.

miles away toward the pole; and, like Nehemiah at the court of Esther, his face betrayed his sorrow of heart, so that not only his wife but his parishioners sought a reason for his troubled looks. His was a secret that could not be kept. By a seeming accident Hans Egede had read of the discovery of Greenland by Norwegian sailors about the close of the tenth century; of the successful preaching of the gospel among the rude people of those climes; of the subsequent ice blockade, and the black pest which, in the fifteenth century, broke off communication, so that for nearly three centuries these poor heathen had been left to relapse into darkness without any man who cared for their souls.

Hans Egede could not say why he should feel such concern for those toward whom no one else seemed to be drawn; but he could rest neither day nor night for thinking of them; and he ventured at last to open his heart to his dear "Elizabeth." But, like many another, she found the home-work a sufficient apology for staying at Vaagen, and could neither sympathize with nor understand this yearning for souls three hundred leagues away. Wife and children and parish were to her field enough for apostolic labors and denials, and she begged Hans to dismiss his anxieties, her earnest pleading waxing at last into virtuous indignation at the mistaken zeal that would turn him from duties close at hand to go on a vague mission to the ends of earth.

God was dealing with her husband, and he could only answer that the Lord would have him do something for Greenland: of that he was sure. He was persuaded to wait, and four years passed away. Greenland seemed to find another ice blockade in Egede's heart. Then came three signs from God; two bishops wrote letters, respectively from Drontheim and Bergen, both urging Egede to take up this mission; and a rich merchant made offer of transportation, and help in founding a colony. Egede felt that God was both thrusting him forth and opening the door; but his reluctant wife was now joined by a sorrowing church, and again Hans Egede consented to wait, but solemnly added: "Twice God has called me—if again He calls, I go."

About a year after, the third call came; and this time it came through his wife, Elizabeth. Thorns had been planted in the household nest, and she was restless and unhappy. Some hostile elements in the parish made her home-life bitter, and Vaagen lost its charm. God was stirring up the nestling and preparing his eaglet for a flight. Half a night was spent on her knees. Then she asked little Paul, her youngest child, whether she should go with his father to the poor heathen across the sea; and out of the mouth of a babe and suckling God spoke once more, for he said, "Yes, let us go; and I will tell them of Jesus and teach them to say, 'Our Father!'" And so; after six years of waiting and watching for God's time to come, the wife, too, felt God thrusting her forth, and now her faith went beyond her husband's.

Early in 1721 the ship was ready to set sail: and when Hans Egede had his foot on the plank to go on board, some sailors warned him that death awaited him if he ventured to those inhospitable shores. They said they had come from Greenland and barely escaped being eaten by those cannibals who dwelt there and who had eaten some of their party. Was this God's voice of warning? The Vaagen pastor took his four children by the hand and turned back. But Elizabeth now led the way, crying, "O ye of little faith!" and boldly crossed the plank. To her this was no sign that they were to stay at home; it was a test, from God, of their worthiness to undertake for Him; and taking her seat in the boat she bade her family follow.

They set sail, and, while the husband and children wept, her face shone as if it were the face of an angel. They undertook as pioneers to preach the gospel in that foreign land, and with some forty settlers founded the Christian colony of which God-thaab, (God's haven) is the capital.

The story of Egede is one of severe hardship, but it is so full of startling marvels that Christlieb has referred to it as one of the many instances which modern missions furnish of that supernatural working which seems to reproduce the apostolic age. Those stupid dwarfs, like the icebergs and snowfields about them, seemed frozen into insensibility; and, feeling that only some sure sign of Divine power could melt their stolid apathy, Egede boldy asked for the gift of healing, and was permitted in scores of cases to exercise it, while his wife received the gift of prophecy, predicting in the crisis of famine the very day and hour when a ship should come bearing supplies!

SCRIPTURE TESTIMONY

God gave signs and wonders through the apostles

ACTS 5:12

When Christian VI. disbanded the settlement on account of the severe hardships and bitter disappointment of the half famished colonists, the work of Egede seemed to have come to naught. But by a very marvellous leading of God, where the mission of Egede ended, Moravian missions began. For, in 1731, at the coronation of Frederick's successor to the throne, the young Count Zinzendorf represented the Saxon court; and meeting two Eskimo converts of Egede, learned that the mission work was to be abandoned. This was one of the main influences that, in the next year, moved the young count, and through him the Brotherhood, to send to the West Indies Dober and Nitschmann, and to organize a mission work that should know no limits but the wide world.

Count Von Zinzendorf—The Moravian Apostle.

1700-1760.

To Philip James Spener, head of this pietist school, and to Francke, his greater disciple, this Moravian bishop's spiritual lineage must be traced. His grandfather, an Austrian noble, had for the Lord's sake given up all his estates, and that heroic example of self-denial his grandmother and aunt had emphasized by such holy training, that the lad, at four years, formally covenanted with his "dear Saviour," "Be thou Mine and I will be Thine." He so longed for communion with his unseen Lord, that in childish simplicity he was wont to write letters to Jesus, in which he laid bare his heart, and, confident that He would get and read them, tossed them from the castle window.

When but ten years old, the pupil of Francke at Halle, we find him forming prayer circles, and the Order of the Grain of Mustard-seed, whose members were to sow in other hearts the seed of the Kingdom. Though drawn to classic pursuits and tempted by rank and riches, his life-motto was that of Tholuck after him: "I have one passion; it is He and He alone:" and it was this, that amid the gaieties of Paris and the snares of Dresden, held him fast to Christ. To this, even the new passion of love was at once brought into subjection; he would marry only in the Lord, and his unique covenant of wedlock involved a mutual renunciation of rank, a consecration of wealth, and a dedication of self to the Lord and His work. From this marriage-altar two pilgrims went forth, as from the paschal supper in Egypt, with loins girt and staff in hand, for a new Exodus.

On their wedding-tour, they found the Moravian exiles taking refuge at Berthelsdorf, and welcomed them to build there, Herrnhut; and the seal of the *Unitas Fratrum* became the count's true coat of arms—a lamb on a crimson ground with the cross of resurrection, and a banner of triumph, with the motto: "*Vicit agnus noster, eum sequamur.*"— "Our Lamb has won; let us follow Him." Zinzendorf began with the resolve that wherever the Lord had need of him he would find his native land; and a little later could say that he would rather be hated for Christ's sake than be loved for his own.

His history merges into that of the Moravian Brotherhood, which at the hundred and fiftieth anniversary of its mission work, in 1882, had sent forth 2,170 missionaries, planted 113 stations, 211 schools, and 89 Sunday schools, with a total of 23,000 pupils, and expended 52,000 pounds yearly, at a cost of only three per cent, for administration.

The Unitas Fratrum is the pioneer church in missions. This brotherhood is in the direct line of descent from the Bohemian martyr, Huss, and his contemporary Chelczicky. In 1467, a few Bohemians formed themselves into an apostolic Church.

Tradition traces the ordination of their first bishop to a Waldensian priest; and so the Moravians are linked to the martyrs both of Bohemia and of the Vaudois valleys. Their doctrine took form both in the mould of Luther and of Calvin, as became a Church that was to be known alike for its vigorous faith and its spirit of reform. Persecution wrought the red cross into the Moravian robe, and in 1722, Christian David, the carpenter, led a mere band of eleven exiles across the frontier into Saxony.

How God teaches us not to despise the day of small things! They remind us of the eleven Apostles at Jerusalem and of the twelve Baptists at Kettering. Five years after they settled on the site of Herrnhut, they were but three hundred strong, with Zinzendorf practically at their head; and August 13, 1727, is still kept as the spiritual birthday of the renewed Church. Ten years later the count became their bishop, and for twenty-three years, until his death in 1760, their "advocate." To his leadership is due more than human annals record. Each morning gives a new text as a watchword; and certain members of the band keep up the hourly prayer, as vestals guarded the sacred fires and lamps. Death is a joyous home-going to be announced with song and trumpet.

The Brethren caught the spirit of their leader; the "seed corn" at Halle has grown into the "*Diaspora*" at Herrnhut, whose principle, as its name implies, is Dispersion. God has given to the Moravians to prove the power of the spirit of missions, and to make real what too many even yet treat as an impracticable ideal. The *Diaspora* is one hundred and sixty-seven years old, has over sixty central stations, numbers over seventy thousand members, and stands for the home mission. To contact with its working force the Wesleys and Whitefield owed their kindling of evangelistic zeal.

But it is the foreign missions of the Herrnhut band that furnish us our most pertinent example. When in 1732 the settlement was but ten years old and numbered but six hundred, Dober sailed for the West Indies; and, soon after, the United Brethren were planting the cross in Greenland and Lapland, the Americas and Africa. Less than one hundred and sixty years later, there were one hundred and thirty-three stations and filials; three hundred and forty-three missionaries and nearly fivefold as many native helpers; thirty thousand communicants, and nearly twice as many more baptized adults; and two hundred and thirty-two schools with twenty thousand pupils.

All Christendom may well stop to gaze at the unique spectacle of a Church, having in its missions almost three times as many communicants and baptized adults as in the home Church of its three provinces: British, German and American; a Church, which, while Protestant Churches at large send one member out of five thousand to the foreign field, sends one out of ninety-two! A like ratio throughout the Churches generally would put in the regions beyond three hundred and eighty thousand Protestant missionaries!

Let us fix in mind the leading features of this foremost missionary Church.

First, its *Evangelistic Basis*. It holds itself in debt to a lost world, and in trust with the gospel: as trustees to discharge the obligation of debtors. All are trained to service, to work for the common good of the Brotherhood and the redemption of the race; to have few wants, frugal habits and readiness for self-sacrifice. Missions are thus not the exception but the law. Prompt obedience to any clear leading of God is the base-block of daily life. Zinzendorf asked a brother if he would go to Greenland. "Certainly." "When?" "To-morrow." Any Church destitute of the spirit of missions is considered dead, and every disciple without service, an apostate.

Again, *the law of preference*. The worst and most hopeless fields have the first claim. Mary Lyon reflected their unselfishness when she advised her students at Holyoke to be ready to go where no one else would, or as a poor negro slave phrased it, "where dere is most debbil." It was Moravian blood that impelled William Augustine Johnson to choose Sierra Leone, because it was the worst field known; and so Hans Egede became an exile in the land of eternal snow, Dober offered to sell himself into slavery to reach the slaves of St. Thomas, and later martyrs have scaled Thibet's mountain walls to unfurl the flag of the cross above the shrine of the Grand Lama.

Again, *zeal for Divine approval*. Wordly ambition is ruled out of the Moravian life. Evangelism, not proselytism, is their principle. Increase of numbers is no object; and hence there is no counting of converts or overlooking of quality in quantity. Of denominational growth they are not jealous, and rather prefer not to extend their borders. To them alone belongs the rare distinction of a litany with this unique petition:

> "From the unhappy desire of being great,
> > Good Lord, deliver us!"

Holy living, ceaseless praying, cheerful giving, constitute their conception of discipleship, and the open secret of that Brotherhood, which, fewest in numbers and poorest in resources, leads the van of missions.

Christian Friederich Schwartz—Founder of the Native Christian Church in India.

1726-1798.

Here was another of Germany's contributions to the mission field. When at the University of Halle, he studied Tamil that he might superintend the issue of a Bible in that tongue; and, though this purpose was not carried into effect, he was unconsciously fitting for a singularly useful work at the centre of oriental missions. Francke, knowing that he had learned Tamil, urged him to undertake a mission to India; and in January, 1750, the meridian year of the eighteenth century, he set sail, unaccompanied even by a wife, that he might be the more single-eyed in his devotion to His Master's work.

He was successively identified with Tranquebar, Trichinopoly and Tanjore. But Schwartz left his track over all India, and he can be traced in footprints of light after one hundred and fifty years. Such was his influence as a man of God that both friends and foes alike looked upon him with an awe akin to worship. He was a day's man betwixt contending parties, a whole court of arbitration in himself. He acted as embassy to treat with Hyder Ali and saved Tanjore. The cruel and vindictive despot gave orders: "Let the venerable Father Schwartz pass unmolested!" When, after nearly half a century of work in India, he was not for God took him, he was mourned by a whole nation. The prince of Tanjore wept over his bier and the Rajah himself built him a monument.

Bishop Heber described him as "one of the most active, fearless and successful missionaries who have appeared since the Apostles," and it is a curious example of apostolic succession in missions that William Carey had been five years in Serampore, when Schwartz was translated to a higher sphere.

"Father Schwartz" wielded a sceptre in India more potent than even Zeigenbalg, who landed at Tranquebar twenty years before Schwartz was born. It may be worth while to notice the steps by which such a career was prepared. born in 1726, he was left motherless while yet an infant. But, as his mother died, she gave her boy into the hands of her Lutheran pastor and weeping husband, with this solemn charge, which recalls the story of little Samuel: "For this child I prayed, and the Lord hath given me my petition which I asked of Him. Therefore, also, have I lent him to the Lord. So long as he liveth he shall be lent to the Lord. Take him, and foster in him any aptitude which he may show for the Christian ministry. This is my last legacy."

The dying commission of this modern Hannah was fulfilled. His father trained young Schwartz to simple, self-denying habits; sent him at eight years of age to the grammar school at Sonnenberg, where he got a good start in Latin, Greek and Hebrew; then eight years later he transferred him to a higher school at Cüstrin. There unhappily, his youthful passions, not yet under the discipline of moral restraint, led him into dissipation, and it seemed as though his mother's "last legacy" would not prove also a prophecy.

But God remembered his covenant. The lad was kept back from presumptuous sins. He came under Francke's influence, became interested in his orphan houses, and studied at the university where Francke taught. That marvellous man drew him with cords of love, led him to a true consecration, and introduced him to Schültze who had been twenty years in India, and was then at Halle to print the Tamil Bible. Under the contagious enthusiasm of this saintly missionary, the seed planted in the boy's heart by his mother found its growth in the man's life and character.

But its full ripeness was reserved for the oriental clime. On the voyage to India, his remarkable linguistic powers were again brought into play, for he so acquired the English tongue as to be able to preach in that language on his arrival at Tranquebar. Within four months, he preached with ease in the native dialect; then mastered Persian, and so had access to the greatest of Mohammedan princes; by his acquaintance with Hindustani, he became invaluable in the service of the British Government; and further acquired the Hindu-Portuguese, that he might reach the mixed race descended from this double ancestry.

His passion to save men made all labour and sacrifice seem little. He studied the habits, modes of thought and idioms of speech, and even the mazes of mythology, which are the paths to the hearts of the Hindus. But above all he set himself so to live in God as by his life to compel men to think of God. No hindrance was or is so serious to mission work as the utter and often shameless wickedness of those who in the eye of the native population stand for "Christians." The Indians of the West said of their Spanish conquerors in Central America, "If they are to be in heaven, we prefer hell;" and the Indians of the East replied to those who preached to them purity, "If only the pure in heart can see God, it is sure that your countrymen will not be found in heaven."

But the character of Schwartz was a sermon that convinced the gainsayers. He spared not himself nor counted his own life dear. With an energy and unselfishness that have almost no parallel, as they had almost no limit, early and late he gave himself to work, and what his hands found to do he did with his might. His discourse before a small native congregation was prepared with as much care as if for courts and crowned heads of Europe. The country became dotted with native churches.

He was but forty years old when events occurred which stamped his career as unique, even in the history of mission enterprise. The Society for Promoting Christian Knowledge chose Schwartz for its new mission at Trichinopoly. His whole allowance was fifty pounds a year. He lived in a small room and on a diet of rice and vegetables. A church was built to hold two thousand people, but he would not allow his work in an English garrison to hinder his greater work among the natives. With the humblest of them he conferred and counselled, and the proud

Brahmans were often won by his arguments, though they, like the Pharisees, feared to confess Christ, lest they should be put out of their "synagogues." In 1769 he so charmed Rajah Taljajee by his thanks before meat, and his holy conversation, that when Schwartz left Tanjore, the Rajah persuaded him to return; and so great was his influence on the Rajah's subjects that they declared that if their prince would set the example his followers would all become Christians; and the Rajah might perhaps have confessed Christ but for the violent opposition of his court.

Henceforth Schwartz went by the name of the "Padre," and was free to go where he would, preaching and teaching. His life was a living epistle of Christ, a whole volume of Christian evidence and apologetics. One young nabob said, "Until you came we thought of Europeans as godless men who did not know the use of prayers." When chosen as the only man fit to treat with Hyder Ali, lest his hands should even seem defiled with presents he would take nothing beyond bare travelling expenses; and his candour and courtesy won even that tyrant, so that on a subsequent occasion he said, "Send to me none of your agents, for I trust neither their words nor pledges: send me the Christian missionary and I will receive him." In the awful famine when Tanjore was laid waste, the Rajah said, "We have all lost our credit; let us try whether the people will trust Schwartz," who was authorized to arrange as he could; and in two days a thousand oxen and eighty thousand measures of rice were ready for the starving garrison.

This one man, by the simple force of his piety, was not only preacher and pastor, but patriarch. He made laws and gave judgment. He ministered to living and dead. When punishment for slight offences became necessary, the culprits besought that he might himself inflict the penalty, and from his judgment there was no attempt or desire to appeal. When, in 1787, the Rajah died, his influence prevented the suttee at the funeral. All unsought by him, the magistracy of the country was in the hands of this saintly missionary. Freedom from deceitfulness and selfishness made him the organizer of cosmical order in the midst of social chaos.

After forty-eight years of consecrated service he died, his clear voice still ringing out his favourite hymn:

"Only to Thee, Lord Jesus Christ."

The Rajah's heir, Serjofee, could not be kept, even by Hindu custom, from taking his place as a chief mourner; and three years later, at his own cost, built him a superb marble monument, executed by Flaxman. The epitaph he himself wrote, the first English verse ever known to be written by a native Hindu:

"Firm wast Thou, humble and wise,
    Honest and pure; free from disguise;
    Father of orphans, the widow's support;
    Comfort in sorrow of every sort.
    To the benighted dispenser of light,
    Doing, and pointing to that which is right.
    Blessing to princes, to people, to me,
    May I, my Father, be worthy of Thee,
    Wisheth and prayeth thy Sarabojee."

WILLIAM CAREY—PIONEER IN ORGANIZED MISSIONS.

1761-1834.

To the Paulerspury "cobbler," the famous missionary, Orientalist, translator, has long been conceded a front rank among pioneers of modern missions and the new apostles.c

He was born the year after Zinzendorf died. At fourteen years of age a shoemaker's apprentice, he was converted at about eighteen, and soon after reaching majority joined the Baptists; three years later he was ordained minister, serving churches first at Moulton and then at Leicester; then in 1793, going with Thomas, as the first missionary from Britain to India. When he died at seventy-three he had for half a century been the leading spirit in modern missions to the heathen.

Several significant stages of progress are noticeable in this leadership. First the kindling of the fires in his own soul and the feeding of them with the fuel of facts; then the carrying of the live coals to other fireless altars, fanning the embers until they burned and glowed, and guarding the feeble flame lest it be smothered by the ashes of apathy, dampened by the atmosphere of selfishness, scattered by the breath of ridicule, or quenched by the wet earth of open hostility. A very distinct stride forward was taken in organizing that parent society at Kettering, among whose original twelve we strangely miss Carey's own name. Then, the next year he became its first representative, and actually arrived at Serampore to give forty years of service to the field in India.

Carey's life is luminous with lessons. First of all, we learn the worth of hard work. He disclaimed genius, but claimed "plodding," as his secret. He dug down deep into God's word to find His will. In the reading of Cook's "Voyages," he went with him "round the world," to learn man's state and need, and so he yearned to bring God's word and that world together, that human want might find its supply, and human woe its solace. From shoeshop at Hackleton to pulpit and chair at

Serampore, he was the same tireless plodder. Up to 1832 he had issued more than two hundred thousand Bibles, wholly or in part, and in forty dialects, beside other printed matter, including valuable grammars and dictionaries of Bengali, Mahratta, Sanskrit, etc. For twenty-nine years he was Oriental professor at Fort William College in Calcutta.

Carey's force lay in character. What he wrought as a missionary pioneer must find its main explanation in what he was, as a man of men, a man of God. Not what one seems, but what one is, fixes the limit of power; the level beyond which the stream never rises is the character which is its source and its spring. "To *be* or not to be, that is the question." Reputation is at best but the reflection of character, and often very imperfect and unfaithful; the echo, faint, feeble, far off; but if the man be what he ought, others may filch from him his "good name," but he is not made poor.

Because of what Carey was, he bore without harm the brunt of a hard, long fight; even the keen blade of unsanctified wit, when used against him, only dulled its edge and blunted its point upon the shield of his manly aim and faith in God. To all accusers, traducers, ridiculers, his life gave the lie.

The energy of his will, every purposeful soul may emulate and imitate. Life that is aimless is both restless and forceless. On the walls of society how many a trumpet hangs, as we saw in the case of young Raimund Lull, useless, voiceless, rusty! it has no lustre and gives forth no music, and is losing the power to emit sound. What an hour of redemption, when some brave warrior lays hands on the long unused instrument, puts it to his lips and blows a bugle blast!

Young men—you whose life hangs idle, aimless, mute, while the right is battling with the wrong, would that some hero-spirit might set you quivering and resounding with the clarion-peal of a holy purpose to serve God and man! No work is so wearisome as doing nothing, no self-sacrifice so costly as self-indulgence. Could you wear the "magic skin" which makes sure the gratification of every selfish whim, it would shrink with every new carnal pleasure and so at last crush out all true life.

From the cradle to the grave an indomitable will, yoked to a consecrated aim, bore Carey onward, upward, like the black horse of the rail, over torrents, up mountains, drawing after him more passive and less positive and resolute

souls. With little teaching he became learned; poor himself he made millions rich; by birth obscure he rose to unsought eminence; and seeking only to follow the Lord's leading, himself led on the Lord's host.

Carey had passion for souls, and, therefore, enthusiasm for missions: for human uplifting makes toil sweet, and loss, gain. Self-denial was his habit, and all the accumulations of his life in India were turned to the cause of God; when his income reached £1500 he reserved less than fifty for his personal expenses, devoting the rest to the purposes of the mission. This reminds us of Wesley, who kept his personal outlay down to twenty-eight pounds a year, though his income rose from fifty to five hundred.

Carey's companions felt that God was behind him, and this constrained them no longer to resist what at first seemed the wild scheme of a fanatic, lest haply they should have been found fighting against God. Dr. Ryland confessed that God himself had infused into him that passionate solicitude for the salvation of the heathen which could be traced to no other sufficient source. He who, like Bunyan, had been given to dishonesty and profanity; whose untamed tongue had been too familiar with the serpent-slime of filth and lies, was from the hour of conversion a new man. His native aptitude for linguistic study early led him to search into Latin, Greek, Hebrew, French and Dutch; and his deep sense of human need and gospel power, drew him into painstaking investigation into the state of the heathen, and into the Bible as the secret of saving grace.

Holy zeal consumed him. For ten years, with increasing ardour and fervour, he urged in private and public prompt and united effort for a world's evangelization. Whether mending a shoe, reading a book, or teaching a boy, he was "absentminded," for his thoughts wandered to the ends of the earth; he saw a thousand millions of lost souls without Bible, or preacher, or knowledge of Christ. He read Cook's "Voyages" till he knew as much as the writer, of the degradation and destitution he had seen; then he bought what other books he could, and borrowed what he could not buy; until he had picked up in fragments a mass of information so incredible that he became a living encyclopedia of missions, and even Scott was glad to stop at "Carey's College" as he went from Olney to Northampton, and so the commentator sat at the cobbler's feet to be taught.

Andrew Fuller found him at Moulton, a mapmaker. Out of such crude materials as a cobbler's shop could furnish, with paper, paste and ink, he had outlined the countries of the world, representing to the eye the appalling facts about the race and the awful darkness and death-shade in the various lands of cruelty and idolatry and superstition. It was thus that he was prepared, when but thirty-one years old, to publish his powerful "Inquiry into the Obligations of Christians," and in the same year at Nottingham to preach that great sermon which has given a movement and a motto to missions for a century past, and which led to the great step at Kettering, the same year, which proved the turning point of missionary organization.

Behold the strange retributions and revolutions of history! Sydney Smith put Carey and his comrades in the pillory, and pelted them with pitiless mockery. To-day, not the Church only but the world honours with homage the name and memory of that "sanctified cobbler." Let men ridicule! There is a Nemesis of Providence whose hand holds a scourge, not of small cords, but of scorpion stings. The "apostates of the anvil and the loom" have become God's apostles of the new Acts, and their witty clerical reviler is now in the pillory!

Ah, ye humble working men, who, like those primitive disciples who forsook ship and tax bench to be Christ's heralds, have left shoe-shop and shepherd's fold, forge and anvil, plough and shuttle, for the sake of the Kingdom, what crowns of glory await you when the final day of awards rights the wrong of the ages!

Robert Morrison—The Apostle of China.

1782-1834.

This famous "last-maker" of Morpeth always brings to mind one who was born twenty-one years in advance of him, the cobbler of Hackleton: for as Carey wrought on boots, so Morrison wrought on boot-trees. Like

SCRIPTURE TESTIMONY
Spiritual burden for a lost people group to be saved
ROMANS 9:1-3

Carey, he had but an elementary education, and yet had such burning passion for knowledge that he worked at his trade with book open beside him and gave to study the spare hours even of the night. At fifteen years of age he joined the Scotch Church, and at nineteen—again like Carey— was digging deep among the roots of Latin and Hebrew tongues, and the more intricate mysteries of theology.

While at Hoxton, Morrison chose the mission field, and in 1804 was accepted by the London Missionary Society and designated for China. Two years were given to special preparation, studying that strange language under a native teacher. He who undertakes the mastery of the Chinese tongue will find his patience and perseverance tested. It has been said to demand "a head of iron, a chest of oak, nerves of steel, the patience of Job and the years of Methusaleh." And yet we find Morrison plodding away undismayed at the task he had undertaken and laboriously copying Chinese manuscripts in the British Museum.

In 1807 he sailed for the Middle Kingdom as an ordained missionary at the age of twenty-five. But Chinese hostility to everything British compelled him to go by way of New York City, from which place he bore to the American Consul at Canton a letter from the United States Secretary of State, James Madison.

Reaching Canton in September, he took lodging in the humblest quarters, adopting for the time native habits both of dress and of diet. Forbidden to preach, he made closer search into the perplexities of the native language, and in 1810, three years after landing, he actually put in print the first copy of any portion of the Scriptures ever issued by a Protestant missionary in the Chinese tongue. Four years later he had completed the translation of the whole New Testament, and with the aid of Richard Milne, who joined him in 1813, in four years more he had ready the entire Old Testament also. It seems incredible, but it is true, that in 1821, less than fourteen years after he set foot on Chinese soil, this one man gave to the Celestials the complete Word of God in their own vernacular. This was a herculean labor, and can be appreciated only by those who have undertaken a similar task amid circumstances equally discouraging, disheartening and difficult.

But this missionary Hercules has other "labours,"as worthy to be reckoned among gigantic achievements. During the eleven years between 1807 and 1818, he had also prepared and published a Chinese grammar of three hundred pages, quarto; and a "View of China," for philological purposes. Verily, there have been giants, even in these modern days, who have confronted, undismayed, foes more formidable than the Anakim with their chariots of iron. To create a new version of the Scriptures—a first attempt, without either helpful precedents or adequate linguistic helps—was an undertaking from which any man but Morrison or Carey would have shrunk back dismayed.

These labours were literally colossal. The Old Testament alone formed twenty-one volumes duodecimo; but even such tasks were followed by a greater, for he compiled a Chinese dictionary, which he published in the same year with the completed Bible, and which cost the East India Company five thousand pounds sterling to issue!

When Morrison died in 1834, he had devoted twenty-seven years to China as a missionary teacher, translator of God's Word, and distributor of a new and sacred literature. He had laid at Malacca in 1818 the foundations of the Anglo-Chinese College, which was afterward removed to Hong-Kong; and himself gave toward the buildings and the support of the infant enterprise, twenty-two hundred pounds.

The University of Glasgow sought to pay a tribute to his great intellectual worth, when it conferred upon him, at the early age of thirty-five, the degree of doctor in divinity; and the nation honored him eight years later by making him a Fellow of the Royal Society; and George IV. granted him a special audience, on which occasion he presented the king with a copy of his translation of the Scriptures into the Chinese tongue.

But these honours pale beside the crown which God placed upon his head in permitting him to be the great pioneer in that most huge and hoary empire of

Asia. What a conspicuous example is Morrison of that grand truth, so needful to be learned, that no man's true work can be measured by man's yardstick. Morrison was only a pioneer. He led the way, and that is all. The end of his work as a philologist and translator was but the beginning of the work of evangelization and education which others have done after him and are now doing. Morrison toiled hard but saw little fruit of his toil. He broke up the fallow soil, sowed the seed, but never saw the harvest and put in the sickle. The same year in which he gave the New Testament to the people, he baptized the first Chinese convert, and for four years Tsai-a-Ko adorned the doctrine, until he was called up into the true country of the Celestials. But Morrison's reward was postponed for a future day. He ordained to the ministry Leang-Afa, after eight years, during which he had tested his fitness for the work. To present a nation whose population represents one-fourth of the human race, with the entire Bible; to lay the foundations of a Christian college among them; to gather to Christ the first convert, and ordain the first native evangelist, is enough for one man. But, be it remembered, that as this work of missions is all "God's building," he who lays the foundation-stones, down deep, out of sight, and whose work may be forgotten by man in the grandeur of more conspicuous and famous achievement, has in God's eyes equal honour and shall have equal reward with him who lays the capstone upon a completed structure amid shouts of joy and triumph. The rough base-blocks lie beneath the surface, hidden from human gaze—but they hold up the whole building. But for them the stately column with its delicate tracery, the graceful arch, the sculptured frieze and cornice, the tapering spire or pinnacle, or the glorious dome, were impossible. And so, when China's evangelization is complete, and the temple of God stands in perfect beauty, Robert Morrison's work will receive both its full recognition and reward.

Samuel J. Mills—Founder of Missions, in America.

1783-1818.

Here is another example of spiritual heredity. This son of a Torringford minister was from birth the subject of pious instruction; but the influence that shaped his character antedated even his birth, for his mother declared that she had consecrated him, while yet unborn, to the service of God as a missionary. And from the hour of conversion, he felt an unconquerable desire, which might better be called a passion, for service in regions beyond. This passion instead of cooling with years rather burned more hotly, and during his college career at Williamstown, from 1806 to 1809, was a consuming flame. There he formed the little band whose professed purpose was to "effect in the persons of its members a mission to the heathen"; and in 1810, at Andover, Hall, Newell, Judson and Nott joined him in that memorial to the General Association of Massachusetts which led to the formation of the American Board, the pioneer of all societies, on this side of the sea, for carrying the gospel to the world.

This man, little known as he is even to this day, was the moving spring behind much of the machinery of missions both at home and abroad. President Griffin of Williams College declared that, from the mind of Mills and from the little society he formed at college came not only the great Missionary Board, but the American Bible Society, United Foreign Missionary Society, and African School under care of the Synods of New York and New Jersey; and all the impulse given to Domestic Missions, to the Colonization Society, and to the general cause of benevolence in both hemispheres.

The name of *Samuel J. Mills* thus stands high in rank, for he was in a sense the father and founder of missions in America. About the time when Carey was dreaming, over his cobbling, of the thousand millions without Christ, Mills was born, in 1783. Before birth a godly mother, as we have seen, consecrated him to missions; at fifteen the Spirit's "demonstration," with its swift logic of the lightningflash revealed to him his lost state and his Saviour; and from the hour when he knew himself a miracle of grace, like Saul of Tarsus he had but *one* aim. Conversion was, with him, consecration, illumination, revelation, all at once. God had plainly set him apart to a missionary career, but none the less did he set himself apart. *Active benevolence* was the one law of his life, and wherever he was or went, he found a field for his activity.

His life was apparently a *failure* to carry out his original design. What *at first he willed to do* he never lived to work out; it remained like the unfinished statue of the sculptor, where the chisel has just begun to show the beauty of the ideal form. And yet no man's life was ever a truer success. In a way wholly unforeseen and unique, he fulfilled God's purpose, audit proved larger in scope and grander in result than his own. From the age of sixteen he flamed with one passion: to bear the gospel to the heathen. If ever a man's holy passion was a prophecy of a life-work, his absorbing ambition was the promise of a mission in foreign lands, though he never *actually entered* on the work he had chosen. Yet the disappointment was God's appointment; for God meant that he should fulfil a far wider mission.

This was the work of Mills: to show that when the true spirit of missions , it can be pent up by no restraints, quenched by no seeming failures. Mills was everywhere a missionary. Humble as he was, his motto was, not to "rest satisfied till he had made his influence felt in the remotest corner of this ruined world." He waited for no new doors to open but went into the doors that were opened. No dreams of a field, more to his liking, kept him from tilling the field at his feet. In college he was planting trees of righteousness; and so the famous haystack at Williamstown was consecrated by his meetings with a few like-minded fellow-students, and in its shelter was formed the covenant that sent Newell and Judson to India and Burma, and became the origin of the American Board.

Mills died at thirty-five. Few lives at seventy-five can compare in work for God. Perhaps no man ever started moving more vast and varied schemes of Christian work, and so projected the lines of his influence to the ends of the earth and perpetuated it to the end of the age. His mind was overwhelmed with the deep night-shade of paganism. He made himself master of facts, and then used them as shot and shell to beat down the walls of carelessness and indifference. He yearned to enter at once the thousand gates to fields of holy work, to have every limb a tongue, and every tongue a trumpet to spread the sound of the gospel! He found in every new fact a new *force*, to impel to new work. He met the poor heathen lad from Hawaii, and that led him to form the foreign mission school to train such as him for service. When not yet ready to go to foreign lands, he could not wait in idleness. He leaped into the saddle and for months explored the half-settled South and West of the United States. Hardships hindered him not. He swam streams swollen with rains and then stopped to dry his wet clothes and pushed on, making way through dense forests, wading through swamps, hungry and drenched, daring wild men and wild beasts, that he might learn the destitution of the people and supply them with the word of God, preaching and conversing as he went; and then coming back to the Eastern coast to organize Bible societies and home missionary effort. Like a warrior fresh from the battle-field, he went everywhere trumpeting in Christian ears the awful spiritual wants of the seventy-six thousand families he had found without even a Bible. His charity began at home, but it did not stay there. He felt that he must pass the limits even of those great states and territories. He felt himself "in a pinhole" even in the great Mississippi valley, while the broad earth lay beyond with its destitute millions. He waited not, like another Micawber, for opportunity to turn up; he *made* opportunity. Being for a little time in New York City he made explorations in the metropolis as thorough as in his Southern tours. When all eyes were turned to Africa, and the colonization scheme was formed, he threw his energies into *that*, and himself sailed for the Dark Continent on a mission in its behalf, and on his return voyage died and was buried at sea.

For the young men of this generation I can find no finer example of a consecrated life. At thirty-five years his life-work on earth closed. Yet already he had lived a century, if life is measured by its aims and achievements. Most of us do not begin to live until we begin to die. Most men think of life as all before them at an age when his was all behind him. He packed the years with noble work for God and man, and made every day a week, and every week a month, and every month a year, in the reckoning of service. Like a comet whose brilliance increases so fast as it nears its perihelion, he moved nearer and nearer to his Lord, and his life grew brighter and more glorious, until its lustre was lost in the sun of righteousness into whose splendours it was merged.

ADONIRAM JUDSON—APOSTLE OF BURMA.

1788-1850.

When God thrust Judson forth to serve Him in the field of missions, He knew His man, for He had trained and fitted him for His work. His genius was not inferior to that of Duff; his industry, to that of Carey; his piety, to that of Wayland; his spiritual instincts not less keen than those of Schwartz. His career embodies the romance of heroism, touched and tinged with the pathos of severe suffering.

God meant Judson to be a pioneer at Burma, and he combined the qualities needful in leaders of great enterprises,—self-reliance tempered with humility, energy restrained by prudence, activity anointed with unselfishness; and, withal, that patience and passionate love for souls which no man knows until he is devoted to a holy purpose and is absorbed in God.

Judson was one of the five now famous men whose offer of themselves for work abroad became the nucleus of the American Board of Commissioners for Foreign Missions. On the way to India, the radical change of his views on the subject of baptism became the germ of a new movement, the organization of the American Baptist Missionary Union; so that providentially he led the way in the formation of two of the most efficient and successful among all the existing missionary societies.

Like many another of God's heroes, disappointment met him at the outset. India was his chosen field, but he was driven further on to Burma, and so became there the first missionary of the new Baptist Board, thus doubly diverted from a Presbyterian mission and from India, that he might found a Baptist mission in Burma. It was another illustration of the Higher Power that is back of contrary winds. God drove him out of his course as he had planned it, to drive him into another course, as God had planned it. There was a barrier that suffered him not to go into Bithynia, that he might obey another call and enter an open door into Macedonia.

Four facts stand in the foremost rank in the furnishing of this Burmese apostle.

First, the fact of his conversion. Of this he had that clear assurance, for lack of which nothing else will compensate. Whether poets are "born" or "made," there is no doubt about a true missionary. He must be born from above. He can never be made by man. No native genius or acquired scholarship, no endowments of nature or attainments of culture, can supply the place of regeneration. Nay more, it is the men who are saved and *know* it, who by their experience give life and power to their testimony. The message needs the man to back it; the Bible needs the believer behind it. The righteousness of God is revealed from faith in the preacher, to faith in the hearer.

Secondly, the fact of his call. The work of a missionary was his vocation. The voice of conviction and of consciousness affirmed it. With Paul he could say, "It pleased God who separated me from my mother's womb, and called me by His grace, to reveal His Son in me, that I might preach Him among the heathen." From the very first he heard and heeded that voice, and went out not knowing whither he went. Because it was an example of the obedience of faith, he went on in the midst of disappointments; the retrospect might be dark and the aspect darker, but the "prospect was as bright as the promises of God."

Thirdly, the fact that he had the word of God. To him the Bible was God's own book; he believed in it throughout, and loved it. His devotion to it reminds us again of the famous Tuscan sculptor's fondness for that relic of the Athenian Apollonius in the Vatican, for Judson studied the Bible from every point of view, as M. Angelo did the torso.

His reverent affection for God's word made it a constant delight to study it. Compared with its infallible oracles, "the tradition of the elders" was nothing, and his aim was to construct his own character, and build in Burma an Apostolic Church, in all things according to the pattern showed him in the holy mount. That this word might mould the people, he became translator, and so joined the noble army to which belonged Waldo and Lefevre, Wyclif and Tyndale, Luther and Bedell, Carey and Eliot, Morrison and Hepburn.

Fourthly, the fact that he held a scriptural idea of missions. He had learned that to preach the gospel to unsaved souls is the one grand business of the Church. Too many seem to count this but as one of many forms of benevolent work, and they talk of missions as an organization of the Church. But Judson saw that the converse is true; that the Church is both the result and fruit of missions; and his life motto was: The Church is both constituted and commissioned to preach the gospel to the world. Of course, then, the chief work of the missionary is put beyond doubt. Though a man of the instincts and the culture of a scholar, finely fitted for a teacher, true to his principles, he made it his one great work to preach Christ, and all else held lower rank.

To estimate Judson aright we must emphasize his scriptural idea of a Church. To him it was no worldly association or religious club of respectable moralists, or people whose claim to membership rested upon their baptism in infancy. It was no lawless democracy, or lordly monarchy, or titled aristocracy; no mutual benefit society or social community for religious and ethical culture. He believed the Church to be a divine institution, composed of converted souls; its threefold end, spiritual worship, holy living, and unselfish service. He sought, therefore, first of all to preach that gospel by which souls are saved; then out of converts to form New Testament Churches, and make them self-governing, self-supporting, self-propagating; and to raise up a native ministry as the condition of their normal development.

He particularly interests the student of missions, as one who projected a biblical theory of missions and put his theory into effective practice. His plan was essentially Pauline, and it led to and fed an unselfish heroism. The mission field offered a tempting bait to ambition and avarice, as it became plain even to the Burmese powers what a high order of man this humble missionary was. But Judson lived and died poor. He illustrated the self-abnegation which is the cardinal law and primary condition of a missionary life. As Dr. Maclaren finely says, "The chord that vibrates most musically is itself unseen while it vibrates."

The apostle of Burma believed every man's life to be a plan of God, and that he should study to find out and fill out that plan. The result was, as it always is, an increase of power. His weak will was energized by the stronger will of God, and his sphere was constantly expanding as his capacity was enlarging; as God gave him more power to work, he gave him more room to work. Another result was a constant deepening of joy. Partnership with God made easy to him patient doing, bearing, and—what is hardest—waiting. And last of all came certain success, for God never fails, nor does he who sides with God.

Blessed is he who, like Judson, learns to call Jesus not only Saviour, but Lord. The clear eye to see, the prompt will to obey, the total self-surrender to serve, at whatever cost of sacrifice and suffering—these are the steps whereby we keep to God's plan, and get that enduement of power which both brings and is, success. When the daughter of Pastor A. G. Brown, of London, was asked what led her to China, she said: "I had known Jesus as Saviour, Redeemer, Friend; but as soon as I knew Him as Lord and Master, He said to me, ' Am I thy Lord and Master? then go to China.'"

When Judson died, hundreds of baptized Burmans and Karens were sleeping in Jesus, and over seven thousand survived, in sixty-three churches, under oversight of one hundred and sixty-three missionaries, native pastors, and helpers. Judson had finished his Bible translation, compiled a Burmese dictionary, and laid the basis of Christian character deep down in the Burman heart.

In the Baptist meeting-house at Malden, Massachusetts, one may read upon a simple memorial tablet:

"In Memoriam.
Rev. Adoniram Judson.
Born August 9, 1788,
Died April 12, 1850.
Malden, his Birthplace,
The Ocean, his Sepulchre;
Converted Burmans
and
The Burman Bible His Monument
His Record is on High."

Captain Allen F. Gardiner—Pioneer of Tierra del Fuego.

1794-1851.

It was a striking saying of the Hon. Ion Keith Falconer, the noble martyr of the mission at Aden, that we must not fear to be called "eccentric." That word means "out of centre," and if we are in the true centre as to God, in the orbit of obedience, we shall be out of centre as to the world.

Allen Gardiner was an enthusiast, a fanatic, but in the eyes of God he was fired with a divine passion. His enthusiasm was an "en-the-ism." While an officer in the English navy, the death of his young wife left him free to give himself to missionary service, and he shrank not from pioneer work among the worst heathens. After a trial of other lands he turned to South America, but there was no open door, for priests of Papal Rome stood between him and the wild pagan tribes of the far South, until, at the Southern Cape itself, he found the island of Tierra del Fuego, so remote that Spanish Jesuits cared not to keep up their pursuit.

Dr. Flint says of the gospel, that its divine origin is seen in its universal adaptation. Here is the magic mirror in which the Eskimo and Maori, Fuegian and Fijian, Melanesian cannibals and Australian aborigines alike see reflected what they are, and what they may be. The message of Christ crucified and risen has captivated alike the wisest sage and the simplest child; because meant for the universal man it finds a reception wherever it gets a hearing. Darwin himself, who found, in the natives of this "Land of Fire," the missing link between man and the monkey, has left on record his testimony that "the lesson of the missionary is the wand of the enchanter."

Against all conceivable obstacles Allen Gardiner persevered. Nature herself was inhospitable; the climate forbade his approach: winds and waves, summer rains and winter sleet, drove him back. Man gave him no welcome. The Patagonians had low foreheads, but lower minds and morals, wretched hovels and scant clothing; they seemed incapable of any high impulses or real improvement. At times they were like brute beasts; at others, treacherous robbers. At first he was compelled to retreat, and return to England. But, if he could not land on the shore, he could float on the sea; and so we have that unique illustration of a new method in missions, in Captain Gardiner's two-decked boats at Banner Bay, where, with two catechists and two more pious sailors, he undertook to do pioneer work among the natives, from his floating home. Everyone of his party perished, never again seen alive by an Englishman. Starvation slowly slew them, and only their dead bodies and their diaries were found to tell the awful tale. One by one, and Gardiner last of all, they had succumbed to hunger.

Yet there had been no whining nor murmuring. The farewell message of the last survivor bore testimony: "Poor and weak as we are, our boat is a very Bethel to our souls, for we feel and know that God is here. Asleep or awake," wrote Captain Gardiner, "I am, beyond the power of expression, happy." Instead of vain repining or lamenting, he left behind only earnest entreating that the mission should not be abandoned, and left a brief plan outlining future operations.

Such was his passionate love for God that, even while starving, he could record nothing save marvels of mercy, and declared that after five days of fasting he felt neither hunger nor thirst. And over the place where he lay down to die he had inscribed, on the rock, from the Psalms, this precious motto:

> "Wait, O my soul, upon God!
> For all my expectation is from Him."

He died, having seen no results of his work. He had sown in tears, but not a blade appeared. It was, however, no failure; for to-day among the heathen tribes of Paraguay there is springing up a plenteous harvest. Hope was deferred, but not lost; faith was tried but not tired, and triumphed.

It was a very strange way by which God led Allen Gardiner. His love for maritime adventure led him to a naval college, and into service in the navy. Little did he know that the curiosity which drew him to a heathen temple in China to witness the superstitions of idolaters, was to be the means of quickening the seed 'sown in his heart by pious parents. He saw what heathenism was, and he took his stand boldly for Christ and the Gospel. He began to seek the salvation of his shipmates, who were practically pagans; then as the ship touched at various ports he obtained leave of absence and explored the region near by, and so made himself familiar everywhere with the spiritual condition of the natives.

The passion for mission work became more intense. In 1834, he went to Zululand, but was driven thence three years later by the cruel war between Chief Dingaan and the Dutch farmers. A whole year was spent in fruitless effort to get entrance for the gospel into New Guinea; then for ten months he was on the Falkland Islands, and while there visited Patagonia, where he besought the Church Missionary Society to plant a mission; and in 1845, he himself with Robert Hunt, anchored in Gregory Bay; but Chief Wissale's "petulance, cupidity, treachery, dishonesty and extortion" again compelled withdrawal, and even as they were conveying their few effects on board an English bark, this dastardly chief was plying his thieving arts.

In the same year, 1845, nothing daunted, Gardiner with Mr. Gonzalez went to Bolivia, daring the Atacama desert for the gospel's sake. Again met by disheartening obstacles, in 1848, he headed a small pioneer party of five, whose destination was Tierra del Fuego, where the hopeless hostility of the natives, led on by Chief Jemmy Button, convinced him that "*The missionary establishment must for the present be afloat!*" Often perplexed, he was never in despair, and nothing could kill his imperishable faith and hope. "Being with him was like a heaven upon earth: he was such a man of prayer," said Joseph Erwin, his boat carpenter.

Captain Smyley's journal and Captain Morshead's letters gave the public the awful facts about the experience of this starved party of missionaries—how from June 22 to Sept. 6, when Gardiner must have died, they had been out of provisions. Men who read or heard this pathetic tale, knew not which emotion was the mightier, horror at such a tale of suffering, or admiration at such dauntless heroism.

Secretary Despard published far and wide the decision of the Patagonian Society, that "With God's help, the mission shall not be abandoned;" and the *Allen Gardiner* left Bristol in 1854, and in 1855 once more anchored in Spaniards' Harbour. A few days later, at Earnest Cove, a new mission party had "the mournful satisfaction of standing on the spot where the remains of Gardiner were found," and, with appropriate memorial services, of setting up a tablet: "In memory of the lamented missionary martyrs."

The period of trial was not yet past. In 1858, a suitable site was fixed upon for a mission, which was named Wycliffe. But Capt. Fell and brother, and Mr. Phillips, the catechist, were brutally murdered, and the *Allen Gardiner* was found in Beagle Channel a perfect wreck, with one survivor, the cook.

Again the wrecked vessel being repaired, another beginning was made, and since 1872 the work has gone steadily forward. On Keppel Island, Fuegians are boarded and trained. El Carmen, on the coast, has been a medical mission for thirty years past. The *Allen Gardiner* still goes on its mission cruises, and it has been so demonstrated that brutal Patagonians and Fuegians may be evangelized, civilized, christianized, that Admiral Sulivan, at the annual meeting of the South American Missionary Society in 1881, stated, after residing at the Falkland Islands, that he had informed Darwin of the great changes which had taken place in his human monkeys—of kindness shown to shipwrecked crews by the converted natives—how fowl-houses remained unlocked without even the theft of an egg; and stated, that in reply Darwin had candidly confessed, "I could not have believed that all the missionaries the world could ever have made the Fuegians honest."

So remarkable is the testimony of this great naturalist, who was, however, no "supernaturalist," that with his oft-quoted testimony we close this brief sketch. He had said after his visit to Patagonia, "Nothing can be done by means of mission work; all the pains bestowed on the natives will be thrown away; they never can be civilized." This was Darwin's opinion until proofs of the facts confronted him, and then he candidly admitted he was wrong, and added: "I had always thought that the civilization of the Japanese is the most wonderful thing in history; but I am now convinced that what the missionaries have done in Tierra del Fuego, in civilizing the natives, is at least as wonderful." And from this time Darwin himself regularly subscribed to the society's funds.

John Williams—The Apostle of the South Seas.

1796-1839.

How curious are the coincidences of history! It was only six weeks after Williams was born, when *The Duff* sailed for Tahiti, as though the ship that was to introduce the gospel to the Southern Seas waited until the coming apostle of those island groups was born, before it unfurled its sails!

The life we now outline covered only about forty-three years, from June 29, 1796, to Nov. 20, 1839. But it was crowded with the wonderful works of God. At twenty-one years of age, John Williams was sent to Eimeo, thence removing to Huahine and Raiatea. After five years of apostolic success, he visited the Hervey group, founding a mission at Raratonga, where he prepared books and in part a Bible translation. Then in a boat, built by himself, he explored most of the surrounding archipelago, establishing the Samoan mission. Four years were spent in England, from 1834 to 1838, publishing his story of the South Seas and his Raratongan New Testament, raising five thousand pounds for a new missionary ship, and planning for a high school at Tahiti, and a theological school at Raratonga for training native evangelists. With sixteen recruits he returned to his most loved work, visited Samoa, sailed for the New Hebrides to start a new mission, and, on the shores of Erromanga, fell a martyr. Twenty-two years—from the ironmonger's forge in London to the savage's club at Dillon's Bay! But what a unique mission, and what a lustrous record on high!

Williams, though generally and deservedly known as the Apostle of the South Seas, was not the pioneer in those waters. Captain Cook's voyages had turned toward these island clusters many eyes besides those of William Carey and the Countess of Huntingdon. When, in 1795, the London Missionary Society was founded, such interest had been awakened in this archipelago, that as early as August 10, of the next year, *The Duff* set sail for Tahiti, under command of that devoted Christian, Captain James Wilson, and with thirty missionaries aboard. More than twenty years had gone by before John Williams followed, but his career was so exceptional, that without it the work in Polynesia would be a drama without its main actor.

The religious revolution wrought under his very eyes has, for rapidity and range of result, no parallel. The prophecy was literally fulfilled:

> "The isles shall wait for His law:
> As soon as they hear of me they shall obey me.
> The strangers shall submit themselves to me."

A year after Raratonga was discovered by Williams, idolatry was in ruins; a whole people called upon themselves the name of the Lord, and built a place of worship six hundred feet long, where Aitutakian chiefs were the main speakers. Greater wonder still,—all this, before one English missionary had yet taught on the island! God had used, to work this transformation, two plain, untaught natives! Here, ten years after Williams had sailed for Eimeo, he met the largest concourse of worshippers he had ever seen outside of his own country; and as they moved past him they laid at his feet fourteen huge idols as gospel trophies!

SCRIPTURE TESTIMONY

Believers exchange superstition for faith in Christ

ACTS 19:18-19

The Raratongans kept their Sabbaths as he had never seen the Day of Rest kept before. Prayer saluted the sunrise and the sunset, as though to punctuate holy time with worship, and the hours between were full of studies in the Word of God, for the people made notes of all the sermons they heard, that they might search, like the Bereans, into the truths they were taught. New codes of laws were built upon the corner-stone of this teaching; marriage was hallowed and polygamy proscribed. One island after another became a sanctuary, vocal with prayer and praise. Chiefs presided at holocausts of idols, stripping the gay trappings from their former gods, and feeding them as fuel to the fires. There were cases in which a few *hours* sufficed, to complete the destruction of all false gods and idol fanes, and to lay the foundations of chapels for Christian worship.

One scene it is well to delineate as an example of many. Tomatoa and his followers approach Opoa. A crowd is at the beach to seize the usual captives of war. But a herald shouts from the canoes, "We bring to you no slain victims; we are all praying people who worship the true God; these"—holding up the books prepared by missionaries—"these are our victims and trophies of war."

When the war-god, Oro, was disrobed, and his temple burned by converts at Opoa, the heathen party built a huge cage of wicker-work in which to burn all the Christians alive. Unceasing prayer brought such plain help from above, that in the ensuing struggle even the enemies of the Lord felt that His hand was against them, and they threw down their weapons and fled, panic-stricken. They looked only for vengeance from their Christian conquerors, but found instead a sumptuous feast prepared for them, and for sheer astonishment could not eat. Then one of the vanquished heathen party rose and said: "Others may act as they will; but never again will I worship gods that could give no help in the hour of danger. We were four times as many as these praying people, and yet they have defeated us with the greatest ease. Their god must be the true God. Theirs is a religion of mercy. Had we won the victory they would now be burning in that cage; but instead of burning us, they feed us. I will go and join this people!" Such was the power of these words that every one of the heathen party bowed that night in prayer to the God of the Christians, and praised Him for giving to His own praying people the victory! And the next morning, after prayer, all united in destroying, in Tahua and Raiatea, every Marae, so that within three days not one vestige of idol worship was left!

John Williams' career was one triumphal progress. At Savaii, for instance, tears of joy greeted him; and he met a people ready formally to renounce paganism. Malietoa, the chief, begged him with all speed to go to his native land and bring back teachers. How pathetic was his plea: "Come back as soon as you can; for before you return many of us will be dead."

The Maruans, who were wont to trace every evil of any kind to bad spirits, turned to God, and proved the sincerity of their faith by ruined Maraes and broken idols. Spears that had once impaled children and borne them as trophies to the temples, were now turned into pulpit balustrades, and Oro and other grim idols of wood were used as props to common wood-sheds and cook-houses. Unchaste songs and gestures gave place to hymns of praise and bowed knees.

The changes which the apostle of the South Seas saw, defied description, and when described seem fables for the credulous. He himself was overawed by the proofs of the hand of God. At Tahiti, over fourteen years had gone by before one convert was made; and at New Zealand, twenty years, before there seemed to be one honest inquirer. Yet Williams witnessed changes nothing short of a radical revolution, within twenty, eighteen, twelve months, and sometimes within as many days. He went to islands where all were heathens; he visited them later to find chapels with thousands of worshippers; he found them without a written language, and left them reading in their own tongue the wonderful words of God!

Williams was of great service in furnishing elementary primers, translations of the gospels and epistles, and creating a Christian native literature. He trained converts into evangelists, who made tours among the surrounding islands until no heathen settlement remained unvisited. He taught converts the grace of giving, and when they had no money, they marked their pigs or other possessions, with the Lord's sign, and sacredly put into His treasury whatever they brought in the market.

One comprehensive statement may serve to summarize this marvellous story of apostolic success. Five years before he fell, no group of islands, nor single island of importance, within two thousand miles of Tahiti, had been left unvisited.

This martyr's death was doubtless due to a misapprehension. The natives of Erromanga had come to hate the sight of foreigners, because of recent wrongs at the hands of a crew, whose vessel touched at those shores. But history has her unique compensation as well as retribution. Fifty years after Williams fell, the son of his murderer was laying the corner-stone of the martyr's memorial, while another son was preaching the gospel for which that martyr died!

Louis Harms—The Missionary Pastor.

1808-1865.

This man was another of God's pioneers, but his personal field was the parish of Hermannsburgh. His divine vocation was found in furnishing an example of what one man and his congregation can do in the furtherance of the world-wide work.

When that disabled *candidat* came to that obscure parish in Hanover, and told his simple tale of the wants and woes of the heathen, little did he know that, though laid aside from the work himself, he was there lighting a fire which was never to be quenched, but to spread far and wide. When the heart of Pastor Harms was kindled with new zeal for missions, the people whom he led felt the fire burning within them also; and, though but a few and feeble folk, mostly occupied with farming and such like work, and too poor to give large sums of money, they responded to his appeal. He said first of all to himself and to them, "Why should we not help missions?" This question soon prompted another, "Why may we not plan missions of our own?" There were incredulous spirits that, like the Samarian lord, asked, "If the Lord would open windows in Heaven, might this thing be!" But faith and prayer and self-sacrifice prevailed, and a moral miracle was wrought.

The simple Hermannsburghers began by offerings of money, but they soon found it easy also to offer themselves. One man gave his farm, and the farmhouse became a training school, where missionary candidates, who willingly volunteered for service, began to be educated for the fields abroad. Then a sailor suggested the building and launching of their own ship, to bear their missionaries to other lands, and sail to and fro, as a medium of communication; and so the *Candace*—first of mission ships—was built and manned by themselves, and became a shuttle to weave threads of practical contact between the Church at home and its workers abroad, and carry mutual messages of love and sympathy.

This was not all. While sending forth scores of men and women to be its heralds and tell the old story of the cross, the Church scattered yet increased, until its membership reached ten thousand and it became the largest Church in Christendom. Not content with supplying workmen and caring for their wants, it set up its own printing-press, printed its own missionary magazine, and thus became in itself a whole board of missions, with its own training school, mission treasury, vessel and periodical, and all the apparatus of a well-organized and thoroughly conducted missionary society; and although for nearly thirty years Louis Harms has been dead, the work remains to witness to the Church and to the world.

That one man, and he but forty years old, and with a simple rural parish, should start such a work, has been a problem to all who do not know the power which comes from the Spirit of God in answer to prayer. Though the undertaking was formally inaugurated in 1849, for years before, the foundations had been preparing in the heart of Harms. While in charge of his father's private school, six years earlier, and as his assistant in parish work, he wielded a sceptre of influence over the people which showed him to be one of God's anointed kings. Alike in private converse and public address, he swayed the hearts of those poor peasants. When, in 1844, he became his father's assistant and was ordained, his hold on the people became stronger. His holy zeal, his passionate ardour and fervour, his intensely human sympathy, brought him into close contact with their hearts, and led to a great religious awakening, which was, as it always is, accompanied by a new missionary spirit. In fact, it is hard to say which was first in order of development; for Harms had so long felt the leverage there is in missions to raise spiritual life to a higher level, that he sought to arouse new interest in the heathen as one means of raising Church members to a higher plane. And when thus the parish had been made ready, it was only needful that the external circumstances should favour, in order for the work to be actually inaugurated.

While acting as his father's assistant, Louis Harms felt under restraint, but at his father's death, he was appointed pastor, and so the building whose baseblocks had long been laid began to rise toward completion.

To trace the history of the Hermannsburgh Society would be impracticable within these limits, and would not serve our present purpose. In 1890, there were some sixty stations, with a total of about three hundred missionaries and native helpers. But it does concern us to learn the lesson which God surely means to teach by this new chapter in the Acts of the Apostles. If a single Church, under the leadership of one man, and he broken in health, a chronic invalid, and his people for the most part only the Lord's poor, could work such wonders, who shall tell us what some other pastors and Churches might achieve for God, where large wealth and large numbers, intelligence and culture, social influence and every other help and encouragement exist to assure a wide work and a grand result!

Pastor Harms drank in the missionary spirit in the secret place where God dwells. Prayer brought him very close to that heavenly altar where God's own fires eternally bum, and the angel at that altar touched with a live coal both his heart and his lips. The first impulse to his missionary heroism was found, not in the appeal of human need, but in the celestial spark which needed only a knowledge of facts to find ample fuel for a consuming flame. The man who knows not how to pray and how to lead his people to pray, may construct an organization, but he cannot put into it the motive power that moves its machinery and makes it mighty to effect results. Because Louis Harms prevailed with God, he also prevailed with men. He took the great facts about a world's need, to the mercy-seat, and held them up in the light of the Divine Presence, until in the mystic Shekinah fire they burned and glowed. Then he held them up before the eyes of men until he compelled others also to feel their awful force, and until indifference could no longer endure to confront them, but was melted into zeal.

Notwithstanding the poverty of his peasant parish, Harms from the first would allow no canvassing for funds, and modern methods of appeal and of raising money have always been repudiated upon principle. And yet money has been provided by methods and in measure surprising to worldly minds. The enterprise that had such obscure and unpromising beginnings, was scorned by the wise and great of this world; it survived, however, not only the death of its founder, in 1865, but the schism in the Hanover Church thirteen years later, and the deposition of Theodore Harms in consequence of his loyalty to his conscience in refusing conformity to the customs of the State Church. He was followed by his people in his independent course, and thus was formed the nucleus of the Free Church of Hanover. These and many other causes combined, threatened to wreck the mission cause, but those simple Hermannsburghers have persisted in their devotion to the work of God, and the society is still sending forth its messengers to the region and shadow of death.

God thus writes upon His shining scroll another name unknown to fame, as men rank greatness; but, like Christ's forerunner, great in the eyes of the Lord, and one to whom it was given to prepare His way among the people!

David Livingstone—Africa's Pioneer.

1813-1873.

The hero of Blantyre furnishes another example of spiritual heredity, for his parents, however humble, were devout, and his father bequeathed to him both his thirst for knowledge and his spirit of enterprise. Though at ten working in the cotton factory, and there continuing for fourteen years, David was so eager to learn that he studied Latin by night, and in his daily labour gathered up the smallest fragments of time, often less than a minute—that nothing be lost. "Dick's Philosophy of the Future State" kindled his missionary fervour, and then he got a medical training, intending to go to China. War with Britain closed that door, but "Moffat's Appeal for the Dark Continent" opened another, and so in 1840, he sailed for Kuruman, little suspecting what a unique career was before him.

Livingstone outranks all others as Africa's apostle. His life spans but sixty years. Converted at twenty, he was in heart and aim thenceforth a missionary; perhaps no life since the Apostolic age has poured forth upon the feet of Jesus more of the costly ointment of consecrated service.

He was a man of such singular force that Sir Bartie Frere thought that "any five years of his life might have established for him in any other occupation, such a character, and raised for him such a fortune, as none but the most energetic can realize." His last public utterance in Scotland gave in five short words the double secret of his life: "Fear God and work hard." That explains his thirty thousand miles of travel and the unrivalled series of discoveries: Five lakes, rivers, falls that outrank Niagara, high ridges that flank Africa's central basin; that motto accounts for the perseverance that searched into the geology and hydrography, the fauna and flora of the continent, and that fought the two great foes of man and beast—fever and tsetse—with such persistency, that he declared that these two words would be found at death graven on his heart.

Force weds industry, if it does not beget it. Though his native abilities were mediocre and his early opportunities meagre, like Carey, he could plod. Economy of time and resolute patience were the steeds he yoked to his life-car, and so he made such progress as even genius does not often secure. What carefulness in details is seen in that famous lined journal of eight hundred quarto pages, with its plain, neat writing. And what versatility is that, akin to genius, which makes it possible for one man in turn to master questions such as the desiccation of Africa, the utilization of her river highways, missionary organization and Bible translation! Book-making alone failed to arouse his enthusiasm; it was a mere task, partly from the long exile that forbade contact or converse with white men.

Livingstone's services to the race are too great for immediate recognition. What he was as a scientist and explorer, traveller, geographer, zoologist, botanist, physician, the future must measure. In accuracy of detail few have ever equalled him. His astronomical observations, exact orientations, and manifold contributions to natural science in all its great departments, show a many-sided man. He could tell the Chamber of Commerce of a score of vegetable products entirely new to them; the geographical society decorated him with their gold medal, and three cities honoured him with their "freedom."

As in all mighty men, the finest elements of his character crystallized about a strong will. If he failed, it meant new and more patient trial. "If I live," he said in 1866, "I must succeed in my undertaking; death alone will put a stop to my efforts." When half starved, his medicine-chest stolen, at the mercy of foes like a warrior without weapons, and thrice in one day barely escaping death—not one man in a million would have pushed forward as he did in the heart of Africa. When in 1872, Stanley urged his return with him to England, though a strange presentiment weighed upon him that he was on his last journey and would never get to its goal, he flinched not in his resolve but pressed on, praying that before he fell he might work out his purpose.

He was a man whose great faith in God was the pole star of his life. He saw that great crises turn on trifles as great doors swing from small hinges, but that there was a Divine Workman who knew how much he could safely hang on such a hinge; and so he was wont to watch the seemingly trivial events that shape character and destiny. And on what apparent trifles Livingstone's career turned! the chance reading of Dick, the appeal of Gutzlaff, the visit of Moffat, the friendly word of a director of the London Missionary Society. One text gave to his spiritual vision telescopic range and microscopic delicacy: "In all thy ways acknowledge Him and He shall direct thy paths." Under such guidance trial and trouble were God's angels, calamity was His storm signal; and that nameless sorrow, which in his dear Mary's death smote him, only drew out once more his "Fiat, Domine, Voluntas Tua!"

He was at heart simply a humble missionary. On that altar of service his whole self was laid, and better to know and meet Africa's wants, he entered that broader sphere that unconsciously made of the missionary a general and statesman. He saw that the true plan for Africa's evangelization must be broad enough to take in the whole continent and its whole future. Hence he sought to explore and develop the resources of the country, devise facilities for travel and traffic, and abolish the awful curse of slavery. That he never lost sight of his original aim is plain from his own sage saying: "the end of the geographical feat is the beginning of the true enterprise."

To further this ultimate end he was willing to go anywhere, provided it be only forward, and to do anything provided it were preparing the whole field for the harvest. His gauge of missionary success was, not so many converts per pound sterling, but the wide diffusion of godly principles—results which no statistics can exhibit.

The hero of Blantyre was Conscience Incarnate. His watchword was duty. To keep his word and do his work faithfully was the double law of his life. But duty was softened by love, and lost all asperity. And it was one of God's gifts to him that his sense of humour was so keen. He enjoyed immensely the superstitious fright of the natives when they watched the figures, shown on the screen by the magic-lantern, mysteriously appear and disappear; and the Soko was to him so hideously ugly, that he could conceive no use for him save to "sit for a portrait of Satan."

Livingstone's habitual indifference to worldly applause and advantage was the unique trait in his character; he was in some respects the counterpart of that Soudan hero, of whom Mrs. Charles says, "Not that he tried to renounce the poor prizes of this world; like Joan of Arc, he simply did not value them." Money was to him no bait, and he hated to be lionized. He turned his back on the praise of men and would not even read what was written in his honour. The world's gold was tinsel, its glory a fading laurel: he was after what was better, and he got it. He belonged to no conventional society: his citizenship was in Heaven. And when in that little grass hut at Ilala he died, alone with God, in prayer for Africa, as Schmidt had before him—that close to his life was poetically and pathetically fitting, more in accord with all that went before it than if he had died in a palace amid fawning courtiers. But, as a martyr's grave drew Bishop Heber to Calcutta, that heart that is buried in Africa will yet be like a new Mecca to thousands of pilgrim saints.

Livingstone's self-oblivion was sublime. The treasures and pleasures of Egypt were to him nothing if he might, like Moses, lead out God's oppressed people from under the slave yoke. For Africa he could spend his last penny, and his last drop of blood. Such was the man whom an intimate acquaintance pronounced the best man he ever knew, and whom history already crowns as Africa's best friend. His life was one grand sermon. The golden pen of action, held in the hand of resolve, wrote out its sentences in living letters on the eternal scroll, for all to read. Both by witness and suffering he ranks with the martyrs. His sacrifices were noble, though he declared he had never made any; yes, the man who had been soaked with drenching rains, had made his bed in damp grasses and his food out of roots, who had been forty times scorched in the furnace of fever, and buried his wife in Africa's bosom; even when on a sick bed, without human helper and in a horror of great darkness, neither talked of self-denial nor halted in his work for Christ.

No wonder if his master passion was to abate and abolish all slavery and slave traffic. The horrors he saw defied description and made him feel that he was in hell. Everywhere he sought to rouse the dormant Christian conscience to the devilish atrocity of this crime; and, the memorial slab in the great Abbey, as is fitting, mutely repeats his memorable words:

"All I can add in my loneliness, is, may Heaven's rich blessing come down on everyone—American, Englishman or Turk,—who will help to heal the open sore of the world!"

Alexander Duff—Pioneer of Education in India.

1806-1878.

The remarkable student of St. Andrew's, from whom this Lectureship takes its name, combined in himself the courage of Knox, the force of Chalmers and the fire of Erskine. He was doubly a pioneer, for he was the first missionary of the Church of Scotland to India, and he led the way in higher education among the Brahmans. He was almost equally conspicuous as an orator, an organizer and an educator. Twice wrecked on his way to India, he saved his Bible from the sea—a fact regarded by him as significant and symbolic of his whole life-work.

He struck out upon a new path. The corner-stone that he laid he himself cleft and shaped in a new quarry. His aim was to open up to the native Hindus, not only purely religious truth as such, but to introduce into the centre of the Orient the science and learning of the Occident. His plan was novel, and it signalized a new era in Indian missions.

A new idea finds slow entrance, especially in the religious sphere, for all new coins are handled with suspicion. Duff met with misrepresentation and opposition, but his school stood the storm like a cedar of Lebanon, and fierce winds strengthened its roots and toughened its boughs. A few years sufficed for his work to win golden opinions, even from scholars and princes. After five years, illness drove him home, but after five more, he came back to find seven hundred pupils instead of the few with which he started: and when, in the year of the disruption, his lot was cast with the Free Church, and his college passed into other hands, he began anew, and organized on a new and ampler scale his whole educational and missionary work.

Dr. Duff ranks with Carey and Livingstone as one of the great missionary triad of the new age. He was, on Indian affairs and Christian missions, an authority. His service to the Church at home was as great as to the vast Oriental Empire beside the Ganges. In 1834, and again in 1849, he was compelled to return to Scotland, and, in 1863, to abandon India altogether; but such a man was anywhere and everywhere a missionary. He was another Peter, the Hermit, sounding the signal of the new crusade, urging and leading God's people onward toward a nobler missionary consecration. He twice filled the Moderator's chair, but this was only a sign of his hold upon the Free Church, and no man since Paul has done more to fan and feed the fires of a holy enthusiasm for world-wide evangelism.

If Duff owed his pious aptitudes to his godly parents, it was the joint influence of Chalmers and Inglis that afterward shaped his mind for work in India. Thomas Chalmers, in 1812, before the Dundee Missionary Society, had held up the inspired Word and the living herald as God's twin agency for spreading the gospel; and, two years later, before the Scottish Propagation Society, had given the testimony of experience to the utility of missions; these sermons left impressions on young Duff that could not be effaced—impressions deepened by personal contact with that greatest of Scotia's sons, in the University. Then when, in 1825, Dr. Inglis made his fervent plea for workers abroad, Alexander Duff could no longer stay at home; and God, who in Carey had given to Schwartz an "apostolic heir," gave in Duff an heir to Carey.

For the period of a whole generation he carried the assault against the citadel of oriental idolatry and superstition, instituting new educational methods for reaching the Brahmans, founding missions not only in India, but in Syria and the New Hebrides. But even this grand and complex achievement is perhaps surpassed in permanent value by his influence over the Church of Christ on both sides of the Atlantic. He made the very pulse of missions to beat quicker, shaping missionary effort and moving hundreds to *go*, as well as tens of thousands, to *give*.

Never will his mission tour in the United States in 1854 be forgotten, and when all those are dead who then heard him, his tracks will yet be left upon the history of American missions; His short career was like a prairie fire, sweeping hot and fast over the land. The enthusiasm he kindled was intense and glowing. At a time when material interests absorbed attention, when the development of a new territory and the growth of a young Republic engrossed thought, he widened the horizon of American disciples, and gave such impulse and impetus to work in other lands as no man since has ever equalled; the most ardent and fervent appeals for missions seem but as a faint echo of that clarion voice that shook the continent forty years ago!

Perhaps in the age to come, Scotia's great pioneer in India will be most thought of, like Raimund Lull, as a great missionary advocate; and yet he had few of the studied arts and self-conscious graces of the ideal orator or finished declaimer. He would not have been set up as a model of rhetoric or oratory; if he had any code of rules, he broke the whole decalogue at once. His gestures, when he used any, were uncouth and grotesque. His muscles took rigidity from his mental tension. He twitched his forearm, hitched his shoulder, swung his long arm around, catching up and holding his coat-tails, while he left the other arm free to do the pounding necessary for emphasis.

But his unique attitudes and motions fitted his unique oratory. For hours he held audiences entranced. Words flowed in a tumbling torrent—a torrent of fire. Facts stood up at his command in ranks and regiments. His courageous fancy dared the loftiest flights, and his contagious enthusiasm set his whole audience aflame. The expense in vital force was immense, and left behind it exhaustion to the point of peril; and yet he did not roar or rant—it was not thunder, it was lightning.

He was a master of climax. His long sentences have been likened to an auger or corkscrew, boring into the minds of men, at every turn and twist bearing down deeper, until at last, as when a cork is withdrawn, pent-up feeling finds vent in tears, in sighs, in shouts of applause. To take down such speeches was impossible. As well attempt to report a terrific storm at sea, with cyclone winds, mountain waves and waterspouts, varied with volcanic explosions, a glorious sunset, and concluding with an aurora borealis and shooting stars! The reporters gave it up, and with heads resting on their hands, fixed eyes and mouth agape, resigned themselves to the charm of a speaker, who, instead of having to say something had something to say.

It might be invidious, among thousands of illustrious names, to assign to any one absolute pre-eminence. But in more respects than one, Alexander Duff shines in the firmament of missions as a star of the first magnitude. No missionary of modern times has laid on God's altar a choicer offering of genius. His mind was at once like Brougham's and like Canning's; as a convex mirror it scattered light in every direction; as a concave mirror it gathered and concentrated all the rays into one burning focal point. With a memory, a store of information and a versatility, equally marvellous, his sagacity was equal to his capacity, which is still more uncommon; and it will take more than one-half century to dim the lustre of that name which has made so glorious the record of Scottish missions.

It was fitting that this apostle of Christian education in India, one of the originators of the Calcutta Review, one of the founders, and for years the virtual governor, of the University of Calcutta, and the most eloquent missionary orator of this century, should leave as his last legacy to missions the cornerstone upon which this Lectureship is laid. May God make it ever a pillar of witness, in Duff's native land, to the vital need of missions in directing and developing the life and power of the Church of Christ!

III.

The New Apostolate of Woman.

A MARKED FEATURE of the New Acts of the Apostles is the apostolate of *woman*. From the day when Gabriel announced to that Virgin of Bethlehem her destiny as the human mother of the Son of God, woman has taken a new rank in history. Mary of Magdala, to whom first He appeared after His resurrection, was a forerunner of the thousands of her sex who should bear the good tidings of a risen Saviour. That outcast of Sychar who forgot her water-pot and hastened from the well to tell even the men of the city about the Messiah, forecast the myriad women who should forget themselves and all secular cares in the ministry to souls.

These were prophecies of woman's work, and have been fulfilled in a startling manner in this new era. As the new age of missions moves toward the final goal, more and more does Christian womanhood come to the front. To-day, more than one-third of the entire force in the foreign field is composed of godly women. At home women's organizations, the outgrowth of the last quarter century, have had an increase so rapid, an influence so wide, and an impulse so forceful, that no other agency compares with them in value and virtue. They have created and scattered cheap and attractive leaflets on missions, stimulated consecration of home life, and trained up a new generation of self-devoted missionaries; and, amid all the varia-

tions of values, and crises in the money market, kept up a constant advance in the scale of gifts to the Lord. To the increased activity of these women who still follow the Master and minister to

SCRIPTURE TESTIMONY
Body of Christ is made up of many members
I CORINTHIANS 12:12-31

Him of their substance is mainly owing the decided advance of missionary enterprise during the thirty years past.

This theme demands a separate treatment, for the field it opens is too broad to be otherwise surveyed. The bare mention of the names, only, of the holy women, single and married, who have adorned the annals of modern missions, would require much space; but to attempt even the briefest sketch of the heroines of the mission field would demand a volume. In some cases they have been wives and mothers, like those three grand women who in succession shared the work of the devoted Judson in Burma, and one of whom laid the cornerstone of Siamese missions. Others have been single women like Fidelia Fiske in Persia, Eliza Agnew in Ceylon, Mary Whately in Cairo, Matilda Rankin in Mexico, Mary Graybell in India, Clara Cushman in China.

Mary Moffat for a half century bore with her husband the yoke of toil and sacrifice among the Bechuanas. Maria Gobat for forty-five years was Samuel Gobat's invaluable helper in Abyssinia and Malta, and finally in the bishopric of Jerusalem. Hannah Mullens, daughter of one noble missionary, was the wife of another, and has left her lasting footprints in Indian zenanas. Judith Grant spent but four years in Oroomiah, and was but twenty-five years old when she died, but her husband found that her life was the most powerful sermon ever preached in the land of Esther. The work of Mary Williams is scarcely less illustrious than that of the martyr of Erromanga. When Dorothy Jones at twenty-four years of age returned to England from the West Indies a childless widow, after a year of service among those degraded negroes, she had passed through a shipwreck whose frightful agonies had distorted her face beyond recognition, yet she could only say, "I have never once regretted engaging in mission work." Anna Hinderer spent seventeen years by the side of her beloved David, in the Yoruba country, and so captivated the women that they almost worshipped her, and so inspired heroism in her converts that they dared torture for Jesus' sake. Rebecca Wakefield spent but three years in Zanzibar, but her heroic fight with hardship and privation, and all the foes of a hostile climate and a pagan society, won for her the crown of a courage "loftier than that of Joan of Arc." Sarah B. Capron not only took equal part in her husband's long service in India, but after his death trained scores of Bible women for zenana work, and has now given her maturest days, in the Bible Institute at Chicago, to the training of candidates for mission work, both at home and abroad.

Out of all this illustrious company of women, in the field of missions, we take, almost at random, a few names as examples of this modern apostolate of woman.

Hannah Catharine Lacroix Mullens

Was born in India. The women of that vast peninsula were therefore doubly her sisters, and nobly did she redeem the debt of sisterhood. As a girl of twelve she was already about her "Father's business," teaching native girls at Bhowanipore. At nineteen she became the wife of the Rev. Joseph Mullens, of the London Missionary Society in Calcutta, and from that time forth the very roots of her being struck deep into the work of a missionary, and absorbed all her energy. Her aid in her husband's study of Bengali, her work in the boarding-school for Hindu girls and in the Bible classes for native women, her sanctified pen, fit companion to her anointed tongue—all these are but hints of the varied and abundant service that made that life overflow with usefulness. She has sometimes been called the pioneer of zenana work; but, before her day, when Rev. John Fordyce was in India, the movement for penetrating the closed doors of Hindu homes had begun; yet Mrs. Mullens has an indisputable share in the glory of securing wider access to the exiled women of India, and of winning them to Christ. And when, after sixteen years as a missionary's wife, she was suddenly called up higher, at the early age of thirty-five, her last day had been spent in writing a book for the native women.

Emily Chubbuck Judson.

Long before "Fanny Forester" had met her husband, her zeal for missions had kindled over the memoir of Ann Haseltine Judson; and when, in 1845, he first met her and asked for the service of her graceful pen in preparing the memoir of the second Mrs. Judson, little thought either of them that the interview would lead to marriage. The few years of her experience in Burma were crowded with self-sacrificing service; and when in 1850 Dr. Judson's fast failing health made a sea voyage needful, though she scarce knew how to breathe apart from him, and was herself in an apparent decline, she heroically stayed behind. Left with three children in her charge, and one of them her first-born infant of two years, and expecting within one month her second experience of maternity, she cheerfully bade her husband farewell. Three weeks after he sailed, she gave birth to her little "Charles," and soon after laid him in his grave, little knowing that his father had made the sea his sepulchre ten days before his infant son had departed; for there were four months of terrible suspense before she knew whether her husband was alive or dead. Yet she leaned hard on Jesus, and, with a patient heroism which, for pathetic interest, is unsurpassed in the annals of missionary life, "endured as seeing Him who is invisible!"

MARY CHAUNER WILLIAMS.

SCRIPTURE TESTIMONY
Disciples are devoted to Christ above anything or anyone
MATTHEW 4:20-22 · MATTHEW 16:24-25 · MARK 1:19-20 · MARK 8:31-38 · MARK 10:28 · LUKE 9:23-27 · LUKE 9:57-62 · LUKE 14:25-35

John Williams always said that, without his wife, he knew not what he would have done. Beside all her loving, conjugal and maternal ministries, her lofty spirit made radiant even the most menial offices of cook and housemaid, and withal she was a teacher. From her the women of Raiatea learned the arts of household life, while every such lesson became a channel for higher instruction. She searched out the aged, half nude and altogether despised and neglected, placed them under proper care, and led many of them to find a new staff for their old age and a new light at life's evening-time. The younger women she diligently taught and catechized until they were trained in the words of faith and good doctrine. Whether with her husband in his "circumnavigation of charity," or staying behind to care for interests that would suffer in their absence, she was the same unmurmuring servant and burdenbearer of the Lord: and, when seven of her babes were sleeping on the various isles of the Pacific, this handmaid of the Lord could still say, "Be it unto me, according to Thy word!" In poverty or peril, sickness or suffering, she was alike undaunted and undiscouraged. Awakened at midnight with the awful news of her husband's tragic death at Erromanga, and while so prostrate with a paralysis of grief, that even friendly visits of sympathy were a torture, she admitted, among the first who entered that chamber of sorrow, Malietoa, the chief. He was himself overwhelmed by the loss which put all Polynesia under its pall. Frantically he appealed to her not to kill herself by indulging grief, pleading with her to live for the sake of himself and his poor people, and crying out, "If you too are taken, O what shall we then do!"

FIDELIA FISKE.

SCRIPTURE TESTIMONY
Christians are generous and hospitable
ACTS 16:14-15 · ROMANS 12:13 · I TIMOTHY 3:2 · HEBREWS 13:2

Born the same year that Williams sailed for the South Seas, at twenty-seven years old, this noble woman went to reproduce in the land of Esther the system of instruction which at Holyoke, Massachusetts, made Mary Lyon's school for girls so famous. There are various types of bravery, and none more heroic than such as this refined and delicate woman displayed, as for Christ's sake she dared the unutterable filth and countless army of vermin encountered in the huts of Oroomiah.

When in 1843 she arrived in Persia, about forty schools had been opened on those plains, but for the most part reached only the boys; and the girls' school, that Mrs. Grant had founded five years earlier, had dragged out a half dead existence. It was for this humble daughter of Shelboume, niece of the Syrian missionary, Pliny Fiske, to become the real pioneer of woman's education in Persia.

God laid it on her heart, to lift up out of the horrible pit and miry clay of unspeakable degradation, Nestorian womanhood; but to do it she must herself go down into the pit. She saw that to raise womanhood, she must first lift girlhood to a higher level. So she began with the daughters, and courageously took measures to gather, into a family school, a few whom she would cleanse and clothe, feed and train. She sought for six girls with which to begin, and, while as yet she knew but one Syriac sentence, she used that to beg parents to "give their daughters." On the proposed day of opening, though fifteen day scholars offered, not one "boarder" was secured. Mar-Yohanan, however, came, leading two little girls of seven and ten; and to this first "gift of daughters" additions were slowly made until they numbered twenty-five—all she could then accommodate.

Thus, on foundations laid in prayers and wet with tears, was reared that New Holyoke which has been to Persia a pearl of great price. For sixteen years she carried on her apostolic work, and when illness drove her home her one wish was to get back to the land of the magi. Cancer ate at her vitals until, not yet fifty years old, she died, in 1864. Yet, while thus weary and worn, feeling this vulture gnawing at her heart, she not only pleaded ceaselessly for missions, but actually took the principalship at Holyoke, Mass., that with her dying hand she might still sow in youthful soil the seeds of missionary consecration.

Of Fidelia Fiske the venerable secretary of the American Board has said: "In the structure and working of her whole nature she seemed to me the nearest approach I ever saw, in man or woman, to my ideal of our beloved Saviour as he appeared on earth."

The work which began with the repulsive task of literally cleansing from filth and purging of vermin the very bodies of Persian girls, found its reward when, in the three years from 1844 to 1847, an outpouring so copious visited her seminary that it could be compared to nothing but the first Pentecost. All the girls above twelve years were converted, and many of them became missionaries in these Persian homes. The school was so obviously blessed in lifting women above the low level of the donkey, and ennobling that character which is the secret of all betterment of condition, that persecution only showed its worth and multiplied its supporters and so made necessary enlarged accommodations. During the closing days of Miss Fiske's stay in Oroomiah ninety-three converted women, in one meeting, greeted her as first-fruits of a life whose motto was, "Live for Christ."

We may well thank God that, after for centuries being kept in the background, Christian womanhood is finding its true sphere of work, and wielding its golden sceptre of influence. Missions have shown the normal status of woman in the Church and in the world; and how closely her identification with her Redeemer is also linked with family life and social life, so that without her there can be no holy household nor reformed society. And her deep sense of infinite debt to Christ, not only for salvation, but for her redemption from her domestic and social thraldom, prompts her to undertake a mission to her degraded sisters in pagan, heathen and moslem lands, which can by no one but a Christian woman be done at all. Perhaps God suffered zenanas and harems to be locked against men so that women might the more feel His providential call for their service to their sex.

Woman's work for woman no human gauge can measure. When Dr. Eli Smith of Syria was giving theological students his reasons why, ordinarily, missionaries should take a wife, he spoke not only of her contribution to her husband's home comforts, and her power to shelter him from moral suspicion, but he added with earnest emphasis, that the wife often does full as effective work in the foreign field as her husband, and that nothing is needed more, as a living lesson to these degraded and ignorant idolaters and victims of vicious social surroundings, than the practical exhibition in the Christian woman herself of what the religion of Christ does for her as daughter and sister, wife and mother. The common witness of the most heroic and successful missionaries is that the holy lives and tireless labours of devoted women have been indispensable to the highest results of missions. There was a time when woman was regarded as little more than man's helper, if not servant: but Paul wrote, "*Help those women* which laboured with us in the gospel," as though they were now leaders, and the men were to go to their help!

IV

The New Lessons.

WE MUST not leave this department of our great theme without looking back and asking what new lessons God would have us learn. And, first of all, this history of modern missions has been writing in large letters the lesson of the *power of pious parentage.*

Rev. J. Murray Mitchell, LL.D., has told how he once ascended to a high summit in India in search of the source of the Godivari River: how at last a spot was reached where so few were the drops that trickled from the rocks that they could for some seconds be held in the hollow of his hand; and at that point one could in a few moments scoop out a new. channel and turn the whole stream in a new direction. From such an insignificant rill sprang one of India's noblest rivers. The little stream he saw, flowing down the slope and gradually broadening: then running eastward toward the Bay of Bengal, growing wider and deeper, gathering volume and momentum, until it became the secret of fertility to thousands of acres otherwise dry and desert.

That river is a parable of human life. "The king's heart is in the hands of the Lord, and he turneth it whithersoever He will." He who learns the secret of the Lord, like Him, gets at the point in the stream, near the heart, where life's issues begin to flow outward, and where character, conduct, history and destiny wait for a shaping hand. Thackeray reminds us how we sow a thought and reap an act; sow an act, and reap a habit; sow a habit, and reap a character; sow a character, and reap destiny. So then he who begins back where thought is forming, moulds the seed of that last, eternal harvest.

No lesson learned from these lives of the new apostles is more awfully solemn than this: They prove to us the power of spiritual ancestry—the faith which, first dwelling in a godly mother or grandmother, has given many a Timothy to the field of missions. The Samuels are to be accounted for by the Hannahs, and the pioneers of our Lord have been nurtured by some Zacharias and Elisabeth. There may be no inheritance of godliness, but there is certainly a heritage of grace; aptitudes are transmitted, if character is not. Let every father remember how from his loins may come a future Judson or Marsden, a Williams or Wilson, a Patteson or Hannington. Let every . mother think how the child she bears and rears may be one of God's destined kings or queens, and that it is her hand that is to give shape to the plastic clay for one of God's chosen vessels. We have only to remember Ziegenbalg and Zinzendorf, Schwartz and Livingstone, Paton and Mills, Gulick and Scudder, Judson and Jessup, Duff and Hudson Taylor, to learn how much hangs on the holiness and heroism of the parents, if the children are to become holy and heroic.

Another lesson taught is that of *unrecognized greatness*. The new apostles, like the old, have not always been recognized, and have sometimes been rejected, by their own generation; and this lack of appreciation of God's anointed men and women by their contemporaries is one of the significant lessons of the New Acts of the Apostles. Carey bore the sneers of unhallowed wit; Stoddard was charged with throwing away his fine culture amid Persian wilds, as Livingstone was, with wasting great powers amid African forests. Williams falling at Erromanga, Hannington shot on the borders of Uganda, Mackay dying yet in youth among the cruel savages of Mwanga's realm, Riggs retiring into scholarly seclusion at the Golden Horn, and three peerless women following Judson to Burma—to many all this is sheer waste; but history reverses many of our verdicts, and the judgment-seat of Christ will reverse many more.

It was not in vain that Morrison wore the queue and burned the midnight lamp at Canton, that Wilder "buried himself" for thirty years in India, that Carey left Leicester for Serampore, that Hunt exiled himself at the Fiji group, that Patteson fell at Nackapu, that McAll spent his last twenty years in tireless labours amid the commune, in Paris.

Again, we are taught *obedience to the will of God*. The plan of God is the only ultimately successful scheme; and to find out that plan and fall into our place in it, is to come into our true orbit round the Sun of the universe—to enter into, to become part of, a system of harmony in which all things work together for good. There, all things are ours, even death as well as life, things present as well as things to come—for we are Christ's, and Christ is God's. Life's length is not measured by its years, but its yearnings, its prayers, its measure of unity with God and conformity to His purpose. All life is long if it reaches the goal God means for it.

The new apostles have been men and women who have sought to hear God's voice and heed divine visions, and move along the lines laid down in the word of God—who have waited God's time and wrought in God's way. The founder of the China Inland Mission heard a voice plainly saying to him, "I am going to open central and inland China to the gospel, and will use you if you are ready to come into My plan;" and from that day he has known no will but that will. God cares not for the many, but He uses the few who are wholly His—who in that calling wherein they are found abide with God; whose eyes are unto His, glad to be guided by His eye, and needing not bit and bridle and rein and whip to compel them to obey His will, like the dumb horse or stubborn mule. He who is content to be drained of selfishness, to lose himself in God, as content to die as to live, if death means life to others; ready, like Ignatius, to be ground between teeth of lions to make bread for God's people—he is the man upon whom the Spirit comes, and with whom, as was written of Gideon, He "clothes Himself," as a warrior with his coat of armour.

Yes, the inner secret of service is the sharing of God's Spirit, and so of His power. Herbert Spencer was right, for "by no political alchemy can we get golden conduct out of leaden instincts." Influence will not be grandly noble when character is basely ignoble, and all efforts to make up in culture for what the soul lacks in renewed nature, will be worse than waste. The builder should not construct ornament, but ornament construction; and he who wants beauty of character needs only to see that there is something solidly built and firmly based, on which to have beauty appear. Otherwise the best appearances are like frost-work on the window-pane that melts away before the sunbeam.

Again, what a lesson may be learned from the *diversity of spheres* that have furnished God's workmen. Coleridge at Christ's hospital felt ambitious to be a shoemaker's apprentice, because from this, more than any other handicraft, eminent men have gone forth to serve the world. Jesus Christ was a carpenter at Nazareth, and His life as a mechanic was a prophecy of the host of those who from the workshop of the common tradesman would go forth into fields of wide usefulness and heroic service. Any place may furnish training and any tool may become, like Moses' rod, God's means to work His signs. The heart needs only to be God's—then "what is that in thine hand?" A shepherd's crook, a carpenter's hammer, a mason's trowel, a shoemaker's awl, or the needle of Dorcas,—these God can use as well as the tongue of the orator or the pen of the ready writer, to glorify Him.

PART III.

THE NEW VISIONS AND VOICES

I.

The Leading Voice—The Voice of the Master.

"AFTER THIS, I looked, and behold a door was opened in heaven; and I heard a voice, as it were of a trumpet, talking with me."—*Revelation*, iv. i. The Apostolic age was both pictorial and vocal: it was an age of visions and voices of God. A door was opened in heaven. Such sights the eye beheld, and such sounds the ear heard, as left no doubt with saints, and sometimes with sinners, that God was in close touch with man. As through a rent veil flashed the hidden glory; and, whether the sound was that of a trumpet, or of the "still small voice," it was awe-inspiring and soul-subduing. The gospel message itself was the voice of God, and, as was fitting, it was emphasized and accentuated by other utterances clearly divine. Both by His providence and by His Spirit He spake so often, so loudly, that the whole age of the Apostles echoed with these divine voices. In effect the visions were voices, for as messengers of God they were vocal, only that their language entered the city of Mansoul through eyegate rather than eargate.

Not even in the time of the ancient Theophanies has God more manifestly appeared and spoken to men. Nor were these visions and voices vain. They mark, in the history of missions, turning points, both critical and pivotal; hinges whereon the golden gates of the kingdom hung and swung. Nor were they meant for that age only. A mere glance at the Acts of the Apostles shows that what God taught the early Church was a lesson for all time: He was giving signs and signals for all ages. To a devout reader this book records and reproduces what primitive disciples saw and heard, somewhat as the photograph and phonograph may yet serve future generations.

One mark of the close analogy between the age of modern missions and that of the Apostolic, is found in the new visions and voices of God, which though less characterized by the purely miraculous or supernatural element are no less unmistakable in their purpose and purport. Every page of these new chapters is thus illustrated and explained by the Divine Teacher; and the fact is both curious and significant that the main lessons, thus taught the Church in our day, follow the same lines as those of that first century. The Heavenly Schoolmaster, like the earthly, finds needful to use repetition for the sake of impression; and so, after the long interval of centuries, we are still in God's school, learning the same old lessons from the same old text-book, only it is a new edition with notes by the Author, illumined by new illustrations, its teaching enforced and vivified by new arguments and appeals.

The first voice we hear in the Acts of the Apostles is that of the Lord Jesus Himself. His words have a double value; as His last words before He was taken up, they form the sum and substance of all His previous teaching; and as His first words before the new age of missions opens, they, like a table of contents, give the sum and substance of the history that is to follow. All other voices and visions found in this book are meant to fix in the minds of believers what they saw and heard when the Lord last appeared unto them before His ascension,—to echo, explain, amplify, illustrate His great commission. Because every word that He then spake is a little world full of meaning, let us write His farewell message in large letters:

> "DEPART NOT FROM JERUSALEM,
>   BUT WAIT FOR THE PROMISE OF THE FATHER
>   WHICH YE HAVE HEARD OF ME;
>   FOR JOHN TRULY BAPTIZED WITH WATER,
>   BUT YE SHALL BE BAPTIZED WITH THE HOLY GHOST,
>   NOT MANY DAYS HENCE.
>   YE SHALL RECEIVE THE POWER OF THE HOLY GHOST
>   COMING UPON YOU,
>   AND YE SHALL BE WITNESSES UNTO ME
>   BOTH IN JERUSALEM AND IN ALL JUDEA,
>   AND IN SAMARIA,
>   AND UNTO THE UTTERMOST PART OF THE EARTH."

Here then is the loud and leading voice of the Apostolic age, and how majestic and commanding! In this final word of our ascending Lord three things stand out conspicuous like lofty peaks against the horizon:

First, the work of witness is the duty of the whole Church. Second, the field of witness is the territory of the whole world. Third, the force of witness is the baptism of the Holy Spirit.

Again we affirm it, this farewell message is all-comprehensive. From it was omitted nothing vital to the Church's great mission; to it nothing has been, or can be, added. The keynote is struck, and the divine melody is sung; all that follows is but a variation upon this theme, the harmony which only makes more conspicuous the melody. The chapters that succeed add only emphasis to this first chapter, and so it will be of the unwritten records yet to follow; every failure or success in our mission work only gives fresh force, heavier stress, to this great message of the departing Master.

Immediately, with but ten days of interval, the farewell word of the Lord, and the promise of the Father, find fulfilment in the outpouring of the Spirit. Pentecost was both a vision and a voice, emphasizing and confirming what Jesus had said.

The *work* of witness now began. Hundreds of tongues, like a chorus of silver trumpets of jubilee, proclaimed in unison the acceptable year of the Lord; and, although at times this work has suffered contraction through unbelief and worldliness, it has never entirely ceased, nor will it, until the end of the age.

The *field* of witness now began to be first seen in its true length and breadth. Peter officially said, "The promise is unto you and unto your children, and to all that are afar off, even as many as the Lord our God shall call." And this he spake not of himself; he had little conception of the meaning of his own words, as subsequent events prove. It was the voice of the Spirit, repeating and enlarging the covenant promises of a former dispensation; repeating them for the sake of Jewish believers; enlarging them for the sake of the gentiles, who had hitherto been aliens from the commonwealth of Israel and strangers from the covenants of promise. Christ had made the field of witness to embrace the uttermost part of the earth; and so now the Spirit leads Peter, still fettered with Jewish exclusiveness, to add, "and to as many as are afar off!" The golden links of prophecy connect the Hebrew race with a larger grace, that is to touch the whole family of man. And so this same Peter was led, a little later, to say to the unbelieving Jews, "Repent ye, therefore, and be converted, so that times of refreshing may come from the presence of the Lord." The reclamation and restoration of God's elect people is a condition, preliminary and preparatory, to that last great time of refreshing which is to come upon all flesh. In Abraham's ".seed shall all the kindreds of the earth be blessed!" but that promise made to the father of the faithful will be fulfilled only when Abraham's seed, receiving the Messiah they despised and rejected, become witnesses to the nations. And so Paul adds his testimony to Peter's:

"Now, if the fall of them be the enriching of the world, and their diminishing the enriching of the gentiles, how much more their fulness! For, if their rejection be the reconciling of the world, what shall the receiving of them be but life from the dead."—*Romans*, xi. 12-14.

The field of witness was not only now first seen to be the world, but in a peculiar way its occupation began. From every quarter of the inhabited globe had gathered those representatives who, on the day of Pentecost, received the word and the blessing; and going back to their far-off and widely separated abodes they naturally became witnesses unto the peoples among whom they dwelt. The sheaf of first-fruits thus laid on that Pentecostal altar, supplied seed for the sower to scatter in regions beyond.

The power of witness was now for the first time revealed in its fulness. Pentecost emphasized our Lord's words by bringing the promised baptism, the chrism of power, the nameless charm and virtue which make all witness effective. Then began the great endowment and enduement, so indescribable yet indispensable; through human tongues the Holy Spirit spake, with a demonstration of truth far beyond all the demonstration of logic, making simple witness to Christ to accomplish what all the wisdom of the schools has never been able to effect. And, from that day onward the secret of power to testify for God, to convince and persuade men, has been the same, namely, to be filled with the Holy Ghost.

We have thus seen that the first two chapters of the Acts furnish the key, not only to this book, but to all missionary history. Our Lord's last words describe the work of witness, define the field of witness, and reveal the force of witness; and the third person of the Trinity adds His confirmation of the word of the Lord Jesus, by leading disciples to begin the work, to enter the field, and to use the power. Where God thus teaches three lessons, and stamps them as of such supreme importance, it must be our duty to learn them thoroughly. We therefore tarry to study them with more care and closeness of application.

II.

The Call to All Disciples.

THIS FIRST lesson taught in the Acts of the Apostles, that the *work of witness belongs to the whole Church,* dominates the book; so emphatically, so repeatedly enforced, that it must constitute one, if not the only, design of its records. Those who believed were from the first sent forth as witnesses. It is of the very genius of Christianity that it implies and compels testimony; "I believed and therefore have I spoken; we also believe and therefore speak." This is not only the logic of missions; it is the logic of spiritual life. The Church of God is an army, always to be mobilized in readiness for action,—more than this, always in action. Livingstone said, "The spirit of missions is the Spirit of our Master; the very genius of our religion. A diffusive philanthropy is Christianity itself. It requires perpetual propagation to attest its genuineness."

How far this conception of a witnessing Church is the controlling law in the structure of the Acts of the Apostles, only careful search will show.

The introduction to this book refers to that "forty days" of communion between the risen Lord and His disciples, the object and result of which were fourfold:

First, to leave in them no doubt of the fact of His resurrection; secondly, to give them instruction touching the Kingdom of God; thirdly, to prepare them for His unseen presence and guidance; fourthly, to inspire them with the true Spirit of missions.

Then, as soon as the Spirit was outpoured, we find the bold outlines of early Church history confronting us, the record of active, aggressive testimony, pushing its lines from Jerusalem into all Judea, then into Samaria, and so farther and farther into the remotest regions beyond.

1. The witnessing Church at Jerusalem and Judea. Chapter i. 13 to vii.

Ten days of prayer are followed by the Pentecostal enduement for service, persecution by Pharisees and Sadducees, Stephen's martyrdom, and the dispersion of disciples; the voluntary community of goods, division of work, and the institution of the diac-onate.

2. The witnessing Church in Samaria. Chapter viii. Under Philip, the evangelist-deacon, Samaria receives a blessing, essentially a repetition of the Pentecost at Jerusalem.

3. The witnessing Church moving toward the uttermost part of the earth. Chapter ix. to the close.

The conversion of the eunuch represents evangelism begun in Ethiopia; and that of Saul of Tarsus, the chosen apostle to the gentiles, raises up the greatest evangelist the world has ever seen, whose especial passion it is to reach the regions beyond. Among the Romans at Cesarea, then among the Greeks at Antioch and at Ephesus, Pentecostal blessings descend with marvellous signs and wonders; and the first gentile Church formed at Antioch becomes the starting point for foreign missions. Paul's three mission tours, with their ever widening circles, are outlined, and the book closes with the Cilician apostle teaching and preaching at Rome, the third great centre of Christianity.

In the latter part of the Acts, Paul comes to the front, while Peter disappears entirely. The reason is plain. The obvious object of the book is to trace the beginnings of missions to the nations of the wide world. To Peter it was given to unlock the door of faith, first to Jews and then to gentiles; then he goes to the dispersion or scattered tribes of Israel; and Paul, whose commission is to the nations at large, the typical world-missionary, naturally becomes the main actor in the scene.

Attention has already been called to the fact, that Luke treats both the gospel which he wrote and this book of which he is the declared author, as parts of one connected, continuous, complete narrative. A careful study will show the links of unity. The purpose of the Spirit, in these two sketches, is to outline gospel history from its infancy in its humble Judean cradle to its mature growth as a world-wide power; to trace the seed of the kingdom, first sown on Syrian soil, then scattered widely beside all waters and borne upon the various streams of civilization to the heart of the heathen world.

Thus, from first to last, this combined narrative is the story of missions. In the gospel our Lord offers the good news to the Jews; and then seeing their actual rejection of Him and foreseeing their continued refusal of His message, He commands and commissions His disciples to go everywhere and witness to every creature. In the Acts we see the commission and command actually carried out; the preaching of the gospel to the Jews by both Peter and Paul, and its repeated rejection by them; with its subsequent and consequent proclamation to mankind as such at the great centres of population.

The Gospel according to Luke opens with Christ's incarnation, and closes with His resurrection and ascension. The promise of enduement with power "not many days hence," is the last link left to connect with the after narrative. In the Pentecostal fires the new links are forged for this chain of events, and so the Acts of the Apostles joins on to the gospel, beginning with the natal day of the Church at Pentecost and ending with Paul's work at Rome.

Now, confining our gaze to the Acts, as a whole, we observe at least ten marked features, all indicating the mission, committed to the whole Church, of a world-wide witness.

1. The waiting for the Holy Spirit. The enduement from on high was also an endowment, fitting for the work of witness; the type of other effusions which followed and which indicated that not only Jewish converts but gentile believers also were to be thus endued and endowed.

2. The substance of this witness was Christ crucified, risen, exalted and glorified, as the only Saviour; pointed prominence being given to the Old Testament prophecies and the exact correspondence of New Testament history; and to that glorious second Coming of our Lord which is to put the capstone upon all prophecy and history. The book is full of Christ, Messiah foretold, Saviour revealed.

3. The resolute persistence of Christ's witnesses in face of organized opposition. The Jews led by Sanhedric rulers, the gentiles led by such as the Ephesian Demetrius, drive disciples to face, if not to fight, that worst of all wild beasts, the mob. Persecution bares her red right arm and whets her cruel sword, warning disciples what price they must pay for free speech. But they "cannot but speak the things which they have seen and heard." And so this story of the Acts becomes the first book of Christ's martyrs. Stephen's angel smile shines amid a hail of stones. James' head drops under the axe of Herod Agrippa. Peter, kept for a like fate by the same despot, is loosed from prison, at the beck of One before whom even iron fetters fall and iron gates open of their own accord. Yet neither can bribe nor force stop the mouth of Christ's witnesses. God is obeyed and man is defied.

4. Church life itself is moulded by this mission to mankind. Believers so commonly accept this work of witness that personal and private interests are merged into this wider and nobler service. The community of privilege and responsibility is emphasized by a more remarkable community of goods. With an unselfishness that has no other example in history, believers part with worldly possessions and pour the proceeds into a common fund, to be distributed according to the wants of each and all. Not only duties but burdens are shared alike.

5. The witnesses disperse more and more widely. Those who were sojourners in Jerusalem went back to their separate abodes with the new message of life burned into their souls by the Spirit's fire, and burning on their tongues; and so light began to shine in the darkness. If we may trust tradition, the eunuch whom Philip guided to the blood of the Lamb and the water of baptism, founded the Church of Alexandria and baptized his own queen. The converted blasphemer from Tarsus, swept over a wider and wider arc, until his mission tours touched not only Ephesus, Athens, Corinth and Rome, but possibly Spain and Britain.

6. The open secrets of Apostolic success may be read upon every page of this short story. Apostolic activity moves toward its goal of world-wide missions with so rapid strides, that in one generation it reaches the remotest parts; yet it treads no strange road. All along the way God's lights are hung, that he who will may follow. How simple the methods of work! Childlike faith in the promise of God and the power of His word and Spirit; believing and united prayer that laughs at the giant Anakim with their chariots of iron, and cares not for high walls and strong gates, and foes many and mighty; a heroic obedience that asks only for "marching orders," and then dares all obstacles and opposers, moving on into -the "valley of death," to "do and die"—such are the simple clew to the whole maze and mystery of Apostolic missions.

7. The unseen divine presence pervades the whole history. To Christ's last command was closely linked a last promise, "Lo, I am with you all the days, even to the end of the age." This book is the record of the fulfilment of that promise. Wonderworking miraculous signs, divine interpositions, so abound that the uncommon becomes common, and the supernatural seems no more unnatural. As we cross the threshold of the story we meet the tongues of flame that tell the power of God; then each chapter is a new chamber of marvels. The healing of the lame man, of the divining damsel, of Eneas at Lydda; the raising of dead Dorcas; the healing virtue that invests the body of Paul and the shadow of Peter; the prison doors thrice opened, twice by the angel, once by the earthquake as God's angel; miracles of judgment as well as deliverance; Elymas being blinded, and Ananias, Sapphira and Herod struck dead;—at every step we tread on enchanted ground.

8. The power of the gospel is everywhere conspicuous. Sinners are converted sometimes as in masses; saints are edified and educated, and the body of Christ grows strong. Even those who are neither converted nor convicted seem compelled to hear and to make some decision; they may not bow to Christ, but they cannot maintain the stolid apathy of indifference. Stephen's stoners are cut to the heart, for his words are swords; Felix says "go thy way," but he "trembles;" Agrippa will not yield but is "almost persuaded." Those who "gnashed on him with their teeth"

"could not resist the wisdom and the spirit with which" the first martyr spake; and Saul, who stood by consenting to their deed, never forgot that shining face which prepared him for the glory that smote him near Damascus!

9. This is the book of the Holy Spirit. Throughout, there runs the stream of His subtle, unseen, mysterious, resistless working. Omniscience, omnipotence, omnipresence, find here the field for their display, promising and prophesying similar results, whenever and wherever like conditions obtain. Here God shows that in grace as in nature He has chosen channels for His power and energy, and if those channels are not obstructed, He who is the same yesterday and to-day and forever, will still work wonders.

10. No undue emphasis is here laid on numerical results or apparent success. In the story of primitive missions the whole stress is upon obedience, not consequence, not on succeeding but on serving. The work is God's, the instrumentality only is man's; the whole responsibility is therefore with the Master Workman, and whether success or failure, defeat or triumph, be the apparent outcome, all is well.

No lesson taught in these chapters is more sublime, or more needful than this. In every age disciples need to learn it anew. So long as our eyes are dazzled by the glittering trophies of victory, and our hearts depressed by seeming disaster, we shall be in a state of chronic worry. Our joy and hope, our courage and confidence, will be like the waves of the sea, tossed up and down by every change of wind, and driven to and fro by every turn of tide. The work of missions is God's work. Man did not plan it, cannot carry it on, cannot make it a success. As Dr. McLaren says, "the results are so poor as to show that the treasure is in an earthen vessel; so rich as to prove that in the earthen vessel is a heavenly treasure." We are therefore simply to do our duty, and with a holy abandonment, a sublime "carelessness," cast ourselves and trust our work upon Him whose we are and whom we serve.

Some of these ten principal features of this book will receive more attention further on; but at this point we have sought to look at them as at the features of one face, striking for the unity and harmony of their combination and impression. And they serve to characterize the Acts of the Apostles as the typical history of the witnessing Church during its first generation, wherein God teaches the philosophy of missions by a historical example.

This book of the Acts teaches that in this witness *every believer is to take part*. A duty is involved from whose obligation no disciple is excepted; a privilege from whose enjoyment and enrichment no believer is excluded. The opening miracle of Pentecost writes this lesson in letters of fire upon the doorway of this historic record, for it brought that twofold gift of converting and anointing grace, and the anointing came upon all that little company, even upon the women. The gift of tongues was both a sign to the unbelievers and a signal to believers. What is the tongue but the great instrument of testimony? The message was spoken with many tongues to teach disciples that their witness was to reach every nation, whatever its language; and possibly that gift of tongues fitted them for such witness, without the tedious mastery of foreign speech. And the tongues were of fire to remind them that faithful testimony was to be attended by a new force, an energy not of man but of God.

So plainly is the tongue of every disciple thus set apart for testimony, that it is a fact beyond explanation that the Church should ever have lost sight of God's purpose, that witnessing shall be the prerogative of all believers; and it is one of the startling proofs of a rapid decline from a primitive piety, that so few modern disciples feel the burden of personal responsibility for souls.

The study of words reveals ethics in language. Error and truth find crystallization in current forms of speech, and so this habitual carelessness that shifts the work of soul-saving upon other shoulders has become coined into popular phrases, fixed forms of expression.

For instance, let us look closely at that dangerous term, "division of labour." It is often said that the Acts of the Apostles encourages and enjoins this principle; and the institution of the diaconate is cited to prove it, because the Church was bidden to look out honest men to serve tables, leaving the Apostles free to give themselves to prayer and to the ministry of the word.

Let us beware of too broad an induction from so narrow a basis of particulars. There is a great gulf of difference and distinction between *division* of labour and *distribution* of labour. Division hints at partition and separation; distribution implies only a special assignment or allotment of work. Expediency and convenience may set apart some to a particular service, in order to free them from all entanglements, and to assure a more competent and thorough attention to that branch of work; but it is quite another matter to build up a dividing wall, or draw even a dividing line, which practically parts disciples, and which they come to think it improper to cross. Service is to be so distributed, that each may have his own sphere and work, and no department be overcrowded or under-supplied. But never, during Apostolic days, was there found asserted in the Church of Christ any law of monopoly, clerical caste, or exclusive right. Whatever such notions or customs have since grown up, "from the beginning it was not so." All believers had, and exercised, an inalienable and undisputed right to proclaim Christ to lost men. Experience of grace was the sufficient warrant for witness to grace; and the only limits to such witness were those of ability, opportunity and consecration.

The appointment of deacons was wise and needful. Material and temporal wants demanded supply, and such cares must not collide and conflict with purely spiritual offices and ministries; and, because provision for God's poor was a form of service to Him, it must be in charge of men, not only of honest report and of wisdom, but full of the Holy Spirit.

The same need still exists. The ministers and missionaries to whom is committed as their one absorbing trust, the curacy of souls, must not be hindered and hampered by the stem necessity of ministering to the temporal needs of their own and of other families. There is a "business side" of the Lord's work which calls for men with a practical talent for finance and business. Some who are *not* called to give themselves wholly to prayer and the ministry of the word, may unshackle those who *are*, relieving them of needless tax on time and strength, by taking care of poor saints, and by providing a sound financial basis and bottom for evangelistic and spiritual work.

How often a noble structure of missions has come to wreck and ruin from dry rot in its timbers, because there has been no one to look after supplies! The war is God's, but it needs money and *materiel*. Brave Captain Gardiner, at Tierra del Fuego, led a little band of seven against Satan's seat in Patagonia, but had to turn back, and died of starvation at the very gates of his stronghold, and in the very crisis of the assault, because of lack of the necessities of life. Had some well organized body of men and women at home kept up the "line of communication" between the base of operations and the source of supplies, Allen Gardiner might not have fallen at Spaniards' Harbour in 1851, and the victory might not have been postponed for half a century!

Let it be noted, however, that the appointment of the seven deacons to serve tables, did not shut them out from preaching or even baptizing, as the records of both Stephen and Philip clearly show. Distribution of labour did not divide disciples, nor debar any from taking part in evangelizing. Over the doors of the early Church the Master wrote in letters so large that he who runneth may read at a cursory glance, "Go ye into all the world, and preach the gospel to every creature." The command was and is to all disciples'. Those who cannot go in person, must go in the person of others who can; and with no less self-denial, prayer, self-offering, must they who tarry by the stuff support those who go to the battle, than if they themselves went to the field. Only so will they share alike in the work and the reward. Let this one law of service be framed into churchlife, and all will be alike missionaries.

In that Samarian Pentecost, God laid new emphasis upon the truth already taught, that the commission of disciples was not limited by priestly lines nor confined within narrow channels. The sharp distinction between priests and people, found in the days of Judaism, disappears in the Christian Church; the barriers were down between the court of the gentiles and the court of Israel, and the middle walls of partition between the court of Israel and the court of the priests perished with the old Temple, and has no place in the Church of Christ. Nay, the veil is rent between the Holy Place and the Holiest of all, and all believers approach alike without hindrance or hesitation to the mercy-seat. What means all this if not a plain assertion of a certain equality of right, dignity and privilege? No assault is designed, in the calm recording of these convictions, upon the views or practices of fellow-disciples; but candour and loyalty to truth demand of us, that as honest students of this great missionary charter of the Church, we shall accept and defend its plain teachings. If we are in earnest to perfect the missionary methods of our own era, we must with open eyes see our present defects, and own our departures from the primitive standard. The prime condition of all spiritual progress is a candid mind. That a custom exists is no warrant for its right to exist; it is at best but a presumption in its favour. As Cyprian said, "Consuetudo vetustas erroris,"—Custom may be only the antiquity of error. And if in the Church any notions or practices have found root and growth which are not of God's planting, and whose fruit is not of godly savour, however marked by old age, the sooner we cut them down and extirpate them, root and branch, the better. And surely whatever hampers or hinders all believers from bearing witness for the gospel, must find sanction outside of the Acts.

God used persecution to reveal the true value and need of what is somewhat invidiously called, "Lay-agency," in the world-wide work. The Spirit records with marked particularity how in this wide scattering of disciples the Apostles were excepted; so that the fact might be more emphatic that it was the common body of believers who being scattered abroad went everywhere preaching the word. God may yet use persecution to repeat the same lesson, that, as there is to be no distinction among those who need the gospel, so we are to deny to no believer the prerogative, which is a sort of birthright, of telling the gospel story as best he can. It needs all believers to reach all unbelievers. The silver trumpet which peals out God's year of jubilee is wrought of the whole Church, every believer adding material to the trumpet and volume to the sound. The Church is God's golden lampstand, and everyone who is taught of God is part of that framework, helping to lift the Light of the world higher and give its rays more range and power. Because we believe, therefore we speak, is the reason for missions. Every one of us is needed in the work: the Church, the world, God, have need of us, and we ourselves need the work for our own growth.

The Church, as primitive piety declined, built up priestly barriers about the "clergy" and taught the "laity" that it was impertinent intrusion for those who are not "ordained," to preach the good tidings. But in all great epochs of spiritual power, believers have burst these bonds like cords of burnt tow, and claimed the universal, inalienable right to tell lost souls of Jesus. Such false restraints are cerements of the tomb; they belong not to the living but to the dead; they have the odour of decay, and, like other grave-clothes, should be left behind in the sepulchre. When Christ's voice calls the dead to life, and one comes forth bound hand and foot with ceremonialism and traditionalism, even his mouth bound about with the napkin of enforced silence—the Lord of Glory says, "Loose him and let him go!" As well force him back into the sepulchre and roll the stone to the door as to leave a converted soul bound! Let every live man be a free man. Stand back! ye who would fetter a disciple's utterance. He is one of God's witnesses. Teach his tongue, but do not bind it! Train him for service, but do not hold him back! Ye, who are preachers and pastors, become ye teachers of teachers, trainers of workers! turn your churches into recruiting offices, barracks, armouries, where disciples enlist for the war, and are put through the drill and discipline of soldiers; where they put on the whole armour of God, and then go forth, led by you, to fight the good fight of faith!

Do we, with needless repetition, seek to emphasize this lesson of the common duty and privilege of believers to preach the gospel? Mark how God repeats it in this book. That Samarian Pentecost was a new voice of God teaching this truth. All that great work of grace revolved about Philip the deacon, a man set apart indeed, but not for preaching or baptizing; and God set his own sign and seal in a wonderful way upon the ministry of this lay evangelist. What a divine rebuke to all unscriptural notions, whether sacerdotal or sacramental! The age of missions holds a blessing so large, that it cannot be confined within priestly lines and limits. The vast host to be reached defies us to overtake their destitution while we rely upon a few thousand educated, ordained, highly trained workmen. Millions sink, unsaved and unwarned, while we are waiting for experts to come to their rescue with all the most improved life-saving apparatus of the schools. If for these souls in wreck we cannot command the rocket and gun, the swinging-basket and life-boat, let us have the strong arm of the swimmer, the plank—anything to save a sinking man!

Let us thank God for the age of a Reformed Church! For fifteen centuries the vicious ecclesiasticism that found deep root in Constantine's rule, overshadowed the Church, and some remnants of it still survive. Too often, with the average Christian, the practical conception of duty is fulfilled if he attends Church-worship, supports the preacher, gives to benevolent work, and lives an upright life, leaving to the minister to do the preaching and to take care of souls.

Such notions find no native soil in the Acts of the Apostles. There, from first to last, we find one truth taught and one duty done: all who believed were expected to take part in spreading the faith; many, not fitted to lead and teach, could, at least, tell the good tidings. In every age, and above all in an age of reviving missionary activity, this fact needs anew to be wrought into the convictions of God's people, that in this sort of "preaching" every believer is to have part. No golden chalice, costly and rare, polished and jewelled, is needed to bear water to those who are dying of thirst; a tin cup or a broken potsherd will do, anything that will hold water.

In our day, new voices of God, loud and clear, are calling disciples to share in this active, aggressive crusade for Christ. God's Providence is the new "Peter, the Hermit," that goes through Christendom, shouting, "Deus vult!"—God wills it! The one great feature of our century has been *the growth of consecrated individualism*; and as a natural, necessary sequence, has come the breaking down of all false barriers that, in direct work for souls, fence in ministers of Christ and fence out members of churches. While the ministers are no less needed and no less busy, in all churches where true life throbs common believers have come to feel that every man is his brother's keeper; and that to shirk personal work for souls is not only culpable neglect of the lost, but serious risk of spiritual loss to the neglecting party!

It is just a century ago since, in 1793, France called all loyal citizens to rise and resist the flood of invading foes that threatened the destruction of the nation. All were bidden to take part in the work. The older men could forge arms and the younger bear them; the women could make tents and uniforms, and even the children could scrape lint and prepare bandages. The God of Battles calls all alike, old and young, men, women, children, to a share in the work and war of the ages. He tells us in unmistakable terms, that those who think of nothing beyond their own salvation, are scarcely saved, if at all; and in answer to His summons, a new generation of disciples is coming forward trained to an unselfish consecration to soul-saving.

1. If we seek some examples of this modern development of personal activity in Christian service, let us hear God's voice in the modern *Sunday-school*, Robert Raikes had originally no aim beyond the occupation of the idle, ignorant children, who made the Lord's day noisy with their mischief. But God was behind the movement that started in Gloucester, and by it He was leading out believers into new fields of work. And now in the Sunday-school, the humblest disciple may

find a little congregation for teaching saving truth, a little parish for exercise of pastoral oversight, a little field to sow and reap in the Master's name. So universal has the Sunday-school become that no church is complete without this nursery of young plants for the Lord's garden.

2. The *Young Men's Christian Association*, now completing its first half century, has a like providential mission. Its rapid growth and world-wide extension reveal its place in the plan of God. Already it has wrought three marked results: it has brought believers together, encouraged Bible study, and trained lay workers.

It belongs to the very basis of this great organization, that it lifts into prominence only the grand truths which evangelical disciples hold in common; and so, leaving out of sight those minor matters of creed or polity which have often proved divisive and destructive of unity, it unifies all believers by magnifying their agreements and minimizing their differences.

Then this association directly stimulates systematic search into Holy Scripture, putting the word of God into the hands of young men as their text-book in holy living and serving, and teaching them that its contents are to be mastered and utilized for growth in grace and usefulness. The last half century is the era of the Bagster and the Oxford Bible as the habitual companion of Christian young men.

These two results contribute to a third, yet more important—the raising up of a generation of young men competent to take intelligent part in soul-winning. Even the Apostolic age may safely be challenged to show any parallel development in this direction. Within fifty years hundreds of thousands of young men have been brought to think, not of denominational distinctions, but of fundamental, saving gospel truths; led to give themselves to personal study of the word of God, until they have attained marvellous mastery of its contents and facility in its use, and then have been drawn to feel the duty and delight of direct work to save others, and to engage directly in active personal service for Christ.

It is a sublime sight to behold this vast army of young men, prayerfully searching the Scriptures, and then going forth to use their knowledge of the inspired word to guide others to Christ, and train them for similar service. To this lay-activity the whole providential history of this world-embracing organization has so rapidly and directly led, that even those who were once incredulous and suspicious are constrained to see in it all, the will and working of God. Just now there is, perhaps, a risk that in the new stress laid upon athletic skill, intellectual culture, social standing, moral excellence, the ultimate end which God obviously had in view may be sacrificed or obscured. If the Young Men's Christian Association should degenerate into a mere religious club; if spiritual development is made subordinate to any other end; if Bible study, training for service and actual soul-saving are ever pushed to the rear to make way for other practical objects however laudable, the unique place which this association has filled in history will be sacrificed, and it will be no longer the important factor and mighty force it has been in the purpose of God. As one who has been identified with this organization for forty years, and who has lovingly and thankfully watched its growth, the writer of these pages thus leaves on record his warning word against those devices of the devil which endanger the future of this wonderful outgrowth of this missionary century.

3. It must not be forgotten that Young *Women's* Christian Associations are the natural result of the other, seeking to do for the sisterhood what the companion associations have done for the brotherhood; and there is coming to be, not the *unsexing*, but the *unbinding* of woman. In the kingdom of God there is to be "neither male nor female." Fetters of unscriptural restriction are fast falling off from the gentler as from the sterner sex; and where man finds a closed door, woman's suasive tenderness and delicacy touches the secret springs of power.

4. Another example of God's call to general activity in behalf of souls is found in the *Young People's Society of Christian Endeavor.*

In the year 1881, somewhat more than thirteen years ago, a young New England pastor felt that something must be done among the younger members of his congregation to educate them into habits of witnessing and working for Christ. He must unloose tongues spiritually dumb, and arrest the drift toward the Dead Sea of idleness and stagnation. So he formed in his own church the first society of Christian Endeavor. Its simple secret was a pledge regularly to attend its meetings and habitually to take part in some way in their exercises. Around this mutual covenant, as a nucleus, the society rapidly grew; and so well did the new plan work that neighbouring pastors and churches followed the lead, and formed societies of a like sort. And so it has come to pass that live coals from the altar at Portland, Maine, have been borne from church to church, until, as we write, the number of these organizations is already legion, and the total membership reaches 1,725,000. Rev. F. E. Clark, D.D., who all-unconsciously kindled this first fire, has been on a world-round tour to visit, as bishop, the hundreds of societies which are belting the globe!

5. What shall be said of the *"Salvation Army"* which, notwithstanding its crude notions and strange methods, has left in the rear all other organizations for carrying the gospel to the most destitute? After an existence of twenty-eight years, it reports 4,397 mission stations; seventy-four homes of rest for officers whose health is broken down; sixty-six schools for the training of officers; sixty-four slum posts; forty-nine rescue homes for fallen women; twelve prison-gate homes, fifty-two food and shelter depots; thirty-four factories and employment offices; and five farm colonies.

Who can look at such developments of our own day and not see God's way of working? How plainly do all these, and other similar voices of God, unite in one loud testimony! He is evoking all the latent energies of his Church for the work of witnessing to all men the gospel of His grace, with a rapidity and energy that remind us of the Apostolic age; the forces He had set in motion have swept away artificial barriers between young and old, male and female, and thrust all alike into the field of service. He who watches the signs of the times must see God in history and will have no doubt which way His march is moving. He is summoning and leading all willing followers to a combined assault on the strongholds of Satan and the powers of hell.

III.

THE VISION OF THE FIELD.

OUR LORD's farewell words taught that great second lesson, that the *field of witness is as wide as the world.*

"Unto the uttermost parts of the earth" must disciples go. Dispersion is the next lesson to be learned, and learned anew in every age. Pentecost prepared for the scattering of those whom the Spirit endued, as they went back to the four quarters of the inhabited world with the life-giving word.

When the disciples, thus endued with power, returned to their separate abodes, this dispersion was itself a missionary campaign. The annual Passover at the national capital was a mighty magnet whose attractive force was felt wherever the scattered remnants of the Hebrew race were found. Great was the concourse, and from many lands. The procession of pilgrims was like the flood, swept through dry riverbeds by the latter rain, and for miles around the sacred city houses and hamlets were crowded, and in every valley and grove tents thronged like a camp. When those who thus came up to keep the feasts of Passover and Pentecost went back with the enduement of power, God was in unforeseen ways multiplying the channels for far-reaching and effective witness. What human wisdom could have planned a scheme whereby the experience of one day in Jerusalem should thus touch so quickly the very ends of the earth!

The persecution that arose about Stephen was another event, vocal with a new command for dispersion. Disciples were prone to congregate and concentrate at Jerusalem; it compelled them to separate and scatter. It was natural for the Jewish Christian Church to gravitate toward the old centre of the hierarchy and of worship, where the tribes had been wont to gather. But the centripetal attraction has always been the fatal foe of missions. Love is a centrifugal force, and He who taught us the supreme lesson of love, said, "Go ye into all the world; as My Father hath sent Me, even so send I you." When this message was in danger of being unheeded, and the old tendency to selfish centralization and religious seclusion was asserting itself, God, by His providence, repeated with stem emphasis the lesson that the Church was to disperse far and wide. It was done as by a peal of thunder and the shock Of earthquake. Persecution with explosive violence drove disciples from the Holy City to the very bounds of Palestine. The Church was shattered that it might be scattered, and fragments were found at Antioch and throughout Syria, at Cyprus, and throughout Phoenicia. And so persecution became the parent of early Christian missions. Strange parentage! "Out of the eater came forth meat!" The devouring lion furnishes supplies to the hungry.

Thus, for all time, God's voice was heard, and the lesson is left on record that, in all this age of evangelism, the policy of His people is to be diffusion and dispersion. No favoured, favourite capital is to become our chapel-of-ease, our earthly rest, even though it could be an earthly Heaven, while hell is found raging in the regions beyond. Even the joys of Christian fellowship may become too absorbing. Selfishness in its most refined forms must yield to the unselfishness which resigns such companionship for ourselves that it may become possible to introduce the most depraved, degraded and destitute to the fellowship of saints and of God. Any influence, any combination of causes, implies a curse to the believer whenever it makes the Church a cradle to rock God's children to sleep with the soft lullaby of "Home, Sweet Home!"

Other visions and voices fastened the impression of this second lesson that the witness of disciples is to find in the wide world, its field.

1. Peter's trance on the housetop at Joppa was both a vision and a voice, teaching most impressively this truth. A parable was enacted, the Divine hand being back of the shifting scenery. The sheet, let down from heaven by its four comers, in which were found all manner of creatures, wild and tame, clean and unclean, was a speaking symbol of the Church, not of man's device but of God's design, let down from heaven and to be caught up again into heaven; its four comers hinting its universal character, reaching ultimately to the four corners of the earth; within whose ample folds are to be brought all classes and conditions of men, from all quarters and climes, nations and grades of society, and representing all varieties of intellectual and moral degradation and development.

No pictorial lesson ever before or since has so taught the value and dignity of man as man! The vision was itself sufficiently vocal, yet it must have a voice to interpret it, and that voice three times spoke the same words:

"Whᴀᴛ Goᴅ ʜᴀᴛʜ ᴄʟᴇᴀɴsᴇᴅ,
   Tʜᴀᴛ ᴄᴀʟʟ ɴoᴛ ᴛʜou ᴄoᴍᴍoɴ!"

Blow after blow of God's heavy hammer, to break into pieces and beat into powder, the adamantine walls of Jewish exclusiveness, and the brazen gates of religious bigotry!

Peter was a representative Jew, and, unlike Paul, seems never as yet to have strayed beyond the bounds of the Holy Land. He was an ecclesiastical aristocrat. To all such as he, the law of separation obscures the law of love. This voice and vision were meant for more than himself. They were the lasting rebuke of that spirit of Caste which upholds invidious distinctions, and upbuilds impassable barriers between man and man.

Of caste, it is not too much to say that it has been the one giant foe of world-wide missions. Very early in Church history God's own hand wrote upon the wall, in letters of fire, such as struck awe to the hearts of the Babylonian revellers—

"What God hath cleansed, that call not thou common."

The whole race will never be reached with the gospel, until we learn what is meant by "all the world," and "every creature." In God's eyes, and therefore in our eyes, no line is to be drawn which limits love or labour for human souls; no discrimination allowed, save in favour of the least and lowest, most destitute and degraded. We are to call or consider no man common or unclean; in love's impartial ministry, no one is to be evaded or avoided; and so far are we to be from such narrowness and selfishness that those are to have the first claim upon our sympathy and succour, who are most in need and most without help.

Peter's vision marked a new stage, a new epoch in Church history. Years have sped by since the Lord went up and the Spirit came down. Yet, despite the great commission and the great effusion; notwithstanding the wide diffusion of the witnesses, by their return to distant homes, and the wide dispersion of persecuted disciples, two barriers yet remain to hinder the world-wide work: the tendency to centralization and the principle of exclusion. The Jew had not yet learned that other places were lawful for worship and solemn assembly beside the Temple of Jerusalem, and that wherever worshippers meet in the Spirit, God is to be found.

The old exclusive policy and spirit survived. As Thales, wisest and best of Greeks, looked on all outside of Greece as "barbarians," so, to the Jew all beyond the circle of the covenant were aliens to be shunned, if not foes to be hated. That phrase, "The Jews have no dealings with the Samaritans," is the key to a chamber of curious and shameful customs and prejudices. The road between Jerusalem and Galilee lay through Samaria, and the Jew must needs go that way or cross the Jordan; but he held his very garments free from the defiling touch of the inhabitants whom he despised as a hybrid, bastard progeny of heathenism and Judaism. By proximity a neighbour, the Samaritan was by hostility a foe, and the Jew would hesitate to point the lost traveller to the road or the thirsty pilgrim to a spring, if he belonged to that unclean race!

What wonder if such barriers had to be broken down before the work of missions could be done or the spirit of missions could have sway! The walls that shut Jewish disciples in, shut strangers and foreigners out. Obstinate holding on to Jerusalem meant equally stubborn casting off of all outsiders. The lines of caste were in effect fatal hindrances to all world evangelization, barriers scarcely less rigid and frigid than those which part the millions of India.

We have seen how the Providence and Spirit of God battered down these walls as with shot and shell by the explosive force of persecution, and how Philip's work in Samaria and his word to the Ethiopian eunuch crossed caste lines; and now, not as by earthquake, storm or flame, but in the still small voice of solemn rebuke and repeated remonstrance, God speaks to Peter, that he may echo it to the whole Church, that God's cleansing leaves no man common or unclean. Then followed at Caesar's palace and before a Roman audience, a display of grace that illustrated and enforced the lesson on the housetop, and forbade the Jew ever to dispute the right, even of the hated conqueror of his nation, to a full part in the great salvation.

That lesson on the housetop was *thrice* taught perhaps because it concerned the work of the Triune God. The Father's electing grace, the Son's atoning blood, the Spirit's renewing power,—all cleanse believers equally and guarantee their equality of right. But one thing is sure: so long as any man is to us common or unclean, we have not caught the divine passion of universal missions. Conversion implies contact, and contact, approach. To Peter, because he was appointed to open the kingdom to all believers, as the representative Apostle, the Divine Preacher gave this picture-lesson with its interpreting voice. The vision and the voice are equally for us. They teach that before Him who is no respecter of persons, all men are on the same moral level; that as to condemnation there is "no difference," "for all have sinned and come short of the glory of God;" that as to gracious invitation there is "no difference," for the same Lord over all is rich unto all that call upon Him; and as to actual salvation and sanctification there is "no difference," for He purifies the hearts of all alike by faith. The first formal proclamation of this fact of the universality of gospel grace was to be made in the palace of Roman aliens, before a gentile centurion and his company, and Peter was to announce it. Hence the thrice-repeated lesson which compelled the impetuous and wilful Jew to learn human equality before God.

When these new chapters in the Acts of the Apostles were to be written, in our age of missions, the old lesson was retaught, and if possible, with heavier accentuation of its central truth. In heathen lands caste lines and limits are frigidly rigid like ice barriers. The Brahmanic system has been aptly characterized as "a cellular structure of society in which the cells never interpenetrate." The different classes, which are by a hoary superstition connected with different parts of the body of Brahm, are like strata of rock, petrified into immobility and immutability. Nothing short of an earthquake convulsion, upheaving the whole social order, could break up this strong fatality of social status. No personal worth or intellectual attainment or heroic achievement, no service to the nation or to its religion, can lift a Hindu above the level of caste in which he was born, though a trifling violation of petty rules may sink him to a lower level as an out-caste. Customs so absurdly unreasonable and inflexible become barriers to mutual fellowship, even between converts at the table of the Lord, and in work for souls.

Thus it is not too much to say that the most formidable obstacle to oriental missions is caste. The Tabu system found prevailing in the islands of the sea was essentially identical with it, forbidding wives to share a meal with their husbands, and making it a capital crime for an inferior to cast his shadow upon his chief by inadvertently passing between him and the sun!

Caste lines are not confined to heathen, pagan and moslem territory. In countries, called Christian, we find arbitrary distinctions scarcely less formidable as hindrances to practical fellowship and common service. In some Protestant communities there exists an aristocratic social structure, where partition walls still effectually divide patrician and plebeian classes, nobility and commonalty. True, it is possible for a man to rise higher the common labourer sometimes becomes the master-workman, the merchant prince, the member of Parliament or of the ruling class. But ascent is not easy, and we all need Peter's lesson reiterated: What God hath cleansed, that call not thou common. Republics as well as monarchies, democracy as well as aristocracy, prove human nature still to be depraved, for in the best social state we find caste walls existing. What is more despotic than the aristocracy of wealth, that hangs one's social rank on the chance of a business venture; or the aristocracy of fashion, that makes Brummels princes, and character something worn on the back, to be bought at a tailor's shop; or even the aristocracy of culture, which weighs manhood in the scales of refinement and confounds morals with manners?

God saw how much there was needed a new lesson even in this missionary century, a lesson to be taught repeatedly and emphatically, that the only real, ultimate standard of value is that which is within reach of all, namely, *moral worth*;

and that as to accidents of birth or blood, of poverty, culture and social position, the Scotch poet was a moral philosopher when he sang,

"A man's a man for a' that!"

That social system which most allows men to breathe and move freely, affording inspiration to hope and scope for growth, is the most perfect. The lamented President Garfield, himself an example of one who had risen far above his native level, used to say that the ideal state is one where we find, not "as in the land, fixed and immovable layers of soil or rock, but as in the sea, conditions so elastic and flexible, that the drop which to-day touches the sand at the bottom may to-morrow glean upon the wave's crest." If in any man there be the force that bears him onward and upward, love forbids us to hold him hopelessly down. The Church should present an ideal state, where all have equal rights, and equal claims upon all that can uplift, emancipate, educate body, mind, soul; where aspiration has full play, and advancement finds favouring conditions.

When King James sent the poor poet, Ben Jonson, a present of a crown piece, Jonson sent back word by the bearer, "The king sends me five shillings because I live in an alley. Go tell him that his soul lives in an alley!" Modern missions have written in letters of light this noble lesson, that many a man who is clothed in purple and fine linen, lives in an alley; and many a beggar who lies at the gate, asking alms of charity, is on his way to the King's palace. See how the Divine Teacher has taught the inherent dignity and royalty of character, in choosing for leaders of the Church universal, Carey from the cobbler's bench, Williams from the ironmonger's forge, Marsden from the blacksmith's anvil, Livingstone from the cotton mill, Hunt from the farmer's plough, Johnson from the sugar refinery! Let us beware how we foster the spirit of caste. Charles Darwin pronounced the Patagonians the missing link between man and the monkey, and thought that not even the lever of Christian missions could uplift them; the French papist who ruled on the Isle of Bourbon told the pioneer missionaries to Madagascar that to convert the Malagasy was as hopeless as to convert oxen, sheep, or asses. But even so enlightened a man as a Canon of Westminster ranked the aboriginies of Australia so low that it was not worth while to expend labour upon them. In appeals for Africa, how often have we been met by the objection that it is a waste of men and money to preach to the fetish worshipers, because they have no capacity to understand or receive spiritual truth, and the image of God, if it ever existed in them, is not only defaced but effaced!

The whole history of modern missions is a vision and a voice in favour of man as man. God has shown by the proof of facts, by that most conclusive argument—experiment—that no human being is too high to need the gospel, or too low to be reached by it. The most signal triumphs and glorious trophies of the good tidings have been among the very classes whom our scepticism would account beneath the reach even of saving grace. The most fertile fields for the seed of the kingdom have been those previously the most barren of good, or desperately fruitful in evil. Man would have turned to the higher classes, appealing to intelligence and capacity. But while they have turned from Christ with contempt, behold the debased demon worshipper in whom all ideas of true worship seem obliterated; or the degraded cannibal, without natural affection, implacable, unmerciful; or the brutal savage, whose religion was a mixture of lust and lies, robbery and cruelty, bloody wars and lawless violence, who cared neither for the virtue of womanhood, nor the innocence of childhood, nor the helplessness of old age—behold such brought to bow at Jesus' feet, and then going forth to tell of Him to others! We can scarce believe our own eyes as we see the modern miracles of missions, of which no pen has ever told the half. Those who glutted their avarice by pillage, their revenge by slaughter, their appetite by feasts on human flesh,—these have been found believing in Jesus and heralding His power to save! Let God speak, ye who think even the worst of the race beneath your respect and unworthy of Christian effort! "God hath made of one blood all nations of men;" and by one blood hath He redeemed all peoples. Therefore, He says, "Go ye into all the world and make disciples of all nations."

Yes, the century is vocal with divine appeals for man as man. Enthusiasm for humanity, that divine passion for souls, must sweep away the hollow, shallow distinctions which part men asunder. In every human soul we must see the potential saint, outranking angels in the closeness of bond with Christ. Without such enthusiasm for humanity, missions must languish.

Peter's vision on the housetop was the forecast; the modern Church is the prophecy fulfilling. In the sheet let down from heaven every class of mankind is already embraced. Wild beasts have been tamed and turned into obedient bullocks, ready for plough or altar; unclean birds of prey are changed to gentle doves, celestial songsters, birds of paradise; crawling reptiles that crept along the earth are transformed into erect men who walk with God. What the Apostle saw in anticipation, we see in realization.

2. Paul, as well as Peter, was taught a divine lesson on the universal need of man. How different his experience at Athens from that of Peter at Cesarea, yet both essentially impress one great lesson.

That "altar to the unknown God" in the very centre of Greek art and wisdom, beauty and philosophy, brands as a failure any civilization that knows not God, because it has no savouring or saving element— no salt of salvation. It reminds one of Heine's comparing beautiful women without religion to flowers without perfume—cold, sober tulips in china vases, looking as though they were also of porcelain, and seeming to say that it is all-sufficient not to have a bad odour, and that a rational flower needs no fragrance. Athens stands in history as the tulip in the vase, coldly beautiful, lifelessly aesthetic—having no savour or flavour of high moral virtue or piety. And Paul's comparative ill success at the Greek capital, and the apathetic hearing at Mars Hill, serve to remind us that stagnant indifference is as bad as violent opposition, and that blasphemers and barbarians go into the kingdom of God before scholarly sceptics and cultivated worldlings. As yet not many wise, mighty, noble, are called. God chooses the foolish, weak, despised nothings to bring to naught the somethings. And yet as the Countess of Huntingdon said, let us thank God it is not true that not any, though not many of the wise and mighty are called. There was one Areopagite, Dionysius, who clave to the Apostle, so that the address on Mars Hill won one convert even from the philosophers. The loftiest as well as lowliest need the gospel, and we are to proclaim it at Corinth and Athens as well as at Nazareth and Gadara.

That sermon to the Areopagite wise men should be studied, for it addresses universal and conscious instincts of man's religious nature. It was a unique address, wholly unlike any other Paul ever delivered. In it he spoke to those who knew not the true God nor the sacred writings of His prophets, nor the words and works of Jesus, His Son. Hence he had to go further back and deeper down than when he spoke to Felix or Agrippa, to Jews at Jerusalem or Greeks at Antioch. He appealed to seven universal instincts:

1. The *Filial*: "For we also are His offspring."
2. The *Fraternal*: "He hath made of one blood," &c.
3. The *Theistic*: "Your altar to the unknown God."
4. The *Judicial*: "A day in the which He will judge the world."
5. The *Religious*: "In all things ye are very religious."
6. The instinct of *Worship*: "Ye ignorantly worship."
7. The instinct of *Prayer*: "Should feel after Him," &c.

In modern days, sagacious missionaries have learned from Paul at Athens, that in every clime they may find classes of men who know not God, but to whose instinctive religious nature they may appeal.

The universal belief in God, which, however obscured, seemed never obliterated, furnishes a basis for preaching the gospel to all men. Fred. Stanley Arnot found everywhere in Africa two existing notions: First, of a supreme power over all; and secondly, of a future life beyond death. To these he could always safely appeal.

And even in Mohammedan lands where little has yet been done, encouragements are not wanting; for the followers of the Prophet are not idolaters, and claim to be monotheists, and to accept even the Old Testament. Among them we have the religious instincts comparatively pure.

3. Paul's night vision at Troas was literally vocal, for the man of Macedonia prayed him, saying, "Come over into Macedonia, and help us;" and from that vision and that voice he assuredly gathered that the Lord was calling him to a new field in the regions beyond. And so the gospel first entered Europe.

That vocal vision was for the whole Church, and it means that we are never to rest, whatever has been done, while more yet remains undone. However wide the sweep of our mission tours, if beyond this circle of effort there is a region where the gospel has not reached, this fact constitutes a trumpet peal of God. And especially if the peal be also a personal appeal; if, as in so many cases, human need finds a voice wherewith to call, as Mtesa did from Uganda, as Chulalangkom did from Siam, as Pomare did from Tahiti, as Ranavolona II. did from Madagascar, as McAll did from France,—how prompt should be the response from the Church of Christ! When out of the region of darkness and death-shade, heathen and pagan peoples clamour for Christian teachers; when fields are ready for the sower and there is no one to scatter the seed, or ready for the reaper and there is no one to put in the sickle; when doors open fast and wide, and no labourers enter some of them, and in other cases, too few, why do we not assuredly gather that God is calling us to go and carry the cross with us? Why are we so slow to push the schemes of holy work into new territory, and send or bear the bread of life to starving souls? How can God set before us a wider and more effectual door than when the heathen themselves are ready to hear the gospel, and make appeal to us to come to them?

This is the paradox of missions. Where are our sandals of alacrity that we speed not as on wings of love to fly to the help of the perishing! Had we the true passion for souls, Satan would no longer be the hinderer, though he piled up obstacles in our way. We should overleap all self-denials in our zeal to relieve soul-wants. It is one of the irreconcilable contradictions of history that the instinctive human sympathies have more readily responded to the appeal of flood or famine, pestilence or plague, than the Christian heart to the awful need of those who perish of hunger for living bread, or who are swept away by the flood of sin and smitten with the leprosy of self-consuming lusts! Temporal wants and woes are real to our sluggish sense, but we are dead to the spiritual poverty and misery of humanity.

That night vision at Troas has been a thousand times repeated within the last century. That man of Macedonia may be seen whichever way we look, and the voice calls to us from every quarter of the horizon. Who that watches modern missions does not feel that what Paul saw and heard at Troas has become the vision for all believers, and the voice from all lands? Let the eye sweep round the whole world, and on the coasts of Corea and Japan, from the depths of Inland China, from the hills of Burma and the rivers of Siam, from India's coral strand and Persia's plains, from the borders of the Red Sea and the valley of the Nile, the banks of the Congo and the vast stretch of the Soudan, from papal countries and pagan communities, there comes one loud voice: "Come over into our Macedonia and help us." Were our eyes not dull of vision, and our ears, of hearing, through the flare and glare and blare of this world, we should see and hear this "man of Macedonia," standing at every point of the horizon, stretching forth hands in appeal, and calling for help.

King Mtesa, whose request for teachers found such voice through Stanley's letters that it pealed across thousands of miles of land and sea and was heard in Britain and America, was only a representative of the race. The needs of Siam have been referred to; there, cities as large as Birmingham and Edinburgh, Leeds and Leicester, are asking vainly for one evangelist to come to their hundreds of thousands, and tell how God loved the world. Burma and the Karens have never had all the helpers which the field demanded. Japan, the modern marvel, suddenly threw open her long-locked sea gates forty years ago; and China, India, Central America, Papal Europe, became likewise open fields for missions—all within a twelvemonth! And yet the devil has shown more zeal to take possession than the children of God. Read the story of the South Seas, and see how the consecrated energy of John Hunt and John Williams, of Geddie and Marsden and Selwyn and Patteson and Paton proved unequal to the meeting of the demands for Bibles and men. From that day to this the same experience has been repeated elsewhere. For centuries, where Rome ruled, the open Bible was flung into the flames and the Protestant missionary dared prison cell, if not martyr's stake. Now France has over a hundred and thirty McAll mission *salles*, and might have a thousand but for want of money and men; and the land of the Inquisition is growing harvests for God in the very fields which Torquemada and Valdez, Deza and Ximenes unconsciously fertilized with the ashes of thirty thousand saints. Think of Bible carts in Madrid unable to supply books sufficient for those who would buy; and a few elect messengers of the cross struggling to meet the wants of hundreds who are deserting the crucifix! When Ethiopia thus stretches forth hands unto God, when China's millions call for missions, and Corea's valleys begin to be vocal with praise; when the capital of the papacy has thirty Protestant chapels within its walls; when from the kingdom of the sunrise to the land of the sunset, there goes up one call for Bibles, schools and churches, teachers and preachers, what is it but the call from Macedonia repeated like a thunder-peal all around the circle of the earth!

There are hindrances, no doubt, in the way of missions, but they are most serious *within the Church*. We are not so ready to send messengers and Bibles as the unevangelized often are to receive. If the response of the Church were as quick as the appeal from the world is loud, within our generation every hill and valley of the earth might be sending up to God the incense of prayer and praise.

The slowness of our forward march is saddening, but no words can fitly characterize the sin and the crime of going *backward*. The call for "*retrenchment*" is like the tolling of a death-knell from the belfry of our missionary boards. Think of it! For lack of men and means, we cannot go a step ahead even to enter new doors, but must go back and leave fields already occupied! We cannot advance but must retreat—abandoning vantage-ground already gained, and, instead of taking new strongholds, evacuating those strategic positions now held! Think of closing preaching stations, shutting up schools, turning adrift native evangelists, locking up Christian presses with silence, calling in our forces and beating a retreat! It seems incredible; but every time the cry goes forth, retrench! it means all this and a great deal more!

When Judson was in the very crisis of his work in Burma, the appropriation for the mission was ten thousand rupees less than the current expenses required. Instead of any advance, he could not even hold his already-gained positions. With a disappointment that bordered on despair, he solemnly recorded as his "growing conviction" that "the Baptist churches in America are behind the age in missionary spirit. They now and then make a spasmodic effort to throw off a nightmare debt of some years' accumulation, and then sink back into unconscious repose. Then come paralyzing orders to retrench; new enterprises are checked in their very conception, and applicants for missionary employ are advised to wait, and soon became merged in the ministry at home." And so letters, which ought to have been like a soft and cooling breeze to a heated brow, came upon him like a sudden tornado, sweeping away the plans of missionary evangelism. He said in his agony, "I thought they loved me; and they would scarce have known it if I had died! I thought they were praying for us; and they have never once thought of us!" And so it seemed to the missionary in his unsupported work.

4. God has in every nation, elect saints; because the gospel message is for man as man, converts are gathered out of most unlikely fields. How significant, therefore, were that vision and voice at Corinth, when the Lord spake to Paul; "Be not afraid but speak, and hold not thy peace; for I am with thee, and no man shall set on thee to hurt thee; *for I have much people in this city.*"

That vision and voice were for the whole Church and for all time. Often has God shown that even where human hate builds huge walls against the truth, and human wrath builds hot fires for its witnesses, He has much people; and that the faith that fears not, can face the foes of God and of His gospel with firmness and unfaltering fixedness of heart, still witnessing to the cross. While martyrs have burned, they have been snatching brands from worse burning to become branches of the true vine; and by their death have brought life to their very murderers, as Stephen's stoning was, perhaps, the secret of Saul's conversion.

This lesson has been taught us so repeatedly in the New Acts of the Apostles that it must be reserved for special treatment when we come to consider the New Signs and Wonders. Suffice it now to repeat that in our age of missions, God has thus in many ways taught us by voices and visions this second great lesson: that the field for a witnessing Church is the whole world and embraces every creature. Man's universal need gives forth its conscious echo in response to the good tidings. The worst men show capacity to repent, believe in Christ and receive the Spirit. Religious instincts, though buried, are not dead, and when exhumed, revive. Even in ruins, souls have a dignity and majesty which forbid caste lines to exclude even the lowest classes from the hope of saints and the love of the brotherhood. In every nation God has accepted souls.

IV.

The New Lesson of the Power.

THE THIRD great lesson of the Acts of the Apostles we found to be, that the secret of power in witnessing is the Holy Spirit of God; and about this, as the central lesson, all others cluster.

A remarkable inversion will be noticed, which cannot be without meaning. When Luke concludes the gospel narrative, he makes our Lord to say:

"Ye are witnesses of these things;

"And, behold, I send the promise of my Father upon you;

"But tarry ye until ye be endued with power from on high."

Contrast this with Luke's account of our Lord's final message before His ascension:

"Ye shall receive the power of the Holy Ghost coming upon you;

"And ye shall be witnesses unto Me."

Here the order of the former thought is exactly reversed. In the close of the gospel, it was first the work of witnessing, then the promise of power. In the beginning of the Acts, it is first the power, then the work of witness. The meaning of such inversion is not enigmatic. In the former message, the Lord followed the order natural to the commission of a trust; first, the thing to be done; then the secret of its well doing. But in the latter, the trust having been committed to disciples, the all-important thing is to fix the mind upon the only power which can assure the effective execution of the trust. And so with us. The command being once for all given, not to be repeated, the one matter in all subsequent time to engross attention, is, that we may be so filled with the Spirit of all power, whose infilling, if not outpouring, is forever new, that we may fulfil our Lord's great commission.

Power is, in every sphere of work, the one all important requisite. There are about man two great constituent elements: a body, fearfully and wonderfully made—the outward, visible, material and perishable part; and the spirit, still more fearfully and wonderfully constituted—inward, invisible, immaterial, immortal. In the original creation, "God made man out of the dust of the ground, and breathed into his nostrils the breath or spirit of lives, and man became a living soul." What a divine tribute to the dignity, superiority, majesty of the spirit, as constituting the real man, of whom the body is but the house of habitation.

This truth is typical and suggestive. About all else that pertains to man there is, first, what is outward, and then, what is inward; what is visible, audible, palpable, and somewhat beside which evades all sense tests; somewhat that is transient, and somewhat that is permanent. Intelligent speech has its body— the spoken word; and its soul—the thought which only thought can catch and hold. The printed page is a body created by human machinery, but enshrining an invisible something, emanating from the author's secret life. All man's work has a body, or outward form of utterance, action, effort; but that which gives it value is the subtle spirit that pervades it.

In the "spiritual" sphere, whose very name carries a lesson—this distinction is vital. The prayer of the lips is but an empty form, unless the Spirit of God intercedes through and prevails in it: the witnessing word becomes the power of God to salvation and edification only when it is the body which He fills and thrills. What we call "unction" is not merely a fragrant chrism as of ointment poured forth; but an imparting of an essentially new and divine *force*, which brings and is, power. Hence, Pentecost was the condition of all true service, so essential that disciples were bidden to "wait for the promise of the Father," to "tarry until endued with power from on high;" for until that power was given no force or true energy could be exerted.

It is often said that it is worth while to wait upon God for the Spirit's infilling, because of the increase of power thus secured; but the Acts of the Apostles shows us a far deeper truth, that up to the point of this enduement with power, *work is waste*. We shall find, like the Greek philosopher who experimented upon a dead body, that we are trying to give to a lifeless form the erectness and energy of a living body; and, like him, be compelled to confess that it lacks—*something within*.

When James writes, "The body without the spirit is dead," he gives us one maxim of the wisdom that is from above. He turns, our thought back to that primal mystery of man's creation and the parallel mystery of his dissolution; with the spirit, there is a living body, a corpus; without the spirit, a dead body, a corpse—a mere mass of dead matter. It may still retain its fine and beautiful form and feature and exquisite organization; but it has no power. It cannot work, or walk, or stand erect; there is no light in the eye, no hearing in the ear, no response to touch, no thought in the brain—what was the temple of mind is the chamber of death.

But the inspired writer teaches a deeper truth, of which this is but a parable: "So faith without worlds is dead also"—a profession of faith is but a lifeless form, however fair, until the spirit of life vitalizes and energizes it, and makes possible the works of God. The Scripture maxim teaches a lesson broad enough to cover the whole world of man's activity and duty. His creed, his character, his worship, his service, even his sacrifice—all are dead, unless and until, behind, beneath, within them all, the spirit of life is found. The form of sound words without the spirit of faith and love in Christ Jesus, is dead orthodoxy. The form of worship, however decorous and devout, is, without the spirit, dead formalism, ritualism—a censer, it may be of gold, set with gems, but empty of all incense. The form of godliness without the power of the spirit, becomes dead works, a self-righteous, soul-deceiving morality or external piety, as different from true godliness as a tomb is from a temple. Even godly service and self-sacrifice may in God's eyes be a dead body, inspired by no spirit of loyalty to Christ or charity and sympathy toward men; empty of soul as the sound of a brass trumpet or the clangour of a silver cymbal, worse than emptiness—*nothing*!

Is there no reason that this most vital truth be taught at the very opening of the Acts of the Apostles? What more important lesson than this which touches all effective service;—this base-block of all missions: that only when God's Spirit possesses and controls, can we work or witness with power! Until then, the best we can do is but a body without soul, a form of service without the force which gives it power and assures to it success. That lesson God thought so needful, that in this great book of primitive missions it is the first taught, and taught with tongues of fire!

Witnessing to Christ is therefore the Spirit of God using a human voice. Let the Spirit be lacking, and there may be wisdom of words, but not the wisdom of God; the power of oratory, but not the power of God; the demonstration of argument and the logic of the schools, but not the demonstration of the Holy Spirit, the all-convincing logic of his lightning flash, such as convinced Saul before the Damascus gate. When the Spirit was outpoured and disciples were all filled with power from on high, the most unlettered tongue could silence gainsayers, and with its new fire burn its way through obstacles as flames fanned by mighty winds sweep through forests.

The study of the universe discloses to us a mysterious quality, as in man. The whole creation of God as a whole, consists of a body and a spirit—matter and force. Matter is inert and motionless—powerless to effect results, whether for good or evil, until force lays hold on it. There is nothing to be feared in all God's universe but force. What are the huge mountain without gravitation, the blackest masses of storm-cloud without electricity, the gigantic sun without light and heat, the earthquake's awful violence without chemical affinity, the shock of colliding orbs in space without momentum? And as only force is fearful, only force is forceful. If we seek power we must go not to matter, that in itself has not even power to *lie still*; but to that by which matter is held, moved, swayed, ruled, and which is the nearest to what in man we call spirit.

No more wonderful fact confronts us in our actual experience of contact with this universe of God than the power He has given to man of commanding and controlling these eternal forces. They all move in obedience to certain conditions or in certain channels or modes of activity, which we call "laws;" and, therefore, intelligent beings can discover the secret of wielding them. If man, in ignorance of these laws or in daring disobedience to them, transgresses, disregards or opposes them, these forces are destructive beyond description. Gravitation dashes him to pieces, heat blasts him or consumes him, even light tortures and blinds him; chemical affinity and repulsion are his enemy and bring instant and awful ruin to him and his finest work; all nature becomes his deadly foe, and unites all her gigantic and resistless forces to overwhelm him with swift destruction.

On the other hand, let man but obey the law of THE FORCE, AND THE FORCE OBEYS HIM! He obeys the laws of light and it becomes his servant, the deft artist that with unerring hand draws for him, with the sunbeam as its pencil, the face of a friend or the scenery of nature, delineating with the skill of perfection every line and lineament, the delicate tracery of every leaf or blade of grass. Man observes the laws of heat, and it becomes the refiner and purifier of his precious metals, melting, moulding the most stubborn material into any desired form. He calls on gravity, and it comes as a master mechanic with a Titanic hammer to beat the rocks to powder, and as his smith to work night and day at the forge. Man learns to control chemical attraction and repulsion, and effects marvellous combinations which make the universe his laboratory; or nitrogen, the lazy giant, comes with explosives to open the very bowels of the earth and reveal all mineral riches. Heat turns water into one of the greatest motive powers known, and drags his chariots over land and his vessels over the seas as though thirty thousand horses were yoked to them. Man obeys the laws of magnetism and it becomes his pilot over trackless wastes of waters; or he calls the very lightning to serve as motor, messenger, illuminator.

Let us follow the analogy to a higher plane. God says, "Concerning the work of My hands command ye Me!" Stupendous mystery! The Spirit of God has His chosen channels and methods; and this Supreme Force of the universe offers Himself to serve man for the ends of the Work of God. Is it not still true, and may it not with reverence be said, "Obey the law of the divine force and the force obeys you?" When God's Spirit controls the man, in a sublime sense the man controls the Spirit; that is, he wields spiritual power. This paradox, like many others, is a truth. "God hath given the Holy Ghost to all that obey Him,"* and he who has the Spirit of God, wields the power of God. Let any humble disciple submit wholly to the Spirit's sovereign control, and He becomes to that disciple all and more than all that nature's forces become to humanity when guided by scientific intelligence,—his artist to delineate for him things divine and celestial, his refiner and purifier to purge away the dross from character and mould him into a chosen vessel, his giant helper to subdue all foes before him, his pilot over life's unknown sea, his motive power in holy enterprise, his messenger between earth and heaven, and his illuminator in the darkness of midnight and mystery. The Spirit of God bows low and condescends to offer to be the servant of those who serve God, to shape character after a divine pattern, and make our works the works of God. And therefore it is that our Saviour bade His disciples *wait*, tarrying until endued, for up to that point power was not theirs.

Of this first lesson of the Acts the whole book is the illustration which constantly repeats and enforces the lesson by examples of power from on high. Pentecost was the outpouring of the Spirit from on high; the Apostolic age traces the flowing and widening and branching out of His streams. These chapters are channels revealing His power, new examples and proofs of what the Spirit can and will do, when He actually dwells in, works in and works through disciples.

---

*   Acts, v. 32.

V.

The New Ministry of the Spirit.

THIS BOOK may well be called the Acts of the Holy Ghost, since He is here thus pre-eminent. Out of all the references to the Spirit of God found in the New Testament, four-fifths are found here. He filled disciples with His own power, separated and sent forth missionaries, appointed overseers in the Church, and witnessed with disciples. But more than this, this is the book of His *personal presence*. He was so among them that they walked in His comfort—in his paracletism; that is, He became actually the Paraclete, the personal substitute for Christ's own self. And how beautifully is this personal presence acknowledged at that first council at Jerusalem: "It seemed good *to the Holy Ghost and to us*"—He meeting with and counselling with them, and all coming to a common conclusion! How august, yet how precious, such a sense of His actual personal presence, when Peter can say to Ananias, "Why hath Satan filled thine heart to *lie to the Holy Ghost,*" as though He stood there behind Peter as the real presiding officer! Yes, there He was, the Holy Spirit, making more than good to them Christ's absence, so that in Him their ascended Lord had come back to stay and dwell among them and in them; to plan for them, and send them where He would have them go; to embolden them in presence of foes, and encourage them by stretching forth His hand to heal and save. Here, indeed, are the Acts of the Spirit, for without Him not a step is taken. The Church is the body of Christ, and Christ is the head, and the Spirit of Life is the vital power filling the body, guiding its movements, and working through its members.

Within the compass of this book the Spirit may be seen exercising all His gracious offices, in the new birth of regeneration, the nurture and growth of sanctification and edification, the enduement and endowment of service, convincing gainsayers and converting even persecutors, and both edifying and multiplying the Churches.

So all important is this ministry of the Spirit that it is the only law of consecration known in the Acts. Every person and place and time which He touches becomes sacred. Every worshipper whom He guides is a priest, every spot he fills with His presence is a sanctuary, and every day becomes sacred because His work pervades it. We look in vain here for any traces of ecclesiasticism, ceremonialism, sacramentarianism; or, if found here, they are only as relics of a perverted Judaism or leavening paganism, curiosities, interesting only to antiquarians and befitting a museum.

Prayer and preaching make a sanctuary wherever believers gather, and wherever souls are new-born is a new shrine of the Nativity. Even temple courts have no longer a monopoly of worship. The house of Mary, the gateway at Lystra, the jail at Philippi, the school of Tyrannus, market-place or theatre, street corner or river side, if only praise and prayer go up and blessings come down, become hallowed, and believers say, "Surely God is in this place; this is none other but the house of God, this is the gate of heaven."

1. One most marked effect of the Spirit's presence was seen in the *unselfish spirit* which He breathed into saints. "Sacrifice," as Mr. Froude has said, "is the first element of religion, and resolves itself into the love of God. Let the thought of self intrude; let the painter but pause to consider how much reward his work will bring to him, and the cunning will forsake his hand, and the power of genius will be gone. Excellence is proportioned to the oblivion of self." In witnessing for Christ His image so filled disciples as to displace that last idol— self; and the Spirit so filled His own temple as to pervade it with an atmosphere of self-forgetfulness.

Observe, for instance, the absence of all money considerations or salaried offices. No soft-lined nest allured the self-denying worker; no tempting bait drew the preacher to bite at the devil's hook of greed; no increase of stipend cleared his eye to read the doubtful call of Providence. As yet no "crozier golden" had made "bishops wooden." Service seems to have been, if not gratuitously rendered, supported only by free-will offerings.

Is there no possible voice here for the Church of to-day? Is not jealousy for money compensation any hindrance to true missionary work? Imagine Philip sending ahead a financial agent to secure proper remuneration for his evangelistic work in Samaria; or Barnabas, that son of consolation, charging so much a week for his ministry to new converts at Antioch; or Peter, hesitating at Joppa till he knew whether the fee for his visit to Cesarea would at least cover expenses and entertainment; or Paul, taking a collection at Mars Hill, or asking offerings to cover rent for his hired house at Rome. While it is lawful that they who preach the gospel should live of the gospel, that law may easily become a cloak for avarice. We must go outside of this short history of early missions to find a vindication for growing rich upon pew-rents, while a thousand millions are dying without the bread of life; or, for paying hired singers and operatic "stars" enough every year to put three or four more missionaries into the field. Satan never won a greater victory than when he made the pulpit a horse-block whereby to vault into the saddle of ambition; or the pastorate a comfortable hammock of luxurious ease; or the service to souls an avenue to wealth. Such perversions have gone far both to destroy the simplicity of a life of faith and the power of an unselfish witness to Christ.

This voice and this vision must once more waken the Church. Everything depends upon having the Spirit with us in His presence and power.

2. He alone can *supply new apostles*. What a divine voice is heard in the conversion of Saul! Suddenly arrested in his persecuting career, threatening and slaughter are exchanged for prayer and preaching; the fiery breath of the Cilician dragon gives place to ardent, fervent witness to Jesus. The arch-persecutor and destroyer becomes foremost of Apostles and pioneer of missionaries. Hear God's voice in this event, proclaiming the sovereignty of that gracewhich snatches from the hands of Jewish rulers the chalice full of the poison of their wrath, and makes of it God's chosen vessel to bear before gentiles and kings, yea, and the very Israel which those rulers represented, the hated name of Jesus.

The Spirit alone can separate His saints for missionary service. He is therefore the ultimate Source of supplies for the field. The same Barnabas and Saul, sent forth by the Church, were also sent forth by the Holy Spirit, and in this double fact we have God's voice, announcing the twin condition of all successful missionary ministry: that the labourers shall be closely linked with the Church as its representatives, and be qualified as well as commissioned by the Spirit of God. The authority of the Church is secondary to that other and higher authority; but both are needful as conditions of the highest service. We must not be reckless of forms, but must seek a higher than any formal ordination or separation. Where workmen are independent and irresponsible, amenable to no authority, their zeal is sometimes without knowledge, and they are more active than efficient. Not a few who entered by no regular door but climbed up some other way, have proved more adepts in subtraction and division than in addition and multiplication, in missionary mathematics. To keep the Church in close touch with the field, the missionary must be sent forth by the Church, as one who is known, loved, trusted; then the work at home and abroad is bound together by a living bond, like the nervous system in the body with its effluent and refluent action.

But, on the other hand, no human election, education, ordination, can *qualify* for God's work. The Spirit says, "*Separate Me*—for the work whereunto *I have called them*." Instead of our appointing labourers and then asking for them proper qualifications, must we not invert the order? and first waiting to see whom the Spirit appoints and anoints, send them forth. Laying hands suddenly on no man, laying stress on graces more than on gifts, we must value above all else the one qualification which makes all others needless—namely, that they who go forth have been under the tuition and bear the commission of the Spirit of God.

The Church that is prepared by prayer and fasting to hear and heed the Spirit's voice will be a missionary Church. But that is always a still small voice, and is drowned by the voices of worldly clamour, of contending passions and hollow mirth. The Moravian Brotherhood has led the van, both in proportion of workers sent forth and of gifts contributed to their support, because in the constitution, worship and working of the "Unitas Fratrum," the Spirit finds less to hinder Him from being heard when He speaks. And so it is out of revivals of religion that missionary impulses have been born or revived. Meetings for fasting and prayer, and for deeper spiritual life, have been the matrix where missionaries have been moulded. While Laodicean churches have lulled their members to sleep with an easy religion of the world and a monotonous drone of ritual, and religious club-houses have drawn disciples into the snares of luxurious indulgence and refined selfishness, the purer, and generally the poorer, Churches have been fertile mothers of missions all over the world.

3. The Spirit uses His own schools and teachers for training His servants. Witness that significant record of the service rendered by the tent-makers of Corinth to the eloquent Apollos. When that gifted Alexandrian Jew, so mighty in the Septuagint Scriptures, came to Ephesus, like certain other disciples whom Paul found in Diana's capital, he had not got beyond John's baptism of repentance. And Priscilla and Aquila, who made tents for a living, turned their home into a theological school for this one pupil; and it was in their humble lodgings that this silver tongue was taught to expound the way of God more perfectly, and, with a new baptism of the Spirit, mightily to convince the Jews that Jesus was the Christ. What a lesson on missionary trainingschools, when some obscure saint gives the finishing touch to God's choicest workman!

4. The Holy Spirit makes every work a divine calling. Tabitha's resuscitation at Joppa was another voice of God proclaiming that service depends on no sphere, and is limited by no narrow circle of work. All forms of honest labour may witness for God, and alms-deeds have no stereotyped, model. Dorcas may have been a chronic invalid, dumb or palsied and bedridden. But she had left to her, hands

that could hold a needle; and the coats and garments that she made to clothe widows and orphans were as true signs of a missionary as the sermons of Peter or the tours of Paul. Whoever in his calling abides with God, is a missionary. If there be first a willing mind it is accepted, according to that a man hath and not according to that he hath not. Then the willing disciple, like Hercules, is a victor, whether he walks or works, stands or sits.

5. The Spirit of God is heard all through the Acts, teaching that witness to Christ is natural and necessary to a true disciple, and is a condition of His full salvation. The tenth chapter of Romans presents God's scheme for universal missions: a message of faith, heard by the ear, entering the heart, and then going out by the gates of speech to find its way to another ear, another heart, another tongue; and so each hearer, who becomes a believer, becomes also a witness. What can be more sublimely simple and more quickly effectual! A word of life winging its way from lip to ear, from ear to heart, from heart to lip, and so in endless circles till the last unbeliever hears the message.

Here is an Apostolic succession, indeed! And observe that he who hears and believes, but does not confess and proclaim, *breaks up the succession*, and like a wheel whose inaction clogs the machinery, so far as he is concerned, stops all the other wheels and disturbs the divine order. He who believes but does not testify, is not only hindering the growth of the Church, but its continuance; for without witnesses there can be no new generation of believers. Missions are the nursing-mother of converts and Churches. Love seeks not inlets, but outlets, and is jealous of limits.

6. The Holy Spirit's administration in the Church will make both giving and going easy. He so unites saints in one body that members have care one for another, and move together, in common work for common ends.

The death which Agabus foretold was a voice of God, calling disciples to send relief to hungry saints in Judea. Infinitely more, then, is world-wide famine of the Bread of Life, God's call for prompt and ample provision for poor and starving souls. All believers form one community, and suffer or rejoice together. There must be no schism in the body. And the whole race is by nature one family, and what some lack, the surplus of others must supply, until, as John Howard said, "Our luxuries give way to the comforts of the poor; our comforts to their necessities, and even our necessities to their extremities." No want must plead in vain.

Each, according to ability, should contribute willingly and cheerfully; and remoteness of abode must become neighbourhood of need. When this lesson is learned as only the Spirit can teach it, even our poverty will abound unto the riches of our liberality. Nature and sin have made all men akin. "He that withholdeth corn, the people shall curse him;" man's inhumanity to man still keeps countless thousands mourning their own awful destitution. Missionary meetings must not only "work up" the missionary spirit, but "work it down," deeper and deeper, till it reaches our selfishness and casts it out. To this only the Holy Spirit is equal. When He actually resides in the Church, and presides over it, every appeal in behalf of lost souls becomes a plea in Jesus' name; nay, Christ becomes the pleader, and it becomes easier to respond than to refuse.

A new standard of giving will be adopted by the Church whenever the Spirit once more pervades it with His living power. Greed is to-day dominant even among disciples. It is changing some of them into coin, so that they have a metallic ring and will drop into the coffin with a chink. The ministry of money is not understood or appreciated; men are purse-proud because they have no sense of stewardship; they think of their gains as their own, and of giving as an act of merit; and so become arrogant and sometimes defiant in their avarice. How quickly when God's Spirit possesses us do we see that nothing is our own, and even we ourselves are slaves paid for in blood and made free at a great price; and so we, and all we have, belong to our Redeemer! To such a man hoarded gains seem heaps of cankered coin whose rust is an accusation.

There is another and more awful side to this matter. Ananias and Sapphira died for the sin of sacrilege in trifling with their stewardship. Achan was guilty of a similar sin and suffered a like judicial death. Something devoted to the Lord and His by right was kept back from Him for selfish ends. *That was all!* But at these two turning points in sacred history there stand two cairns of black stones —mute warnings that just there is the point of peril, where the step, the slip, may prove fatal. When God in any way calls for our gifts, at our peril we withhold; no sudden death-blow may fall, but a subtle putrefaction or silent petrifaction attacks character and leaves spiritual life to awful decay and deadness.

7. When God's Spirit moves in the Church there is a holy cessation of all undue carefulness as to results. However much we rejoice over converts, we are not unduly depressed when Paul's experience at Rome is repeated; when notwithstanding untiring toil and testimony in preaching and teaching, some believe not, or even harden themselves in rejection of the truth.

To some the same divine word which is a savour of life to others, becomes a savour of death unto death; not wings by which to soar, but weights by which to sink. God drops down roses of paradise, but when they touch hard hearts, they become like burning coals of fire. The book of the Acts is a narrative of missionary labours, but records as many failures as successes. But in God's eyes our failures are often successes, and our successes are often failures. Duty is ours—let Him take care of all other issues.

The New Acts of the Apostles abounds in voices and visions of God. But not every one hears or sees. Once He spoke in thunders, now in whispers; once He was seen in flashes of light, now He reveals Himself only to the vision of faith. They who walk the crowded thoroughfares with the worldly and the frivolous, amid the din of Mammon worshippers and the blaze of fashion's superficial glory, will neither hear the voice nor see the vision.

The drift of the age is toward the idolatry of self, and no man can serve two masters. We must make our choice. He who often seeks God in the secret place and keeps silence before Him, will hear voices that wax louder and clearer until the closet of communion becomes the audience-chamber of the King; and will get such glimpses of the glory of God, that to him a door will again be opened into Heaven itself.

PART IV.

THE NEW CONVERTS AND MARTYRS

I.

The Miracle of Conversion.

Art may borrow models from nature and imitate her; but life itself defies all rivalry. Between Alexandria and Cairo is a row of palms, planted at equal intervals and meeting overhead, which suggests whence architecture gets its columnar forms with their capitals and arches. But however elegant and graceful, sculptured forms are stiff and dead. God's palms differ from art's pillars, for they are living growths.

Conversion is God's perpetual miracle. There are transformations in the lives and souls of men which cannot be counterfeited. They are not wrought by human hands as by hammer and chisel; but are growths of a hidden seed of new life, the planting of the Lord that He might be glorified. Reformation of outward conduct may be due not to grace but to selfishness, for manners and morals are a passport to good society, while profligacy is the foe of respectability. Amid the death-shade of heathenism, a high type of morality has been sometimes found, because it was believed to be the price of favour with the gods. But regeneration, which changes not only outward habits and conduct, but the inward nature and character, so that new tastes, affections and affinities control; the conversion which is transformation, which turns hate to love, and former preference to abhorrence—this is re-creation—as truly a miracle as the first creation. This is God's everlasting sign, never cut off, whatever other signs fail.

The Ethiopian cannot change his skin, or the leopard his spots; but if they could, the one would still be an Ethiopian and the other a leopard. Differences of race, genus, species, lie deeper down than the colour or markings of skin. But for Ethiopian to become Caucasian or American, or leopard to become lamb, means a miracle.

In the Acts of the Apostles, wonders of transforming grace constantly confront the reader. The opening miracle of Pentecost was a new creation on a grand scale, of three thousand souls in one day. Such miracles of changed character as these pages record are meant as a type and prophecy of things to come, and hence instances enough are given to represent all future cases and classes of converts. Pentecostal converts may stand for the multitudes that at one time flock like doves to their windows. The "great company of priests" who became obedient to the faith, hint the gospel triumphs in making inroads upon the very shrines and temples of false gods, and bearing away their priests as trophies. The eunuch's conversion forecasts thousands who, led by the word of God, feel after God and need some man to guide them. Saul is an example of the power which can turn foe into friend, and persecutor into Apostle.

Side by side with Saul's conversion we may set that of the Ephesian magians as a sign of divine power.

Around that famous fane of Diana, which was one of the seven world-wonders, the masters of curious arts naturally gathered. Yet, so mightily grew the word of God and prevailed, that even these seers and sorcerers confessed their tricks of trade and impostures upon popular credulity, and crowned their confession by burning before all men, the costly books which contained their secrets, and whose market value was a fortune for those days— fifty thousand pieces of silver!

With Apostolic days we associate a series of such marvels of convicting and converting grace. This brief book of the Acts records some twelve individual cases, and no two alike: The cripple at the beautiful gate, the eunuch of Ethiopia, Saul of Tarsus, the centurion of Cesarea, the proconsul of Cyprus, Lydia and the jailer at Philippi, Dionysius and Damaris at Athens, Crispus at Corinth, and possibly Timothy and Æneas. The ignorant and the cultured, Jews and gentiles, men and women, those in high life and in low life, the best and the worst, yield alike to the gospel, to show that the message is adapted to reach all classes.

Furthermore, the emphasis is unmistakably upon multitudes. The evident intent is to impress upon the reader the fact that, even within the first generation, the world proved a fertile field for gospel harvests. At least twenty times the stress is put, though not unduly, upon the large numbers of converts. At Pentecost, three thousand; soon after, five thousand; a little later, "multitudes both of men and women;" again, the number of disciples was multiplying; and again, "was multiplied in Jerusalem, greatly, and a great multitude of the priests were obedient to the faith." In Samaria multitudes gave heed with one accord to Philip; all they that dwelt at Lydda and Sharon turned to the Lord; at Joppa, "many believed in the Lord" at the raising of Dorcas; at Cesarea "all who heard the word" believed;

"a great number" at Antioch in Syria; "many Jews and proselytes at Antioch in Pisidia; at Iconium "a great multitude both of Jews and Greeks;" "many disciples" at Derbe; at Thessalonica, "a great multitude of devout Greeks, and not a few of chief women;" of Bereans "many believed;" and likewise of Corinthians, as also of Ephesian magians. The Lord made daily additions to believers, so that James at Jerusalem could point to "many thousands" (myriads) of believing Jews. Such repetitions have meaning. Converts multiplied in large numbers; large households with servants or retainers, and even villages and wider districts yielded to the gracious sway of the Spirit. The power of the truth wielded by such a divine arm is massive—Jerusalem, Samaria, Joppa, Lydda, Sharon, Cesarea, the two Antiochs, Iconium and Derbe, Thessalonica and Berea, Corinth and Ephesus feel the mighty movings of grace.

The new chapters of the Acts add records scarcely less wonderful. Individual examples quite as marked, as varied, as significant, abound, to prove converting power, and in every field multitudes have at times been gathered. Of this we shall cite examples and proofs; but here again the embarrassment of riches compels a resort to the principle of selection. First, a few marked individual instances will be cited from countries, communities and surroundings widely different; and then we shall glance over broader fields, where results are seen in the transformation of whole communities.

In explaining the parable of the sower our Lord prophesies a yield of thirty, sixty, an hundredfold increase. It sometimes seems as though His words had already been fulfilled. The Pentecostal gathering of one hundred and twenty had added to them, that same day, about three thousand souls—a thirtyfold increase. The South Sea work, from 1817 to 1839, and that in the Hawaiian Islands especially, probably exceeded any previous in-gathering in number, variety and rapidity of results; and this may represent sixtyfold increase. Half a century later, the greatest single harvest of Christian history was reaped in Southern India, and may well stand for the hundredfold. The new chapters of the Acts continue the older record, and chronicle similar marvels. Not only do they record individual conversions equally remarkable, but they tell us again of multitudes turning to the Lord.

II.

NEW CONVERTS AND MARTYRS.

KAYARNAK—THE CONVERTED ESKIMO.

MISSIONS AMONG the stolid, stupid Greenlanders seemed for long years as hopeless as melting the icebergs of the Frozen Pole. One hundred and sixty years ago, Matthew Stach wrote home: "We have found here what we sought, heathens who know not God, who care for nothing but catching seals, fish and reindeer, and for this purpose are constantly roving about."

SCRIPTURE TESTIMONY

Believers will suffer terrible things for the sake of Jesus' name

MATTHEW 24:9-14

The Eskimo religion was the lowest type of paganism. Without temples or idols, they believed in a great spirit, Tongarsuk, and priests or wizards, his Angekoks. Fear seemed to be their only religious emotion, and their supersti-tions fostered it. Christian truth had apparently no power to impress them, and the native tongue had no words to convey spiritual ideas. Not one missionary in a hundred would have borne what Matthew Stach and Frederick Boehnisch and the heroic John Beck who had already been in prison for the Lord's sake, bore from those natives. The Eskimos shunned them with aversion, blamed them for the scourge of smallpox which had raged for nine months and made New Herrn-hut the centre of a desert, and they adopted a systematic course of annoyance. Whatever the missionaries said, was travestied and ridiculed; whatever they did, was caricatured and grotesquely mimicked. In the midst of earnest exhortations, they feigned sleep and snored; or they would feign pious desire to hear hymns

142

sung, and then drown the singing with howls and beating of drums. But farce and comedy were not sufficient—and personal insult and violence threatened a tragedy. For five years they sought to wear out the patience of the missionaries by a series of persecutions. They laid siege to their huts, broke their furniture, stole their food and manuscripts, pelted them with stones, and broke their boat which was their last hope of subsistence. And when starvation was threatening these noble Moravians, with monstrous ingratitude and cruelty they would not even sell them one morsel of food, though they themselves had abundance.

Seldom has mission work held out less hope. The Eskimos were repulsive dwarfs, with minds and hearts even worse dwarfed than their bodies. Their looks were ugly, their habits filthy. Mothers licked their children as cats do their kittens, and they all wallowed like swine in the mire of their uncleanness. Hans Egede had found all his efforts for their uplifting met by resistance, doggedly stubborn and malicious. They invoked the aid of their Angekoks to destroy him with their wizard arts, and when these failed they thought he must be chief of wizards, as his Master has been called Prince of Demons. But the motto of these brave men was thus "Lose thy way, but lose not thy faith," and they held on to God and persevered in prayer.

The first sign that God's summer sun was melting these icy hearts was when John Beck's infant daughter drew their eyes to the beauty of Christian homelife. Once more the prophecy was fulfilled:

> **SCRIPTURE TESTIMONY**
>
> *Salvation transforms*
>
> 2 CORINTHIANS 5:16-17 · GALATIANS 6:15

"And a little child shall lead them." Her lisping lips somehow softened their rudeness and warmed their coldness; and when the Eskimo mothers heard her singing holy hymns, they yearned to hear their little ones sing like her, and began themselves to learn those simple gospel songs which Beck and Boehnisch had written in the native tongue.

Then in 1738, as Beck was in his humble hut preparing an Eskimo Bible, a company of Greenlanders from the South came in and watched him at his work, wondering that a piece of paper could be made to hear, remember, and repeat the words of God. He read to them from his manuscript translation of the gospels, and once more the story of the cross broke hard hearts. One of these men, Kayarnak, came nearer and looking up into Beck's face, said, with pathetic earnestness, "How was that? Tell it to me once more; for I too want to be saved."

The ice was breaking, and the long winter was feeling the first touch of spring. Beck's soul, so tried during these years of fruitless toil, could scarcely believe what his ears heard. There was at last one seeker after God. His joy overflowed in tears and in speech; again and more fully he told the tale that never loses its charm. And when his fellow-missionaries returned from work in the districts round about, they found him in the midst of a group of Greenlanders, whose open ears drank in his words, while their hands were laid on their mouths, to express amazement at the strange and wonderful things, never before heard.

From that day Kayarnak could be found daily at the mission hut, with cheeks wet with tears, with heart opened to attend unto the things which were spoken, and yearning to be taught, as no Greenlander had ever been known to yearn before him. He clung fondly to his Moravian teachers, remaining with some twenty companions, through the winter, and aiding in the translation of the gospels. On Easter morning, 1739, in presence of a large assembly of natives, he, with his wife and two children, confessed Christ in baptism. And so the first fruits of that long-delayed harvest-field began to be gathered.

The return of spring compelled Kayarnak to start again on his search for seals; for the ocean is the field which the Eskimo cultivates. His boat's keel is his plough, and seals and fish are his crop. With no little fear Beck and his brethren let this new convert go forth to his work with heathen companions. But a year later he came back, not only having fast hold upon his newly-found Jesus, but bringing with him his brother and his family, having been so long absent in hope to gain them as converts to the Lord.

The conversion of Kayarnak we have thus given in detail, because it marks a new era in missions to that north land. Beholding this man healed, the opposers of the gospel could say nothing against it. The miracle wrought in his changed heart and life put a sudden stop to the mockery that had made Stach's heart burn with holy indignation; and the spirit of earnest inquiry, which flamed in Kayarnak's breast, kindled a like spirit among the people. Instead of keeping aloof, or coming to scoff and jeer, they became constant and reverent hearers, and learned and loved the sacred songs and gospel readings which Beck had written for them.

The whole life of the people now underwent a change. Brutal cruelty gave place to considerate kindness; past ill-treatment was confessed, and forgiveness was sought; care for the wants and woes of others, and even of strangers, took the place of heartless indifference. For instance, if the women of Greenland hated anything it was suckling a motherless babe; yet even this they were found doing gladly, so sweetly had the gospel taught them the grace of unselfish service to the most needy and helpless. If their language had no word for gratitude, their transformed conduct made up for the lack of their speech by its own peculiar dialect; and the newly converted natives found some words to express their new views and feelings which their foreign teachers had long sought in vain. It need not be said that the charms of the Angekoks were now broken and the reign of superstition was at an end.

Kayarnak, the learner, became also the teacher. He taught even the missionaries; he helped them so to understand the language as to correct the errors and blunders of earlier teaching and translating; and they learned from him a still more valuable lesson; for he led them to stop trying to convince unbelievers by mere argument, and to trust to the patient and prayerful presentation of the mere facts of redemption; to depend not on the logic that appeals to the reason, but on the demonstration of the Holy Spirit.

Kayarnak himself was permitted only to lead the way in this new era. At the end of a year of most exemplary piety, amidst a living testimony, that in its faith and fervour and rich experience was apostolic, he fell asleep; but the work went on. In 1747, twenty-five years after Hans Egede had landed at Ball's River, the first church building in Greenland was erected, where three hundred were wont to gather. As the Moravian Brethren saw the church and school and singing class; as they beheld the very land itself yielding to culture, and the changed aspect of the whole country; and most of all as they saw the desert of human hearts turning into the garden of the Lord, they could only say, "The Lord hath done more for us than we knew how to pray for. A stream of life is now poured upon this people. As we speak or sing of the sufferings of Jesus they are so sensibly affected that tears of love and joy roll down their cheeks. Though they may happen to be from four to six leagues away, almost all come to our Sunday service; and candidates for baptism can scarcely wait patiently for the happy hour."

Other missions and missionaries followed, and progress was in geometrical ratio, for at Lichtenfels four years saw as much advance as fourteen at New Herrnhut, and the largest of the congregations was gathered at Lichtenau. For thirty years John Beck was spared to watch the seed which his own hand had sown ripening into harvests. He had made a solemn vow to follow the Lord wholly in that land of ice and snow, to do all and bear all as unto Him —and sacredly had he kept his covenant. He had asked one soul saved, as the seal of God's approval, and that prayer was answered so abundantly that all the settlements throughout Greenland are now Christian, and it is now forty-five years ago since at Proven the last professed pagan died. Kayarnak was the leader of a host; and Beck's Bible became the base-block on which was built a new Christian State. Over the icy castles of the frozen north floats the flag of the cross, and again the prayer and pains of the missionary have their recompense of reward!

Africaner—The Hottentot Terror.

Africaner was known as the "Bona-parte of South Africa." This notorious Hottentot chief had become the terror of the whole country. The Boers had at

SCRIPTURE TESTIMONY
Salvation transforms
2 CORINTHIANS 5:16-17 · GALATIANS 6:15

some time wronged or offended him, and in revenge for their insult or injustice, with characteristic rage, he carried on a constant, cruel, relentless war with the natives living near the mouth of the Orange River. He was a terrible foe, feared by everybody, deaf to remonstrance and appeal. He stole cattle, he burned kraals, he took captives only to enslave those whom he did not destroy.

When in 1817 Moffat started for Africaner's kraal his friends warned him that this savage monster would make a drum-skin of his hide and a drinking cup of his skull. But the noble hero of Namaqua-land was not to be dissuaded even by the tears of the motherly dame who wept for the danger and death into which he was rushing.

Africaner was originally a Hottentot in the service of a Dutch farmer at Tulbach, near Cape Town. His usual work was the care of cattle; but he and his sons were often sent on raids of plunder against unarmed tribes further inland, a good school of robbery and of murder, where this Hottentot proved a quick learner; and on a slight provocation he shot his employer and his wife. Then Africaner fled as an outlaw, across the Orange River, keeping near enough to harass the Boers, but far enough away to be safe from arrest and punishment. From this time his hand, like that of Ishmael, was against every man. It mattered little whether white or black, native or foreigner, Namaqua, Hottentot, or Boer; whoever crossed his track he hunted down like a wild beast, and fire and sword were his merciless weapons. The authorities of the colony would have paid any reasonable price for his head; but where was the man daring enough to attempt to capture or kill such a monster? It was like fighting a dragon. He might tolerate missionaries, but they could not hope to change him, and gave it up in despair.

Robert Moffat won this hard-hearted monster, and it was by the same old gospel that has broken so many other hearts of stone and melted so many other hearts of steel. Into the very soul of Africaner this truth of God entered, and until the day of his death there was no break in the harmony of this strange friendship. During Moffat's sickness, it was Africaner whose hands ministered to his needs, furnished his food and the best of milk. And when Moffat found it needful to go to Cape Town, although there was still a premium upon his head, Africaner went with him. That whole journey is one of the romances of history. When the missionary stopped on his way at the house of a farmer who had been his host as he journeyed to Namaqualand, he had no little difficulty in convincing him that he was Moffat, for the man had heard that the Hottentot chief had murdered him, and knew a man who had "seen his bones." But when he saw Africaner, who had killed his uncle, and witnessed the change in his whole character and demeanour, the farmer could only exclaim, "O God, what cannot Thy grace do! What a miracle of Thy power!"

The sensation produced by Africaner's appearance at Cape Town defies description. Here was an outlaw, a robber, a murderer, for whose capture such large rewards had been vainly offered, himself coming back, risking arrest, trusting himself among them, a changed man. The lion had become a lamb. The governor sent for him, and the reward offered for the seizure of the outlaw was actually spent in gifts for himself and presents for his people. As Moffat found it vain to attempt further work in Namaqualand, Africaner went with him to the Bechuanas. He first moved Moffat's goods and cattle and sheep to his new home at Lattakoo, and then, having faithfully fulfilled his trust, went back for his own movables, that he might settle beside his beloved teacher. But his end was near, and he died shortly after at his old kraal.

Kapiolani—The Hawaiian Female Chief.

Kapiolani, of the Hawaiian Islands, was the most noted among female chiefs, and had large landed possessions. When first seen by the missionaries she was seated on a rock oiling her person, and was found to be dark-minded, superstitious, intemperate, repulsive. Yet, when the gospel touched her heart, this degraded daughter of heathen kings was found attending the place of prayer, becomingly dressed, dignified in deportment, devout and meek, but resolute and courageous. She received the messengers of the Lord at her house with the courteous cordiality of Lydia, and with them planned for the improvement of her own people in condition and character with the ardour and candour of Catherine of Sienna. Like Catherine, she was inspired with the heroism of a reformer. From the sanctuary of Keave, the sacred house of deposit, she bore away the royal relics which were worshipped with divine honours, and hid them in inaccessible caves near the head of the bay in the side of a precipitous rock. When Charles S. Stewart, chaplain of the United States ship of war, "Vincennes," was leaving Kaawaloa at midnight, she insisted on going with him to the shore, that with warm hand-shake and many tears, she might accompany him to the ship, as Ephesian elders did with Paul. This heroic woman, with her husband, strove to uproot the most tenacious idolatrous notions and customs. Without counting costs to herself, she put down murder and infanticide, theft and Sabbath-breaking, lust and drunkenness, and sought to reform morals and religion. And when, in 1841, she died, had no other gem for the crown of the great Conqueror been dug up on Hawaiian soil, this woman's conversion sufficed to prove that the gospel is, as truly as in Apostolic days, God's power unto salvation.

One act of her life will ever stand out in conspicuous pre-eminence. She knew that the famous crater of Kilauea was believed by the people to be the residence of the awful goddess, Pele. The superstitious hold of this goddess upon the people must be broken. And she determined to lay hold upon the very pillars of this temple of the Hawaiian Dagon and bring down this superstition into ruin. In 1825 she made a journey of a hundred miles to this volcanic crater, and there openly defied this false deity, at her throne and shrine. She not only refused to offer even the sacred bean as a propitiatory offering or in any way avert or appease the wrath and power of Pele, but she made the crater ring with the praises of Jehovah, as she sang hymns to the only true God. She had made the journey on foot with numerous attendants, who were awe-struck at the open indignity with which she defied the dreaded goddess. And those who know with what awful terrors such pagan deities are clothed in the common mind, and with what tenacity these superstitions continue to hold even professed converts, can imagine what holy courage faith must have begotten in this Hawaiian heroine. It was eleven hundred years before her (723), when Boniface at Geismar in Upper Hesse, boldly, with axe in hand, hewed down the gigantic and venerable oak sacred to Thor, the Thunderer, defying the superstitions which held the people in bondage, and the idolatrous associations of centuries; and, as blow after blow fell, the pagans looked to see the bolt of the avenger smite the profaner of his sacred grove dead. That was a heroic deed, but Boniface had never been under the thrall of this idolatry, and had no superstitions of his own to fight. But this woman was herself only just delivered from the chains of lifelong idolatry, and had no band of clergy around her to encourage and share her act of open profanation.

Kho-thah-byu—The Karen Evangelist.

<table>
<tr><td>

SCRIPTURE TESTIMONY

Jesus taught with authority

MATTHEW 7:28-29

</td></tr>
</table>

One man is selected out of the Karens, or wild men of Burma, as an example of the transforming power of the gospel, mainly because he was the first convert among his people. He was a poor man and a slave, and one of the degraded people of a debased nation, a man of very ordinary abilities, and yet most useful and uninterrupted in his labours. The first of his nation to be baptized, he lived to draw hundreds and thousands to follow his own steps. He is a singular example of what ordinary faculties will accomplish when wholly consecrated. He aroused the whole nation to Christianity. born in 1778, and baptized in 1828, he was fifty years old when he took up the cross. Until he was fifteen, he was at home, but wicked, wilful, ungovernable. After he left his parents he became a robber and a murderer; and was, no doubt, at least accessory to no less than thirty murders. His natural temper was vicious.

After the Burmese war he went to Rangoon, and got into Mr. Hough's service, by whom the first religious impressions were made upon his mind. He followed Adoniram Judson to Amhurst, and was taken into the family of Ko-shway-bay, who, having paid for him a debt, took him into his family as a servant, according to Burmese law which makes the debtor slave to the creditor. His master, who was also an inquirer, became discouraged with regard to doing him any good, and could not retain him in the family on account of his immoral character. He was, however, transferred to the family of the Rev. Francis Mason, and soon after began to pay attention to religious things, though he had fits of violent temper. Soon signs of repentance appeared, and faith in Jesus. His dark mind slowly took hold of the truths of Christianity, and his violent temper often caused him great discouragement and depression, and deferred his baptism. He was, however, baptized on the 16th May, 1828, as we have said, at fifty years of age. He had already studied with great diligence, in order to read the Burman Bible, and became immediately very zealous to bear witness to the Saviour whom he had found. Immediately after his baptism, accompanied by two of his country-men, he left Tavoy to visit the Karens in the valley of Tenasserim, preaching and explaining the catechism, and with immediate results in the conversion of other Karens, Moung Khway being the first.

Nearly a whole village ultimately became Christian through the influences started by this converted Karen. From this time, so long as his strength allowed, he was accustomed to make tours among his brethren, from which he would return with converts prepared for baptism, the numbers running all the way up from six to one hundred and fifty. He obtained the ears of the people of whole villages, and remarkable changes took place under his ministry. He was unwearied in labour, would often talk of the gospel till near midnight, and absolutely spared not himself. His preaching carried with it conviction, and compelled others to say, "Truly this is the word of God." After Mr. Boardman had preached in Burman he would interpret as much of the discourse as he could remember into Karen. Though a naturally weak man he became magnanimous, because the Spirit of Christ and the love of souls inspired him. His wife was likewise baptized in 1828. She had formerly been very ignorant and very wicked, but the influence of her husband had been blessed to her entire transformation. His tours lasted from a week to six months, spent in itinerating with perpetual labour, day and night. Most amazing results often followed his ministry. For instance, when the mother of the baptized Karen headman died, in fear that other relatives of the deceased would wish to perform heathenish customs in connection with her burial, he proposed to erect a preaching zayat near the grave, and invited Kho-thah-byu to hold forth the word of life there. At one time this Karen evangelist projected a journey into Siam, and actually started to visit the Karens in that country, but was not suffered to cross the border, and was compelled to return.

After Mr. Boardman became unable to labour, the whole care of the church and the instruction of the inquirers devolved on this simple-minded convert. He taught school and showed diligence in every department of labour. His pupils could repeat verbatim whole Burman tracts. His boldness in attacking idolatry was remarkable. The town of Shen Mouktee is famous for the idol which it contains, which was said to have grown miraculously from a little brass image of a few inches high, to the full size of a man. It was as sacred to the Burmans as Diana was to the Ephesians. When this old man had been left to rest in one of the zayats he was found surrounded by a large congregation of Burmans, and, holding them under a peculiar fascination, that was compared to the influence of a serpent over a brood of chickens. And the first words that were heard by Dr. Mason as he approached, were, "Your God was a black kula;" that is, a foreigner. The peculiar look which accompanied these words could never be forgotten by the beholder. If ever a man hated idolatry, that man was Kho-thah-byu. No fatigue, no obstacles, could prevent his seeking out his fellow-countrymen, and when he could not reach the Karens he would attack the Burmans and their idolatry with unmerciful energy, utterly heedless of their ridicule. His ruling passion was for preaching, and once, when he was in danger of losing his life by drowning, his only solicitude was lest he might never more preach the gospel to the Karens. He was not only a man of very ordinary abilities, but he was actually, in some things, ignorant to the verge of stupidity. His own pupils outran their teacher in their attainments. His adaptation was for a pioneer, and God permitted him to become, in succession, the first Karen preacher to his countrymen in the districts of Tavoy, Maul-main, Rangoon and Aracan. The son born to him in Tavoy he named Joseph, the first Christian name ever conferred by native Karens; and his great desire was that that son might live to become a preacher to his people.

In his tours he sometimes had to wade streams to his armpits, and sometimes through mud and water where the rain filled the hollows; yet nothing could discourage or dismay him. He was one among a thousand. Sometimes the Karens thronged his house so that there was danger of breaking it down, and their importunity left him no chance for needed physical rest, and scarcely for food. He was chief of all the native Karen assistants employed in the carrying forward of the mission. When his days of itinerating were past by reason of rheumatism and blindness, it was to him the greatest of all his afflictions that he was unable to carry on active work: and when at Sandoway the summons came for him to cease from his labours, on the 9th of September, 1840, at sixty-two years of age, he departed without an anxious thought as to his future state. The blue mountains of Pegu, often the first land seen in India by the approaching mariner, remain his monument; and the Christian villages that adorn their sides constitute his epitaph. If he hated idolatry, he loved the gospel with equal intensity; always planning some new excursion, never so happy as to find hearers for his message. The leading truths of the Bible became familiar as his alphabet, and he sought in every sermon to bring into prominence the vicarious death of Christ. Among his converts there was a more thorough knowledge of justification by faith than can be found among an equal number even in Christian countries.

While it is true that his work was a pioneer work, breaking up the fallow ground and casting in the seed, yet few who have devoted their entire lives to such labours have been the instruments of gathering as many converts to Christ. He idolized his work. It was the only business to which he attached the least importance; and it was this which constituted the charm of his life. His absorption in preaching made him quite insensible to external objects, and he has been known in preaching to be forsaken by every individual soon after the commencement of his remarks, and yet continue with such interest as though he were preaching to listening thousands; and when, at the close of his discourse he found himself alone, without discouragement he would, with renewed zeal and ardour, enter upon his work with the very next individuals he met. He was utterly unceremonious in introducing religious themes, regarding no time or place unsuitable, and though his mental resources were limited they were well directed. He concentrated all his powers upon his work. His success can be accounted for by just four words, "God was with him." He was a man of prayer. It was his practice to read and pray aloud. He has been known to spend all days and, like his Master, whole nights in this way; and, however ignorant upon other subjects, the moment he touched his favourite theme he surprised all his hearers. His baptism in 1828 was the commencement of the mission, which in success exceeds perhaps any other, except that to the Hawaiian Islands. He was never ordained, because he lacked a well regulated mind, and to the last was liable to outbreaks of evil temper, which caused him great sorrow and humiliation.

When the year 1878 completed the centenary of his birth, and the semi-centennial of his conversion, a large new institute building was dedicated to the service of God and Christian education, under the name of the Kho-thah-byu Memorial Hall. That is the true monument of his twelve years of earnest and successful labour. It cost nearly 50,000 rupees, and was the result of ten years of gathered contributions among the Karens of Bassein. It was dedicated without debt in the month of May. It stands on a fine knoll in the outskirts of the town, and is visible for a long distance from the north and west. Its entire length on the south front is 134 feet. The east front and wing measure 131 feet, the west side with the wing 104 feet. The tower is sixty feet high, surmounted by a Greek cross, and on the wall of the south verandah, in carved, gilded, Burmese characters, we read this inscription:

"1828—Kho-thah-byu—1878."

Ranavalona II.—Madagascar's Queen.

When Robert Drury gave the first full account of the savages of this great island, it was under the despotism of wickedness, and might was the only right. Idolatry of the most degraded kind existed, and the island was the scene of perpetual war, lust, slavery and superstition. Thousands of natives were sold every year, and the spot where they caught the last glimpse of home, as they went into hopeless exile, even yet bears the pathetic name, "The weepingplace of the Hovas." Vices were treated as virtues. Punishments were savagely contrived to inflict long torture. The people were a nation of thieves and liars. There were no homes. A native never spoke of family or family ties. The pen refuses to record what was there seen and heard. It should be written in blood and registered in hell. Female virtue was of so little account that it did not even affect the legitimacy of offspring. Idols so filled the land that anything which was not comprehended, though it were but a machine or a photograph, was deified. The French governor of the Isle of Bourbon told the first missionaries that they might as well attempt to convert sheep, oxen or asses.

Madagascar has unenviable celebrity as the scene of a persecution which might have brought a blush even to the cheek of Nero. When Rana-valona I. mounted the throne, murdering all rivals,—the "bloody Mary" of Madagascar, treacherous as Judas, selfish as Cleopatra,—from twenty to thirty thousand victims fell annually a prey to her cruelty. Her chief amusement was a bull fight, and it was said that half of the population perished under her bloody sceptre. At her coronation she took two of the national idols in her hands, and said, "From my ancestors I received you. In you I put my trust, therefore support me." And those idols, in robes of scarlet and gold, were held at the front of the platform to overawe the multitude.

We pass over an interval of years. In 1868, thirty-nine years after the coronation of Ranavalona I., and seven years after her death, Ranavalona II. was crowned. For the first time, Madagascar had a Christian, as well as a constitutional, ruler. He who would see the marvellous transformation in this island need only contrast the coronation of these two queens, one on the 12th of June, 1829, and the other on the 3rd of September, 1868. At this latter ceremony, the symbols of pagan faith were nowhere to be seen. In their place lay a beautiful copy of the Bible, side by side with the laws of Madagascar. Over the queen was stretched a canopy, on whose four sides were as many Scripture mottoes: "Glory to God," "Peace on Earth," "Good-will to Men," "God with Us." Her inaugural address was interwoven with the dialect of Scripture, and now it was idolatry and not Christianity that became a suppliant for toleration;—and all this, seven years after the death of the bloody Mary, whose thirty-two years had been a reign of terror! Astrologers and diviners were no longer to be found at court; Rasoherina's sacred idol was cast out of the palace; government work ceased on Sunday; Sunday markets were closed, divine worship held in the court. The Madagascar New Year was changed from an idolatrous festival to a Christian holiday, and the queen's address declared, "I have brought my kingdom to lean upon God, and expect you, one and all, to be wise and just, and to walk in His ways." One month later this Christian queen and her prime minister were publicly baptized by a native preacher, in the very courtyard where the bloodiest edicts had been promulgated.

When the queen was examined by native ministers, previous to baptism, it was found that her first serious impressions were traceable to a native Christian. One of the four noble men afterward burned as martyrs had thus sown the seed in her own heart. Two days before their baptism, the queen and her prime minister were married, and shortly after publicly joined in the Lord's Supper. Her example was likely to be followed by government officers of high rank; and even the chief idol keeper, the astrologer of Rasoherina, applied for baptism. The congregations multiplied beyond all means of accommodation. A hundred new buildings were in demand. There was an increase of sixteen thousand worshippers in a year, and the royal chapel was erected in the very courtyard of the palace, where to-day that beautiful house of prayer may yet be seen. In gilded letters upon two large stone tablets forming part of the surbase of the structure, appears engraven the following royal statement, read at the laying of the cornerstone in 1869:

"By the power of God and grace of our Lord Jesus, I, Ranavalomanjaka, Queen of Madagascar, founded the House of Prayer, on the thirteenth Adimizana, in the year of our Lord Jesus Christ, 1869, as a house of prayer for the service of God, King of kings and Lord of lords, according to the word in sacred Scriptures, by Jesus Christ the Lord who died for the sons of all men, and rose again for the justification and salvation of all who believe in, and love Him.

"For these reasons this stone house, founded by me as a house of prayer, cannot be destroyed by any one, whoever may be king of this my land, forever and forever; but if he shall destroy this house of prayer to God which I have founded, then is he not king of my land Madagascar. Wherefore I have signed my name with my hand and the seal of the kingdom.

"RANAVALOMANJAKA, QUEEN OF MADAGASCAR."

MASKEPETOOM—THE INDIAN CHIEF.

The Rev. Mr. Rundle, of the English Wesleyan Missionary Society, was the pioneer, who, at great personal risk, visited the Cree tribes of the North American Indians, that he might bear to them the message of salvation. These tribes were, perhaps, the most numerous and powerful among the Indians that roamed over the vast regions of the Canadian northwest, before the scourge of epidemic disease had mowed them down by thousands.

We put on record here the simple story of the most powerful chief among those tribes, known as Maskepetoom, or the crooked arm, from the fact that one arm had been so hacked and wounded in close conflict with his ferocious neighbours, the Black Feet Indians, that, in healing, the muscles had contracted and stiffened, and permanently crooked the arm. This chief was a born warrior. His special delight was found in the excitement of Indian conflict, in cunning ambuscades, and strategic movements. He did not hesitate to practice those barbarities and cruelties upon the captives of other tribes that have given to the Indians a character as specially vindictive and inhuman.

> SCRIPTURE TESTIMONY
>
> *Forgive, or you will not be forgiven*
>
> MATTHEW 6:14-15 · LUKE 6:37

The Rev. James Evans, in his marvellous trips through the magnificent distances of this northwest, visited and faithfully preached the gospel to Maskepetoom and his warriors; and, although some accepted the gospel, and became Christian believers, the warlike chief himself was found impervious to the message of peace. Some years later, the Rev. George Macdougal, at one of the camp-fire services, read as his Scripture lesson the story of Christ's trial and crucifixion, and came to the prayer which the Saviour offered for his murderers: "Father, forgive them, for they know not what they do." He stopped to dwell especially upon this prayer, for the Indian spirit feeds upon retaliation. If there be any attribute of the Indian character that has become historically and proverbially conspicuous, not only prominent but overtopping all others, it is the disposition to revenge real or imaginary injuries upon the perpetrators of them. And, having in mind the fact that this quality was so regnant in the hearts of his Indian hearers, he attacked the evil stronghold, and plainly told them the conditions of divine forgiveness: "If we forgive not men their trespasses, neither will our heavenly Father forgive our trespasses;" that if they really expected forgiveness from the Great Spirit, they must be able to pray such a prayer as Christ offered on the cross. The dark-eyed warrior listened with profound attention, and was deeply moved, but nothing more was said to him that evening.

The next day, as the great company led by him, and composed of many hundred Indians, was riding along over the beautiful prairie, a subordinate chief rode quickly to the side of Mr. Macdougal, the missionary, begging him, in an excited manner, to fall back into the rear, lest he should be compelled to witness the horrible torture and violent death of a man who was approaching them in a little band of Indians, seen in the distance, although so far off as scarcely to be distinguishable to a white man's vision.

The warning of this chief was occasioned by the fact that, months before this, Maskepetoom had sent his only son across a mountain range, or pass, to bring a herd of horses home. Among the foot-hills of these massive mountains are many fertile valleys where there is grazing all the year round, and in one of these the great chieftain had kept his reserve of horses. One of his warriors was selected as the comrade of his son, to aid him in his work. It transpired that this man, having a chance to sell these horses, was so excited by the bait offered to his cupidity, that he actually murdered the son of the chief, disposed of the herd, and for a time concealing his booty, returned to the tribe, telling a plausible story that in one of the dangerous passes in the mountains the young chief had lost his foothold and been dashed to pieces over an awful precipice, so that he, being left alone to manage the herd of horses, had been compelled to see them scattering wildly over the plain. As nothing was at the time known to the contrary, Maskepetoom and his followers were compelled to accept this improbable story; but it subsequently transpired that, unknown to the murderer, the tragedy had witnesses; so that for months a horrible vengeance had been preparing when the offender should come within the control of the exasperated chief. And now the awful day had come when the vengeance might find opportunity of execution, and the bereaved father was actually approaching the band, among whom was the murderer of his only son. As he advanced the very warriors held their breath. He quickened the speed of his horse, and rode on in advance. Mr. Macdougal, anxious, if possible, to prevent the execution of such dire revenge, spurred his horse forward, and rode up just in the rear of the mighty chieftain, uplifting his prayer to God that the wrath of man might at least be restrained.

When the two bands approached within a few hundred yards of each other, the eagle eye of Maskepetoom caught sight of the murderer. He drew his tomahawk impetuously from his belt, and rode still faster till he came face to face with the man that had treacherously inflicted the greatest injury that was possible upon the father; then, with a voice tremulous with suppressed emotion and yet with admirable command over himself, the chieftain looked in the face the man that had broken his heart and murdered his boy, and said to him, "You have killed my son, and you deserve to die. I selected you as his trusted companion, and gave you the post of honour as his comrade, and you have betrayed my trust and cruelly murdered my only boy. No greater injury could you have done to me and to my tribe. You have not only broken my heart, but you have killed him who was to have been my successor. You ought to die, by all the laws of Indian tribes; but I heard from the missionary last night at the camp fire, that, if we expect the Great Spirit to forgive us, we must forgive our enemies, even those who have done to us the greatest wrongs; and but for this I would have buried my tomahawk in your brains at this instant You have been my most cruel enemy, and you deserve death; but," he added, as his voice trembled with still deeper emotion, "as I hope the Great Spirit will forgive me, I freely forgive you. But go away from me and from my people, and let me never again see your face." Then Maskepetoom hastily pulled up over his head his war bonnet, his voice completely broke down, and actually quivered with the feelings that were tearing his heart, but which he had for the time suppressed; the gigantic form bowed low over the neck of the horse, and he gave way to an agony of tears.

This great chieftain not only became a devoted and consistent Christian, but for years afterwards lived a becoming and beautiful life. He gave up all his old warlike habits. He mastered the syllabic characters in which the Cree Bible was printed. He made the word of God his daily solace, his counsellor, and his joy, and the remainder of his days were spent in service to God and man. He delivered thrilling and earnest addresses to his own people, urging them to give up all their old sinful ways, and become followers of that Saviour who had so grandly saved him. They listened to his words, and many, like him, abandoned their old warlike habits, and settled down into lives of peaceful quiet. He was so desirous even to benefit his old enemies, the Blackfeet, and to tell them the story of a Saviour's love, that he actually went fearless and unarmed among them, Bible in hand. His end was the end of a martyr, for a bloodthirsty chief of that vindictive tribe saw him approaching, and, remembering some of the fierce conflicts they had waged in other days, and, doubtless, having lost by the prowess of Maskepetoom some of his own relatives in those conflicts, he seized his gun, and, in defiance of all rules of humanity, not to say magnanimity, he coolly shot the unarmed and converted Christian chieftain in cold blood.

And so fell a man who was a wondrous trophy of the cross, a chieftain whose conversion did a vast amount of good, showing how the gospel can change the hardest heart, eradicate the most deeply rooted habits, and enable a warlike savage so thoroughly to conquer the besetting sin of the Indian character, even under the most extreme provocation and where few could have found fault if the price of blood had been exacted and the murderer executed, as actually to forgive the offender. This is the more remarkable, because revenge, like cannibalism, has its root in a religious or superstitious conviction. Dr. S. McFarlane says that cannibalism can be accounted for in no way satisfactorily but as a religious practice. He gives many proofs of this position. It is not due to appetite for human flesh, nor simply to vindictive feeling toward enemies. They regard the devouring of an enemy as the means of incorporating into themselves the strength of a slain foe, and all the ceremonies of cannibalism are invested with the sanctities of religion. And so we may say, of the Indian character, as to revenge; it is not regarded by them as a vice, but a virtue, as the quality of a manly, brave, and noble spirit; as a form of justice, not simply of hateful passion; and something to be cherished, not to be suppressed. An Indian without revenge is a coward in the tribe, and there is nothing from which an Indian shrinks more than from the charge of cowardice; and so, when the gospel overcomes in a man like Maskepetoom the instinct of revenge, and especially when revenge could be justified as a judicial act, inflicting punishment upon a murderer, it is one of the marks of the miracle-working power of the gospel of Christ.

Ling-Ching-Ting—The Chinese Opium-Smoker.

Rev. James Main was so shocked at the vacuity of a Chinaman's face that he declared there was in the very look of a Chinese audience somewhat that seemed to say that the consequence of

> **SCRIPTURE TESTIMONY**
>
> *Jesus is able to save to the uttermost*
>
> HEBREWS 7:25

not having heard the gospel was a loss of all capacity to receive and understand it.

Thirty years ago, in Foochow, a man, of about forty, found his way into the little suburban chapel at Ato, and his eyes and ears were fixed upon the Rev. S. L. Binkley, who was preaching on the all-sufficiency of Christ to save. For some reason this poor Chinaman's attention had been strangely riveted to the truth, and he tarried at the close of the service to converse with the missionary. He said, "This Jesus I never heard of until now, and I don't know who He is; but did you not say that He can save me from all my sins?" "Yes," replied Mr. Binkley, "I said exactly that." "But then you did not know me when you said so. I have been for many years a liar, a gambler, a sorcerer, an adulterer, and for twenty years an opium-smoker, and no man who has used opium for so long a time was ever known to be cured. Now if you had known me, you would never have said what you did, do you see?" Of course the missionary could only repeat with emphasis his former declaration, about the power and willingness of Jesus to save his believing people from even such a multitude of sins!

The opium-smoker was struck dumb with amazement. His mind was in bondage to ancient superstitions; the poison of lust was in his very blood; and worse than all, he was sold in hopeless slavery to the awful drug and his will was in chains to a habit of twenty years, and he had never yet known any such victim to be set free. The thought of such a deliverance as even possible, of salvation from all his sins, was too much—he was dazed by the glory of such new freedom and dared not believe such statements to be other than extravagant fancies or tormenting illusions. And so he went away; but he came back the next day, and day after day, to hear more of this wonderful Saviour, and to look into this gospel of salvation that promised to free even an opium-slave. Weeks passed by; and one morning impetuously rushing into the missionaries' room, before his tongue could speak his radiant face had told of his new discovery: "I know it now! Jesus can save me from all my sins, for He has done it."

SCRIPTURE TESTIMONY

Beaten for preaching the Gospel

ACTS 5:40 · ACTS 14:19-20

Yes, so quick had been the victory of faith that the last and worst enemy was destroyed; the habit was broken, and even the desire was gone. He no longer felt the bonds under which he had hopelessly struggled for so many years. Christ had made him free; and such deliverance demanded a declaration. The opium slave must speak, for he believed; he must go back to Hok-chiang, where his companions in sin lived, and tell them of this Jesus who could save them from all their sins. Friends sought to dissuade him from preaching this doctrine of these foreign devils; or, if he would, let him stay at Foochow, where he would be safe, and not risk the riotous mobs at Hok-chiang, who would take off his head, and then there would be a stop to all his talking. But, no! Ling-Ching-Ting would go to his own people, and with no weapon but the word of God. He went. He told the story of a great salvation for the worst of sinners, and held up himself as an illustration—like Paul, a pattern for other believers. Pelted with clods and stones, beaten and bruised, driven from place to place, his witness could not be stopped. At last his persecutors brought him before a cruel district magistrate at Hok-chiang, and false witnesses preferred against him the vilest charges; and the corrupt judge, glad to deal out revenge against this foreign sect, actually sentenced him to receive two thousand stripes! and upon his bare back the cruel bamboo was mercilessly laid, until the flesh lay in strips. He was borne to the mission premises almost dead, and the doctor declared that such injuries he had never before seen inflicted by the bamboo.

When Dr. Baldwin sought to comfort this martyr of Christ, before he could find words with which to address him, the suffering saint, so lately the chief of sinners, said with a smile: "Teacher, this poor body be in great pain, but my inside heart be in a great peace." Then, to the astonishment of the missionary, lifting himself a little on his bloody cot, he said, "If I get up again from this, you will let me go back to Hok-chiang, won't you?"

For some time his recovery seemed doubtful, and then improvement slowly began. While yet but half healed, and scarce able to walk, he stole away, and suddenly appeared at Hok-chiang to preach again to his hateful persecutors; and it was not strange that words of witness, sealed by such experiences of blood, brought his very foes to his Saviour.

Ling-Ching-Ting for fourteen years kept on preaching. He was ordained in 1869. He won hundreds of converts, and a score of native preachers learned from him to tell the old story of full salvation. In 1876, failing health gave the signal of his approaching end; but when too weak to stand, he still gathered around him those to whom he could bear witness to the Saviour, and passed away, singing, in the joy of an unclouded hope.

Narayan Sheshadri—The Brahman Apostle.

From the converts of India we select this remarkable man who became the first convert of the Free Church of Scotland, under the ministry of Dr. John Wilson, and Dr. Murray Mitchell, fifty years ago. He spent some years as a missionary, teacher and preacher, and was then ordained by the Presbytery of Bombay, and for the rest of his life this highly educated Brahman devoted himself to a ministry of love among the outcast Mangs of the Deccan centre of India. He left ordinary British territory that he might undertake to annex the great native state of Hyderabad to the kingdom of Christ. This was in the year 1863, when he was about forty years of age. His evangelistic work was unceasing and untiring. He secured a tract of some three hundred acres near Jalna, and formed a Christian Church and community which he called by the name of Bethel. After ten years of toil he visited Scotland and America that he might interest the churches in his work and raise money for necessary enlargement. Those who saw him in his native Indian dress and white turban will not soon forget the impression that he made in the assemblies in which he moved. His face was charming, and his personality magnetic. His command of the English tongue was such as left little distinction between himself and the natives of Scotland. He had an extremely pithy and impressive way of speaking, and his earnestness was both captivating and contagious. He was at the Presbyterian Alliance in Philadelphia in 1880. He was made doctor of divinity by the University of Montreal.

There were no pews in the Bethel Church in India. The congregation sat on the floor in rows, devout and attentive, while the babies crawled about everywhere. An hour or so after service the catechists and Bible women met. Bands went forth under Dr. Sheshadri's training to preach in the villages round about Bethel; and in this way small communities were formed. He carried on work amid the thirty-three villages where Christian converts resided, and, in 1890, reported 1,062 living members, beside 649 adherents. These native Christians keep all their primitive simplicity, and are not Anglicised by their Christianity.

Dr. Sheshadri was a teacher as well as a preacher, singularly facile in his interpretation of Scripture, and acute in meeting objections brought by Hindus and Moslems against Christianity. He sought to train over a thousand converts into intelligent disciples and workers. He left Bombay for Japan on account of impaired health, in February, 1891, and visited America; but on his return, while *en route* for Glasgow, died, and was buried in mid-Atlantic. Here was a Brahman lad who confessed Jesus Christ before the Supreme Court of Bombay, and who was blessed to lead some 2,000 of his countrymen to Christ. What has been done in the case of one educated and accomplished Brahman, who in his youth had been identified with the gods and entitled to worship, may yet be accomplished among thousands and millions of his fellow-countrymen. His first confession of Jesus Christ was in the presence of the Civil Court. In 1843 two brothers left the fire worship of Zoroaster for the service of Christ, and the Civil Court was appealed to. The two Brahman brothers clung to the new Saviour they had found. They were Narayan and Shripat. The younger was not sixteen years old, and Sir Erskine Perry handed him over to the Brahman priests, sneering at his plea that he had arrived at the age of discretion. Tom from the arms of the missionary, Nesbit, he sobbed forth the question, "Am I to be compelled to worship idols?" It was thus a Christian judge drove this lad back into Brahmanism, and he was compelled to swallow the five products of the cow that he might be restored to caste; but his older brother, Narayan, being confessedly of age, could not be hindered, and started on his new career as the Brahman apostle.

Joseph H. Neesima—The Japanese Educator.

Fifty years ago, there was born in the Sunrise Kingdom a boy for whom God had decreed a future which was to bear wrought into it, as into the crusader's cloak, the red sign of the cross. He was but five years old when he renounced idol worship, though he had not yet found a faith that fed his soul-hunger. Then a stray copy of a sort of Chinese Bible fell into his hands, and that opening sentence: "In the beginning God created the heavens and the earth," struck his youthful mind as more sublimely simple and satisfactory than any account of the origin of all things that he had ever met. The transcendental philosophers tell us that the owl comes from the egg, and the egg from the owl, but fail to answer the question, where did the first owl come from that laid the first egg? But here young Neesima found a great First Cause.

Thus he first got a glimpse of the Christian God, and began to feel after Him, if haply he might find Him; and untaught by' man, he prayed, "O, if you have eyes, look upon me; if you have ears, listen for me!" A glimpse of an atlas of the United States had also awakened a desire to see more of that Western World, and he thought, if he could get away from Japan, he might both see America and learn more of this new faith. And so, in disguise, he sailed for Shanghai, and thence worked his way to Boston, on the voyage studying English and reading a Chinese New Testament which he bought in Hong Kong.

As in the first verse of Genesis he had found God the Creator, so in John iii. 16 he found God the Saviour. Arriving at Boston, he fell in with a copy of Robinson Crusoe, and was taught by the prayer of Crusoe in shipwreck how to draw near to God. Nothing happens by chance; and it was a part of God's strange ordering that the owner of the ship in which he had come to Boston should be Alpheus Hardy, one of the most benevolent and missionary-spirited men then in America. Hearing of young Neesima from the captain, he sought out the Japanese stranger, and gave him a name, Joseph Hardy, declaring that God had raised him up to be to his own people a saviour, like Joseph in Egypt. Mr. Hardy's help secured to Neesima a Christian collegiate training; and the result was that he developed so beautiful a character that when President Seelye was asked for a testimonial to his worth, his sufficient answer was, "You cannot gild gold!"

While he was studying theology in 1871-2, the Japanese Embassy, at Washington, secured his services as an interpreter, and the year he spent with them visiting the American cities and European capitals was radiant with his shining example of Christ-likeness. These distinguished men secured him a pardon for leaving his own land without leave, and when he returned to Japan, they were at the head of government, and gave him aid in his projects for the Christian education of his countrymen.

> **SCRIPTURE TESTIMONY**
>
> *Disciples are devoted to Christ above anything or anyone*
>
> MATTHEW 4:20-22 · MATTHEW 16:24-25 · MARK 1:19-20 · MARK 8:31-38 · MARK 10:28 · LUKE 9:23-27 · LUKE 9:57-62 · LUKE 14:25-35

Joseph Neesima became the first native evangelist of his race. He not only preached Christ boldly and taught the truths of the gospel, but before he left America, had secured the money with which to lay the foundations of the Doshisha, the training college of Kyoto, for Japanese pastors.

Urged by his friends of the embassy to take a prominent and lucrative part in the government of the New Japan, he could be drawn aside by no bait of money, position or personal gain. He bore the cross to the heart of the Island Empire, first preaching Christ in the interior; and persistently wrought at his great educational enterprise for fifteen years, facing all obstacles, and patiently and prayerfully holding on to his "one endeavour," as Doshisha implies, until, before his death, he had seen more than nine hundred pupils in his school.

His perseverance was Apostolic. When as yet the Bible could not openly be taught, he taught Christianity under the disguise of moral science. When to put up buildings for a Christian school was pronounced even by friends to be as hopeless and chimerical as to "attempt to fly to Mars," his faith was so courageous that in four months the buildings were opening and the objector was taking part in the dedication! He used to say that he could have been nailed to a literal cross with less suffering than his labours for Christ had cost; yet nothing but the hand of death ever arrested his work or even dampened his ardour. To the last he was planning new enterprises for the evangelization and education of his countrymen. Death overtook him, as it overtook Goujon, the sculptor, who, with chisel in hand, had his eye fixed on a half-carved statue. He was dictating final messages to his school and the missionary society: and, like a great general, with maps of five provinces before him, was marking the strategic points, and issuing orders for a grand campaign.

His funeral marks an era in the history of Japan. The foremost convert, the apostle of Japan, was dead. Seven hundred students of the Doshisha, seventy graduates from all parts of the empire, government officials, and even a delegation of Buddhist priests from Osaka, thronged the procession that followed to its resting-place the body of the man who, not yet fifty years old, had made upon the empire a mark such as no other had ever left for good.

Burial could not be permitted beside his father in the Buddhist Temple grove; but the refusal was itself the most splendid tribute to his worth; for the assigned reason was that Neesima was the very chief and head centre of Christianity in Japan, and must not, therefore, find a grave in the sacred cemetery of Buddhism!

SUSI AND CHUMA—"LIVINGSTONE'S BODY-GUARD."

The work of David Livingstone in Africa was so far that of a missionary explorer and general, that the field of his labour is too broad to permit us to trace individual harvests. No man can thickly scatter seed over so wide an area. But there is one marvellous story connected with his death, and which has to do with individual character, the like of which has never been written on the scroll of human history. All the ages may safely be challenged to furnish its parallel.

On the night of his death he called for Susi, his faithful servant, and, after some tender ministries had been rendered to the dying man, Livingstone said, "All right; you may go out now." And reluctantly Susi left him alone. At four o'clock next morning, May 1, Susi and Chuma, with four other devoted attendants, anxiously entered that grass hut at Ilala. The candle was still burning, but the greater light had gone out. Their great master, as they called him, was on his knees, his body stretched forward, his head buried in his hands upon the pillow. With silent awe they stood apart and watched him, lest they should invade the privacy of prayer. But he did not stir; there was not even the motion of breathing, but a suspicious rigidity of inaction. Then one of these black men, Matthew, softly came near and gently laid his hands upon his cheeks. It was enough: the chill of death was there. The great father of Africa's dark children was dead, and they were orphans.

The most refined and cultured Englishmen would have been perplexed as to what course to take. They were surrounded by superstitious and unsympathetic savages, to whom the unburied remains of the dead man would be an object of dread. His native land was six thousand miles away, and even the coast was distant fifteen hundred. A grave responsibility rested upon these simple-minded sons of the Dark Continent,—a burden, to which few of the wisest and ablest would have been equal. Those remains, with his valuable journals, instruments, and personal effects, must be carried to Zanzibar. But the body must first be preserved from decay, and they had no skill nor facilities for embalming; and, if preserved, there were no means of transportation—no roads or carts; no beasts of burden available—the body must be borne on the shoulders of human beings; and, as no strangers could be trusted, they must themselves undertake the journey and the sacred charge. These humble children of the forest were grandly equal to the occasion, and they resolved among themselves to carry that body to the sea-shore, and not give it into any other hands until they could surrender it to his countrymen. And, to insure safety to the remains and security to the bearers, it must be done with secrecy. They would gladly have kept secret even their master's death, but the fact could not be concealed. God, however, disposed Chitambo and his subjects to permit these servants of the great missionary to prepare his emaciated body for its last journey, in a hut built for the purpose on the outskirts of the village.

Now watch these black men, as they rudely embalm the body of him who had been to them a saviour. They tenderly open the chest and take out the heart and viscera: these, with a poetic and pathetic sense of fitness, they reserve for his beloved Africa. The heart that for thirty-three years had beat for her welfare must be buried in her own bosom. And so one of the Nassik boys, Jacob Wainwright, read the simple service of burial, and under the moula-tree at Ilala that heart was deposited; and the tree, carved with a simple inscription, became his monument. Then the body was prepared for its long journey; the cavity was filled with salt, brandy poured into the mouth, and the corpse laid out in the sun for fourteen days to be dried, and so reduced to the condition of a mummy. Then it was thrust into a hollow cylinder of bark, over this was sewn a covering of canvas, the whole package securely lashed to a pole, and so it was made ready to be borne between two men upon their shoulders.

As yet the enterprise was scarcely begun—and the worst of their task was yet before them. The sea was far away, and their path lay through a territory where nearly every fifty miles would bring them to a new tribe, to face new difficulties. Nevertheless, Susi and Chuma took up their precious burden, and, looking to Livingstone's God for help, began the most remarkable funeral march on record. They followed the track their master had marked with his footsteps when he penetrated to Lake Bangweolo—passing to the south of Lake Liembe, which is a continuation of Tanganyika, then crossing to Unyanyembe. Wherever it was found out that they were bearing a dead body, shelter was hard to get or even food; and at Kasekera, they could get nothing they asked, except on condition that they would bury the remains they were carrying. And now their love and generalship were put to a new and severe test. But again they were equal to the emergency. They made up another package like the precious burden, only that it contained branches instead of human bones—and this with mock solemnity they bore on their shoulders to a safe distance and scattered the contents far and wide in the brushwood, and came back without the bundle. Meanwhile others of their party had repacked the remains, doubling them up into the semblance of a bale of cotton cloth, and so once more they managed to get what they needed and get on with their charge.

The true story of that nine months' march has never yet been written, and it never will be, for the full data cannot be supplied. But here is material waiting for some coming English Homer or Milton to crystallize into one of the world's noblest epics; and it deserves the master-hand of a great poet artist to do it justice.

See these black men, whom your scientific philosophers would place at one remove from the gorilla, run all manner of risks, by day and night, for forty weeks; now going round by a circuitous route to insure safe passage; now compelled to resort to stratagem to get their precious burden through the country; sometimes forced to fight their foes in order to carry out their holy mission. Follow them as they ford the rivers and traverse trackless deserts, daring perils from wild beasts and relentless wild men; exposing themselves to the fatal fever, and burying several of their little band on the way; yet, on they went, patient and persevering, never fainting or halting, until love and gratitude had done all that could be done, and they laid down at the feet of the British Consul, on the 12th of March, 1874, all that was left on earth of Scotland's great hero, save that buried heart.

When, a little more than a month later, the coffin of Livingstone was landed in England, April 15, it was felt that no less a shrine than Britain's greatest burial-place could fitly hold such precious dust. . But so improbable and incredible did it seem that a few rude Africans could actually have done this splendid deed, at such cost of time and risk, that, not until the fractured bones of the arm, which the lion crushed at Mabotsa thirty years before, identified the body, was it certain that these were Livingstone's remains. And then, on the 18th of April, 1874, such a funeral cortege entered the great Abbey of Britain's illustrious dead as few warriors or heroes or princes ever drew to that mausoleum. And those faithful body-servants, who had religiously brought home every relic of the person or property of the great missionary explorer, were accorded places of honor. And well they might be. No triumphal procession of earth's mightiest conqueror ever equalled for sublimity that lonely journey through Africa's forests. An example of tenderness, gratitude, devotion, heroism, equal to this, the world has never seen. The exquisite inventiveness of a love that on the feet of Jesus lavished tears as water, and made tresses of hair a towel, and broke the alabaster flask for His anointing; the feminine tenderness that lifted His mangled body from the cross and wrapped it in new linen, with costly spices, and laid it in a virgin tomb— even this has at length been surpassed by the ingenious devotion of the cursed sons of Canaan. The grandeur and pathos of that burial scene amid the stately columns and arches of England's famous Abbey loses in lustre when contrasted with that simpler scene near Ilala, when, in God's greater cathedral of Nature, whose columns and arches are the trees, whose surpliced choir are the singing birds, whose organ is the moaning wind,—the grassy carpet was lifted and dark hands laid Livingstone's heart to rest! And in the great cortege that moved up the nave of Westminster, no truer nobleman was found than that black man, Susi, who in illness had nursed the Blantyre hero, had laid his heart in Africa's bosom, and whose hand was now upon his pall. Let those who doubt and deride Christian missions to the degraded children of Ham, who tell us that it is not worth while to sacrifice precious lives for the sake of these doubly lost millions of the Dark Continent,—let such tell us whether it is not worth while, at any cost, to seek out and save men of whom such Christian heroism is possible!

III.

Transformed Communities.
The Pitcairn Islanders.

BY HIS book alone, God has wrought wonders of transformation.

We have been wont to think the presence of personal agency an essential condition of the work of conversion; and perhaps, in view of the emphasis laid by God Himself upon the living voice and the believer's witness, we are not likely to give any undue importance to personal contact with souls. But we must not forget that God's choice of human channels for His grace does not leave Him absolutely dependent upon them. In more instances than one, He has set His peculiar seal and sanction upon His own inspired word as the means of softening hard hearts and changing foes to friends.

<table>
<tr><td>SCRIPTURE TESTIMONY

Salvation transforms

2 CORINTHIANS 5:16-17 · GALATIANS 6:15</td></tr>
</table>

The story of the Pitcairn exiles is an illustration of the power of the Bible alone, as the seed of God, to raise up in the most sterile soil and amid most hopeless conditions a harvest for the kingdom. For He has two sorts of seed—one is the word of God; the other the children of the kingdom. (Mark iv. 14; Matt. xiii. 38.)

In the mind and heart of the mutineer, John Adams, God's way may possibly have been prepared by early parental training of which we have no record; but, so far as we know, no human hand wielded the subtle moulding influence that turned that abandoned sailor to God. In this case the solitary cause which wrought such miraculous effects on Pitcairn Island was the written word of God. And other facts are fast coming to the surface and demanding thankful recognition, which prove that, quite apart from the voice and presence of the living and witnessing believer, the Bible is doing its own peculiar work. Where the feet of no other missionary have yet left their tracks, this living word, which liveth and abideth forever, has sometimes proved the pioneer missionary and evangelist.

Pitcairn Island lies solitary in Pacific waters, and is about seven miles in circuit. Carteret discovered it over a century and a quarter since, and named it after one of his officers who caught the first glimpse of it. There for more than sixty years the mutineers of the *Bounty* and their descendants found a habitation. In 1790, nine of these mutineers landed there, with six men and twice as many women from Tahiti. At that time the island was found uninhabited, though relics of previous occupancy were afterwards discovered.

Among these settlers of a century past, quarrels violent and bloody broke out, and the flames of passion, fed by strong drink, burned so hotly that when the dawn of the new century came, it looked down on desolation: all the Tahitian men had perished, and all but one of the Englishmen. John Adams was, of the mutineers, the sole survivor. He had rescued from the wreck a Bible and a prayer-book. Destitute of all other reading, and left without former companions, he turned to these two books for occupation, comfort and counsel. As he read the word of God, he began to be conscious that he was looking in a magic mirror—he saw himself in his hideousness, and remorse for past sins and crimes began to sting his conscience as with a whip of scorpions. And from contrition he was led to conversion—from fear to faith—and all this without any man to guide him. He became not only a true believer in Christ, but a witness to His grace and a missionary. With the aid of these two books, he undertook to teach those grossly ignorant women of Tahiti, and the children that were left of this mixed parentage. Mark the result! Upon this lonely island grew up a Christian community so remarkable that all travellers visiting those shores have borne common witness to the gentleness of character and virtuous simplicity of conduct which were there displayed.

This story of the Pitcairn Islanders thus stands quite unique in the history of missions. Here was a bastard community—a progeny whose parentage was mutiny and lust, from the beginning doubly accursed. Of all the common institutions of the gospel, which we significantly call "means of grace," there was complete destitution— no clergymen or Christian laymen, no churches or Sunday-schools, no restraints of law or religion. One stray copy of the blessed book of God, and of that Book of Common Prayer, which is so largely permeated with that word of God,—and even these in the hands of a reckless, godless mutineer,—first became means of blessing and salvation to him, and then to that degraded class by whom he was surrounded.

The Colonists of Sierra Leone.

<table>
<tr><td>

SCRIPTURE TESTIMONY

Christians are generous and hospitable

ACTS 16:14-15 · ROMANS 12:13 · I
TIMOTHY 3:2 · HEBREWS 13:2

</td></tr>
</table>

When William A. B. Johnson went to this Mountain of Lions, in 1816, he found the refuse of slave ships there gathered. If the horrors of that "middle passage," in which four hundred wretches were crammed into a hold, twelve yards long, seven wide, and three and a half high, had crushed their minds and moral natures into as narrow a compass as their bodies, they could have not been more hopeless subjects for labour. They were manumitted slaves, but in all but name were still in most abject bondage. These liberated captives represented tribes so numerous that samples of one hundred and fifty dialects might have been found at Queen's Yard in Sierra Leone. Johnson found himself at Hogbrook, with fifteen hundred half-starved, diseased, filthy Africans, dying at the rate of two hundred a month, and already dead to all response even to human kindness. He held a Sunday service with but nine attendants, and these nearly nude. The fact is that, like the victims of Spanish treachery in Central America, they had so suffered at white men's hands, that even the gospel was unwelcome at white men's lips, and the idea of Heaven, if white men were to be there, was almost as repulsive as hell would be without them.

This simple-minded German fed them daily with their allowance of rice, and patiently showed them loving sympathy, and so won their confidence for himself. Then they thronged his cottage to hear the gospel until he had to resort to the open air as a meeting-place. His school was likewise full to overflowing, and those pupils who had never seen a book or known a letter, in less than a year were reading the New Testament. With unceasing labour, and, better still, unceasing prayer, fighting the deadly climate and the enfeebling fever, seeing his fellowhelpers falling beside him till the graveyard at Kissy was full of bodies, he persevered, telling the simple gospel story. And when, in 1819, his wife's illness drove him to England, he left at Regents Town a model state, like Eliot's Nonantum and Duncan's Metlakahtla. The natives had laid out a settlement, properly organized, with decent homes, and all the signs of a Christian community. They had built a church, which held 1,300 and overflowed with habitual attendants at three services each Lord's day. He had 263 communicants, a daily service attended by from 500 to 900, and hundreds of cases of as deep conviction of sin and as genuine conversion to God as any field ever produced. At the very time when his courageous faith almost gave way before the gigantic obstacles he had to surmount, and he had sought the retirement of a forest to indulge in sorrowful thought, he heard one of these poor slaves praying for the liberty of a son of God, and he knew that the hour of victory was at hand. Even the secular authorities were constrained, in their report to the British Government, to confess, like Pharaoh's magicians, "This is the finger of God." As they contrasted the former state of the colony, "grovelling and malignant superstitions, their greegrees, their red water, their witchcraft, their devil houses," with the existing sincere Christian worship, they wrote, "The hand of Heaven is in this!" It is "a miracle of good which the immediate interposition of the Almighty alone could have wrought." And they added, "What greater blessing could man or nation desire or enjoy than to have been made the instruments of conferring such sublime benefits on the most abject of the human race."

Johnson was so impressed with the simple childlikeness of their faith and the obvious groaning of the Spirit in their prayers, that his journals are full of these records. Their devotion to him was pathetic and romantic. Hundreds of them went on foot with him to Freetown, five miles off, and when the sea prevented their going with him further, they said, in their broken English: "Massa, suppose no water live here—we go all the way with you—till feet no more." And when he came back, and his arrival was announced in the church at night, some could not wait to go out the door, but leaped out through the window. Some went that night to Freetown to meet him, while others could not sleep, but sang the night away.

Again, in 1823,-he was compelled to seek rest in England. And now over a thousand scholars were in his school, seven hundred of whom could read. He had four hundred and fifty communicants, and they had their own missionary society. And when it pleased God that seven years of work should close with his burial at sea, Sara Bickersteth,—the first of her nation to taste the grace of God, his own child in the faith,—watched by his berth, read to him the twenty-third Psalm and prayed beside him, heard his dying words and closed his dying eyes. And so, dying, like Mills and Hunt, at thirty-five, this man in seven years, and amid a community as hopelessly ignorant and unimpressible as ever a missionary confronted, actually laid the basis of a Christian state, where, thirty years after his death, Bishop Vidal confirmed three thousand candidates, and where, in later years, parishes with native pastors, a college and a vigorous life of its own, pushed missions into the interior and along the Niger.

Tyndall has called attention to the wonders of crystallization. "Looking into this solution of common sulphate of soda, mentally, we see the molecules, like disciplined squadrons under a governing eye, arranging themselves into battalions, gathering round distinct centres and forming themselves into solid masses which, after a time, assume the visible shape of this crystal." But there is something far transcending this in wonders, when, out of a community such as Johnson found at Sierra Leone, or Hunt at Fiji Islands, a well-ordered Christian state is organized. A secret, unseen, mysterious power, which none can define or describe, is at work. Around the name of Jesus the disorderly and confused elements of a moral chaos arrange themselves in symmetry and beauty, and society becomes crystalline and reflects the glory of God.

The New Zealand Converts.

The New Zealanders were alike objects of fear and hate, when the devoted Marsden pleaded their cause with the Church Missionary Society and laid the basis of one of the most successful missions of the modern era. They were perpetually at war, and with brutal murders revenged the treachery and violence of white men who touched at their shores. But while Samuel Marsden was yet at New South Wales, he met many from these islands who visited Paramatta, and he detected in them something which promised a nobler life. When the mission was first projected, no clergyman could be found ready for an enterprise so heroic; and two skilled mechanics undertook to win a way for the gospel by the arts of civilization. At the end of thirty years' toil, Marsden declared that civilization is not necessary before Christianity, but will be found to follow Christianity more easily than Christianity to follow civilization; and, he added, that with all its cannibalism and idolatry, New Zealand would yet set an example of Christianity to some nations then before her in point of civilization.

Certain outrages by a sea captain at Whangaroa Harbour had provoked horrible retaliation on the part of the natives, and this led to subsequent acts of vengeance on the part of a whaling vessel. The excitement ensuing postponed missionary effort; but at length, the two mechanics ventured to New Zealand and were well received. Marsden now yearned to follow in person, but could not find a ship captain to take him at a less cost than six hundred pounds for the risk; so he bought a brig and set sail, landing on those shores unarmed, and with but one companion.

As he lay awake that first night, excited by the awful environment of paganism and cannibalism, he saw above him those brilliant constellations, the Southern Cross and the Southern Crown, which served to remind him of One who bore the cross for all men and who would yet wear the crown of universal empire. And on the Christmas-day which soon followed he preached the first sermon in New Zealand, using a native interpreter. His text was, "Behold I bring you glad tidings of great joy;" and around him were gathered a motley group of men and women and children and chiefs. For years no converts crowned the work, though the natives seemed to desire the Pakehas, or Englishmen, to settle among them; and ventured to assure Marsden that they would not be killed and eaten, as they were such salt eaters that their flesh was less savoury than that of the Maoris—a statement which did not diminish the quantity of salt eaten by the English. At length the spirit of religious inquiry was awakened, and truth found such root and room to grow that even chiefs began to be baptized. And when Marsden made his sixth visit, the east and west shores of the bay where he landed presented one of those strange and eloquent contrasts often seen where the gospel has won a partial victory. On one side, naked savages, their hands red with blood, yelling like demons, and the moans of the wounded and dying: on the other side, a peaceful community, decently clad, assembled for worship, and using devoutly the Church service printed in their own tongue. Here at one glance were the anticipations of heaven and hell—the misery and wretchedness of paganism confronting Christianity with its trees of righteousness and plants of godliness. When, at seventy-two, the patriarchal missionary paid his last visit, his coming was the signal for ecstatic delight. In his arm-chair before the mission house, he received the thousands who from great distances thronged to do him honour; and on re-embarking they bore him on their shoulders six miles to the shore. Since then, when, on the unconscious verge of another sea on whose unknown waters he was so soon to set sail, the apostle of New Zealand lifted his hands in a farewell benediction— since then, fifteen thousand native Christians bear witness that the introduction of Christianity into the cannibal islands on Christmas-day, 1814, was not in vain. Three years after Marsden's death Bishop Selwyn reported a whole nation of pagans converted to the faith.

The Ferocious Cannibals of Fiji.

We have before referred to the atrocious cannibals of Fiji, the slaves of a religion of organized cruelty, that fattens on blood, crushes conscience, and kills sensibility as a red-hot iron burns out the very eye-ball. For a hardened Fijian to be brought to tenderness of heart and sensitiveness of conscience is as much a miracle as to replace a maimed limb or restore a withered arm. Hunt saw two conversions wrought at Viwa. One from paganism as an idolatrous system, to the Christian faith; that was wonderful, like opening a blind eye or straightening a crooked form. But the other was more marvellous: it was a conversion from the love and guilt and power of sin to God and love of godliness. It was comparatively easy to secure a profession of Christianity; but this was like a resurrection from the dead.

When this Wesleyan farmer saw in these pagan monsters penitence for sin as sin, deep conviction of guilt and agonies of godly sorrow; when for days and nights together they were racked with wildest grief until from sheer exhaustion they fainted, and recovered only to swoon again after another agony of prayer, he said, this is the work of God.

John Hunt goes on his circuits of a hundred miles a month, telling Christ's story, forming schools to train converts for teachers, "turning care into prayer,"working hard on his Fiji New Testament. Who can tell what that lonely servant of God had to overcome in facing hostile, cruel chiefs without force or threat, mastering a difficult tongue without grammar or lexicon, teaching such savages when their pagan tongue supplied no fit terms to convey divine thoughts!

God had much people even there, and when His fit and full time came He knew how to lead them out. The priests predicted an awful drought as the judgment of the gods on the sin of those who confessed Jesus; but the failure of the prophecy shook popular faith in the pagan idols. The Queen of Viwa, and the "Napoleon" of Fiji, Verani, became Christians,— and Verani a preacher and winner of thousands of souls.

This lesson of God's power has been taught us, repeatedly, in the new chapters of the Acts. The story of *John Hunt in the Fiji Group* is the all-convincing example and illustration. When he went there in 1838, the moral aspect of those hundred islands was as hideous as their material aspect was lovely. If nature had lavished her bounties and beauties so that every prospect was pleasing, how vile and repulsive was man. Treachery and ferocity, raging passion and devilish cruelty, were branded on the very faces of the Fijians. One who had shuddered at the sight has sought to paint the awful portrait: "The forehead filled with wrinkles; the large nostrils distended and fairly smoking; the staring eyeballs red, and glearning with terrible flashings; the mouth distended into murderous and disdainful grin; the whole body quivering with excitement; every muscle strained, and the clenched fist eager to bathe itself in the blood of him who has roused this demon of fury."

If one could dip his pen in the molten brimstone of hell's fiery lake, he could still write no just account of the condition of the Fijians fifty years ago. Two awful forms of crime stood like gates of hell to let in demons and shut out gospel heralds. Of all children born at least two-thirds were killed at birth, and to make sure of their death there was a *system* of organized destruction, and every village had its authorized executioner, to repeat the tragedy of Bethlehem's babes. Of course, infanticide and parricide go together; and so if the parents did not spare their offspring, neither did the offspring spare the parents, but despatched them when old or feeble.

Cannibalism,—the most atrocious form of pagan ferocity, that breaks the whole decalogue at once, the climax of theft, sensuality and murder,—was not only a custom, but a sacred religious rite, and the children that were allowed to live, were trained to dishonour and devour the human form divine. Mothers gave their babes a taste of the horrible feast, as a beast her cubs, to excite a relish for the horrid meal; and not only dead bodies, but living captives, were given over to young children as playthings on which to practise for sport the art of mutilation and dissection. It became a pride to Fijian chiefs to boast of the number of human bodies they had eaten; and Ra Undreundu's pile of stones, in which each stone stood for one such victim, contained nine hundred! The Fijian word for *corpse*, "vakalu," suggests also the idea of a meal, as the Greek word for rejoicing suggests a banquet ($\chi \alpha \rho \alpha$). All the life of these people, civil and religious, was inwrought with the destroying and devouring of helpless victims. A building of a hut, a launching of a canoe, a burying of the dead, and events of far less moment, were the signals for a banquet on human flesh. And if the plump form of a favourite wife, or the tender flesh of a little child promised an unusual delicacy, without compunction or hesitation the husband and father called his friends to a feast on the dainty morsel!

It was among such a people that the ploughboy of Lincolnshire landed in 1838. He soon found that the half of the inhuman cruelty and devilish butchery of this people had never been told him; and yet he went to Somosomo, whose people were the worst of all. When the youngest son of the King Tuithakau was lost at sea, sixteen women were strangled and then burned in front of the missionhouse, notwithstanding Mr. Hunt's entreaties that they should be spared; and when, some months after, eleven men were dragged by ropes to be roasted in the ovens, these demons, who were preparing the feast, threatened to burn down the missionary's house, because his wife closed and blinded the windows to shut out the sickening sight and smell of burning bodies!

Not one Christian among a hundred would have counselled Hunt to attempt work among such incarnate monsters, when the king himself forbade his subjects under pain of death to "lotu" or profess the new faith, and when even the readiness to confess Christ seemed to be due to mere greed of gain in cutlery and firearms. Captain Wilkes of the American navy, in 1840, witnessed the trials of their seemingly hopeless work, and besought them at least to let him carry them to a more hopeful field; but John Hunt had heard a divine voice—"Fear not, for I have much people in these islands"—and he stayed. Three years at Somosomo sufficed so to change the horrid life about him that at least a bloodless war was waged, a large canoe launched and a great feast held for weeks without one human sacrifice; and this last with no direct interference of the missionary.

The last six years of John Hunt's short career of ten, were spent at Viwa, near Mbau, the head centre of Fiji power. King Thakombau, "the butcher of his people," was a fierce foe, and his wars and hostility to the missionary seemed to make all success hopeless—yet here again the patience of God's saints was rewarded. Even among this city of demons, God had much people.

THE LAND OF THE BRAHMAN.

Even India, the Malakoff of heathenism, is not deficient in signs of divine power in furnishing her quota of converts and martyrs. The greater part of a century has passed since the directors of the British East India Company put on record their conviction that "the sending of Christian missionaries into our Eastern possessions is the maddest, most expensive, most unwarranted project that was ever proposed by a lunatic enthusiast." No arraignment of the entire principle and policy of modern missions to the Hindus could have been more sarcastically severe. Observe the terms, which indirectly accuse those who favoured and furthered such a project, as not only lacking good sense, adequate justification, or business economy, but as enthusiasts, madmen and lunatics! But, what is worse—at that time, now more than eighty-five years ago,—this outrageous assault upon obedience to our Lord's command was not repudiated by the great body even of English Christians, and found positive support even among members of parliament and ecclesiastical dignitaries. A few disciples, full of faith and prayer, dared, notwithstanding all this violent opposition, to send messengers and give money for this insane purpose.

And now it is not too much to say that popular sentiment has undergone such a complete revolution that even the secular newspaper has become the advocate and vindicator of missions to India. The testimony of such men as Sir Bartle Frere, Sir William Muir, Sir Monier Monier Williams, Sir Herbert Edwardes, Max Muller, Sir Richard Temple, Sir Donald McLeod, Sir William Hill, Lord John Lawrence, the Earl of Northbrook, Hon. W. E. Baxter, and a host of others, who have had ample time and large facility for forming an intelligent judgment, have left on record words so weighty that, in comparison, all sneers or charges against missions in India become light and frivolous, if not 'contemptible and dishonest. Such men as these, who could be misled neither by ignorance nor motives of policy, have borne singularly unanimous witness to the number and worth of native converts; and to something even more important—the fact, that Christianity is forming a new nation in the land of the Brahman; that while every other faith is decaying, this divine gospel is alone beginning to run its course; that the changes taking place under the benign influence of Christianity are, for extent and rapidity of effect, far more extraordinary than anything witnessed in modern Europe by us or our fathers. Shortly since, Sir Rivers Thompson, Lieutenant-Governor of Bengal, testified that "Christian missionaries have done more real and lasting good than all other agencies combined." And to all this testimony there still remains to be added, before an intelligent verdict can be made up, the testimony of the native Hindus themselves—not Ganga Dhar, Abdul Messeh, Tulsi Paul, Narayan Sheshadri, Keshub Chunder Sen and others like them who have been converts or open advocates of Christianity, but the native rajahs and princes; from the Rajah of Tanjore, who built a monument to Schwartz, down to the first Prince of Travancore, who in 1874, publicly said:

"Marvellous has been the effect of Christianity in the moral moulding and leavening of Europe. I am *not* a Christian; I do not accept the cardinal tenets of Christianity as they concern man in the next world; but I accept Christian ethics in their entirety. I have the highest admiration for them."

Four years before this, a learned Brahman had candidly said: "Where did the English-speaking people get all their intelligence, and energy, and cleverness and power? It is their Bible that gives it to them. And now they bring it to us and say: ' This is what raised us. Take it and raise yourselves!' They do not force it upon us, as the Mohammedans did their Koran, but they bring it in love, and translate it into our languages and lay it before us, and say, ' Look at it, read it, examine it, and see if it is not good.' Of one thing I am convinced,—do what we will, oppose as we may, *it is the Christian's Bible that will, sooner or later, work the regeneration of this land.*"

India has presented perhaps the most formidable barriers ever encountered in any of our mission fields. The subtlety and acumen of the Brahmanic priesthood, and their power over the superstitious and ignorant common folk, the rigid restraints of caste—itself a wall of ice, mountain high against the approach of the gospel, and a system of frigid immobility which, like a vast polar zone of frost, locks in eternal winter the whole society it girdles—the long sway of that religious faith which is one of the purest and best of Oriental religions, notwithstanding its practical corruptions—these are some of the hindrances Christian missions have had to meet. And yet notwithstanding all, the gospel is slowly razing these high walls, undermining these strongholds, and, like the resistless summer sun, melting these ice castles.

The seraphic Henry Martyn, eighty years ago was so horror-struck at the gross idolatries and nameless atrocities connected with the pagodas and pageants of Juggemath, and the blazing fires of the suttee, that his exquisite sensibilities shrank back in revolt at the sight, and he said, "I shivered as if standing, as it were, in the neighbourhood of hell. The fiends of darkness seem to sit in sullen repose in this land!" Now ruined pagodas have become Christian temples, and where demons were once worshipped, prayer ascends to Him who cast out demons with His word.

Dr. John Wilson, of Bombay, who spent nearly a half century in India, twenty years ago, "tersely catalogued the bloodless triumphs that had been won" on that field, where Carey led the way a century ago. That catalogue we venture to reproduce entire from the masterly work of his eminent biographer.*

---

* "Life of John Wilson," by George Smith, LL.D., p. 35a.

HORRORS AND INIQUITIES OF INDIA REMOVED BY GOVERNMENT.

I. MURDER OF PARENTS.
  (a) By Suttee.
  (b) By exposure on the banks of rivers.
  (c) By burial alive. Case in Joudhpore territory, 1860.

II. MURDER OF CHILDREN.
  (a) By dedication to the Ganges, there to be devoured by crocodiles.
  (b) By Rajpoot infanticide, West of India, Punjab, East of India.

III. HUMAN SACRIFICES.
  (a) Temple sacrifices.
  (b) By wild tribes—Meriahs of the Khonds.

IV. SUICIDE.
  (a) Crushing by idol cars.
  (b) Devotees drowning themselves in rivers.
  (c) Devotees casting themselves from precipices.
  (d) Leaping into wells—widows.
  (e) By Trága.

V. VOLUNTARY TORMENT.
  (a) By hook-swinging.
  (b) By thigh-piercing.
  (c) By tongue-extraction.
  (d) By falling on knives.
  (e) By austerities.

VI. INVOLUNTARY TORMENT.
  (a) Barbarous executions.
  (b) Mutilation of criminals.
  (c) Extraction of evidence by torment
  (d) Bloody and injurious ordeals.
  (e) Cutting off the noses of women.

VII. SLAVERY.
  (a) Hereditary predial slavery.
  (b) Domestic slavery.
  (c) Importation of slaves from Africa.

VIII. EXTORTIONS.
  (a) By Dharaná.
  (b) By Trága.

IX. RELIGIOUS INTOLERANCE.
  (a) Prevention of Propagation of Christianity.
  (b) Calling upon Christian soldiers to fire salutes at heathen festivals, etc.
  (c) Saluting gods on official papers.
  (d) Managing affairs of idol temples.

X. SUPPORT OF CASTE BY LAW.
  (a) Exclusion of low castes from offices.
  (b) Exemption of high castes from appearing to give evidence.
  (c) Disparagement of low caste.

There are reasons to believe that thousands even in India believe, but, like the Pharisees of old, do not confess Christ lest they be put out of the synagogue. Observers who have had rare opportunities to note the facts tell us that secret believers are rapidly multiplying; and that for every avowed convert there are hundreds who, for fear of kin and caste, of ostracism and actual starvation, dare not make such avowal, but are ready when the break shall come. So said "The Indian Witness" in 1889.

THE SLAVES OF JAMAICA.

Who can read the story of Jamaica, and doubt the power of the gospel over even the most degraded negro slaves. When the island was formally ceded to Great Britain by the treaty of Madrid in 1670, the place of the native Indians was taken by Africans, imported by Spaniards, and during the eighteenth century over half a million were brought over to suffer as the heirs of Canaan's curse. The history of these slaves, their poverty, misery, degradation, wretchedness, is among the blackest annals of the race; and when the facts became known in Great Britain, the popular heart of English freemen demanded their liberation. On August 1, 1834, the emancipation began to take effect in the freedom of the children of the slave families; but the midnight of July 31, 1838, was to usher in the complete liberation of the whole slave community; and on that night, led on by William Knibb and James Philippo, fourteen thousand adult slaves and five thousand children joined in prayer to God as they waited and watched for the hour of twelve, midnight, which was to terminate the life of slavery in Jamaica; and as Rev. J. J. Fuller says, who was himself a child of slavery and there present, every coloured man on the Island was on his knees that night.

A mahogany coffin had been made, polished and fitted by the carpenters and cabinet-makers of this slave population, and, as became the great occasion, a grave was dug. Into that coffin they crowded all the various relics and remnants of their previous bondage and sorrow. The whips, the torture-irons, the branding-irons, the coarse frocks, and shirts, and great hat, fragments of the treadmill, the handcuffs—whatever was the sign and badge of seventy-eight years of thraldom—they placed in the coffin and screwed down the lid. As the bell began to toll for midnight, the voice of Knibb was heard, "The monster is dying—is dying"—until, when the last stroke sounded from the belfry, Mr. Knibb cried—"The monster is dead! Let us bury him out of sight forever!" and the coffin was lowered into its grave; and then the whole of that throng of thousands celebrated their redemption from thraldom by singing the doxology! This was the way these black slaves took vengeance on their former masters—not by deeds of violence, lust, rapine, murder; but by burying the remnants of their long bondage and the remembrance of their great wrongs, in the grave of oblivion. Where did those debased Africans learn such magnanimous love, except of Him whose greatest miracle was His dying prayer, "Father, forgive them, for they know not what they do!"

This is not the end of this story. To-day there is not on the island among all the different bodies one church dependent on outside help: they all support themselves, and a large portion of them have for pastors the sons of former slaves. They have also their own independent missionary society, as well as schools, high schools, grammar schools, etc.

On the island to-day there are more than two hundred and seventy Baptist churches alone, seventy of which are ministered to by young men trained in the colleges of Jamaica, children of former slaves; and the Presbyterians, Wesleyans and Episcopalians have their congregations beside. Here, within a little more than a half century, the gospel has not only broken slave bonds, but has developed former slaves into a Christian community of freemen of the Lord, with Christian institutions. Folly and vice, idolatry and witchcraft, ignorance and superstition, were the thick growths that covered the soil half a century since, where now are the trees of righteousness, selfsustaining and self-propagating churches of coloured people, ministered to in many cases by sons of those who were formerly enthralled in slavery. These preachers, developed from a former slave population, side by side with their white brethren maintain the gospel with equal success. To see the difference which the gospel can make, one needs only to contrast Jamaica with Hayti.

OLD CALABAR.

SCRIPTURE TESTIMONY
Salvation transforms
2 CORINTHIANS 5:16-17 · GALATIANS 6:15

When Rev. J. J. Fuller, to whom already reference has been made, left his native island of Jamaica to follow his father in a mission on the west coast of Africa, he landed in the Gulf of Guinea and the Bight of Biafra. This was in 1845. He found neither Bible nor book, not even written language; none of the people had ever heard the name which brings salvation. There was a community of naked, degraded, depraved, ignorant savages, and human sacrifices were the natural apex to a pyramid of cruelties, which were not only common, but sanctioned and supported by superstitions which claimed the rank of religion. These horrid and revolting customs were simply built into the whole structure of society, like pillars into the temple they uphold. Cruelty was a part of the education of the people, and a very efficient school it was in vice and crime!

The people had faith in a future life, but even that faith only stimulated cruelty; for it led to the cultivation of customs supposed to be a protection alike to the dead and the living. If anybody died, somebody else was responsible; accusation followed, and trial for witchcraft by tests which were equally fatal for the innocent and the guilty. Poison was the ordeal that followed accusation. The living infant was buried with the dead mother; and if the mother had borne twins, she was beaten to death and the babes were put out of the way; and so a curse was supposed to be lifted from the land. A king's death meant a wholesale burial alive of men and women who were put into the royal grave. Mr. Fuller, during forty-five years of personal ministry, witnessed the great transformation. A people without God or hope shortly began to feel after God, and a new faith began to dawn over their horizon. Their language was put in written form. Alfred Saker and the Presbyterian missionaries translated the whole Bible for them; and now they have churches, schools and a native ministry. The people are learning to read and write, and coming up to the higher plane of enlightenment. Belief in witchcraft is dead; the ordeal of the Calabar bean, the massacre of slaves, and other like absurd and cruel customs of centuries, have disappeared.

Take one contrast: In 1845, one of the kings of old Calabar died. Into his grave, according to long-established custom, many living people were put to die beside the dead. To-day a grandson of that buried chief is an elder in a Presbyterian church; and every morning, with the open Bible in his hand, he leads his household in family worship.

Mr. Fuller tells of his going into the Cameroons, and how in the morning, looking across the river he saw many canoes with people dressed up in all their war dresses, and their spears and swords were brandished in the sun. They had their war caps upon their heads. He took his glass and looked, and found that the decoration on the bows of all those

SCRIPTURE TESTIMONY

Salvation transforms

2 CORINTHIANS 5:16-17 · GALATIANS 6:15

canoes was nothing else but human heads. He went up to the chief and said to him, "What do you do such cruel deeds for?" He looked very much astonished that any one should ask him such a question, and said, "What deeds?" Pointing across the river, Mr. Fuller said, "Look, yonder. What about that row of human heads on your canoe? Why do you do such cruel things? They are not right." The chief replied: "You people come into this country and live here and you claim to be a good people, and that is true enough; but do you tell me that when I die my sons are going to put me into an empty grave alone and nobody with me?" When Mr. Fuller replied "Yes," he looked at him and said, "You are a fool." Then all his sons came up directly and said, . "What is the matter, father?" And he repeated what he had said to Mr. Fuller: "This man who has come to live in this country says that when I die you boys will put me into an empty grave, alone, with no one with me," and they looked at Mr. Fuller and grinned their savage grin, and then turned away and said,"Father, do not believe him. He is a fool, and he is a foreigner. What does he know? Let him alone." And yet mark it! That same chief lived on until the old custom of burying living people with the dead was completely abolished. In his town, about fifty yards from his own house, stood a little chapel, and the preacher in that chapel was none other than one of his sons, who was preaching the gospel of the Lord Jesus Christ!

If God, in such a short time, can produce such a marvellous change, surely prayers for missions, and for the extension of Christ's kingdom in the world, have abundant proof that they are being answered of God. Think of the present condition of the people, and then of what was their former state, when this missionary first met them in their degradation as naked savages. A letter was recently received from the Church in Cameroons, reporting that they had built a chapel for themselves that will seat one thousand people, and that the membership of that one church had grown to seven hundred; also that they had collected for themselves among their own people one thousand pounds, and had established fifteen different stations in different parts of the country within a year or two, in order to spread the gospel among their own tribe. Africa, with all her degradation and ignorance, desires to have the gospel, and if it is given to this degraded people they, of themselves, in their own country, will spread that gospel. The time will come, and Mr. Fuller believes that it is not far off, when the Dark Continent will emerge from her degradation and darkness. Fifty years ago, up the Congo River, no one had ever heard the gospel, and it was looked upon as a hard soil to work; but to-day the Scripture is being translated into their own tongue, their young men are being taught to read the Bible, Christian churches are being formed, and some of the cruelties that the missionaries met, when they landed first in the

Congo, are gradually being removed; so that the time has already come when a great change is visible among the people.

Mr. Fuller further narrates how he stood at his door and saw one of the chiefs coming toward him. He was a great man, a man of position in his country, but the only covering that he

> **SCRIPTURE TESTIMONY**
>
> *There is salvation in no other name*
>
> ACTS 4:12

had on, was the fibres of the plantain tree combed out and on his head a great cap with parrots' feathers. He had a great bullock horn hung across his breast, and he walked as stately as a monarch. Several of the princes were following him, all of them dressed in the same way. Mr. Fuller called to this man as he passed the door, using his name, "Mikani," but he only looked round, and would not answer. He was called again, but would not answer; and yet a third time, when one of his followers turned and said to Mr. Fuller, "What do you want?" "I only want to speak to him and ask him a question," was the reply. The man said: "He will not answer you. He has just been taking the sacred oath, and has sworn that for nine days he will not speak to anybody except by signs. At the end of the nine days he will go back to the place where he came from, and after that he will converse as of old." It seemed of no use to trouble him any more, but after the nine days were over Mr. Fuller went to his house. He was sitting at the door, and this bullock's horn that he had worn across his breast was hanging across the threshold of his door. His visitor looked at it, and then looked at him, and said: "Do you mean to tell me that a big man like you, in such a position as you are, believes in such a foolish charm as that?" The man was rather insulted. "What do you mean?" he said. "Why! look at that! Do you mean to say that such a thing has any power in it? Let me take my penknife and open it, and I will show you what is in it."

There was nothing there but some red clay, parrots' feathers, dogs' teeth, pieces of the skins of animals, some of his own hair, and a little bit of his own toenail. "Do you mean to tell me that you believe in that stuff?" He answered: "Believe it? Yes. If I have that horn hanging at my door no witch will dare to come into my house. If she came, before she crossed the threshold of my door she would be dead." Mr. Fuller again remonstrated: "You do not believe such rubbish, do you?" "I do. And the reason why you missionaries all die, is that you come into this country, and the witches know that you have nothing to keep off the power of their witchcraft, and so they kill you; but they will not come near me because they know that I have got a charm that will stop them."

Mr. Fuller made it his business to visit that man day after day, and try to convince him; but it seemed of no use. He could do nothing. Six months after that time, he was sitting in his little study and heard the drum that tells of death. He knew what it meant. When a chief dies, the sound of that drum tells the tale, and the missionary has to be immediately on the move to prevent cruelty. He took his hat directly, and started up, and got to the chief's hut. "Mikani, who is dead?" He hung his head down for a minute, and then he said: "One of those princes that were with me on that day." "Why," said Mr. Fuller, "you told me that the man that had got that charm would not die. Did not that prince wear one of these horns?" "Yes." "Did he not have a cap?" "Yes." "Was he not protected by that same charm? Then, how is it that he is dead?" The poor savage hung his head down for a moment. Then lifting it up he looked full into the missionary's face for a few moments and was silent. Finally, he stretched out his hand and took hold of the horn as it hung across the door, and removed it from its place and flung it across the road, and said: "I will try your way." Where is he to-day? Go to the Cameroons, and you will see a native minister there preaching the gospel; but on the right hand of that native preacher sits a grayheaded man, and the very look of that man's face tells us of his inward peace and happiness. *He is the same man.* He has tried and found that there is none other name given among men whereby we must be saved but the name of Jesus Christ. He is the head deacon of the Church, and the membership is now about seven hundred. There is a congregation of perhaps a thousand gathering together there now. Yet when Mr. Fuller landed in 1845, less than fifty years since, these people were rank savages, brutal in every act,—naked, depraved, cruel, vicious savages; and to-day, clothed and in their right mind, they meet as a Christian congregation, with their dark faces and their bright eyes, worshipping the same Saviour that we love;—and if this is true in such a community, we know that the gospel of our Lord Jesus Christ will win its way wherever it goes.

The Pentecost on the Congo.

Few tales of missionary experience surpass for thrilling interest that of the work of the past fifteen years at Banza Manteke. In 1879, Rev. Henry Richards went from England as missionary of the Livingstone Inland Mission, and, at Banza Manteke, one hundred and fifty miles from the mouth of the Congo, and ten miles south of its stream, established a mission station, afterward transferred to the American Baptist Missionary Union.

Mr. Richards came to the United States in 1890, and told of the Lord's work on the Congo,—a story so full of interest that we present in these pages a condensed account, as worthy both of preservation and wider circulation.

When Stanley travelled from Zanzibar across the Dark Continent, for a thousand days, though he met many thousands of people each day, he did not find one who knew the Lord Jesus Christ. In 1879, two missionaries were sent out to penetrate this trackless, desolate region. At length they reached Banza Manteke, and, unable to go farther, decided there to establish a station; for many villages were near by, and the people were friendly.

They had only one tent, and built a hut of the long grass that grew about them. There, in September, 1879, Mr. Richards found himself alone, among people entirely unknown to him, as were also their customs and their language. He began at once to study them and then their strange tongue. Some things, however, he learned only too soon. He found that they all seemed to be thieves, and would take everything on which they could lay hands. They were equally adepts at lying; for when he would look into their faces and charge them with their theft, they would deny it with brazen-faced stolidity.

He gives an interesting description of his experience in learning their language. They had no dictionaries, grammars, nor literature of any kind, and no white man had ever learned their tongue. In a note-book he wrote down phonetically every-thing he heard, with the supposed meaning belonging to the word. In this way he soon had a number of words, phrases, and sentences, which at once he began to use. His hearers often laughed at his mispronunciations and his awkward blunders in putting words together; but he quietly persisted in his effort. Some words he found it very hard to get at. For instance, he noticed the strong affection between mothers and their children, and he sought the word for mother. He thought he had succeeded, but afterward he learned that the supposed word for mother really meant a full-grown man. He was three months in finding out the equivalent for yesterday.

He tried to get hold of the grammar of the language. He began with the nouns, and sought for the way of forming plurals, suspecting it was by some modification at the end of the words, but he could detect no such change. After much experimenting he found that there were sixteen classes of nouns, with as many modes of forming the plural; and in like manner he discovered seventeen different classes of verbs, with many tenses besides the ordinary present, past and future, each having its specific form, the shades of meaning in these variations often being very delicate and beautiful.

The language was found to be no mere jargon, but really very beautiful, eupho-nious and flowing, with numerous inflections. When once acquired, it was easy to preach in it and to translate the Scriptures into it. He says, "If some of our best linguists were to try to form a perfect language, they could not do better than to follow the Congo. It seems to be altogether superior to the people; and there must have been a time when they were in a higher state of civilization, from which in some way they have degenerated."

After learning in this patient way to use the language a little, he began to study into the customs, superstitions and religion of the people. He found that they believed in a great Creator, who made all things, but they did not worship this "Nzambi," because they did not think Him a good God, or worthy of praise and worship. He did not concern Himself about them; He was too far away. They had little images cut out of wood—some like themselves, only with birds' heads, beaks, and claws; others like animals—these are their gods. They trust them to protect from sickness, death, disaster, but expect no direct blessings from them. They believe also in witchcraft, to which they attribute all evils and misfortunes, and which they counteract by charms. They send for witch-doctors, if any one is sick, who with many incantations drive out the demon, or point out some person as the witch, who has to undergo the test by poison, so common in Africa.

Mr. Richards sought to show them that sickness, death and other calamity are due not to witchcraft, but to sin. He gave them the Bible account of the creation and the fall, etc., and tried to show that God is not only a great, all-powerful Creator, but a kind and loving Father. For four years he pursued this course, thinking it necessary to give them some idea of the Old Testament before beginning with the New. But they were just as rank heathen at the end of this time as when he first went among them. There was no evidence of any change. They did not even feel themselves to be sinners.

Then Mr. Richards went home for a season of rest, and, while there, spoke to some who had had much experience in mission work, seeking a clew to his maze of difficulty. He was advised to go back and *preach the law*—for that convinces of sin. So on reaching Banza Manteke again, the first thing he did was to translate the *Ten Commandments* and expound them to the people. They said the commandments were very good, but claimed that they had kept them; and the plainest and most personal applications of the decalogue made no apparent impression. So two years more passed, and the people were no better. He began to be hopeless of doing them any good. He had gained their respect, and they were kind to him, but that was all.

At last, in his discouragement, he began to study the Scriptures anew for himself, feeling that there must be some mistake in his preaching or lack in his living. In the Apostolic days souls were converted; why not now? Surely the gospel had not lost its power. If, in the days of the Acts of the Apostles, heathen turned from idols to serve the living God, why should not these heathen in Banza Manteke? He studied the Gospel and the Acts of the Apostles, and began to see that the commission is not, "Go ye into all the world and preach the *Law*," but "preach the *Gospel*." This was the turning-point in the work of this lonely and disheartened missionary! He determined simply to preach the gospel. Again he noticed that disciples were bidden to wait until they were endued *with power from on high*. He felt that he had not this power. He returned to his work, determined not only to preach the gospel, but cry to God for the promised enduement.

It was needful to decide just what "preaching, the gospel" means. If he preached Jesus crucified, the people would want to know who Jesus was. He decided to take Luke's Gospel as most complete and suitable for gentiles. He

SCRIPTURE TESTIMONY
Give to everyone who asks
MATTHEW 5:42 · LUKE 6:30 · ACTS 20:35 · 2 CORINTHIANS 8:1-2 · I JOHN 3:17

began translating ten or twelve verses a day, and then read and expounded them, asking God to bless His own word. At once his dark hearers proved more interested than when he had preached the law, and he was more and more encouraged. When he came to the sixth chapter of Luke, thirtieth verse, a new difficulty arose—"Give to every man that asketh of thee." But these people were notorious beggars; they would ask for anything that pleased their eye—his blanket, his knife, his plate— and when he would say he could not give these things to them, they would reply, "You can get more." Henry Richards was greatly perplexed as to *what to do with that verse*. He let his helper in translation go, and went to his room to pray over the matter. The time for the daily service was drawing near. What should he do? *Why not pass over that verse?* But conscience replied that this would not be honest dealing with God's word. The preaching hour came; instead of advancing, he went back to the beginning of the gospel, reviewing the earlier part, to gain time for fuller consideration of that perplexing text. Still, on further study, he could not find that *it meant anything but just what it said*. The commentators said, Jesus was giving general principles, and we must use common sense in interpreting His words. But this did not satisfy him. If he interpreted one text in this way, why not all others? "Common sense" seemed a very unsafe commentator.

A fortnight of prayer and consideration drove him to the wall: the Lord *meant just what He said*. And so he read to the people that verse, "Give to every man that asketh of thee," and told them that this was a very high standard, and would probably take a lifetime to live up to it; but he meant *to live what he preached*. After the address the natives began to ask him for this and that, and he gave them whatever they asked for, wondering whereunto this thing would grow; but he told the Lord he could see no other meaning in His words. Somehow the people were evidently deeply impressed by his course. One day he overheard one say: "I got this from the white man." Then another said that he was going to ask him for such a thing. But a third said, "No; buy it if you want it;" and another said,

"This must be God's man, we never saw any other man do so. Don't you think if he is God's man we ought to stop robbing him?" Grace was working in their hearts. After that they rarely asked him for anything, and even brought back what they had taken!

<table>
<tr><td>SCRIPTURE TESTIMONY</td></tr>
<tr><td>Holy Spirit convicts people of their sin
JOHN 16:8</td></tr>
</table>

This humble man went on translating and expounding Luke's Gospel, and the interest continually grew. The climax was reached as he came to the account of the crucifixion of Christ. A large congregation confronted him that day. He reminded the people of the kindness and goodness of Jesus, and of His works of mercy; and, pointing to Him as nailed upon the cross between thieves, he said: "Jesus never would have died if we had not been sinners; it was because of your sins and mine that he died." The impression was very deep. The Holy Ghost seemed to have fallen upon the people!

He continued preaching the gospel and seeking Holy Ghost power. One day as they were returning from a service, Lutale, who helped him in translating, began to sing one of the Congo hymns. His face shone with joy, and he said: "I do believe these words; I do believe Jesus has taken away my sins; I do believe He has saved me." Seven years of toil, weary waiting and suffering had passed, and now the first convert was found at Banza Manteke! At once, Lutale began testifying what the Lord had done for him. But the people became his enemies and tried to poison him; so that he had to leave his town and live with Mr. Richards for safety. For a time there were no more converts, but the people were stirred. By and by the king's son became a Christian. Shortly after, another man came with his idols, and placing them on a table, said, with savage determination, "I want to become a Christian," and he soon began to preach. The work went on until ten were converted, but all had to leave their own homes, as they were threatened with death. The missionary now shut up his house, and taking these men with him, went from town to town preaching the gospel. The whole community was greatly moved; one after another came over to Christ's side. Two daily meetings were held, and inquirers were numerous. The work continued and was blessed, until *all the people immediately around Banza Man-teke had abandoned their heathenism*! More than one thousand names were enrolled in a book of those who gave evidence of real conversion.

After years had passed, Mr. Richards found the converts holding on their way. About three hundred had been baptized, and the native Church was earnest and spiritual. There had been much persecution, but it had failed to intimidate these new converts. Materials for a chapel, provided through the liberality of Dr. A. J.

Gordon's church in Boston, were brought to a point fifty or sixty miles distant, and carried by the people all the way to Banza Manteke, over rough roads. Some of the carriers went four or five times, each trip requiring a week. In all there were about seven hundred loads, of sixty pounds each, and the whole of these loads were borne without charge.

Those who had been thieves and liars before, now became honest, truthful, industrious and cleanly. Witchcraft, poison-giving, and all such heathen practices have been put away. They brought their idols, and at the first baptism had a bonfire of images, destroying every vestige of idolatry! *Laus Deo*!

THE PENTECOST AT HILO.

We have reserved for the last of these sketches of transformed communities, one which deserves a separate setting, as a peculiarly lustrous gem.*

Titus Coan, nearly sixty years ago, in 1835, began his memorable mission on the shore belt of Hawaii. He soon began to use the native tongue, and within the year made his first tour of the island. He was a relative of Nettleton and had been a co-labourer with Finney, and had learned what arrows are best for a preacher's quiver, and how to use his bow. His whole being was full of spiritual energy and unction, and, on his first tour, multitudes flocked to hear, and many seemed pricked in their hearts. The multitudes thronged him and followed him, and like his Master, he had no leisure, so much as to eat; and once he preached three times before he had a chance to breakfast. He was wont to make four or five tours a year, and saw tokens of interest, that impressed him with so strange a sense of the presence of God, that he said little about them and scarcely understood, himself. He could only say, "It was wonderful!" He went about, like Jeremiah, with the fire of the Lord in his bones; weary with forbearing, he could not stay.

In 1837, the slumbering fires broke out. Nearly the whole population became an audience, and those who could not come to the services were brought on their beds or on the backs of others. Mr. Coan found himself ministering to fifteen thousand people, scattered along the hundred miles of coast. He longed to be able to fly, that he might get over the ground, or to be able to multiply himself twentyfold, to reach the multitudes who fainted for spiritual food.

Necessity devises new methods. He bade those to whom he could not go, come to him, and, for a mile around, the people settled down—Hilo's little population of a thousand swelled tenfold, and here was held, on a huge scale, a two years' unique "camp meeting." There was not an hour, day or night, when an audience of from two thousand to six thousand would not rally at the signal of the bell.

---

* Eschol. By S. J. Humphrey, D.D

There was no disorder, and the camp became a sort of industrial school, where gardening, matbraiding, and bonnet making were taught as well as purely religious truth. These great "protracted meetings" crowded the old church with six thousand hearers, and a newer building with half as many more; and when the people got seated, they were so close that until the meeting broke up no one could move. The preacher does not hesitate to deal in stem truths. The law with its awful perfection; hell, with its fires, of which the crater of Kilauea and the volcanoes about them might well furnish a vivid picture—the deep and damning guilt of sin, the hopelessness and helplessness of spiritual death —prepare the way for earnest gospel invitation and appeal. The vast audience sways as cedars before a tornado. There is trembling, weeping, sobbing and loud crying for mercy, sometimes too loud for the preacher to be heard; and in hundreds of cases his hearers fall in a swoon.

> **SCRIPTURE TESTIMONY**
>
> *Holy Spirit convicts people of their sin*
>
> JOHN 16:8

Titus Coan was made for the work God had for him, and he controlled these great masses. He preached with great simplicity, illustrating and applying the grand old truths, made no effort to excite but rather to allay excitement, and asked for no external manifestation of interest. He depended on the word, borne home by the Spirit. And the Spirit wrought. Some would cry out, "The two-edged sword is cutting me to pieces." The wicked scoffer who came to make sport dropped like a log, and said, "God has struck me." Once while preaching in the open field to two thousand people, a man cried out, "What shall I do to be saved?" and prayed the publican's prayer; and the entire congregation took up the cry for mercy. For a half hour Mr. Coan could get no chance to speak, but had to stand still and see God work.

There were greater signs of the Spirit than mere words of agony or confession. Godly repentance was at work—quarrels were reconciled, drunkards abandoned drink, thieves restored stolen property, adulteries gave place to purity, and murders were confessed. The high priest of Pele and custodian of her crater shrine, who by his glance could doom a native to strangulation, on whose shadow no Hawaiian dared tread, who ruthlessly struck men dead for their food or garments' sake and robbed and outraged human beings for a pastime—this gigantic criminal came into the meetings with his sister, the priestess—and even such as they found an irresistible power there—and with bitter tears and penitent confession, the crimes of this monster were unearthed. He acknowledged that what he had worshipped was no God at all, and publicly renounced his idolatry and bowed before Jesus. These two had spent about seventy years in sin, but till death maintained their Christian confession.

In 1838, the converts continued to multiply. Though but two missionaries, a lay preacher, and their wives, constituted the force, and the field was a hundred miles long, the word and work was with power, because God was in it all. Mr. Coan's trips were first of all for preaching; and he spoke on the average from three to four times a day; but these public appeals were interlaced with visits of a pastoral nature at the homes of the people, and with the searching inquiry into their state. This marvellous man kept track of his immense parish, and knew a church membership of five thousand as thoroughly as when it numbered one hundred. He never lost individual knowledge and contact in all this huge increase— what a model to modern pastors, who magnify preaching but have "no time to visit!" It was part of his plan that not one living person in all Puna or Hilo should not have the gospel brought repeatedly to the conscience, and he did not spare any endeavour or exposure to reach the people.

He set his people to work, and above forty of them visited from house to house within five miles of the central station. The results were simply incredible were they not attested abundantly.

After great care in examining and testing candidates, during the twelve months, ending in June, 1839, 5,244 persons had been received into the Church, On one Sabbath, 1,705 were baptized, and 2,400 sat down together at the Lord's Table. It was a gathering of villages, and the head of each village came forward with his selected converts. With the exception of one such scene at Ongole, just forty years later, probably no such a sight has been witnessed since the day of Pentecost. What a scene was that when nearly two thousand five hundred sat down together to eat the Lord's Supper! And what a gathering! "the old, the decrepit, the lame, the blind, the maimed, the withered, the paralytic, and those afflicted with divers diseases and torments; those with eyes, noses, lips and limbs consumed with the fire of their own or their parents' former lusts, with features distorted and figures the most depraved and loathsome,— and these came hobbling upon their staves, and led or borne by their friends; and among the throng the hoary priest of idolatry, with hands but recently washed from the blood of human victims, together with the thief, the adulterer, the Sodomite, the sorcerer, the robber, the murderer; and the mother—no, the monster—whose hands had reeked with the blood of her own children! These all met before the cross of Christ with their enmity slain, and themselves "washed and sanctified and justified in the name of the Lord Jesus, and by the Spirit of our God."

During the five years, ending June, 1841, 7,557 persons were received to the Church at Hilo,— three-fourths of the whole adult population of the parish. When Titus Coan left Hilo in 1870, he had himself received and baptized 11,960 persons.

These people *held fast* the faith, only one in sixty becoming amenable to discipline. Not even a grogshop was to be found in that parish, and the Sabbath was better kept than in New England. In 1867, the old mother church divided into seven, and there have been built fifteen houses for worship, mainly with the money and labour of the people themselves; who have also planted and sustained their own missions, having given in the aggregate one hundred thousand dollars for holy uses, and having sent twelve of their number to the regions beyond.

Christian history presents no record of divine power more thrilling than this of the Great Revival at the Hawaiian Islands from 1836 to 1842. When in 1870 the American Board withdrew from this field, there were nearly sixty self-supporting churches, more than two-thirds having a native pastorate, with a membership of about fifteen thousand. That year their contributions reached $30,000. Thirty per cent, of their ministers became missionaries on other islands. That same year, Kanwealoha, the old native missionary, in presence of a vast throng, where the royal family and dignitaries of the islands were assembled, held up the Word of God in the Hawaiian tongue, and in these few words gave the most comprehensive tribute to the fruits of gospel labour:

"Not with powder and ball, and swords and cannon, but with this living Word of God, and His Spirit, do we go forth to conquer the Islands for Christ!"

IV.

THE NEW WITNESSES AND WORKERS.

THE NEW Acts of the Apostles tells, as we have intimated, not only of converts, but of those who as unmistakably belong to the "noble army of martyrs" as did Stephen or James. Converts from tribes the most debased have given proof alike of genuineness and heroism by the voluntary endurance of suffering, torture and death for Christ's sake.

When the capricious and treacherous King of Uganda panted like a wild beast for the blood of Christian victims, he seized young lads whose only crime or offence was their ardent attachment to Jesus, and the consistency that, in them,

SCRIPTURE TESTIMONY
Killed for the sake of Christ
MATTHEW 16:24 · ACTS 7:58-60 · ACTS 12:1-5

rebuked his fickleness and inconstancy; and they were led away to die. The crowd followed them with jeering and mockery, led on by the "high priest" of the king's cruelty. But ridicule and sneer expended their darts in vain upon the shield of faith borne by these young disciples.

They were, like their crucified Lord, taunted with their faith in God and their trust in His promises, and were burned to ashes to test their new doctrine of the resurrection. But the answer to all this was that of the prisoners in the Philippian jail—prayer and praise to God. The place of their death was the edge of the dismal swamp—Maganja; the bed of their torture a wicker framework built over a slow fire; and the prelude to this awful agony was mutilation—the knife, then the flame. Butchery without mercy—then roasting with fiendish cruelty! Not a murmur of complaint—songs of praise to Jesus, mingled with moans of agony and sobs of

191

anguish; and then the long silence that tells of the end! Yet when another young convert stood by and saw all this and was threatened with a like fate, he only dared these human fiends to do their worst, declaring that he was not ashamed of Jesus.

SCRIPTURE TESTIMONY

Believers will suffer terrible things for the sake of Jesus' name

MATTHEW 24:9-14

Japanese converts have had to risk martyrdom. When in 1876, forty pupils of Captain Janes' school in Higo, in Kiushu, pledged themselves to Christ, it was the signal for open war. The leaders were withdrawn from the school, held as prisoners, some of them for over three months, and subjected to all sorts of intimidation and indignity; parents vowed to commit *harakiri*, unless their sons abandoned the Christian faith; but they stood firm. Their Bibles were burned, their physical strength in some cases failed, and death was threatened; but all in vain. One of them was made the slave of the servants in his own home, and they were bidden to treat him as a devil-possessed man without human rights. He became an outcast in his own father's house, but stood like a rock.

It must be remembered that, notwithstanding all the missionary literature of our day, the history of the work of the past century is but fragmentary, like the Acts of the Apostles. Especially is this to be borne in mind, that most of the facts concerning the development of native disciples on foreign soil have been gathered from incidental references in the biographies of missionaries. The major part of the history of native converts and churches is yet unwritten. For example, there is as yet no published account of Dr. G. L. Mackay's work in Formosa. Who shall tell us the full story of converts and martyrs who belong to the New Acts of the Apostles? We must wait till God's Book of Remembrance is read!

Martyrs—yes, and *missionaries*, too, have come from the ranks of these converts. Not only have noble disciples, but valiant witnesses and apostolic preachers and evangelists, come from the Maoris of New Zealand, the Hottentots of the Southern Cape, the cannibals of the South Seas, the brutal Malagasy, the Australian-aborigines—Nazareths of paganism whence even Christian disciples once thought no good thing—certainly no prophet—could come.

The ministry is the flower of church life, and, therefore, its highest product—its consummate fruit and hope; for in that flower is not only the bloom of the beauty of the divine plant, but its fruit and seed —the secret of propagation. In the Acts, we trace the results of missions in the creation of new heralds who spread missions. And, in the new Acts, converts have scarcely been gathered into churches upon heathen soil, before, by a spontaneous movement of the new life, these converts themselves have been found going to the other unsaved souls about them with the good news—and outrunning the mother churches of Christendom in zeal and activity. The first mission to Micronesia was organized and manned by Hawaiian converts. It was the South Sea disciples that John Williams sent forth as pioneers to new islands and island groups; and they won triumphs and bore away trophies where no white man had ever set foot. Bishop Patteson's ten years' work in Melanesia was full of pathetic heroism; and his native boys proved how sincere was their love to Christ and how ardent their zeal for His kingdom, when they offered to go and undertake work on other islands. The *Southern Cross*, in the year of Patteson's death, bore twenty-nine of them from the missionary college at Norfolk Island to spread gospel light at their homes; and when the year ended, three hundred were at work, and they represented most of the islands from the New Hebrides to the Solomon group.

The total force at work now on the foreign field is close to fifty thousand; and while not more than one-fifth of the number come from Christian lands— including wives of missionaries and other women who are teaching—the other four-fifths are native evangelists, preachers and pastors, teachers and helpers! So that the missions, recently begun among heathens and pagans, have already given to the mission field four times as many workers as the churches at home have sent forth! When converted Raiateans organize missionary associations, establish missions in surrounding islands and support them with offerings of cocoanut oil; when the Samoans surprise the missionary by declaring that they are "Sons of the Word," and in eighteen years every island, within a circle whose diameter is four thousand miles, has heard the gospel, and all this mostly at the mouth of native converts,—the Church may well stop to ask whether mission-harvests have not yielded more of the seed of propagation than the crops that grow at home!

When, from Erromanga's shore, the relics of Williams's devoured body was borne to Upolu, his Samoan converts resolved to rear the cross on the spot where he fell; and at risk of like fate, again and again, they made the attempt. When Bishop Selwyn knelt on that tragic shore to ask God to open a door of access to those debased natives, it was a converted pagan teacher who knelt beside him. And when at length, forty years ago, the chief, whose club killed Williams, surrendered that club as a trophy of missionary triumph, it was two natives from the Hervey group who had effected entrance.

Thus the triumphs of the cross are already to be found among all tribes and races, classes and conditions of men. As Dr. Flint has well said, "Comparative theology is a magnificent demonstration not only that man was made for religion, but *for what religion* man was made." What missions *can* do is sufficiently demonstrated and illustrated by what has already *been* done. The individual is the type of the universal, and one community, of all others like itself. God has chosen enough of the highest from among the heathen to prove that none are so elevated as not to need the gospel; and sufficient from the lowest, to show that none are so degraded as to be beyond the gospel's reach. Whatever doubt may have existed as to the expediency and efficiency of Christian missions, that greatest logician, Experience, has now demonstrated such doubt to be unreasonable and unfounded.

The most hopeless fields have often been the most fruitful in the end, and the harvests that have been longest in ripening have often been the largest in yielding. History is already so fulfilling prophecy as to render the most glorious predictions no longer seem incredible. God has thus emphasized His own command by the encouragements of rewarded toil. Facts are His new trumpets that sound His new signals. The world lies before us, open to access; a thousand millions of human beings wait for the message. To go and give the gospel is to impart infinite blessing, and yet increase our own riches of grace in imparting. Every motive—whether drawn from the voice of authority that spoke on Galilean hills, or from the wail of human woe and want that comes up like the moan and sob of many waters telling of wrecks and drowning souls—every conceivable incentive, whether found in devotion to our Lord or passion for men; in the humane sympathy that would relieve man's present misery, or the holier self-sacrifice that would uplift and redeem immortal souls— every motive and incentive unite to urge us to bear to the earth's utmost end the tidings of the cross. Let us tell men what Christ has done for the world and its sins and sorrows—let us assure them that the Son of David even now rides triumphant and comes near to His temple—that they may meet him with their waving palms, and holy hosannas, and cry, "Blessed is He that cometh in the name of the Lord!"—and so the final Palm Sunday of the ages shall be ushered in when out of millions of mouths of babes and sucklings, new-born into the kingdom, His praise shall be perfected!

PART V.

NEW SIGNS AND WONDERS

I.

THE NEW MIRACLES.

THE LAW of correlation, in nature, finds every capacity filled and every craving fed, so that the bird's wing and fish's fin become prophecies of the atmosphere and the water, as the eye and ear imply sights and sounds. The same law holds true in the spiritual world. The capacity and craving for the marvellous and wonderful is akin to adoration, which is a higher, holier form of admiration. God's work of creation constantly appeals to the sense of the marvellous; and, ever since the creation of the world, His invisible attributes, His power and Godhead, have been clearly seen. Man's own body has been fearfully and wonderfully made and constrains him to adore his Creator. And so it is in the kingdom of providence and grace. It needs but an open eye to see the working of a supernatural Power: the abundant proofs of the divine handiwork leave all observers "without excuse."

It may seem without warrant and even irreverent to apply to the wonders wrought in our age the term "miracles of missions." But a miracle is no more or less than a wonder and a sign combined:—a wonder, for if not out of the common course it would attract no attention; a sign, for if not contrary to, or superior to, the working of natural causes, it would not show to man a higher Hand at work. With such limitations upon the term, we need not hesitate to affirm that modern missionary history furnishes an array of miracles which form the greatest treatise on apologetics ever given to the human race.

To those who deny or doubt a divine mind and method back of the stage of events, with its changes of scene and actors—to all who are sceptical as to a presence and power above man which goes with the gospel, the one sufficient answer is, missions to the heathen!

Proofs and examples of this have not been wanting in previous pages, as seen in the opening of doors, the calling of apostles, the raising up of converts who have proved both evangelists and martyrs. Through the whole study of the theme thus far the golden thread of a divine plan and performance has been traced. He who holds the Key of David, who openeth and no man shutteth, and shutteth and no man openeth, has been seen unlocking the iron gates and bursting bolts and bars. The new Pentecosts reveal the Hand that alone can open the windows of heaven and pour out the blessing which comes only from above. A divine Voice alone could have called out labourers from an apathetic and unwilling Church, and sent them forth at the times and to the points most needful, and only He whose existence and purpose span the ages could have kept up this unbroken succession of Workmen. God has been visiting his people by Voices and Visions, and training them for new service; and the harvests already reaped argue a divine husbandry. All our paths thus far have been through the territory where Jehovah has worked wonders. A Pillar of cloud and fire has gone before the missionary host—and has led them through deep waters on dry ground, past the Burning Bush, the quaking mount, the riven rock, the routed foe— and all the way a table has been set in the wilderness and man has eaten angels' food.

But a large class of divine interpositions and wonder workings, not so far considered, demands special notice, if the *Pleroma*—the fulness of the presence and power of God in modern missions—is to be seen.

Two great miracles, one in the Old Testament and the other in the New, are the evident forecasts both of missionary methods and success, and we feel persuaded that their typical meaning has not been apprehended. One is the *Fall of Jericho*, the other is the *Feeding of the Five Thousand*.

Everything about the Fall of Jericho hints its typical character. The preparation of the people, the circumcision at Gilgal and the rolling away of the reproach—the resumption of the long-neglected Passover Festival, and the courageous crossing of the Jordan—are conditions of the display of God's power. Then Jericho was the *first stronghold* which they encountered and stands for world conquest.

Note the circumstances: Exact obedience to the divine command, circumscribing the doomed city, marching round and round it, till thirteen circuits were accomplished with the "soles of their feet," which was the prescribed law of occupation or taking possession by appropriation. How obviously the blowing of the trumpets represents the sevenfold proclamation of the gospel, the jubilee trump, announcing the acceptable year of the Lord; and what was that shout of victory before the walls fell, but the anticipation of *faith* counting things that are not as though they were, because God had promised! How plainly does the falling of those walls of the doomed city, before one blow was struck, teach us dependence, not on human might or power, but on the good Spirit of the Lord, and teach us that the weapons of our warfare are not carnal but mighty through God to the pulling down of strongholds! How inadequate human means are! God must interpose to do the real work and achieve the real victory Himself. He will not give His glory to another, and the consummation is all His own.

When, from this miracle which stands at the beginning of the conquest of Canaan, we turn to Pentecost, which strangely prefaces the beginning of gospel wars of conquest, we see Jericho interpreted. Peter's sermon was the blowing of the rams' horns, and the immediate and resistless prostration of the walls of Jewish bigotry, self-righteousness and hardheartedness,—was the divine razing to the ground of barriers to gospel entrance.

Now turn to the great New Testament miracle, when the five loaves and two fishes fed the five thousand. Here is the second great lesson of obedience and dependence. A world is to be reached and every creature fed. Our force is inadequate. "What are *all these* among so many?" Nevertheless, "give ye them to eat." District the world, go to work on a definite plan of distribution of field and labourers—bring what you have of money and means, Bibles and workers, to Jesus for His blessing. Take no account of the inadequacy of your supplies, but do exactly as He bids and, with what you have, undertake for Him, expecting Him to multiply as you divide. How often is this lesson taught throughout God's Word! the unwasting barrel of meal and flask of oil, the unexhausted cruise of the widow,* the divine independence of power and wealth and wisdom, of numbers and natural means,— all teach us that things impossible with men are possible with God.

What greater impulse could be imparted to worldwide missions than this—that the Church should recognize and realize that it is her salvation to be in straits! because the utter despair of self-sufficiency teaches her that her sufficiency is of God. Our emergency is His opportunity. If the fewness of labourers drives us to pray the Lord of the harvest, that He will thrust forth labourers into His harvestfield, He will be heard, saying, "Separate Me Barnabas and Saul," and Barnabas and Saul will be found ready. If our poverty of resources leads us to look to Him who alone can supply the ever recurring and increasing need; if the vast host and mighty power of our foes leads us to spread out our case before the Lord, and plead for His might against this great company—success is assured. And, whenever in such spirit, the crises of the kingdom are met, He interposes!

The Acts of the Apostles records God's sure working. Its pages flush with the glory, flash with the lightnings, and peal with thunders of the Eternal Throne.

---

* I. Kings xvii. 9-16; II. Kings iv. 1-6.

Christ's promise became reality, for, as they went forth and preached everywhere, the Lord wrought with and confirmed the word with signs following. It became plain even to foes that God was with them. His seal and sanction was set upon their words by works such as man alone never wrought. From Peter at Pentecost to Paul at Rome, every new chapter is a new challenge to faith, for it is a new display of divine power. Those tongues that flamed with Heaven's message; those sharp sword-thrusts of the Spirit by which penitent sinners were pricked in their heart, and by which Stephen's stoners were cut to the heart; the healing word whereby the cripple, lame from his mother's womb, stood, and walked, and leaped; the prayers that shook the assembly-room at Jerusalem, and the foundations of the prison at Philippi; the judgments that struck the sorcerer blind and the liars dead; the healing virtue that invested with power Paul's person and Peter's shadow; the vivid visions of divine things, which made Stephen's face shine as an angel's, ana Paul's heart peaceful in shipwreck; the close contact with God that taught Philip where to go and what to do, and caught him away with sudden rapture; the personal appearances of Christ to the dying martyr and the living persecutor; Paul's sudden blindness and as sudden restoration to sight; the raising of Dorcas at Lydda, and Eutychus at Troas; Peter's prophetic vision, and Agabus' prophetic warning; the angel visit to Cornelius in the palace and to Peter in the prison; the Apostle's deliverance from the sword of Herod, and the tyrant's deliverance unto the sword of the avenging angel; the supernatural Voice that at Antioch separated Paul to missions, and at Corinth assured him of safety; the healing of the cripple at Lystra and the damsel at Philippi; the outpourings of the Spirit at Samaria, Cesarea, Ephesus as well as Jerusalem! who can walk along this highway of marvels without seeing everywhere the signs and tracks of God's footsteps! We feel that the place is holy ground, the place of the Burning Bush, the Pillar of cloud and fire, the Angel of the Lord. We are hurried on amid a continual and continuous blaze of glory, for we no sooner emerge from the startling splendour of one miracle before we enter the precincts of another.

The whole study of the theme seems to bring us face to face with a divine Wonder-Worker, and the history is the pattern of His thought and plan wrought into the fabric of events. The new Pentecosts are His bestowments of blessing, as purely from God as the rain is from the heavens; the doors which open are His gifts of opportunity and facility; in the modern apostles and evangelists His appointment of spheres and service appears; in the control of His providence all creation is but a host—the armies that obey His bugle call; and in His gracious transformations the perpetual miracle is seen which attests the living God. Christ is on the throne, and at the same time on the battle-field. We seem to see the star of universal empire flashing on His breast, and the white horse of conquest makes the battle-field quake beneath His awful tread.

Have the days of miracles *passed*, or are we still moving amid signs and wonders? If the age of missions does remind us of the Acts of the Apostles in its display of certain divine power, it matters little whether or not the *mode* of God's working is the same. The *fact*, not the *form*, concerns us. The signs of the earlier age may have given place to the signs of a later age. God is not poor in resources; His fund of force is not exhausted; He needs not to repeat Himself, nor does He; His infinite versatility assures infinite variety.

Moreover, it is probable that, for our new age, the signs and wonders wrought will be different, if they are to be equally convincing and conclusive, and equally suited to the present purpose of God and the present needs of man. In His kingdom of grace, as of the nature, the *lower* ever gives place to the *higher*. And, as Dr. Upham says: "Through this invincible law, the lower physical miracles, of the time when our Lord was on earth, gave way before the coming of a higher order of spiritual miracles." The former belonged to a receding dispensation; and in these things is the answer to the question: "Have miracles ceased?" Miracles have passed on from a lower to a higher sphere; from the seen to the unseen; from the world of nature to the world of spirit, where spiritual miracles are daily, hourly, wrought by the Holy Ghost, in answer to the prayer of faith— miracles far greater than those which typified and prophesied of the later and higher miracles. Even if the earlier signs do occasionally reappear, to clamour for them is to long for and hold fast what belongs to a finished age, instead of going onward and upward.

Careful research into the history of modern missions leaves on the mind this ineradicable impression and impress: that the *facts*, abundantly furnished and attested—facts as much above denial or doubt as the most certain events of history—simply defy explanation without admitting a divine factor. These facts are not few, scattered, exceptional, isolated; not done in a comer and lacking adequate authentic witness. They are conspicuous and confident; they move in such masses that the march of their host compels their recognition. In this conviction the most devout and acute observers of missionary history are agreed.

From these modern signs and wonders a *few representative* examples may be selected, drawn from all varieties of sphere and experience. And the few will suffice; when testimony has confirmation from agreeing witnesses, the mere *number* of witnesses adds but little assurance. And, if competent testimony does not carry conviction, it is vain to pour more light upon any eye that only meets more illumination by closer contraction.

Mission history is both a demonstration and illustration of One who is present to preside and provide —a divine Director and Controller. There is an invisible Actor, whose will is wrought out in the changes of events and the control of inferior actors. These instances and evidences of His interposition sweep round the whole circle of the continents and the whole cycle of the ages. We may trace God's intervention particularly in the following particulars:

We may see Him opening doors of access, and removing barriers at critical points and periods. In some cases there has been a sudden subsidence of barriers which can only be likened to the sinking of the land so as to permit the overflow of the sea, as in the Hawaiian Islands in 1819, and Papal France in 1870.

We may see Him preparing the work for the workman and the workman for the work, where such foresight was impossible to man; controlling invention and discovery so as to develop civilization according to a preconceived plan, and furnishing new instruments and agencies in a marked order of succession. We may see Him obviously overruling human mistakes and failures, frustrating the designs of enemies and persecutors; setting the limits and determining the direction of human lives and purposes.

We may watch Him answering prayer and turning great crises to which man was utterly unequal, and when there was despair of all human help.

We may, most of all, see God's power indirectly modifying existing evils, and directly transforming both individuals and whole communities until, as there was *subsidence* of barriers, there is also an upheaval of the entire social level.

All this is no human evolution: it is a divine *revolution*. The strategy is that of a General-in-Chief whose eye commands at a glance the whole field of the world, and the whole history of man, and to whom the future is as present to view as the past. Amid the drift in the direction of a natural scepticism, accelerated by the influence of infidel opinion, nothing more restrains and corrects such tendencies than the unanswerable argument for a personal God supplied by the history of modern missions. He who carefully examines it feels that he treads on enchanted ground, whose mysteries compel a divine solution.

Of course, we are now dealing with matters whose very nature precludes mathematical proofs; not with the science of quantity, but of moral probability, which demands moral evidence. And, yet, practical certainty is attainable, for moral proofs are conclusive when properly used. For example, the law of *coincidence* pertains to a department of moral evidence. God confirms faith in His interpositions by bringing together occurrences which *so correspond* as to exhibit an intentional mutual fitness. Hence, for example, Prayer and its Answer often so fit each other, in time, place and exact correspondence, as to make certain that

God and the praying soul are in contact. And this principle must be admitted if we are to recognize signs and wonders, not appealing to our senses but to our reason. The greatest signs of God's presence in Apostolic days were found not in miracles addressing the eye and ear, but in the wonders of such coincidence. When the first fish that Peter caught contained in its mouth the exact sum necessary to pay the tribute due from Christ and himself, according to Christ's word, the coincidence compelled conviction that it was no accident. When the tragedy of the crucifixion was attended by six hours of dense darkness, and an earthquake; and when the dying cry, "It is finished," and the violent rending of the Temple Veil took place at the same instant, even a Roman centurion could not but say, "Truly this was the Son of God!" The Acts of the Apostles is full of these coincidences, which betray an invisible Hand guiding affairs.

Philip is led to go down to a desert road at the very time when the eunuch is inquiring as to the true faith, and Philip's approach is at the very moment when he is reading aloud the very verse in prophecy which furnished the best text for a gospel sermon. While Peter had a vision on the housetop, the messengers from Cesarea were knocking at the gate to ask him to go to the Romans whom he had thought unclean; and while' many are gathered praying for him, he is delivered from prison and the axe of Herod's executioner. The death of Ananias and Sapphira coming at the instant of an act of lying and perjury against the Holy Spirit, showed that God's judgment was at work; as Herod's awful death at the very time of his accepting divine honours, made plain that God had smitten him. Paul's conversion at the very climax of his triumph as persecutor, and when he was just entering Damascus, left no doubt that he had seen Jesus in the way. These are a few instances of that coincidence which establishes a probability amounting to practical certainty, that something more than the chance of accident had been controlling history. Thoughtless or uncandid persons often foolishly demand on moral subjects what they call, "mathematical proofs," forgetting that such proofs are in the nature of the case impossible, and we must look for quite another order of demonstration. But, when examined in a proper method and spirit, it will become scarcely less certain that God is, and that He is the actual governor in missionary history, than it is that two and two make four, or that the three angles of a triangle equal two right angles.

These "miracles of missions" are so numerous and various that we are again compelled to resort both to classification and selection. They fall naturally into two classes—miracles of *providence* and miracles of *grace*. The first includes all those interpositions of God which concern the control of individual . lives, or governmental acts—which have to do with the general shaping of events, with protecting and providing for His own people, avenging their wrongs, destroying their foes, or raising up for them friends and helpers in crises. The miracles of grace include all direct or indirect influence of His word and Spirit in working transformation of personal character or popular life, and particularly in accomplishing great social revolutions which turn the world upside down and imply an energy superior to man.

When Paul and Barnabas returned to Antioch from their first mission tour, they rehearsed in the ears of the Church all that God had done with them and how He had opened the doors of faith unto the nations: and, as Paul went up to the first council at Jerusalem, he declared what things God had wrought by his ministry, and "when they heard that they glorified the Lord." Mark the repeated emphasis upon *the Lord's doings*—what He had done, how He had opened the doors, what He had wrought—that all glory might be His. There has never been a truly great missionary since Paul, who has not magnified the *Power of God* in the fruits of his work,—who has not known and felt that what results he has seen wrought were accountable for on no other philosophy —and this is the most conspicuous testimony unanimously borne by the most devout missionaries.

Just where such recognition of dependence on God and such confidence in His power have most abounded, the grandest demonstrations of His presence have been seen. Pastor Gossner, at sixty-three, stopped ringing the door-bell of millionaires and rang only the door-bell of heaven—and he put into the field one hundred missionaries who gathered 30,000 converts. Not what great things I have done or suffered for my Lord, but what great things the Lord has wrought for me,—that is the boast of the true missionary.

II.

NEW OPPORTUNITIES AND PREPARATIONS.

CLEAR SIGNS of a supernatural Providence are seen in the new opportunities of modern history. The hidden hand of God has manifestly touched the affairs of men in the unlocking and opening of long shut doors.

The poet Dryden crowned the year 1666 as "Annus Mirabilis," because made forever memorable by such events as the great fire in London, and the naval war with the Dutch and their allies. The Marquis of Worcester entitled the sixteenth century the "century of invention." And a wonderful hundred years they were that saw the globe circumnavigated by the ships of Magellan, that covered the era of Charles the Fifth and Elizabeth, of Henry the Eighth, and Leo Tenth, of Luther and the Reformation, of the wars of France and the rise of the Dutch Republic, of the Diets of Worms and of Spires and of Augsburg, of the Council of Trent, and the final triumph of the Protestant cause, and the birth of religious liberty.

But, in every respect, even as the century of invention, the nineteenth century has far outshone the sixteenth; and as to the "annus mirabilis," that one year, 1858, is probably the most wonderful year in the annals of history, for the rapidity with which on every side new doors opened for access commercially, politically and religiously, to the whole world. During that year, Japan, after two centuries of sealed ports, made treaty with Great Britain; China enlarged vastly the rights conceded sixteen years before; India became part of Britain's worldwide empire, and zenanas were penetrated by Christian women; Italy laid the basis of her new era of freedom; Mexico threw open her doors to the Protestant missionary—all this and much more within a twelvemonth!

In that one "annus mirabilis," two-thirds of the entire population of the globe were suddenly brought within the reach of the missionary who preaches a full gospel and carries an open Bible. It was that same year that the "week of prayer" began, upon recommendation of the missionaries in Lahore, and how quickly came the answer! From that year, missions entered upon an entirely new career. On the walls of history a divine Finger wrote, as in flaming capitals, certain words which should be the motto of all future enterprise for God:

"Behold I have set before thee an open door."
"The fulness of time is now come."
"The King's business requireth haste."
"The field is the world."
"Occupy till I come."

One must read the story of missions with veiled eyes who sees no miracles of providential preparation.

When the *Thaddeus*, in 1820, furled sail in the harbour of Oahu with that pioneer band of eighteen, who went to begin the long, and, as some thought, hopeless fight with a degraded and brutal paganism, what was their astonishment to find that, before they landed, not only had God opened to them a door of access, but He had moved a pagan priest and a pagan king to strike the first blow at Hawaiian idols! Obookiah, the native lad, who in his impatience to get ashore had gone off in a small boat, had brought back to them, while yet on board, the news: "Oahu's idols are no more!" And they could only make the vault of heaven ring with their praise: Sing, O heavens! for the Lord hath done it!

Was there no meaning in this opening history of the work of the American Board in those Pacific waters? Who was it that, before these missionaries had set foot on these islands, and not only without their agency but without their knowledge, had demolished the barriers of a thousand years and left before them a wide and effectual door? They came to Jericho, and before they had even marched around it, the walls are found fallen flat, and the stronghold awaiting easy occupation. When it is remembered that this mission was undertaken by that great missionary society as a sort of test-work, in which the will of God might be seen as to future and similar enterprises, the whole of this unparalleled beginning reminds us of Joshua's interview with the Captain of the Lord's host, who assured him in advance that He was there to lead them on to victory.

Japan, almost at the other limit of the half century thus begun, may be cited as an example of providential preparation. If ever a divine plan and purpose were to be seen, surely it is here. Was it an accident or mere incident that, after two centuries of exclusion and proscription, Christianity should find entrance to the Land of the Rising Sun, at the very time when a great social and political upheaval had unsettled the old foundations, and offered opportunity to establish a new order! In no previous time of Japanese history—certainly not since the year 1600— had such an hour of crisis come. And hence the progress of this Island Empire toward national transformation and evangelization has been more rapid than anything known since the accession of Constantine.

The preparation which Robert W. McAll found in France for his simple evangelistic work, can be compared to nothing but a *sudden subsidence* of barriers, such as we sometimes see when some seismic convulsion sinks the land

> **SCRIPTURE TESTIMONY**
>
> *Unbelievers pleading to hear the Gospel*
>
> ACTS 16:9-10

below sea level and lets the waters rush in upon the submerged territory.

When McAll went to the French capital in 1872, the war with Germany had left desolation behind it. Anarchy and violence had brought a new experience of the revolution of eighty years before, with its cruelties, bloodshed, lawlessness and godlessness. Even atheistic France revolted from the terrors of a society without God. It was a period of transition. The land of La Fayette was breaking her long allegiance with Papal Rome; Gambetta had thundered out his anathema against "clericalism" as "the foe of France;" and the nation, weary of a religion which was a wedlock of formalism and superstition, and whose offspring was hollow ceremonial and utter recklessness, was drifting toward utter denial of God and of all godliness.

Just at this time McAll came to Paris and met that "man of Macedonia" opposite the wine-shop in Belleville, who, in unmistakable words, said: "Come over and help us!" That whole mission work is one of the miracles of modern Providence, raising up and thrusting into the field the right man, at the right hour, in the right place! The round peg dropped into the round hole, and the man and his work fitted each other perfectly. Just when it was needed and prepared for, France got, for the workingmen and the priest-ridden masses, a simple gospel, unencumbered with churchly methods, without priestly forms and without price.

Instances such as these are sufficient to convince even unbelievers that God's Hand is in missionary history. And, even if any one of the many examples of such providential preparation were insufficient to sustain the argument for such divine Providence, their *united* testimony is overwhelming; they are like the threads which, separately unable to bear a heavy strain, may, when wound into one strand, defy any power to break them.

III.

Providential Preservations.

Missionary history abounds in marvels of *preservation*. God does not promise, even to the most faithful of His servants, absolute immunity from disease and death. It may be best that witness should be sealed in blood as well as seasoned with suffering. The servant is not above his Master, and the first martyr may have done more to save souls by his death than Paul did by his life; but God has often stayed the hand of man, and many an imperilled witness to Christ has heard the same voice that Paul heard at Corinth: "Be not afraid, but speak, and hold thy peace; for I am with thee, and no man shall set on thee to hurt thee."

When Martin Luther was asked at Augsburg: "Now, with Pope and cardinals, priests and kings all against you, what will you do?" he answered, "Put myself under the shelter of Him who said, 'I will never leave thee, nor forsake thee! '" Having the same spirit of faith, when Robert Moffat's life was threatened at Kuruman, he bared his breast to his assailants, and calmly replied: "Strike, if you will! but my mind is made up; I stay among you." The life of John G. Paton, that has recently thrilled all lovers of missions with its story of heroism, records perhaps fifty cases in which his life was threatened, or death by violence overhung him; yet in marvellous ways deliverance came, so that his preservation seemed like a perpetual miracle.

It is now nearly thirty-eight years since on August 19, 1856, Rev. William C. Burns arrived at Chao-chow-fu, in South China, on his sacred mission of evangelization and colportage work. Suddenly arrested, and the same night brought before the district magistrate, it was decided to send him to Canton. The relations of China with foreign countries was disturbed. The Tai-ping rebellion threw China into a state of chaos; and Burns arrived on the eve of a war which, that year, broke out between Britain and China. Had he come to Canton only a little later, when the events connected with Commissioner Yeh were in progress, death would probably have been the result. In the diary of Mrs. Stewart Sandemann, of Perth, Scotland, under date of December 28th, that same year, is this entry: "Mr. Burns was safely kept through his arrest and imprisonment in China. Comparing the dates I find that we were met in prayer for him during his dangerous journey under guard of the Chinese officials!"

For more than one hundred and twenty years, the Moravian missionary ship has sailed between London and Labrador, over those exceptionally stormy waters and amid fields of icebergs, yet with such freedom from accident that Lord Gambia declared the continued preservation of this vessel to be the most remarkable occurrence in maritime history that had ever come to his knowledge. During more than one hundred and sixty years, during which about twenty-five hundred Moravian missionaries have sailed for foreign lands, in only eleven cases has any loss of life come by shipwreck; and, of all the children of missionaries sent home to Europe, not one, says Dr. Storrow, has perished at sea.

Missionaries in Africa, India and the Indian Archipelago, have, in hundreds of cases, had to face perils amid beasts of prey and deadly serpents; is there one instance recorded of death by such means? Livingstone was delivered from destruction three times in one day, and once his arm was crushed and he was shaken into insensibility by a lion. To the first missionaries to the Fijians deliverance often came when murderous foes were surrounding them, and their only weapon was prayer. Kapaio, a native of the New Hebrides, confessed that he watched to waylay Dr. Geddie, and when, with club in hand, he had him in his power, he became unable to deal the blow at the crisis when the man he hated and had followed in order to kill, was at his mercy. He confessed that a strange, new sensation came over him and convinced him that a higher power held him back.

A little while ago a company of Breecks, a low, fierce tribe of Karens, made a raid on a Christian village, and carried off as captives, two boys and a girl. They said, "Now we will see; if the Christians' God delivers these captives

SCRIPTURE TESTIMONY

Deliverance from enemies and circumstances

LUKE 1:71

out of our hands we will believe in Him, and all become Christians; but if their God cannot deliver them, we will go over and take more captives."

Just at this juncture Dr. Bunker arrived at the village where all had been praying for help. They quickly told him, and he said: "Well, this is a case of God *versus* the Devil," and he felt strong to say, *"God will deliver them; keep on praying."* He sent a message demanding the release of the captives, and got word back, "Come on; get them if you can; we have guns." He sent then what he called his *ultimatum*: "If you do not deliver up those captives we will leave you in the hands of our God, who can and will deal with you." Meanwhile he and the Christians prayed mightily. His messengers met the Breecks on the road bringing back one of the captives. He then selected one of his preachers and fourteen followers to go unarmed for the other two.

When they got to the village they did not say a word to any of the tribe, but planted themselves in the road. The preacher took out his hymn-book and read a hymn, which they sang; then he read a portion of Scripture and preached, then prayed, and by that time the villagers brought the other captives to them and said: "Now take them, and be gone." This, of course, made a great stir among the Christians, and led them to expect a great ingathering from the Breecks. The captives told them that a brother of the chief who stole the captives, himself an awfully wicked man, talked strongly about the wickedness of the deed, and the wife of the chief begged her husband to make peace while he could,— showing how God was working to bring about answers to prayer.

Let Mr. J. Hudson Taylor tell for himself the story of his first voyage to China.

<table>
<tr><td>

SCRIPTURE TESTIMONY

Ask Me anything in My name

MATTHEW 18:19 · JOHN 14:13-14 · JOHN 16:23-24

</td><td>

He says: "The voyage was a very tedious one. We lost a good deal of time on the equator from calms; and when we finally reached the Eastern Archipelago, were again detained from the same cause. Usually a breeze would spring up

</td></tr>
</table>

soon after sunset, and last until about dawn. The utmost use was made of it, but during the day we lay still, with flapping sails, often drifting back and losing a good deal of the advantage we had gained during the night.

"This happened notably on one occasion, when we were in dangerous proximity to the north of New Guinea. Saturday night had brought us to a point some thirty miles off the land; but during the Sunday morning service, which was held on deck, I could not fail to notice that the captain looked troubled, and frequently went over to the side of the ship. When the service was ended, I learned from him the cause—a four-knot current was carrying us rapidly towards some sunken reefs, and we were already so near that it seemed improbable that we should get through the afternoon in safety. After dinner the long boat was put out, and all hands endeavoured, without success, to turn the ship's head from the shore. As we drifted nearer we could plainly see the natives rushing about the sands and lighting fires every here and there. The captain's hornbook informed him that these people were cannibals, so that our position was not a little alarming.

"After standing together on the deck for some time in silence, the captain said to me, ' Well, we have done everything that can be done; we can only await the result.' A thought occurred to me, and I replied, 'No, there is one thing we have not done yet.' 'What is it?' he queried. 'Four of us on board are Christians,' I answered (the Swedish carpenter and our coloured steward, with the captain and myself); ' let us each retire to his own cabin, and in agreed prayer ask the Lord to give us immediately a breeze. He can as easily send it now as at sunset.'

"The captain complied with this proposal. I went and spoke to the other two men, and after prayer with the carpenter we all four retired to wait upon God. I had a good but very brief season in prayer, and then felt so satisfied that our request was granted that I could not continue asking, and very soon went up again on deck. The first officer, a godless man, was in charge. I went over and asked him to let down the clews or comers of the mainsail, which had been drawn up in order to lessen the useless flapping of the sail against the rigging. He answered, ' What would be the good of that?' I told him we had been asking a wind from God, that it was coming immediately, and we were so near the reef by this time that there was not a minute to lose. With a look of incredulity and contempt, he said with an oath that he would rather see a wind than hear of it! But while he was speaking I watched his eye, and followed it up to the royal (the topmost sail), and there, sure enough, the comer of the sail was beginning to tremble in the coming breeze. ' Don't you see the wind is coming? Look at the royal! ' I exclaimed. ' No, it is only a cat's-paw,' he rejoined (a mere puff of wind). 'Cat's-paw or not,' I cried, 'pray let down the mainsail, and let us have the benefit! '

"This he was not slow to do. In another minute the heavy tread of the men on the deck brought up the captain from his cabin to see what was the matter, and saw that the breeze had indeed come. In a few minutes we were ploughing our way at six or seven knots an hour through the water, and the multitude of naked savages whom we had seen on the beach had no wreckage that night. We were soon out of danger; and, though the wind was sometimes unsteady, we did not altogether lose it until after passing the Pelew Islands.

"Thus God encouraged me, before landing on China's shores, to bring every variety of need to Him in prayer, and *to expect that He would honour the Name* of the Lord Jesus, and give the help which each emergency required."

The following incident is related of a Chinese convert,* who had for many years been a vegetarian, to gain merit and be saved. "He came to the chapel," says the writer, "heard and believed the gospel, and for years has lived a consistent Christian life.

SCRIPTURE TESTIMONY

God answers prayer

LUKE 18:7 · JOHN 15:7 ·
ACTS 12:5 · JAMES 5:15

Some time ago the people collected a large sum of money to be expended in idolatrous work, in order that their houses might be saved from fire, and asked this man to contribute to that fund. He declined, on the ground that he trusted in the living God, and that the idols were not able to save them from fire. No sooner was the idolatrous ceremony over than an extensive fire broke out in the very street in which this man's house was situated; one hundred and twenty houses were burnt down, and when the flames were coming nearer and nearer to his house, the people said, 'Now you see what you have got.' And they wanted to persuade him to take out all his furniture into the street that he might save something. He knew that if he brought the things out into the street, even though they would be safe from fire, they would probably be stolen. But he believed that God was going to preserve him from suffering loss, and he told the people so. While they were hurrying to and fro in all their excitement, he, in the presence of them all, prayed God that He would show that He was the living and true God. And then he watched the fire as it came nearer and nearer, until there was only one house standing between his own and the flames. But just then there was a sudden change in the wind: God had said, ' Thus far shalt thou come and no farther,' and his house was saved."

David Livingstone, returning from Central Africa, told of a great inland sea—Lake Nyassa. The Scottish churches and the Universities' Mission took possession for Christ—money and life were freely spent to evangelize Nyassaland. After several years the envy of Portugal is aroused: she sends Major Serpa Pinto to seize the country, and Cardinal Lavigerie is ready with his priests to station them in all the places where the missionaries have laboured, where the graves of Englishmen and Englishwomen are "the title deeds to Nyassaland." Is all this work for Christ to be overthrown? A spirit of prayer comes upon British Christians, and the Portuguese encroachments are defeated, not by the statesmanship of Lord Salisbury, but by the prayers of those who sent out the missionaries, and who, day by day, cease not to pray on their behalf. Truly, "It is better to trust in the Lord than to put confidence in princes."**

---

* "China's Millions,"Sept, 1883. "Progress in China,"by Rev, A, Foster, p. 52,
** Missionary Review of the World. Vol. iv. p. 26.

In 1574, God, at the siege of Leyden, used the forces of Nature to compel the retreat of the Spanish armies. The Spaniards had derisively shouted to the citizens, "As well might the Prince of Orange pluck the stars from the sky as bring the ocean to the walls of Leyden for your relief;" but, on the night of the first and second of October, a violent gale from the northwest and southwest piled up the waters of the North Sea in vast masses on the coast, and drove them furiously landward, till the ocean swept with unrestrained fury across the ruined dykes, and the relieving fleet sailed up almost to the walls of the city! No wonder, as Motley says, that the enemies of Holland were struck with terror when they saw the hand of God send the ocean and tempest to the deliverance of the besieged city. It was the prayers of saints offered up in those times of great peril that preserved Holland from Spanish fury, as Britain was preserved from the Spanish and French Armadas.

The missionary life of that "veteran of Aniwa" is one almost continuous example of striking answers to believing prayer. When the armed savages approached Nowar's village and the people were panic-stricken, such prayer

SCRIPTURE TESTIMONY

God answers prayer

LUKE 18:7 · JOHN 15:7 ·
ACTS 12:5 · JAMES 5:15

rose to Jehovah as can be offered only by those who stand consciously on the brink of eternity. The savages were only about three hundred yards off when Nowar touched Rev. J. G. Paton's knee, saying, "Missy, Jehovah is here. See, they all stand still!" "We gazed shorewards," says Mr. Paton, "and sure enough they were all standing still. They actually began to turn and enter the remote bush at the end of the harbour." Why they turned back no man can tell. God was interfering to save imperilled lives. At another time when the savages surrounded the mission-house, and set fire to the church and the fence connecting the church and the dwelling, Mr. Paton ran out and tore up the burning fence, while savages raised their clubs and shouted, "Kill him!" At this moment occurred an incident which his readers may explain as they like, but which he traced directly to the interposition of my God. A rushing and roaring sound came from the south, like the noise of a mighty engine or of muttering thunder. Every head was instinctively turned in that direction, and they knew from previous hard experience that it was one of their awful tornadoes. Now mark, the wind bore the flames away from the house, but had it come in the opposite direction no power on earth could have saved them all from being consumed. It made the work of destroying the church only that of a few minutes; but it brought with it a heavy and murky cloud which poured out a perfect torrent of tropical rain. Now mark again: the flames of the burning church were thereby cut off from extending to and seizing upon the reeds and the bush, and, besides, it had become almost impossible now to set fire to the house. A panic seized the savages, and throwing down their torches they fled. Returning to the house Mr. Paton was met by Mr. Mathieson, who exclaimed, "If ever, in time of need, God sent help and protection to his servants, in answer to prayer, He has done so to-night. Blessed be His holy name!"

The reader of the two volumes of the "Life of John G. Paton, Missionary to the New Hebrides," will not need to be told that the whole narrative evinces the interposition of God. No biography has done more in modern days to revive faith in Providential Preservations.

IV.

New Judgments of God.

WE RECOGNIZE wonders of Providential interposition in the defence of His servants and the defeat and destruction of their foes.

From the times that the stars in heaven fought against Sisera, God has not ceased to do battle for His own elect. And in not a few instances His "little flock," few and feeble amid their foes, like lambs among wolves, have had only to stand still and see His salvation. Sometimes the Angel of Death has gone forth at His bidding and smitten the enemies of His people with a destruction as sudden as that which smote Herod in the midst of his fawning courtiers. Kings have conspired to cast away His cords from them, and rulers have counselled together to break asunder His bands; but His sceptre has dashed them in pieces like a potter's vessel.

In Siam, in 1851, and in Turkey twelve years before, at the very crisis of missions, when absolute expulsion of all Christ's witnesses was impending and final disaster threatened their work, sudden death came to the hostile monarchs who had flung themselves upon the bosses of Jehovah's buckler. These two cases may stand as sufficient to represent the class of interpositions we refer to now. In both cases the respective rulers were at the time proposing and preparing to drive out all Christian missionaries and bring their work to wreck and ruin. In both cases, all resistance was so hopeless that prayer to God was the one and only resort. And, in both cases, the death of the stubborn and malignant monarch,

SCRIPTURE TESTIMONY

*Deliverance from enemies
and circumstances*

LUKE 1:71

at the exact time when the plan was ripe for accomplishment, and the crisis of missions had fully come, was felt even by the foes of God themselves to be an interposition of God, and turned the scale.

When Sultan Mahmud thus suddenly died in Turkey, the edict of expulsion found no executive to carry it into operation. On the other hand, Abdul Medjid who succeeded him, on the 3d of November following, in presence of an august assemblage of the nobles of the empire, not only the Mussulmans, but the deputies of the Greeks, Armenians and Jews, together with foreign ambassadors, ordered his Grand Vizier to read the *Hatti Sherif of Gûl Hane*, or first formal Bill of Rights, the Magna Charta of Turkey, and himself led the way in taking the oath of fidelity to this new Charter of Liberty, which prepared the way for the famous *Hatti Humayoun* in 1856! Thus, for more than fifty years missions have been acquiring more and more influence within the dominions of the Sultan of Turkey.

As to that other Land of the White Elephant, the turn of tide is one of the most striking in all history. Maha-Mong-Kut, who then came to the throne, was the one man in the empire who had been prepared by God to be the friend and patron of Christian missions. He had been taught in science and language by a missionary, and in this frequent and familiar contact had become his friend and the friend of his fellow missionaries. He had imbibed from such intercourse a liberality of mind, a catholicity of sentiment, which both fitted and disposed him to favour and further the work of the missionary. He was not, however, a Christian disciple, and had retired to the cell of the Buddhist monastery. But, on the sudden demise of the reigning and reckless sovereign, Maha-Mong-Kut was called from his seclusion to mount the throne of the "Sacred Prabahts," and, for seventeen years, wielded a sceptre so benignant that he has been known as the most enlightened and catholic ruler of all Asia. Before he died he had decreed liberty of conscience throughout all the land, and his son and successor, Chulalangkom, has followed in his steps. More than forty years not only of toleration, but of co-operation toward missions, have been the fruit of one unmistakable act of divine interposition in 1851. Could unwritten history find a record, there are many such interpositions both in behalf of individuals, and of the work of missions as such, which equally reveal the presence and power of Him whose last promise was, "Lo, I am with you alway."

There is something awful in the majesty of divine judgments. God's "great army" has not been disbanded, though the prophet's pen no longer outlines their march and describes their regiments. Caterpillar and cankerworm, locust and palmerworm still obey His behests.

What a desert of devastation, for instance, the locust leaves in his track! Think of an army of these invaders, reaching fifty miles in every direction, and half a mile thick, with one hundred and fifty locusts to the cubic foot, and moving from twelve to twenty miles an hour! It would require seven million vessels, each of six thousand tons burden, to transport such a host; and yet this is but one small detachment of God's "great army!"

God calls for the famine and it does His bidding, and often strangely prepares His way. In India it introduced, in 1877, the greatest ingathering of converts ever known. In China, in the days of Morrison, eight times it did the

SCRIPTURE TESTIMONY

Christians take care of their enemy's needs

ROMANS 12:20

work of an evangelist and made full proof of its ministry by giving God's servants the opportunity to show the unselfishness of the Christian spirit. A heathen people, dying of drought or flood, pestilence or starvation, see their fellows of the same nation and religion, stand aloof in utter indifference, while "foreign devils," inspired by a hated faith, labour night and day, daring all privations and exposures to feed the starving, heal the sick, and comfort the dying; and this goes further to correct false prejudices and win men to Christ than any argument or word of witness. Famine has been so often the precursor of "revivals" that missionaries have learned to think of it as an angel in dark disguise. In connection with that Pentecost at Hilo and Puna, there was a miracle of judgment that will never be forgotten. In a secluded valley of Puna was one small village which was a moral cesspool. Awful as was the heathenism about it, here it was worse, and the labours of Mr. Coan, so rapidly fruitful elsewhere, here, for years were vain and even worse than vain, for the people hardened themselves against God, and even sought to starve out his messengers. At one time Mr. Coan, with a little band of native Kanakas, went there to hold a meeting, and were refused even a half-potato; and at night lay down unable to sleep for hunger. While the villagers thought them asleep, they were seen eating the food which they had denied that they were able to supply for the Lord's servants. In the morning, the missionary left them, literally shaking off the dust of his feet for a testimony against them, saying, "Never again will I come to you until you call for me." Not long after, this village, though forty miles from port where the infection was usually caught, was so visited by a scourge of small-pox, that, save three or four survivors, every inhabitant died; and in 1840, a lava flood swept over the site of the previous visitation of God, and left only a black field of death and desolation behind it. It is to this day a reminder of the destruction that overtook Sodom! The people saw in it God's strange work of judgment and retribution.

V.

General Administration.

Japan is looked upon by the world as one of its modern wonders. The revolution, there wrought within a decade of years, has perhaps no historic parallel. The steps were giant strides: the fall of the dual dynasty, the change of capitals, the death-blow of feudalism, the adoption of a new calendar, and of the weekly Rest-day; the establishment of postal union and savings banks; national mint, lighthouses and coast survey; of railways and telegraphs; the reconstruction of army and navy and educational systems—these were a few of the prominent features of the New Japan, now also crowned with constitutional liberty.

To some, there is in this no hand of God, but only a nation waking from long sleep, shaking his locks, quaffing the new wine of Western enterprise; and, conscious of gianthood, bursting old bonds and taking huge strides forward. But there are circumstances too remarkable to allow any explanation short of divine interposition; some coincidences which are both marks and fruits of a higher plan, in which, as cog fits cog in the wheel of a vast machine, event meets event in a pre-arranged harmony. As in Ezekiel's vision, even events which face different ways move together in one direction.

Commodore Perry's initial act—when he laid an open Bible over the American flag upon the capstan of his flagship, and sent the words of the Hundredth Psalm echoing over Yeddo's Bay—that initial act was a parable in action. The mute guns of his warship spoke of a peaceful commerce displacing warlike invasion. The stars and stripes were the symbol of Western civilization with its liberty, civil and religious; and the open Bible and the sacred psalm forecast gospel triumph. God himself planned all the details of that opening scene, and according to that pattern the work has been built on those shores.

216

All along the subsequent development of these forty years, we see the play of this divine mechanism —the wheel in the middle of the wheel. We shall need only to recur to the story of Neesima, as already given in previous pages. Apparently accidental, really providential — his disgust with idols, his glimpse of the Bible, his taste of a new faith, his escape to America, his contact with Alpheus Hardy, his Christian training, his service to the embassy, his return to his own land, the vindication of his right to teach, the establishment of the Doshisha—are not these the play of divine coincidents and coincidences in an articulated plan?

After Neesima found Christ, and, while asking how he could get back to his country without incurring death for having gone away without leave—the Japanese embassy seek his aid as interpreter. Through them he not only gets safe conduct, but open door to his new mission among his countrymen; for, when he lands in Japan, his former patrons of the embassy are holding the reins of empire, and the decree goes forth to his opponents: "Let Neesima alone!"

Watch the play of these wheels still further. Was it a mere chance that opened Kyoto for the Hundred Days' Exhibition, when Rev. O. H. Gulick made the acquaintance of that friend whose powerful mediation not only furthered Neesima's plans for Christian education, but furnished the site for the Doshisha? And when the "sacred city" would have denied even Neesima the right to teach the Christian faith, it was Tanaka himself, who owed to Neesima his successful study Of the common schools of America,—who was head of the department of education and turned the scale in Neesima's favour; so that he himself could only attribute his deliverance from the "deep muds of the past" to the "unseen hand of God."

Close search reveals in this curious fabric of Japanese history one delicate thread of divine purpose, wrought of countless fibres. Many of these providential events belong to yet unwritten records; but a further example may serve to confirm our faith in this remarkable guidance of God.

Just when this great work of Christian education at Kyoto hung in the balance and final failure seemed to threaten, there came a strange accession of some thirty native Christian students as reinforcements from a most unexpected quarter. In the old province of Higo, in Kuishu, some "Jo-i" men, or "foreign-expellers"— had banded together to form a school for the purpose of keeping out Western ideas, and especially the hated Western religion. A certain Captain Janes, who had come out to teach military tactics, but was without employment, by another most singular chain of events became the teacher. That man, says Dr. Davis, Neesima's biographer, was himself a Christian. Yet so deadly was the hatred of the new faith that for six months he had to keep his Christianity out of sight;

but meanwhile he could not keep its influence from pervading the school—a flower cannot suppress its fragrance even in the darkness. At last he ventured to present the scientific argument for the existence of a God, and was met by a bold challenge from his pupils, "*You lie, sir!*" Two years went by before he dared to ask some more advanced students to study the New Testament with him. The patrons of the school consented because students must understand Christianity *in order to oppose it.*

Behold God's hand placing in the very hotbed of infidel culture, a plant of godliness! and making the foes of the faith to give it room to take root, in order that they might learn how to recognize it and destroy it wherever found! God's armour-bearer is training the opposers of Christ in the knowledge of His own weapons; and, meanwhile, they are compelled to see that no weapon formed against Him can prosper!

Two years more go by. To study the New Testament is to look upon the cross with its Crucified One, and before the infinite pathos of that cross, the winter in their hearts shows signs of melting under the beams of the Sun of Righteousness! And less than five years after Bible study began its work, forty of those young men who had banded to fight the new faith, went up the Hanaoka mountain to set their seal to a new covenant with Christ and each other, to give their lives to Christ for Japan! And these were the men that in the crisis reinforced the imperilled enterprise at Kyoto, and in 1879 were graduated from the Doshisha to become the best native teachers and preachers to mould the New Japan!

There are many other plain signs of the divine working in this well-jointed mechanism. Neesima was a conspicuous man from his connection with the embassy and the Doshisha, and even the opposition to his work only gave his name and fame a trumpet voice. The graduates from his school were found to be commanding the best posts in the empire and controlling affairs by sheer force of character, so that, at the tenth anniversary of the Doshisha, it had proven its mission to be so useful that it had vindicated its right to be. Count Inouye himself gave the address, and so the government recognized a Christian school as a national blessing! Before Neesima died he had, in a large Buddhist temple at Kyoto, pleaded for the new university, and over 60,000 yen had been subscribed. And five years ago the work of the Doshisha had already given to Japan nearly one thousand young workers for God.

This story we have considered worthy of a large place as an example of the wonder-working of God in modern missions. Prominent as is the individual factor, its importance is found only in its connection with Him who alone controls history. This man was the rod of God with which He wrought signs.

Neesima's biographer, already referred to, expresses the sum of all this forty years' wonderworking:

"Let us realize that God still moves in a mysterious way His wonders to perform in the world. The age of miracles of physical healing may be past, but we have before us the fulfilment at the present day of the Saviour's promise: 'Greater works than these shall ye do, because I go unto my Father!'" Then referring to the wonderful chain of events already traced, he adds: "This is as great a 'miracle' as is recorded in the Old Testament or the New, if we except our Saviour's incarnation and atoning work. It is inconceivable that all these improbable things should happen and come together at just the right time, simply by chance!"

The *location and succession of labourers* is another proof of providential administration. Who but God knows what sort of men and women will be needed at any critical and pivotal point of time and place. Yet with what divine prescience the story of missions abounds! God has at the precise exigency raised up and placed at the great centres of influence the exact workmen needed. And they could have had no conscious part in this adaptation, for they did not know the field to which they were going, and still less did they know its peculiar wants. There were obvious pre-adaptations which far transcend all mere human forethought. How little Livingstone knew how his preparations for China were pre-eminently fitting him for Africa and his exact work in the Dark Continent! When McAll was amusing himself with architectural drawing, how little did he dream that his pencil was to be brought into such requisition in planning salles in Paris! When John E. Clough was training as a civil engineer, and persisted in going to India, who but God foresaw that, in 1877, a civil engineer would be specially needed to complete that Buckingham canal, and give perishing Telugus work and wages? Who gave Carey such native love for linguistic study and such passion for Cook's "Voyages," but He who meant him for England's first missionary to India, and the great translator of His Word into the many dialects of that vast empire? Dr. George E. Post little thought, when perfecting himself in medicine and surgery, that he was to wield a worldwide influence from Beirut, and make St. John's Hospital a vestibule to the kingdom of heaven.

Was it no providence of God that at *critical periods* of missions raised up and placed at the great centres of influence the exact men and women needed? What a man was Lord William Bentinck, to take the governor-generalship in India during that memorable seven years, from 1828-1835. It forms an epoch in administrative reform, and in the slow process whereby the population of a province become reconciled to foreign rule, and even attached to alien rulers. With Lord Bentinck *begins that modern history* of British rule in India which introduced a benevolent and fraternal administration, wherein the good of the native population was the supreme end kept in view. Two memorable acts forever adorn his rule: the abolition of suttee and the suppression of the Thugs. So prevalent was the immolation of widows under religious sanction, that, in the year 1817, seven hundred mounted the pyre in Bengal presidency alone; and to-day, each of the little white pillars, so thickly dotting the most holy pilgrim paths of the Hindus, commemorates a suttee. In the face of determined opposition, both from natives and Europeans, this noble magistrate decreed Dec. 4, 1829, that all who abetted the suttee were to be held guilty of "culpable homicide." And when the Brahmans claimed the right to follow their own conscience, which, as they declared, demanded that widows should be burned alive, he calmly answered: "Obey your conscience, then; but I forewarn you that an Englishman's conscience compels him to hang every one of you who becomes responsible for such murder!"

And then, as to the Thugs or Thagi—those bands of secret assassins bound by oath to commit outrages, and basing their vows on the rites of the bloody Kali— between 1826 and 1835, over fifteen hundred of these Thugs were apprehended in different parts of India. And thus gradually the plagues of India abated.

Macaulay's graceful pen furnished that noble tribute engraved on the statue at Calcutta:

"He abolished cruel rites; he effaced humiliating distinctions; he gave liberty to the expression of public opinion; his constant study it was to elevate the intellectual and moral character of the nations committed to his charge."

And so suttee and Thug outrages ceased; and then infanticide—till, in 1863, the last link between idolfanes and State patronage was broken.

VI.

Miracles of Grace.

The remark of Prof. Theodore Christlieb is often repeated, that "in the history of modern missions we find many wonderful occurrences which unmistakably remind us of the Apostolic age." And in view of the fact that, now as then, such hindrances to the gospel exist in the heathen world that the sense of divine things is dulled and blunted, he thought that supernatural exhibitions of power are needed to confirm the message and compel attention. With such a basis of conviction that God's intervention is to be expected, the wonders recorded in the experience of Hans Egede, Spangenberg and Zeis-berger, Kleinschmidt, and the little flock in the Vaudois valleys, will not appear incredible. And, inasmuch as there is no hint in the New Testament that the signs promised as proofs of Christ's presence and confirmations of faith were ever to cease, why are we incredulous as to the reality of the wonders recorded?

The New Acts of the Apostles have recorded similar triumphs of grace. In countless cases the moral miracle wrought at Ephesus has been repeated. Leaders of the people, who have made merchandise of superstition and imposture, have sacrificed both their profits and their prominence, their means of livelihood and sometimes life itself, rather than longer sin against God, or betray even by silence their former victims of ignorance and delusion. Who can count the cost to a Brahman like Sheshadri in India, or a Maronite priest like Asaad Shidiak in Syria, of renouncing a false faith and a lying life, henceforth to teach the hated gospel and bear the shameful cross! Hudson Taylor tells of one such conversion in inland China, where a former leader in atrocious crimes turned the haunts of unbridled lust into the place of prayer, and himself became the witness to those whom he had led astray.

In the Acts of the Apostles, they are the wonders of grace that overawe us, and not those of simple power. When the magicians, already referred to, that clustered about Diana's great temple, were so wrought upon by the Spirit of God that their pride and greed, their lust of power and their lust of gain, were at once renounced, and the flames devoured the costly text-books of their occult arts, there is something in such sacrifices that is sublimer than any mere display of force, though it were sufficient to shake the earth itself. We all know that selfish greed and social rank grapple men as with hooks of steel; and we stand in awe of such proofs of divine working as were seen when all sources of pecuniary gain and superstitious prestige were thus voluntarily abandoned.

<table>
<tr><td>SCRIPTURE TESTIMONY

There are no gender distinctions in Christ

GALATIANS 3:28</td></tr>
</table>

Is it no sign of God's power when moral and social changes which the wisest men reckon among impossibilities are not only actually wrought but with a rapidity that seems fabulous?

For example, when Dr. Duff began work in Calcutta, he found that a cow had more rights and higher rank than a woman, and he said that to try to educate women in India was as vain as to attempt to "scale a wall five hundred yards high." To-day in the province of Bengal alone a hundred thousand women and girls are under instruction, and India's most gifted daughters are laying hold of the treasures of the higher education. Zenana doors have been unlocked by the gentle hand of Christian womanhood, and a transformation is already accomplished which centuries of merely human wisdom and power could not even have begun.

Those sagacious men who are God's seers look on this great change as the hope of this Oriental Empire. Woman was taken out of man, yet even in India as in Eden, woman leads man, and through her heart lies the road to his head. Whatever system of truth or faith captivates woman, in the end captures man. Even those who see, can scarce believe what they see—a moral movement to-day in progress, by which the conditions of a half century ago are being reversed. What then was a wall of hopeless exclusion, the despair of the missionary, is now become a highway of access and the hope of final conquest, as before the victorious Macedonian the walls of Tyre were turned into the mole that joined the island to the mainland.

Henry Martyn calmly said that the conversion of Krishna Chundra Pal, India's first Protestant convert, was as stupendous a miracle as raising the dead. What would he say if he saw the native Christians in that empire of Brahma, increasing eighty per cent, in one decade of years?

When that first convert was baptized, in 1800, the islands of the South Seas thronged with hordes of heartlessly cruel savages. Cannibalism, their shame, was yet their glory; human skins furnished them with water-bags and human skulls with drinking-cups; men's bones were their ornaments, and men's blood moistened their war-paint. How has it come to pass that to-day scarce a trace of these brutal barbarities exists through the vast Pacific Archipelago?

From the commencement of the *Bechuana* mission by Hamilton Read, in 1816, for over ten years no ray of light shot athwart the gloom. The Batlaping had open ears only to what promised temporal gains, and were deaf to all spiritual invitation or warning. When the sorely-tried faith of the missionaries almost gave way, there was a holy woman in the mission who never faltered in her faith. She believed in the promise of an unchanging God, and she said: "We may not live to see it, but, as surely as to-morrow's sun will rise, the awakening will come." When her friends at home would have counselled her to give up her forlorn hope and go to a promising field, and when Mrs. Greaves, of Sheffield, wrote, asking what could be sent her that would be of use—the sublime answer of Mary Moffat was: "Send us a *communion service*; it will be wanted."

At that time there was not the first glimmer of day—it was the forecast of faith; and it took many months for the letter to find its way to England and for the request to find fulfilment. And, meanwhile, the darkness seemed to deepen, and doubts grew graver as to the expediency of carrying on the Bechuana mission; but her faith knew no change: it had its grip on the promises. In 1827, the gray light of dawn faintly appeared, and by 1829, a marvellous quickening began even among these stolidly indifferent natives, and without any human or visible cause. There was "a wave of tumultuous and simultaneous enthusiasm," which could not be due to the "sober-minded and hard-headed Scotchmen," who have a wholesome dread of sensationalism and emotionalism. But in a few months the whole aspect of matters was changed. The meeting-house thronged in advance of the hour of service—songs and prayers instead of pagan chants and dances—all at once eternal realities had come to the front and compelled attention. The dirt and filth and nudity of the natives were exchanged for cleanly habits and decent attire, and such a spirit of inquiry was aroused that the little Kuruman meeting-house resounded with sobs and cries that made it hard to go on with the usual forms of worship. And the first time the table of the Lord was spread in the Bechuana mission, the same number sat down as at the original celebration in Jerusalem! and the very day previous to that appointed for this ordinance, there arrived a box, long on the way, which being opened was found to hold the communion vessels Mary Moffat had asked for nearly three years before—prophesying "we shall want them—send them on!"

William Duncan took seven years—1856-1863—to establish his model state among the wild Red men of North America. When he first went among them he found nine hostile tribes gathered together, and when after six months he undertook to preach his first sermon, he dared not bring them into one assembly, but delivered it nine times the same day to as many different groups; and when Lord Dufferin, Governor-General of Canada, went to see Duncan's Metlakahtla, he could find no terms in the various languages of which he was master, fitly to describe what he saw, but could only exclaim, "What wonders hath God wrought!"

William Duncan went to Fort Simpson in 1856, where he found some twenty houses of fur-traders, and nearly three hundred in along straight line on the Pacific coast, where wild Indians lived.

Not long after his arrival he found a crowd of these savages on the beach actually tearing in pieces, and then eating, a human body. With the aid of an Indian, named Clah, who could speak English, he undertook to learn the languages of these wild men, and get acquainted with their habits. He found two distinct parties—"man-eaters," and "dog-eaters"— but more numerous tribal divisions. He began to visit them at their houses, and after working over eight months, wrote out that first plain sermon which nine times he read to audiences that numbered from fifty to two hundred. He opened his first school in the house of a chief, Legiac. At first he had such conflicts with their unholy rites and pagan superstitions, that even his life was in danger; but he persevered, teaching and preaching and visiting the sick, and the influence of the gospel became apparent. Feathers and paint gave place to decent attire. Even the chiefs were found at school; church-goers were numbered by hundreds. And in 1863, he withdrew with fifty Indians to a retired bay twenty miles off, that he might build there a model state, free from the drunkenness and other vices that were constantly undoing his work at Fort Simpson. Six weeks later, he was joined by three hundred more who entered into the covenant to abandon pagan practices and vicious habits. And so the foundations of *Metlakahtla* were laid. A Christian village grew with surprising rapidity. It was laid out with regularity, but its outward order was but a faint reflection of its moral order.

Chief Legiac was transformed from a fierce and revengeful savage to a quiet carpenter, and became Mr. Duncan's chief helper. The Tsimean Indians developed not only into industrious tradesmen, but into artistic carvers in wood, stone and ivory, and jewellers. The natives bought their own vessel and set on foot their own commerce. Whiskey and immorality were excluded, and Metlakahtla became a proverb for all the most beneficent fruits of Christianity, and put to shame the oldest and best governed communities of Christian lands, by its beautiful example of the Power of the Gospel.

Individual conversions weigh heavily in the scale when we are seeking proofs that God is supernaturally working; but when to these is added the weight of testimony found in these changes that affect the whole domestic and social life, what doubt remains? We must take the whole range of human experience, of the sins and sorrows, curses and crimes of society, when we estimate either human degradation or elevation. *Gesta Diaboli* must be known if *Gesta Christi* are understood.

What lever is that which after thousands of years of worse than slavery is now lifting womanhood to a lofty level? In Asia woman has long found no welcome at birth, no instruction in girlhood, no love in wifehood, no care in motherhood, no protection in old age, no regret in death. In Africa, sold for so many head of cattle, she has often been more brutally treated; and in Persia, loaded like a donkey, she could not easily be distinguished from a beast of burden. Tabooed by caste, denied either freedom or society, counted as soulless, and both incapable of culture and unworthy of respect, she has been shut up in a domestic prison, and treated as a slave for service and a victim for vice.

Where woman is thus dishonoured, we shall not be surprised to find the whole basis of society rotten, and can believe that the road leading to Juggemath's shrine is for fifty miles paved with men's bones, and that the altars of that monster are stained with blood and smeared with obscenity. We shall not find it hard to credit the awful sacrifices which slavery has offered on the altar of human cruelty, though it has bound and slain such a host of victims that their bodies, laid side by side, would thrice girdle the globe at the equator!

Sin has made the earth the habitation of cruelty. When the old king of Eboe died, by the *ju-ju* rites forty victims were sacrificed. Nine of his youngest wives, their ankles and wrists broken, and in excruciating pain, were put at the bottom of the open grave pit, with the dead body, to await death by slow starvation, guards being stationed about the grave with clubs to beat back any of them if they moved from their place. Other human beings were bored through the feet and hung from high trees heads downward to die in agony. And these are but specimen-pages from that bloody book of human history which records deeds of which it is a shame even to speak.

The missionary who has witnessed the power of God unto salvation is not ashamed of the gospel of Christ. He sees it lifting the individual to his true level and putting him in his normal place. Nakedness is decently clad; the hut or hovel, where beasts made their stalls side by side with human beings, gives place to neat and comely houses, where modesty is no longer put to shame, and order reigns. Children are nourished and cherished with loving tenderness, and breathe the atmosphere of a pious, prayerful home. Woman is dignified and honoured, wedlock sanctified, and family life glorified. Honest toil is respected and rewarded; the serf and the slave are made free and independent; ignorance and idleness, the handmaids of vice, are exchanged for virtue's habitual attendants—industry and intelligence.

Isaac Taylor once attempted a catalogue of the great social evils: polygamy, legalized prostitution and capricious divorce, bloody and brutal games, rapacious and offensive wars, death and punishment by torture, infanticide, caste and slavery. From all lands where the cross has been set up and the gospel faithfully preached, these nine gigantic forms of wrong are either retreating or are no more found. A new standard of manhood is also erected, and new lessons in living, taught. So surely as Christ becomes Master, so surely do these owls of the midnight flee before the new dawn.

Instead of polygamy, once more, as at the beginning, one man and one woman become "one flesh." The law, instead of shielding vice by legalizing it, becomes the avenging sword to punish unbridled lust; and easy divorce is condemned as the apology and refuge of "free love." Infanticide is branded as both cruelty and crime, fatal both to natural affection and a good conscience. Aggressive warfare becomes highway robbery and organized slaughter. Bloody and brutal games are considered as lowering man to the level of the brute, if not the demon; and needless torture even of the worst criminal, inflicts a pang upon the community-scarcely less keen than the anguish of the victim. Caste is seen to be an insult to God, because a dishonour to His image in man; and slavery becomes, to an enlightened Christian society, the breach of all duty and love both to God and our neighbour—the violation of the whole decalogue at once—a conspiracy of man to rob and ruin, debauch and defraud, degrade and dishonour his fellow-man—to make impossible a true life for the individual, the family, or the state; to set a premium on lies and lusts, covetousness and cruelty; to cage God's nightingale—the human soul—and put out its eyes, that it may become content behind bars and sing when it can no longer soar!

There are those who dispute the unique claims of the Son of God, and talk of Christianity as one of the great religions, all of which have their right to a seat in the world's parliament. But the difference between the gospel of Christ and any other religion is one not of *degree* only, but of *kind*. Let these claimants to the honour of equal rank bring forth their witnesses. Greece boasted her religion of beauty and art, wisdom and knowledge; Rome, her manly virtue and martial valour, model laws and ideal state. Did the refinement and culture of Athens, even in the age of Pericles, or the noble statesmanship and heroic courage of Rome in the days of Augustus, actually uplift society from moral degradation and depravity? Did these "religions" banish gladiatorial games and the cruelties of the arena, and aggressive wars of conquest? Did they prevent worn-out slaves and even aged parents from being turned out to die; or, the modesty of maidens from being sacrificed at temple altars in the name of religion? Did Athens or Rome build hospitals or asylums for the deaf and dumb and blind and crippled and incurably diseased? Let Buddha, "Light of Asia," and Brahma, India's saviour, tell us whether they made impossible the murder of the innocents, the funeral pyre and the torture fire, the car of Juggernath, the hook-swing, the bed of spikes, the caste walls, the child marriage, the worship of the cow and the trampling of woman?

Now let the Christian missionary testify! Whereever Christ has found a throne, the arena is in ruins. Warfare yields to peaceful arbitration, when it is not needful as a check upon despots or lawless rioters and anarchists. The mercenary spirit gives place to the merciful, and poverty finds pity, and suffering is soothed by compassion. Christian lands build not only schools and colleges, but great homes where sickness and misfortune find refuge and loving ministries. Man's inalienable rights find their *Magna Charta*, and even the animal creation profits by the compassion which Christ teaches. Christianity is the only faith that has ever been able to turn the world upside down, and restore the true and original order, so that where man had become the worshipper of beasts and the slave of his own lusts, he has once more asserted the supremacy of conscience and regained dominion.

The *whole history* of modern missions abounds in the sublime. It is a panorama of wonders. Take one more example out of hundreds that might be cited. In Japan, without any injustice to the others who compose that noble band who have sought the true illumination of the Sunrise Kingdom, we may mention the name of John C. Hepburn, M.D., LL.D., as *facile princeps*. He arrived at Kanagawa October 18, 1859; and, although not the first to enter those ports after the Townsend-Harris treaty of 1858, he has perhaps rendered to the Island Empire the most distinguished service yet permitted to any one man. In December, 1862, he located at Yokohama, doing' daily dispensary and lexicographic work, and teaching on Sundays. For over thirty-three years he has been almost continuously a resident of the Island Empire, even his temporary absences being in the interests of Japanese civilization. During two winters he was in Shanghai printing his dictionary, and has more than once visited America. But over the entire empire for the period of a generation this man has been known as a medical missionary, an educator of the very first rank, whose services were sought in vain at high prices by the Japanese Government; as a Christian statesman and philanthropist untiring in his devotion to the well-being of the nation; but principally as the chief translator of the Holy Scriptures. And no more sublime hour has been reached in the history of this awakening people, than when, after nearly thirty years of patient toil, holding in his hands the two volumes of the completed Word of God, he formally presented the Japanese Bible to the nation.

When Rev. Dr. Inglis, of Aneityum, was asked to make a speech before the General Assembly of the Free Church of Scotland, and was cautioned to be brief, he said:

"Fathers and brethren, we are told that missionaries should content themselves with stating facts, and leave the Church to draw the inference. I wish to bring three facts to your notice.

"*First*, I place on your table," suiting the action to the word, "the Shorter Catechism translated into the language of Aneityum.

"*Second*, I place on your table also 'Pilgrim's Progress ' translated into the language of Aneityum."

Then, taking into his hands a large volume, while he looked longingly on the pages that had cost him years of toil, he laid it on the table, and said:

"*Third*, I place on your table the Holy Scriptures, Old and New Testament, translated into the language of Aneityum, and now leave the Church to draw the inference," and sat down amid a storm of applause.

VII.

Rapidity of Results.

G OD SHOWS His power both in the quality and quantity of His work; and perhaps no proofs of His energy are more convincing in the sphere of missions than those furnished in the astonishing *rapidity* with which results of great magnitude have been wrought.

This may be made to appear most clearly if we take a cursory glance over the entire century since Carey sailed for India, and, without tarrying at any point, sweep round the vast circle of the work accomplished, and get at least a comprehensive glimpse of the stupendous changes wrought within these hundred years.

Ninety-six years have swept by since mission history began in the South Seas. At least fourteen years of labour passed before there was the first convert in Tahiti. Then, and while the missionaries were absent from the island, Tuahine and another of the natives, who had been impressed with the truth while serving in a missionary's family, were found praying to God for a new heart. Then Pomare II. gave up his idol-gods; and, before the missionaries had again set foot on Tahiti, a wonderful upheaval of society had begun. Since that day in 1811, the converts, living and dead, in Western Polynesia, have numbered over a million!

Let us now shorten the period of our survey to the eighty years since 1813, when the American Baptist Missionary Union was formed. Then Judson and his wife were its only representatives and Burma its sole field. For ten years he wrought before he had been able to gather one little flock of eighteen converts into a church. Those ten years seemed comparatively fruitless. But when from across the sea the question was asked, "Judson, what are the prospects?" his faith, undiscouraged, saw only a future as bright as the promises of God! We now look back over this four-score years, and, not excluding the first decade of years of comparative famine, what a glorious harvest the Baptist Union has already reaped! Taking the whole eighty years into our reckoning, one new Baptist church has been organized on heathen soil for every three weeks of the entire time; one new convert has been baptized for every three hours, counting in day and night; and at least one in ten of such converts has become an active worker in the field, himself a seed of the kingdom!

Let us still narrow down the time to fifty years, and see what signs and wonders He has wrought who takes no note of man's calendar of time.

In Turkey, more than twenty translations of the Word of God in the languages and dialects of living peoples have been supplied during the half century: an average of one new translation for every thirty months! By Dr. Cyrus H. Wheeler and his co-workers, the banks of the Euphrates have been dotted with self-sustaining churches; and a standard of giving, so exalted and apostolic, has been erected, that wherever ten disciples could be found, a church could be gathered which would support its own pastor. For each disciple gave a tenth of his income, and out of ten such tithes, a sum could be realized equal to the average income of the givers; and so the native pastor, willing to live on a level with his people, could have enough to keep him from want. Think of such model churches in territory newly occupied for Christ!

When, in 1878, the jubilee of the baptism of the first Karen convert was kept, the Kho-Thah-Byu Memorial Hall was joyfully dedicated, with its capacious audience-chamber and various accessories. But what a host of converts had those fifty years seen gathered to Christ! not less than sixty thousand, half of whom were living to take part in the celebration. Sir Charles Bernard reckons the present Christian community at 200,000, and it has five hundred self-sustaining churches.

In China, the era of missions properly began in 1842; fifty years later, there were fifty thousand converts, and the ratio of increase during the quarter century between 1863 and 1888 was eighteenfold!

SCRIPTURE TESTIMONY

*The Gospel brings light
to the dark nations*

ACTS 26:16-18

The fifty years in the Fiji Islands from 1835 to 1885, saw changes so wonderful that they defy adequate description. When James Calvert went there his first duty was to gather up and bury the skulls, hands and feet, of eighty victims, sacrificed at a cannibal feast. He lived to see the very people who had taken part in that horrible meal seated about the Lord's table to eat of the bread and drink of the cup that are the emblems of His Body and Blood. At the close of that fifty years thirteen hundred churches of Christ could be counted, some of them standing on the site of cannibal ovens, and out of a population of 110,000, 104,000 were habitual attendants at places of worship. And in no part of Scotland could there be found fewer homes where no family worship hallows household life.

Forty-three years were spent by Eliza Agnew at the girls' seminary, in Oodooville, Ceylon. She was called the "mother of a thousand daughters," for she had taken part in the training of three successive generations of Ceylonese girls; teaching the daughters and even granddaughters of her original scholars. When she laid down her work, it was found that not a single girl who had gone through the full course under this saintly teacher had gone back unconverted to a heathen home; and upwards of six hundred whom she had taught were penetrating with the light of the gospel the darkness of Indian zenanas! It may be doubted whether a fuller cup of service has ever been offered to the Saviour of souls by any woman of the century.

Look at the contrasts of *thirty* years in Upper Burma, 1860-1890. When Theebau was inaugurated as King of Upper Burma, at Mandalay, he was a monster of cruelty, and the event was celebrated by a massacre so horrible that several hundred of the nobility, and even members of the king's own family, were among the victims. The sacrifice of human life was so common, that when the city of Mandalay was built, fifty-six young girls were slain, that the eight gates of the city might by their blood be secure from all invaders. To attempt missions in such a locality meant captivity, if not martyrdom, to whoever undertook the work.

Thirty years later, in that same city, the Baptist Missionary Conference was held, and during the conference the Judson Memorial Church was dedicated. Burmese Christians had given eight thousand rupees toward the cost; it was a native Karen choir that led the service of sacred song; and at the closing communion of the Lord's Supper, Tamils and Telugus, Burmans and Karens, Shans and Tounghus, English and Eurasians, Americans and Chinamen, representatives of five hundred churches and 30,000 believers in Burma, sat down together to keep the sacred supper—bound in one bundle of life.

Let us still shorten the time to a *quarter century*. Johann Gerhard Oncken, born Varel, Oldenburg, about 1800, and in early life a domestic servant, in young manhood opened a book shop at Hamburg, joined the English Independents, and became agent of the Edinburgh Bible Society and Lower Saxony Tract Society. In April, 1834, about 34 years old, he asked Dr. Barnas Sears of Brown University, then in Hamburg, to baptize him and six others and form them into a Baptist Church, of which Oncken became pastor; and next year the American

Baptists made him their missionary. Then began a career so remarkable that it can be scarcely believed. He visited all parts of Germany and Denmark, preaching, scattering Bibles and tracts and organizing churches. He faced persecution and was several times imprisoned; but, in 1842, during the great fire, he with his family and congregation so helped homeless sufferers, that the Senate publicly decreed to them the right of unhindered worship, and he gave himself anew to missionary work.

Twenty-five years passed, and sixty-five churches with seven hundred and fifty stations had been established, with nearly ten thousand members and one hundred and twenty ministers and Bible readers; Bibles and tracts had been scattered by the million pages, and fifty millions of people had heard the gospel. Give us two hundred and fifty churches like Oncken's at Hamburg, and we can, in twenty-five years more, secure the preaching of the gospel to every human soul!

Dr. John Geddie was at Aneityum only *twenty-four years*, from 1848 to 1872. On the tablet reared, to his memory we read: "When he landed in 1848, there were no Christians; when he left in 1872, there were no heathens."

John Williams's course reached over but *twenty-two years*, from 1817 to 1839. Five years before he fell a martyr at Erromanga, the gospel had been carried over a circle of four thousand miles diameter, whose centre is Tahiti. There lies a vast Pacific archipelago, within whose circumference of twelve thousand miles are included the Raratongan, Friendly, Cook, Society, Navigators', Marquesas, Union, Austral, Gambia, and Solomon groups of islands, and Low Archipelago, as well as many others. Yet, within *seventeen* years, not only had every group, but every considerable island in every group, been evangelized; the people had burned the maraes, and given up their abandoned idols as trophies to the missionaries. War spears had become pulpit rails for the gospel of peace, and the god of war himself had become a prop for the roofs of the homes where peace found dwellingplace!

Robert W. McAll's sixteen years in France, from 1872 to 1888, finds no parallel in any papal community. In 1872 he opened one little *salle* amid the lawless Communists of Belleville; sixteen years later, he had *112 salles*; and in one year held 14,000 religious meetings, whereby probably a million of hearers had been reached. And even the government held out to him every encouragement in his work, declaring that police force became unnecessary in proportion as McAll meetings prevailed. And all this amazing success was reached without any outward attraction of art. A free gospel for everybody, an open Bible, hearty singing, plain, simple talks, self-denying toil for souls—these were all the machinery.

It is but sixteen years since the great Pentecost in the Telugu country: and the progress of gospel triumph during those years can be compared only with the rapidity of the work in the South Seas. Souls were ingathered with such amazing speed and in such vast numbers, that it has been doubted whether even the first Pentecost in Jerusalem equalled it. The church at Ongole became the largest in the world, numbering with its branches over 30,000 members. And the peculiar feature of this history is that the blessing is perpetual. No one ingathering has perhaps ever been so astonishing from first to last. The revival has known no cessation since its beginning, and nearly ten thousand souls were added to the Church during the eighteen months last reported!

Harpoot—that leading station of the American Board in Eastern Turkey, the seat of the Euphrates College, and the centre of widespread evangelism among the Armenians—has been the scene of a quiet, but powerful work of God. One of its most venerated missionaries, Dr. H. N. Barnum, once gave an account of fourteen years of labour, in preaching, establishing stations, training a native ministry, and carrying on all the work of evangelization and education over a wide territory. The question was asked: "At what cost was all this done?" And the answer was—for a sum less than the cost of the church building in which he was then speaking—an edifice worth probably 150,000 dollars! Fourteen years of such wide-reaching work at an average cost per year of somewhat over 10,000 dollars!

When Mackay, at Formosa, kept his twelfth anniversary, he sought to gather all his living converts at the Lord's table—and twelve hundred kept the solemn feast. Many had died during those twelve years, and much time had been spent at the outset in acquiring a strange tongue; yet, notwithstanding all this, there was this rich living harvest of twelve years' sowing.

Seven years were allotted to Johnson in Sierra Leone—among the chaotic mass of human beings, the refuse from the holds of slave ships, who could hold no converse with one another except through a bastard English dialect; who lived a life of unbridled lust, habitual lying, thieving and quarrelling; who had no honest trades to occupy their time or earn their living, but were fed like paupers and criminals on government rations. Yet, out of such worthless material, by God's help, he organized a Christian community, as out of the filth of earth the divine forces of nature crystallize gems, turning the miry clay into sapphires, the sand into opals, and even the soot into diamonds.

A like period of seven years sufficed to establish among the wild men of North America, William Duncan's model State, or Metlakahtla, a community whose industry, intelligence, virtue and piety were incredible to all who were not eye-witnesses of the marvels of God's grace.

Six years on the Hawaiian Islands saw almost a complete revolution. Seventeen missionaries had landed March 31, 1820, among a people where infant-murder, even by the hands of mothers, was common; where modesty was unknown and traffic in female virtue became a trade, and every foreign vessel a floating Sodom; where no marriage law was known, and the nation was rapidly coming to extinction by its own vices. Yet, even here, in 1826, 10,000 natives met at Kawaihae to hear the gospel; at Hilo and Kailua places of worship were built holding 5,000; and at the dedication of the church at the latter place, the rulers of the nation pledged it to the Christians' God. In every district of the islands, Christian schools were found, with a total of 400 teachers and 25,000 pupils.

Four years, as we have seen already, sufficed at Hilo and Pima to work a transformation that finds no adequate symbol but the volcanic upheavals with which the Kanakas are familiar. The eleven thousand converts, gathered from 1835 to 1839, represent only one evidence of God's miraculous work. The whole reconstruction of the community, from its very base, was a grander result and a clearer proof of a supernatural power. Transient movements of sympathy and sensibility may account for revivals that sweep like sudden tidal waves over a wide territory; but the permanent creation of an orderly, decorous, peaceful Christian State must be traced back to Him who alone can mould lasting spiritual results.

<table>
<tr><td>SCRIPTURE TESTIMONY

*The Gospel brings light
to the dark nations*

ACTS 26:16-18</td></tr>
</table>

Three and a half years of John G. Paton on Aniwa saw a gigantic upheaval of the whole conditions of society. That story is as thrilling as any written in the new chapters of the Acts, and no narrative of missionary toils and triumphs is either more readable or more romantic, more graphic or pathetic, or more abundant in proofs of supernatural power. A religion that in so short a time can transform a cannibal island into a civilized community, with Christian home life, Sabbath sanctities and unselfish ministries; that can develop ignorant, heartless, brutal savages into intelligent, affectionate, devoted Christians, must be more than human. One of the first missionaries to this island, twenty-six years before, had been killed. In 1866 Dr. Paton went there to reside, and there are now 1,300 professed disciples on the islands of the New Hebrides group.

<table>
<tr><td>SCRIPTURE TESTIMONY

Believers exchange superstition for faith in Christ

ACTS 19:18-19</td></tr>
</table>

Two years on Nanumaga wrought results not less marvellous. When Thomas Powell left a native evangelist on the island, the natives kept him waiting for hours on the beach while they sought to avert the wrath of the gods, for permitting him to land. He found literally an idol-god in every house, and began to labour, with no apparent hope of success or hold upon the people. Yet, in two years not an idol could be found; the whole population gathered in a place of worship built for Jehovah, and He was inhabiting the praises of those who had just before been abject slaves of the lowest idolatry. All the native children old enough to be taught were in attendance on school, and it is no exaggeration to say that the entire complexion, and even constitution, of Nanumagan society was changed.

We may shorten the period of survey to a *single year*, and we yet find signs and wonders. Not only does Ongole furnish us an example of 10,000 converts baptized in the one year, 1878, but during that same year, in Tinnevelly and various other places in Southern India, so great was the harvest gathered, that it has been computed that 50,000 turned from idols in that single twelvemonth.

And what shall we say when *one day* proves with God as a thousand years? When Titus Coan, on one Sabbath in July, 1838, baptized over 1,700, it was thought scarcely credible that such oversight and scrutiny could have been

SCRIPTURE TESTIMONY

Take the gospel to the ends of the earth

MARK 16:15 · ACTS 1:8 · ACTS
6:7 · COLOSSIANS 1:23

exercised as to keep out unworthy candidates. But, forty years later, Jewett and Clough baptized in one day over *five hundred more* than Coan had; and that only after the most rigid examination, lest unworthy persons should find their way into the waters of baptism.

Surely the triumphs of grace already recorded in these pages belong to signs and wonders inexplicable by human power. Idolatry, the most degraded in type and the most prolific in fruit, confronted, conquered, uprooted, destroyed! Jeremiah reproached Judah with having gods as many as cities;* but in Nanumaga every hovel had an idol, and in India more deities are worshipped than the worshippers themselves number. Obstacles have been confronted which towered high as mountains and defied either removing or surmounting. Yet see a feeble few seize the very centres and hold the very fortresses of the devil! as earlier disciples dared to go to Ephesus, centre of Diana worship—to Paphos, where Venus kept her shameless feasts—to Babylon and Rome, where vast pagan empires held their capital and carnival! Follow unarmed men and sensitive women as they tread over paths lined with human bones, and walk through valleys of death, to assault the image of a modern Moloch and overturn the shrine of Juggemath! Whether it be to face the despotic Sultan and the ruthless Turk at the Golden Horn, or the cruel ruler of Uganda, or the savage cannibals of the Pacific, or the half idiotic Patagonians,—the same invincible faith and holy heroism!

---

*   Jeremiah xl. 12.

The horrors of heathenism defy any description. Language is not black enough—hell itself is not equal to the needs of such a portraiture. Take infanticide as an example. Mrs. Williams had, at Raiatea, a female servant who, after conversion, gave her an awful glimpse of the customs that swayed all Polynesia. A mother would suffocate a new-born babe with a wet cloth, or with her own hands strangle it, or bury it alive—and feel no pang of compunction; or, yet more like a demon than a brute, break joint after joint of the fingers and toes and then of the arms and legs, and if such torture did not kill, finish the deed by choking it to death. One woman confessed to thus having killed five, another seven, another nine, and yet another, her whole family of seventeen! At a school anniversary an aged chief, before whom six hundred children passed in review, arose under the force of deep feeling, and said: "I must speak! O that I had known that such good was in store for us! my own children might have been among this happy group! But I have destroyed them all— nineteen—and have not one left!" Then turning to the king, his relative, he said, with streaming eyes: "You, my brother, saw me kill them one after another! Why did you not stay this murderous hand! and say, God is about to bless us! Salvation is coming to these shores!"

The island of Raiatea, the centre for Williams's tours, was the seat of both the political power and idolatry of the group; there was the Temple of the Mars, and the Moloch of the South Seas. Idleness and iniquity, cruelty and crime, held high carnival. The mind was blunted by ignorance, and the conscience seared into insensibility. And yet even among such a people he was not ashamed to preach the gospel, and believed it would prove the power of God. It seemed as though association with such brutes would drag him down, but he brought them up to his level, instead of sinking to theirs. He taught them religion, and religion brought civilization, until every house seemed a house of prayer, and naked savages clothed and in their right minds sat down at Jesus' feet. No more a wilderness of wretched hovels, but three miles of comely cottages; useful trades and mechanic arts, and a thrifty commerce. Within a year seven thousand idolaters have flung their gods to the fires and built a great house for God. And so in Samoa five-sixths of the whole population of sixty thousand are shortly flocking to him to be taught. And all this with no aid from the civil power!

And still God's signs and wonders convince not the unbelieving, for some would not be persuaded though one rose from the dead. "Critics of missions" still survive who can look at God's great work, and yet call missions either an "organized hypocrisy, or a disastrous failure!" Such a judgment recalls Dr. Johnson's verdict upon Milton's "Lycidas," that it is "no poem at all;" with Matthew

Arnold's quiet rejoinder that "such a sentence is terrible—*for the critic!*" Some guns kick so badly that, as Dr. Beecher used to say, "it were better to be before than behind them."

We have not written to convince sceptics or silence critics, but to encourage believing and praying saints who find new food for faith and prayer in every new fact that proves a present and a living God. To such, God's signs and wonders are a daily inspiration; and all missionary history becomes one continuous miracle. These signs have not been wrought "in a corner;" they are found everywhere, and attested by witnesses who are beyond impeachment, whether for competency or integrity, and who are too many in number for honest doubt to remain.

A brilliant but erratic American once replied to an opponent in debate,—who sought to discredit his statements of fact, by saying that "of such facts he himself had no knowledge"—"My knowledge, however limited, cannot be set aside on account of another's ignorance, however extensive!" The masterly retort is but too applicable to some who with a superficial denial would sweep away the testimony of that noble band of witnesses who, from Carey to Mackay, and over a field that reaches from Japan to Liberia, and from Greenland to Tierra del Fuego, attest gospel conquests.

VIII.

ANSWERS TO PRAYER.

AS MIGHT be anticipated, this century of missions bears no mark of the wonder-work of God more conspicuous than the multiplied and marvellous *answers to prayer*.

Every conspicuous step and stage of progress is directly traceable to prevailing, believing, expectant supplication. When Jonathan Edwards blew his trumpet blast, calling all believers to united prayer for a new and world-wide Pentecost, Northampton in England echoed the clarion peal of the New England Northampton, and the monthly concert of prayer, established thirty-seven years later, was the beginning of a stated monthly season of such united, organized pleading with God for a lost world.

Carey was the Moses and Joshua of the new movement, both in one; and nothing marked him so conspicuously as the rod of God in his hand—the power of humble, believing supplication. Had Carey not known how to pray, the missionary century had not yet dawned, or had waited for some other praying soul to roll back the curtain of the long night. God has compelled his saints to seek Him at the throne of grace, so that every new advance might be so plainly due to His power that even the unbeliever might be constrained to confess: "Surely this is the finger of God!"

He meant that the century of missions should be to the Church at home as important as to the distant fields of missions abroad; and, in fact, the heart must have a strong pulse if the life currents of blood are to be driven to the fingers' ends. And so no age, since the Apostolic, has been so peculiar for the revival of prayer. Every new Pentecost has had its preparatory period of supplication—of waiting for enduement; and sometimes the time of tarrying has been lengthened from "ten days" to as many weeks, months, or even years; but never has there been an outpouring of the Divine Spirit from God without a previous outpouring of the human spirit toward God. To vindicate this statement would require us to trace the whole history of missions, for the field of such display of divine power covers the ages. Yet every missionary biography, from those of Eliot and Edwards, Brainerd and Carey, down to Livingstone and Bums, Hudson Taylor and John E. Clough, tells the same story: prayer has been the preparation for every new triumph, and the secret of all success; and so, if greater triumphs and successes lie before us, more fervent and faithful praying must be their forerunner and herald!

If this be so, we must fix this fact in mind by repetition, sound it out as with God's own trump, write it as in letters of light, on the very firmament of missions—that the New Acts of the Apostles opened with prevailing prayer, and in each new chapter records its new triumphs.

About the middle of the eighteenth century the fallow soil began to be sown with those seeds of missionary enterprise which came to the surface a half century later. We repeat what has been said, that Carey's movements were only the germinating of what Edwards, and others like him, had planted. When in 1784, at that Northamptonshire Baptist Association, John Sutcliff, of Olney, reported, recommending a stated monthly meeting to bewail the low state of missions, and to implore God for a general revival of pure piety, and a world-wide outpouring of power from on high, the first Monday of each month was the time designated, and John Ryland, Jr., drew up the plan. Soon after, Sutcliff republished Edward's appeal, thus acknowledging that this new advance was the result of seed sown as early as 1747, and wholly due to prayer, which was now formally recognized as the *one hope* alike of the Church and the world.

Three years later, Carey was ordained at Moulton, and five years after that came the compact at Kettering, which was the Magna Charta of modern missions; and the Baptist Missionary Society was born, now mother of so large a family of societies. That small but famous "fund" of thirteen pounds and one half-crown, laid by that little band of twelve on the altar that so sanctified and magnified the gift, was, by God's decree, the small offering it was, and from His poor, because He meant to show that it was not by might or by power, not by numbers or by wealth, but by His Spirit, that this work is to be carried on.

Those who, like Sydney Smith, sneered at the "consecrated cobblers" and "apostates" from the humblest callings of life, who with a hundred halfcrowns would attempt world-wide missions—were blind to the open mystery of God's dealings, who always chooses the base and weak and despised nothings to bring to naught the great and strong and mighty somethings; and who deliberately chooses and uses the few and the poor, the lowly and the obscure, that the excellency of the power may be of God and not of man, and that no flesh should glory in His presence. Had that first roll of subscribers held twelve hundred distinguished names, with some prince of royal blood as patron, and had that sum been thirteen thousand pounds to start with, missions might have waited another century for their real beginning.

Those who knew, and at first opposed, Carey, came to feel that he was a man of prayer and that the God of Prayer was back of him. It was prayer that found expression in the monthly concert, that baptized with power Carey's "Inquiry," that made that map at Moulton luminous with divine light and vocal with a world's mute appeal; it was prayer that led to that sermon in Nottingham and that gathering in Widow Wallis' parlour at Kettering, and to Carey's offer of himself in 1793.

God saw that the Church would never take up, or be *fit* to take up, this Apostolic work without a revival of Apostolic faith in divine power and in the prayer that alone commands that power. Reliance on human patronage, and the kindred confidence in numbers and riches, are fatal hindrances to missions. When Carey preached his now immortal sermon, whose divine quality was found in its unction, he said: "Saviour, Thy greatest things have had smallest beginnings." It was to him a great encouragement that when God called Abraham he was alone. (Isa. 1. 1.) And this same truth of insignificant beginning was illustrated in Widow Wallis' house on October 2d, 1792.

Upon this one form of signs and wonders our minds have need, therefore, to linger, as bees upon a bloom, for the nectaries of our Christian life are here to be found: we refer to these *Answers to Prayer*.

God has taken infinite care to fasten in the minds of believers the power of supplication in the name of Christ to work supernatural results. In the Word of God there are at least ten very marked lessons on prayer; and these lessons are progressive—they advance from the simplest rudiments, in a distinct order or series, in which each step must be taken on the way to the next—each lesson learned, if the succeeding one is to be understood. For instance, if we combine the gospel narratives and observe the development of the doctrine, we shall find that we are successively taught the nature of prayer as asking of God; then the negative and positive conditions of acceptable, prevailing prayer, such as a frame of forgiveness, of faith in God's promise, of importunate earnestness, of devout expectancy, of mutual agreement in the Spirit, of accordance with the will of God, etc. The climax of all these lessons is reached in that expressly new lesson taught by our Lord, as to asking *in His Name*; that is by virtue of our identity with Him.

When prayer is offered in another's name, that other becomes the *real suppliant, whoever presents the request.* And so our Lord teaches us that from the time when our oneness with Him is recognized and realized as based upon our membership in His body, we may ask in His name, by His power, in His stead; so that the petition becomes *the petition of Him in whose name it is* offered, as Esther's writing, when signed and sealed in the name of King Ahasuerus, became his decree. *

Behold these lessons gathered up and woven into the fabric of one superb metaphorical representation in the Apocalypse. In the eighth chapter, the visions of the seer of Patmos open with a solemn and mysterious half-hour of silence in heaven. Before the first of the seven trumpets sounds, the seven angels stand silent before God, as though waiting a signal. And the half-hour of silence seems wholly given to this revelation of the power of prayer.

The Angel of Intercession comes and stands at the altar, holding in his hands a golden censer. Unto him is given much incense, that he should add it unto the prayers of all the saints upon the golden altar, before the throne; and the mingled smoke of the incense and prayers of saints ascend like a sweet savour before God out of the censer. Then the Angel takes the censer, fills it with the fire of the altar, and casts it upon the earth; and astounding results follow—thunderpeals, lightning flashes, voices, and earthquake convulsions.

This parable in action might still have remained an inscrutable mystery but for a divine key that is in the lock, which opens to us its meaning. We are here twice told that it concerns the "prayers of saints" And with this key we may open the doors of this great truth. Laying aside the figurative forms of expression, which are like bronze gates, sculptured with allegorical figures—what readest thou?

Prayers of saints, offered in holy agreement, ascend like vapours, which blend and mingle in pure white clouds. The great Intercessor at the Throne presents them before God, made acceptable by His own infinite merit, and thus they prevail. The power of God is put at the disposal of praying souls; and upon the earth wonderful changes, convulsions, upheavings, revolutions take place. Prayer has gone to heaven, found acceptance, and returned in answers of almighty power, as moisture goes up in vapour and returns in rain. Supplication, when it is according to scriptural conditions, commands divine interposition.

Here, then, we have a vision of *Prayer as a power in the universe of God.* There is a half-hour silence; no word is spoken. But the silence has a voice. It tells an unbelieving Church that whenever great moral and spiritual reformations and transformations, evolutions and revolutions, are witnessed, somebody has been praying, though only God may trace the links between the prayers and the answers.

---

* Compare John xvi. 23-27, Esther viii. 8.

The whole story of missions is the historic interpretation of that Apocalyptic vision: it is the story of answered prayer. If we would trace organized mission effort back not to its *birth* but to its *conception*, we must go farther than Widow Wallis' parlour at Kettering, or even the cobbler's shop at Hackleton, or Edward's appeal in 1747. Nearly twenty years before that trumpet-call to prayer, another great movement had started at Oxford, where John and Charles Wesley, and Morgan and Kirkham, Ingham, Broughton, Hervey and George Whitefield were studying and praying to promote holiness and usefulness. At the end of six years this little company numbered but sixteen. But such were some of the preparations God was making for the birth-hour of modern missions. Upon these few men at Oxford there came suddenly a blessing from on high, which not only changed the whole tenor of their lives, but became the mould of a revived Church and the matrix of modern missions.

If the history of all that prayer has wrought, in the century now closing, could be written and read, it would be as startling as the opening of the books in the last great day. The number is legion, of the movements for human weal whose secret source, unknown to the people, has been in prevailing prayer.

The repeal of the "Contagious Diseases" Act in Britain was a triumph of prayer. Against the advocates of this repeal almost the whole strength of the two houses of Parliament was massed, but throughout the kingdom disciples were giving themselves to supplication. A few men undertook to maintain a stand against the whole nation, and two or three godly women took their stand beside them, hooted at by an insulting rabble and pelted by the daily press with merciless ridicule as the "howling sisterhood!" But prayer prevailed and the abhorrent measure was abolished by unanimous vote.

<table>
<tr><td>SCRIPTURE TESTIMONY

The believer is to be persistent in prayer

LUKE 11:5-10</td></tr>
</table>

Those who in England and America have watched the slow steps by which the way was prepared for the abolition of slavery well know that in that great contest between human rights and the might of organized selfishness and sordidness, Prayer turned the scale. There were some godly women, for example, who met at stated times in Boston to claim from God the freedom of the slave; and, when the wild waves of riot surged against the very doors of their little place of prayer, they remained on their knees and were heard to say: "Lord, the foes of God and of the slave molest us indeed, but they *cannot make us afraid.*" And so the praying saints kept praying, until the fires of God came down and burned the fetters from four millions of manacled hands.

That famous cartoon of the death of St. Genevieve depicts the triumph of

Roman valour with its pomp and pageantry of arms, side by side with a humble deathbed around which praying saints are gathered. But it suggests how much mightier is the power that goes with a few supplicating believers than all the boasted might of armies.

Read the New Acts of the Apostles; linger over the scenes at Hilo and Tahiti, New Zealand and the Fiji isles; pierce to the church of the cavern in the Vaudois vales; follow the Huguenots in exile; study the personal life of Edwards and Brainerd, and Mills and Carey and Judson and Johnson; track to their closets and retreats in the forests and caves, God's praying ones, and you shall know how God's Pentecosts are but the rewarding "openly" of those who have learned how to get hold on Him "in secret."

The Church, when it is once more a praying Church, will boldly claim of God that He shall stretch forth His hand as the only way to give boldness in preaching His word. When it is God's "work" we are doing it is our right and privilege not only to ask, but to "command" Him. (Isa. xlv. n.) Faith not only offers a request, but issues a fiat—and says, it shall be so. Prayer, says Coleridge, is

> "An affirmation and an act,
>   That bids eternal truth be fact!"

The promise makes prayer bold, for God's word cannot fail. Fulfilment is as certain as past events are fixed, and the future becomes a present to such faith. There is a new era of missions yet to be ushered in when the disciples of Christ learn to ask in Jesus' name, by the power of the Holy Spirit, for the glory of God, and with a confidence that counts things that are not as though they are.

Missionary history has exemplified that superbly grand lesson, that prayer, when it prevails, has about it a boldness, a holy audacity, which reminds us of the prophet whose plea was— *"Do not disgrace the Throne of Thy Glory!"* When a saint understands that prayer has three intercessors—the interceding Spirit within, the interceding suppliant, and the interceding Christ before the Throne—he feels himself but the channel through whom a current passes, whose source is the Holy Spirit in his heart, whose final outpour is through our great High Priest into the bosom of the Father; and he loses sight of himself in the thought of the divine stream, and its spring . and its ocean. How can he but be bold? Prayer becomes no more mere lame and timid asking—it is claiming and laying hold of blessing. Nay, it is waiting for and welcoming the blessing, as a returning stream from the heart of God, pouring back into and through the heart of the supplicant. While he calls, God answers—there is converse, intercourse, intercommunication: prayer is not only speaking to God, but hearing Him speak in return. As a Japanese convert said, it is like the old-fashioned well, where one bucket comes down while another goes up—only in this case it is the full bucket that descends! Such prayer a true missionary has to learn, and it is such prayer that brings him the conscious presence promised by his Master, with its outcome of divine wisdom and strength. It is such prayer that brings to our aid that consummate preacher, the Holy Spirit, whose divine oratory convinces and persuades—who has the power of revelation, demonstration, illumination—who can flash instant light into the darkest mind and command life to the dead.

What gracious blessings have come to heathen souls in answer to prayer! The Rev. Griffith John, of Hankow, records a whole Saturday spent in prayer for a baptism of the Spirit of God. The following morning he preached on the subject, and at the close of the service proposed a meeting for an hour a day, during the ensuing week, for special anointing from above. From fifty to seventy of his converts met day by day, and mingled a confession of their sins with supplication for the holy outpouring. The impulse which the native Church then received has never yet spent its force. The mission in China, begun in 1847 by William Burns, has now increased until it has five separate centres, with thousands of converts, with native preachers and pastors and schools and medical missions. Its converts have stood firm against persecution, and the abundant blessing has been reverently traced to the monthly prayer-meeting for China held in the room at Edinburgh.

For some years the writer has been gathering and putting on record authentic and striking answers to prayer. A few of them, which have carried unspeakable blessing to his own heart, he now places on record in these pages:

<table>
<tr><td>

SCRIPTURE TESTIMONY

*All great movements of God
are birthed in prayer*

ACTS 1:14 · ACTS 4:31

</td><td>

Charles G. Finney, in his "Revival Lectures" (page 112), tells of a pious man in Western New York sick with consumption. He was poor, and had been sick for years. An unconverted merchant was very kind to him, and the

</td></tr>
</table>

only return he could make was to pray for his salvation. By-and-by, to the astonishment of everybody, that merchant was converted, and a great revival followed. This poor man lingered several years. After his death his widow put his diary into Mr. Finney's hands. From this it appeared that, being acquainted with about thirty ministers and churches, he set apart certain hours in the day and week to pray for each of them, and also for different missionary stations. His diary contained entries like the following: "To-day I have been enabled to offer what I call the prayer of faith for the outpouring of the Spirit on the ----- Church." Thus he had gone over a great number of churches. Of the missionary stations he mentions particularly the mission at Ceylon. Not long after the dates mentioned, mighty revivals had commenced and swept over that region, nearly *in the exact order of his praying*; and in due time news came even from Ceylon of a revival there! Thus this man, too feeble in body to leave his house, was yet useful to the world and the Church. Standing between God and the desolations of the Church, and pouring out his heart in believing prayer, as a prince he had power with God and prevailed.

The following incident was related at Northfield by the Rev. J. Hudson Taylor: A station in the China Inland Mission was peculiarly blessed of God. Inquirers were more numerous and more easily turned from dumb idols to serve the living God than at other stations. This difference was a theme of conversation and wonder. After a time Mr. Taylor returned to England, and at a certain place was warmly greeted by a stranger, who showed great interest in his mission work. This stranger was so particular and intelligent in his questions concerning one missionary and the locality in which he laboured, seemed so well acquainted with his helpers, inquirers, and the difficulties of that particular station, that Mr. Taylor's curiosity was aroused to find out the reason of this intimate knowledge. To his great satisfaction, he now learned that this stranger and the successful missionary had covenanted together as co-workers. The missionary kept his home brother informed of all the phases of his labour. He gave him the names of inquirers, stations, hopeful characters and difficulties, and all these the home worker was wont to spread out before God in prevailing prayer.

In the recently published memoir of Adolph Saphir,* there is put on record one of the countless instances of divine administration of missions, which we cite because of the many-sided lesson taught.

It is the story of how the mission for the Jews was established in Pesth, Hungary. Prayer is the key to every new mystery in this series of marvels. First, the father of this movement was Mr. R. Wodrow, of Glasgow, whose private diary shows whole days of fasting and prayer on behalf of Israel. The next step was the appointment of a deputation, in 1838, consisting of those four remarkable men, Doctors Keith and Black, with Andrew Bonar and McCheyne, to visit lands where the Jews dwelt, and select fields for missions to this neglected people. The intolerance of the Austrian government seemed to shut the door to any work within its dominions, and so, notwithstanding the large Jewish population there resident, Hungary was not embraced in the plan of visitation. But God did not propose that this land should be longer passed by; and He, by mysterious links, joined the plan of the deputation to His own purposes for Hungary.

---

* Memoir Adolph Saphir, D.D., by Rev. G. Cariyle, M.A., p. 37 et seq.

Dr. Black slipped from his camel's back as they were crossing from Egypt to Palestine, and the seemingly trifling accident proved sufficiently serious to change the homeward route of Dr. Black and Dr. Keith, by way of the Danube. As they passed through Pesth, they made some inquiries as to the Jews there to be found, little knowing what unseen Hand was leading "the blind by a way that they knew, not."

The Archduchess Maria Dorothea, then residing in the Prince Palatine's palace, had some years previously been led, by a death in her family, to seek solace in the Bible, where "she met Jesus." She was, by the imperial law, forced to bring up her children in the Roman Catholic Church; but as she had found the truth, she taught them, with much prayer, the way of faith, and, in her solitude, yearned and besought of God that a Christian friend and counsellor might be sent to her. In a window of her boudoir, which overlooked the city with its hundred thousand people, day by day, for seven years, she had poured out her soul in prayer to God for some one to carry the true gospel to those around her; at times, in agony, stretching out imploring hands to God for at least one messenger of the cross to come to Hungary.

The year of 1840 came, with Drs. Keith's and Black's providential visit to Pesth, and Dr. Keith's almost fatal illness there—and just at this time the archduchess was strongly and strangely impressed that a stranger was *about to arrive* who would bring a peculiar blessing to the Hungarians she loved. There was one fortnight particularly, when, night after night, she awoke at the same hour, with a vivid sense that something was about to take place which was to bring her relief. And when at last she heard that Dr. Keith was in town dangerously ill of cholera, she said to herself, "This is what was to happen to me." And from that hour her sleep was no longer broken. She went to the bedside of the prostrate stranger, and with her own hands ministered to his wants; and, as he became better, told him of her longings and prayers, acquainted him with the state of the Hungarian Jews, and assured him that if the Church of Scotland would plant a mission in Pesth, she would throw about it all possible guards. And so it came to pass that in the very field which the deputation purposely left out of all their scheme, God brought about, by link upon link of His inscrutable providence, the famous mission associated with the name of "Rabbi Duncan," and which was the means of giving, to the Church of Christ, Adolph Saphir.*

Thus came the Protestant gospel into Buda-Pesth: and by what a series of divine leadings! A man's prayer in Glasgow, a woman's prayer in Hungary, a seeming accident On desert sand, a change of route, an almost fatal illness, a visit of an

---

*   Bonar's "Mission of Inquiry to the Jews."

archduchess— who shall dare to doubt that the Hungarian mission was a tree of God's planting! who can wonder that as the first missionaries went to this new field they "felt wafted along by the breath of prayer, and had, from the very beginning, a mysterious expectation of success!"

No recent development of missionary zeal is more startling than the sudden and rapid *uprising of the educated young men* on both sides of the Atlantic, to which has been given the title of the "Modern Crusade."

From the inception of this movement, as having been strangely interlinked with it, the writer can testify that, from first to last, its sole secret is prayer. More than twenty-five years ago, a missionary, after seventeen years of work on the foreign field, lay on his deathbed. Suddenly arousing himself, with great emphasis, he said: "I have a testimony to give, and would best give it now. Tell the Christian young men in America that the responsibility of saving the world rests on them; not on the old men, but on the young. It is past time for holding back and waiting for providences. I used to think that a missionary ought to husband his strength; but this is a crisis in the world's history, and one man by keeping back may keep back others. Reason is profitable to direct, but the man that rushes to duty is faithful. There are times when rashness is the rule and caution the exception. I look upon the Church as a military company: an army of conquest, not of occupation."

Whatever may be thought of this advice, one thing is plain: the heart of a dying missionary is singularly on fire with a passionate zeal for souls; and the dying eyes become gifted with the vision of a seer, who beholds the greatness of the crisis, and would trumpet forth a blast, calling young men to the duty of the hour.

While that dying missionary was leaving behind his last legacy in a message to young men, there was at Princeton, New Jersey, another missionary, returned after thirty years' service in India, who was gathering in his own house, from time to time, a few younger brethren, to urge on them the same .deep conviction—that on them God had laid the burden of beginning a new missionary crusade. He put before them the map of the world, pressed the need of an organized movement among young men to enter the regions beyond; and, while he left them to consider and confer, he withdrew into a neighbouring room to pray. To those prayers we may trace a movement so mighty that already it enrolls on its missionary covenant more than eight thousand young men and women and twice as many in the mighty current of its influence.

In 1886, at Mt. Hermon, Massachusetts, a few hundred students met, at Mr. Moody's invitation, for a few weeks of Bible study and prayer. While there the young men, whose hearts had begun to burn at Princeton, sought to kindle fires on other altars; and the number who chose the foreign field rose from twenty-three to a hundred. Then, after much prayer, a tour of the colleges was undertaken, that two of their number might bring the facts of the world's need to the minds of fellow-students not represented at that gathering. And now, both in Britain and America, the universities and colleges and theological schools are becoming fountains of missions. And the end is not yet—the movement grows rather than loses in volume and momentum, and it looks like one of the great developments of the latter days.*

Prayer—Coincidences.

There are remarkable *coincidences in missionary history* which show a divine hand, as surely as the release of Peter at the very hour when disciples were met at the house of Mary, mother of Mark, praying for him. Let one or two examples suffice to prove and to illustrate this.

<table>
<tr><td>SCRIPTURE TESTIMONY</td></tr>
<tr><td>The believer is to be persistent in prayer

LUKE 11:5-10</td></tr>
</table>

At the precise time in missions to Tahiti, when the labours of fourteen years seemed wholly in vain— when the tireless toil, faithful witness and unsparing self-denial of the early missionaries seemed like blows of a feather against a wall of adamant—when as yet not a single convert had rewarded all this long labour, and abominable idolatry and desolating warfare seemed to reign—one of the clearest signs and greatest wonders of God's power was seen in the South Seas. The directors of the London Missionary Society seriously proposed abandoning this fruitless field. But there were a few who felt that this was the very hour when God was about to rebuke unbelief and reward faith in His promise and fidelity to duty. Dr. Haweis backed up his solemn remonstrance against the withdrawal of missionaries from the field by another donation of two hundred pounds; and Matthew Wilks, the pastor of John Williams, said: "I will sell my clothes from my back rather than give up this work." And, instead of abandoning the mission, it was urged that a special season of united prayer be appointed that the Lord of the Harvest would give fruit from this long seedsowing. The proposal prevailed; letters of hope and encouragement were sent to the disheartened toilers at Tahiti; and the friends of missions, confessing the unbelief that had made God's mighty works impossible, implored God to make bare His arm.

Now mark the coincidence. Two vessels started, unknown to each other, from

---

* The second "Student Volunteers' Convention," held in Detroit, Michigan, in February, 1894, had the largest body of accredited delegates, ever gathered in any missionary conference.

opposite ports—one from Tahiti bound for London, the other from the Thames bound for Tahiti, and crossed each other's track in mid-ocean. That from the South Seas bore the letters from the missionaries, announcing a work of God so mighty that idolatry was entirely overthrown; and the same ship bore also the very idols which a converted people had surrendered to the missionaries. That other vessel from London carried to the missionaries the letters of encouragement that bade them hold on to God and gave pledges of increased prayerfulness and more earnest support. Here was not only an answer to prayer, of the most wonderful sort, but the promise was literally fulfilled: "Before they call I will answer; and while they are yet speaking I will hear."

The great outpouring at Ongole is another proof of a prayer-answering God. In 1853, at Albany, New York, the American Baptist Missionary Union was considering whether the fruitless field among the Telugus should not be given up. Here, again, a few of God's prophets foresaw that if faith could but triumph in this dark hour, a great harvest might yet come even to this desert of Southern India. And the "Lone Star" mission was not abandoned but reinforced; and Dr. S. F. Smith ventured, in a singularly prophetic poem, to predict that the time would come when that Lone Star would outshine all other missions. A bolder prophecy was never uttered by any uninspired seer. Twenty-five years passed by and then God sent a famine among that people, and the promised blessing seemed farther off than ever.

In fact, that famine was, like John the Baptist, a forerunner that prepared the way of the Lord. Dr. Clough had in the interval joined the faithful Jewett —and, being a civil engineer by training, he undertook to complete the Buckingham canal, in order to get work and wages for starving thousands. These great gatherings of gangs of workmen gave opportunity for the simple telling of the gospel story. The great text, John iii. 16, was again, as at Tahiti, sixty-three years before, the "Little Gospel" from which God's love was made known; and, in that very field which had been so nearly abandoned as both fruitless and hopeless, God gave the largest and longest succession of harvests ever yet known to the missions of the Christian Church. These two examples are enough to prove to any candid mind that God is still working signs in answer to prayer.

And, let it be added, that, twelve years before this grand effusion of the Spirit, and when the prospect was darkest, a humble missionary, with his wife and three converted natives, on the first day of the year, climbed the high hill overlooking Ongole, and there, looking down on that large town and fifty surrounding villages sunk in idol worship, knelt, and each in turn asked of God that He would send a missionary there, and make that centre of heathenism a centre of gospel light.

For twelve years God delayed the answer, and then the blessing came, just where it had been besought, only far more abundantly than it had been expected, and it has not yet ceased. In 1869, when there were as yet but 143 members, special prayer was made for an addition that year of 500 converts, and 573 were baptized; and in some twelve years more the Church numbered 2,000. Now it is the largest in the world!

> **SCRIPTURE TESTIMONY**
>
> *God answers prayer*
>
> LUKE 18:7 · JOHN 15:7 ·
> ACTS 12:5 · JAMES 5:15

In 1872, in December, the Church Missionary Society appointed a day for intercession, with special reference to the increase of missionary force—and that day was spent in prayer offered distinctly and definitely for more men. It was immediately followed by offers of service beyond any other period of the Society's history. In the five years following it sent out 112 men, whereas, in the preceding five, it had sent but 51.

In 1880, this same noble society called for very special intercession for more money—as eight years before, for more men. Within a few months, £135,000 were offered to wipe off all deficit, and £150,000 more, specially contributed for extension, as well as other special gifts whereby substantial advance was made upon the ordinary income. Again, in 1884, men were sorely needed, and it was asked of God that the very flowers of society might be transplanted to heathen climes. A day was appointed to pray for this result. The *previous evening* Secretary Wigram was summoned to Cambridge to "see a number of graduates and undergraduates who desired to dedicate themselves to the Lord's work abroad." More than one hundred university men met him, and the next day he went back to the prayer-meeting to illustrate to his colleagues the old promise: "Before they call I will answer; and while they are yet speaking I will hear."

THE TWO LEGIONS.

Ancient tradition has handed down two most interesting relics about the devout soldiers of the Roman army. The story of the Theban Legion, in the third century, may be coloured by fancy, but has, doubtless, a foundation of fact. Twice, it is said, they were decimated by the Emperor Maximian because they would not obey, when ordered to march against their fellow-Christians in Gaul. But no threats nor executions could turn the fixed hearts of the legion. The survivors still held their ground after their fellows had been slain; and Maurice, their leader, respectfully but firmly declared to the Emperor, in behalf of his fellow-soldiers, that, whilst ready to yield implicit obedience in all matters consistent with conscience, death was preferable to the violation of duty to God. And when the Emperor ordered his soldiers to destroy the whole band, they quietly laid down their arms and accepted martyrdom.

The other story is that of the Thundering Legion under Marcus Aurelius. When the Roman hosts were surrounded by barbarian hordes, and the peril was great, these Christian soldiers, mighty in prayer, knelt on the very battle-field and sought from God and obtained deliverance by His hand from the dangers that threatened the forces of the empire.

Whether there ever was a Theban Legion and a Thundering Legion in the days of the Silver Eagle matters little; but the Missionary Army has had both from the beginning. Men and women who would not be drawn or driven from their duty to Christ and lost souls, though the fever, the famine, the sword decimated their ranks, have dared the prison cell, starvation, persecution and death itself rather than abandon their witness to Christ. And the strength of missions has ever been that the Captain of our salvation has always had His Praying Legion; who in the crises of the conflict, took no account of the number or might of foes, but prevailed with God in prayer. It is the central glory of missionary history that it has produced more intrepid and self-sacrificing soldiers of the cross, and more great intercessors like Moses, Samuel, Daniel and Elijah, than any other form even of Church life. Surely between these facts there must be some divine link of connection. A work that develops such courage and constancy, on the one side, and such faith and prayer, on the other, must, in this very fact, bear the peculiar stamp and seal of the King himself.

Thus, by "many infallible proofs," missionary history vindicates its rightful claim as a continuation of the Acts of the Apostles, in the signs and wonders God has wrought. And what shall I more say? for the time would fail me to tell of all the marvels of Providence and Grace which make the whole growth of modern missions a Burning Bush aflame with the glory of the presence of God!

On the long guns of the African moors these words are often found engraven: "For the Holy War if God will." When will disciples learn that they are God's soldiers, and that every power and faculty is to be devoted as a weapon to His holy warfare? What new signs and wonders would be wrought if, in response to the bugle blast of our great Captain, the whole Church would march to the battle-field! All that God has yet shown of His mighty power would be but a small part of His ways. Men would begin to see Omnipotence baring its resistless arm, and the thunder of His power would shake earth and heaven!

PART VI.

THE NEW MOTIVES AND INCENTIVES

I.

THE LOOK FORWARD.

IT WAS a saying of Immanuel Kant that every man should propose to himself three questions: What can I *know*? What ought I to *do*? and for what may I *hope*?

Motive is that which moves, or produces motion. All action is the result of incentives; and the more numerous and powerful the inducements, the more prompt and energetic the activity. *Hope* is, therefore, the greatest motor of human life; it is the very sculptor of character and conduct; the architect of history and destiny. Hope is so connected with happiness that its perfect crown is heaven; and Dante was not less philosopher than poet when he wrote over the gates of the Inferno, "Abandon hope, all ye who enter here!"

The matter now claiming attention belongs at the conclusion of our studies, for it is the apex which, naturally and fitly, forms that culmination.

To tarry, at any point of progress, simply to dwell on past successes, is the forfeiture of further advance. The backward glance is helpful only when the retrospect enables us to apprehend the aspect and appreciate the prospect; when memory inspires and energizes hope; when the review acts not as a sedative and a narcotic, but as a tonic and a stimulant.

Motives and incentives cannot stimulate to action until their value and virtue are felt, and to be felt they must be appreciated. Their weight in the scale will depend upon the attractive power they possess to our minds; for the scale whose beam they turn is the judgment. God will guide with His eye those who keep their eye fixed on His; but the Divine Eye cannot guide without this answering look. Other wise we must be guided by sterner restraints and constraints, like the beast whose mouth is held in with bit and bridle, leather reins in place of gentler glances.

To this closing part of our great theme we may well approach with thoughtfulness, for all new progress in missions finds here the hiding of its power. If the new century, now beginning, is to write new and grander chapters in the Acts of the Apostles we must feel the force of the mighty motives which God puts before us. He means that the hundred years ahead shall be as much more abundant in effort, intelligent in zeal, and glorious in achievement, as the century which began with Carey's sermon at Nottingham surpassed that which went before it. And so countless are the new motives and incentives now yoked to missionary effort, that if they move and draw us as they should, our advance will be not by an arithmetical but a geometrical ratio, and the world's evangelization will go forward not by slow steps but by gigantic strides.

II.

A New Order of Things.

First of all, *a new order of things* has been divinely created for our encouragement. So novel are the conditions of missionary labour that nothing seems old and unchanged but the gospel message and the converting Spirit. Instead of a world locked against us, with walls to be broken down and gates to be forced, an open highway to the heart of Asia and Africa; in most parts a welcome; in almost all, an undisputed entrance. Instead of the barriers of a century ago,—obstacles between the Church and the heathen world, which hindered approach and access, intercourse and impression; and obstacles within the Church itself, which hindered action and co-operation,—an aroused Church, in sympathy with the work of missions, confronting a world-wide field, everywhere inviting the sower with his seed, and in many parts presenting a harvest calling for the reaper with his sickle.

It has been reserved for the nineteenth century to behold the whole world open to the missionary. God has flung wide the gates of India, broken down the wall of China, unsealed the ports of Japan; Africa is girdled and crossed, Turkey and Siam, Burma and Corea, invite missionary labour, and France and Spain, Italy and Mexico, welcome an open Bible and a simple gospel. These long-locked doors God has curiously opened with the keys of commerce and common schools, the printing-press and medical science, as well as arms and diplomacy. In some cases, still more strangely, He has used His "great army" of locusts, caterpillars and cankerworms, famine and fever, drought and flood, to force entrance into Satan's strongholds. What inspiration to holy activity and zeal, when His shining Pillar moves before us to assure of victory through His presence and power! Moreover, our work may now be done, in almost every land, with comparative immunity from danger. M. Schoffler, missionary to Cochin China, was publicly executed at Sontay by order of the grand mandarin, for his preaching of Christ, contrary to the laws of the land, on May 4th, 1851. This was the last such execution in the Flowery Kingdom, and from it dates the new era in Chinese evangelization. Resistance we shall probably continue to meet everywhere, but the more violent, the less likely to be prolonged.

There are three stages of missionary work: First, the *pioneer* period, when as yet the missionary is met with such distrust and suspicion, that little headway can be made; secondly, the period of *action*, when early obstacles have been removed or surmounted, opposition is overcome, and the cross is actually planted, and converts are multiplying; and, last of all, the period of *establishment*, when native churches become self-governing, self-supporting, self-propagating. During the first stage it is vain to send many missionaries to the field; during the third, they may be withdrawn as no longer needed; but during the second they should be especially multiplied; the opportunity is grand but brief, and must be promptly improved; and, in most fields, we have actually reached this middle period, when the need of men and money is most imperative.

Is it no significant sign of the will of God that just at this time of peculiar crisis, such increased capacity should exist in the Church to meet this greatly increased demand? Fewness of numbers and smallness of means the Christian Church can no longer offer as an excuse or extenuation for inaction.

To-day the evangelical Protestant Churches have a membership of nearly forty millions of communicants, One from every hundred, which is a smaller proportion than the small community at Herrnhut actually is sending out—would give us a missionary army of about four hundred thousand—fifty times the present available force. As to money, wealth is in the hands of this vast membership to an extent perilous to piety. From careful estimates, the average income of Protestant Church members, the world over, is reckoned at not less than one hundred pounds annually—a low estimate, considering what hoards of treasure are in the coffers of so many; and yet this yields a sum total of four thousand millions of pounds sterling, or about twenty thousand millions of dollars—a sum too immense for us to conceive.

If of this, a tithe were given, there would pour annually into missionary treasuries four hundred millions of pounds, or two hundred times the amount now given to missions. And imagination fails to paint the grandeur and glory of mission conquests, with a consecrated Church sending nearly half a million men and women into the world field, and furnishing an annual income approaching five hundred million pounds to sustain them in the combat with idolatry and iniquity!

The gifts that idol worshippers lavish upon the fanes and shrines of false gods, put to shame the worshippers of Jehovah. The "Peacock Throne" of the Great Mogul, in the Hall of Audience at Delhi, cost more than two and a half millions of pounds sterling—or twice as much as missions in India since Carey went to Calcutta! And the cost of the new twin temples of Hon-gwan-ji, in the ancient city of Kyoto, Japan, will be as much more. The "Eastern" and "Western" structures belonging to this Japanese fane are superb in expenditure. The latest built of them is erected entirely from freewill offerings of Buddhists; precious woods, metals, money and jewels were given without stint; and the offerings of human hair remind us of the maidens of Carthage and Tyre, who furnished from their ringlets the bowstrings and cordage for archers and war-ships. On one of the platforms could have been seen twenty-four heavy coils of rope, from three to four inches diameter, attached to which was the inscription:

"Since the thirteenth year of Meiji (1880), when the rebuilding of the two halls of the Eastern Hon-gwan-ji was begun, the faithful laymen and lay-women of every place have been unanimous in presenting to the principal temple, Hon-gwan-ji, strong ropes wrought of their own hair, to be used in the work of re-erection. The number of these ropes reached fifty-three, twenty-nine of which became worthless from use. The total length of the remaining twenty-four is 4,528 feet, and the total weight, 11,567 pounds!"

Beside these ropes lay several large coils of hair— several of them gray, the gifts of the aged—which came too late for use, but not too late to express devotion.

One feature of this new order of things is found in the *changed relations of so-called Christian nations to the rest of the world*. God has not only opened doors of entrance to all other peoples, and supplied avenues and facilities for this world-wide occupation; but He has given to the great Protestant peoples of the earth the *sceptre of the race*. To Great Britain, the United States, Prussia, belongs the undoubted supremacy of the world; for, to the nations most deserving to be called enlightened Christian, the rest of mankind tacitly yield homage. Mohammedanism most stubbornly resists the approach of the gospel; yet Dr. Schreiber, of Barmen, says, of 175,000,000 Moslems, that 100,000,000 are already in subjection to Christian powers, and that before long the other 75,000,000 will be. The political downfall of the False Prophet is thus already an accomplished fact.

The great *prominence of missionary literature* supplies another new incentive. When Christ gave his last command, there was not one Christian book— even the first gospel narrative was not yet written. The Church, for nearly a century, had no literature, and had to wait fifteen centuries for a printing-press; and for three centuries more, for any missionary literature outside of the Acts of the Apostles. Some who are yet living can remember when the "Evangelical Magazine" promised its readers a page of missionary intelligence, "as soon as enough matter could be found to fill a page." To-day missionary hymns are in our hymn-books, missionary magazines and reviews throng our mails; and about one-seventh of our religious publications deal either directly or indirectly with missions; and even our secular dailies devote columns and pages to the subject! We have chairs of missions in our colleges and theological schools, and missionary lectureships. There are some three hundred societies organized for promoting missions, and as many translations of the Bible into the languages and dialects of the peoples whom we need to reach with the message.

III.

MEDICAL MISSIONS.

WHAT NEW conditions of success are found in the recent development of *medical missions*! In the Acts of the Apostles, two great aids were granted to the witnessing Church: first, the gift of *tongues*, which fitted the heralds to reach strange peoples without the slow mastery of a foreign speech; and, secondly, the gift of *healing*, which made even opponents favourably disposed toward the herald who first brought such help to the body. In a natural way, the lack of these supernatural gifts is now compensated. Christian scholarship has so far outrun the best learning and training of those earlier days, that grammars and dictionaries of all the leading languages and dialects can be supplied to the student; Morrison could study Chinese in London and Schwartz could learn Tamil at Halle, and Keith Falconer, Arabic at Cambridge—before China, India or Arabia were reached.

Within the hundred years past, at least one hundred tongues that had before no literature, not even an alphabet, have by missionaries been reduced to writing. And the Word of God, in over three hundred dialects, now, like a perpetual Pentecost, speaks to the nations, so that each man may in his own tongue read the wonderful works of God. This reduction of the world's languages to a written form, to a scientific form, is God's modern gift of tongues.

And the medical mission, now finding entrance into all fields, and itself having, in many, as at Corea, held the key that unlocked the doors of entrance— what is this but God's modern gift of healing, which is to go before the gospel to dispose men by the help given their bodies to hear the words which, to all the woes and wants of sinsick souls, bring health!

Medical missions have great capacity of service, both as a means, and as an end. As an end they displace existing systems of so-called medicine, positively useless to reach disease, and positively harmful and cruel to patients. How Christian medical science relieves bodily suffering is shown by such work as that of Dr. Grant in Persia, Dr. Kerr in China, Dr. Post in Syria, and scores of other most successful medical missionaries. No more wonderful story has been written in modern days than that of the St. John's Hospital at Beirut, as given to the World's Conference in 1888. But medical missions are also a means to a higher end. They are destructive of superstition and idolatry, for false faiths are so bound up with false science, that to attack one is to attack the other, and they must go down together. The ignorant devotee who finds that his medicine men and conjurors have only been adding to his pains and sufferings, and that the Christian doctor both brings help and cure, naturally feels drawn to the new faith he teaches; and so medical missions are not only destructive of superstition and false religion, but they are constructive of a new faith and life. God is now singularly using this new agency both as a handmaid to the gospel and as a power to unbar long shut gates to the ambassador of Christ. The healing art is still the preparation for conversion to the great Healer.

The sudden emphasis, so singularly laid on medical missions within the last sixty years, has solved one of the greatest problems of missions. Of course there has never been a period in which preaching of the gospel has not been closely allied to the healing art. Mackay, of Uganda, was right when he said, that "All genuine missionary work must be in the highest sense a healing work." Body, soul and spirit have all been poisoned and diseased by sin, and redemption must bring salvation to the whole man. We cannot sever sin from sickness, and we cannot but feel that there is more than a link of language between holiness and wholeness, or health. Christ went about preaching the gospel of the kingdom and healing all manner of disease; and in commissioning the seventy and the twelve, healing the sick was conjoined with saving souls.

Yet as a feature of *missions*, the medical mission is just sixty years old. The first regularly trained and designated medical missionary was Dr. Peter Parker, who, in 1834, went to Canton, under commission of the American Board; followed shortly after by Benjamin Hobson, sent out by the London Society to Macao.

Dr. Christlieb has called attention to the fact that it was an English physician, Gabriel Boughton, M.D., who really laid in the East the foundations of British civilization and dominion nearly 260 years ago. In 1636, a princess of the great Mogul's court was badly burned, and he was the means of her cure. Whereupon, in his magnanimity declining all personal compensation, he asked as his reward only that his countrymen might have leave to trade with the great Indian Empire. And so the healing art spoke the magic word which caused the iron doors to swing open. Was not Dr. Otis R. Bacheler, sent out to Orissa by the Free Baptists, also one of the first missionary physicians?

The Medical Missionary Society of Edinburgh multiplied its income more than fourfold in the ten years from 1871 to 1881. Before 1861, the number of missionary physicians in all heathen lands did not exceed twenty; and ten years later, not over double that number. Seven years after, the number closely approached one hundred; and in another seven years, there were nearly two hundred regularly qualified medical missionaries; by this time, ten years later, that number has again about doubled. And yet, how inadequate! New York City alone has 3,000 doctors, or one to about five hundred people: the unevangelized world has about one to every three millions!*

---

*   It may be well, in order to make these statements and statistics, so far as practicable, complete up to date, to add, that the British missionary societies, in 1893, reported 139 fully qualified physicians engaged in mission work, of whom 13 were women. The Medical Missionary Record of New York, after gathering with great care a list of all medical missionaries in the world, gave in 1893, the following as facts:
There were in the entire world field, up to 1893, 359 fully qualified medical missionaries, of whom 74 were women.

Presbyterian Church, U. S., has	48
A. B. C. F. M.,	32
Methodist Church,	30
C. M. S.,	25
Free Church of Scotland,	20
United Presbyterian Church,	10
Church of Scotland,	8
Presbyterian Church, Canada,	8

This list apportions to the U.S.,	173
to Great Britain,	169
to Canada,	7
to Germany,	3

As to Countries, China has	126
India,	76
Africa,	46

IV.

The New Activity of Woman.

WOMAN'S PRESENT prominence in Christian work provides a new incentive of immense value and power. The progress of Christianity has made in woman's estate a complete inversion. Once, by a strange perversion of God's creative word, she was accounted a helpmeet for man—not his correspondent or *counterpart*, as the original implies, but his subordinate and servant, or, at best, his helper—that is, man, the superior and sovereign; woman, the subject and servant. And so, even in the Jewish body of believers, woman scarcely ever comes to the front. Miriam, Deborah, Anna the prophetess, are the rare exceptions in Hebrew history, in which woman is submerged and out of sight. With a curious significance Paul writes: "Help those women which laboured with me in the gospel," as though they were now leaders in holy service, and men must come to their help. Through Christ and His gospel she who was first in transgression, is becoming first in holy consecration and missionary devotion; in the family, the radiant centre of attraction; in the Church, the disseminator of missionary intelligence, the kindler of enthusiasm, the organizer of systematic benevolence. Woman goes abroad as teacher, nurse and medical missionary, and in endurance and endeavour rivals the most patient and valiant; or, as wife and mother, shows what Christ makes of her sex; and not only joins her husband in work, but sometimes equals and even outdoes him in service. One-third of the unevangelized can best be reached by woman, and a large part of them can be reached by her only, as they are inaccessible to man.

Medical missions afford a new field for the sisterhood of Christ. From the reach of this noble auxiliary to *missions*, the women of the Orient, and especially of India, were long shut out by the rigid laws of the zenana, the seraglio and the harem. Even heathen doctors had to them no access. In Syria a physician was called to prescribe for a favourite wife of a dignitary, but was not allowed even to see her tongue or feel her pulse; and when he insisted that no medical aid could be given without such examination, a female slave was made to thrust out her tongue and reach out her hand through a rent in the curtain, that he might examine his patient by proxy. And so, as late as 1878, Mrs. Weitbrecht wrote: "All Hindu women are, in time of sickness, utterly neglected. Prejudice and usage banish medical help." And hence, fever, ophthalmia and other contagious ills bred their awful progeny unchecked among women and children.

But now, what a change! All India clamours for capable women who are trained nurses and qualified physicians. The Presbyterian Female Hospital at Lucknow, opened ten or eleven years since, had thirteen patients the first year; but three years later, 212, beside 2,712 outside patients and 6,930 distributions of medicine. The movement has ceased to be provincial and become national; the work at Lucknow and Lodiana, Travancore and Amritstar, is extending over the great empire.

Five years ago, the medical missions of China were scarcely less numerous than in India, extending from Hong Kong and Canton to Peking, and even into Manchuria and Tartary and Formosa. The whole force then at work, male and female, was upwards of eighty. The hospital at Swatow, opened by Dr. Gauld in 1863, had in 1888 two hundred inmates, treating six thousand patients a year.

It is a strange fact that the law of sex runs through all Christian work. The feminine element is needed as well as the masculine. Man may be aggressive, bold, strong, fitted to pioneer, organize, administer; but woman is patient, impressive, tender, sympathetic, fitted to win, to soothe, to comfort, to minister. Both together bring to the work the complete furnishing that leaves no element of adaptation lacking. And hence, when less than fifty years ago women began to organize work among themselves, gather money, scatter information, send out women and undertake their support, qualify for medical missionaries, and educate their own sex for intelligent co-operation in securing the spread of the good news, the effect was felt from the centre to the circumference of the whole sphere of Christian service. And the end is not yet!

V.

NEW LESSONS FROM EXPERIENCE.

THE MODERN age of missions furnishes new incentives in the exhibition of the *relations of Christian missions to Christian life*, which could be understood only when experience had both proved and illustrated those relations. Long since, Solomon wrote: "There is that scattereth and yet increaseth; and there is that with-holdeth more than is meet but it tendeth to poverty." That is one of the great truths of the wisdom from above, but to the worldly man it is folly. No paradox Christ uttered is more inexplicable to the natural and carnal heart than this: "He that saveth his life shall lose it, and he that loseth his life for My sake and the gospel's, the same shall save it." To increase by scattering, and grow poor by withholding; to save by losing and lose by saving—is the climax of absurdity, yet it is the first principle of divine philosophy. Selfishness withholds and gets poorer by the attempt to grow richer. Benevolence scatters, and in imparting increases—in giving, gets.

Missions sustain Christian life—a relation both of sustenance and satisfaction—they supply the one most complete avenue for service and for satisfying joy. There are returns, though they are not carnal nor material—the channel which conveys our gifts outward, conveys joy inward—like the mutual action of arteries and veins. Worldly pleasures are sweety for a season, but they lose relish and give place to bitter dregs at the bottom of the chalice. The worldly mind is a mirror turned downward, reflecting only what is earthly, sensual and sensuous, material and temporal. The spiritual mind is the mirror turned upward, reflecting heaven with its stars. Worldly pleasures lose charm; so shallow that you can look through them and see the mire at the bottom of the stream from which you drink; so hollow that, as you grasp them, you have a sense of their unsubstantial, unsatisfying character. Adolph Monod, dying at fifty-four years of age, in 1891, left in a brief, dying sentence, the sum of his legacy to his survivors: "All in Christ, by the Holy Spirit, for the glory of God! ALL ELSE IS NOTHING."

The Church has found missions needful for its own full *arousing to activity*, for such work is the preservative of life. Nearly one-third of our existence is passed in that sleep which for all active purposes of life is a blank, but which helps to replenish waste and supply energy to exhausted brain and brawn. But while in the physical sphere there is no antagonism between sleep and life, in spiritual things sleep is death. All activities of the vital spirit cannot cease without cessation of life itself, for motionless members become atrophized; as Dr. Solander said of travellers amid the snows of a Norwegian winter: "Whoever sits down there will sleep, and whoever sleeps will wake no more." The sleep of the soul arrests spiritual circulation and respiration. Piety cannot survive absolute inaction.

When missionary activities cease, ritualism and formalism intone their monotonous chant, and by their mechanical uniformity induce hopeless sluggishness and spiritual death. There is but one source of safety, even to disciples. Apathy brings apostasy, lethargy palsies and kills. To have a healthy, alive Church, all must be at work for souls; each, like Arnold of Rugby, studious to learn the evils and needs of his own generation and serve the whole race.

Missions are thus inseparable from the *salvation of the Church*. The Hawaiian Islands undertook the mission to Micronesia to arrest decline and decay among native converts. The sagacious pioneers in Tahiti and the Fiji group encouraged the newly-organized churches to send labourers at once to other clusters about them as a means of their own development. And it has always been so. Not one of the ancient Churches survives in purity that was not a missionary Church; all the rest are to-day dead. And if, at this time, the forty millions of Protestants should give up all missions and concentrate all effort on denominational extension and self-preservation, it would be the surest, quickest way to promote decay. Ruin would result, perhaps so rapid, that in a century we should have relapsed again into the Dark Ages.

Daniel Webster, some years before his death, made an extensive tour to the extreme west of the United States, and on his return, expressed in four words his impression of the country's peril: "Abundance, Luxury, Decline, Desolation." A sagacious seer and prophet was this, our American Burke. He saw that this boasted abundance and luxury were the summit of a hill beyond which the descent was awfully rapid and dangerous. Numerical strength may be weakness, and wealth, impoverishment. What saved the Church of the seventeenth and the first half of the eighteenth century from the apostasy that threatened, was the *birth-hour of missions* which gave the Church a new remedy for its ills. And the only thing that can save the Church of the nineteenth century from another apostasy, will be a new consecration to the work of a world's evangelization, proportioned to our new measure of knowledge and opportunity. For be it remembered that fidelity has no fixed standard; it varies because light has its degrees of clearness, and ability has its varying measure. What would have been faithfulness in Carey's day is neglect now; what would have been zeal then is indifference now. As the world opens to us; as our numbers and resources multiply; as our knowledge of human need increases; as our facilities are indefinitely enlarged, so our readiness, promptness, fulness of devotion, must keep pace; otherwise we are unfaithful. If, when I have wealth, I give no larger a proportion than when poor, I really keep a far larger proportion for my indulgence; if, when I have far more incentives to duty, I am no more active, I am the more unimpressible and irresponsive. So, of this age to which so much more is given, God will require the more.

Frenchmen have accomplished the feat of actually plating a dead child with a metallic shell. The corpse is prepared by a bath of nitrate of silver and the vapour of phosphorus, and then electricity is employed to lay on the thin shell of copper, aluminium or gold. The tendency of our day is to a plated Church—to leave the corruption of this world, and the coldness and lifelessness of a secular selfishness, within, and gild over with fashionable formalism and polite culture. To leave this tendency unchanged is to have, in the end, a corpse with a gold shell!

There certainly is a crisis in Church life just now which gives to watchful saints no little alarm. It is an age not only of doubt, but of declared doubt; an age of scholarly inquiry, but audacious rationalism and impudent irreverence; an age of unrest, insatiate avarice and reckless ambition; an age of fashionable indulgence and unrestrained selfishness; an age of formality in religion and prayerlessness; an age of religious extension, rather than of holy intensity; an age of secular churches and wide-spread neglect of the real sanctities of holy living.

Reference has been made already to John Owen's "Pneumatologia," and to what he says of every age, "that it has its own *test* of fidelity or infidelity." Before Christ's advent, the great testing truth was the oneness of God's nature and His monarchy over all. At His advent, whether a Church was orthodox hung on this—whether it would receive or reject the Son of God as divine, incarnate, sacrificed, glorified according to prophecy and promise. But, now that the Church has been outgathered, the test is, "*how the Church receives the Holy Spirit*," so that a body of disciples who hold tenaciously to the unity of God and the trinity of the persons of the Godhead, and accept Jesus Christ as Son of God, Saviour and

Lord, may yet in God's eyes be apostate, because practically . rejecting the Holy Spirit in His divine offices!

The remark is alarmingly true, and there is no sign of such apostasy more convincing than the absence of that missionary spirit which is the practical evidence and expression of the abiding of the Spirit of Christ. If at once the whole Church of God should enter upon the work of a world's evangelization with a zeal proportioned to the present claims of duty and opportunity, there would be a sudden cessation of the widespread doubt, due to the leaven of German rationalism, under polite names of Biblical criticism; we should find it once more true, as Shaftesbury said, that the antidote to all this scepticism and uncertainty is to be constantly and wholly absorbed in work for soul-saving. All minor questions are forgotten when major issues come to the front; as two animals that have been fighting will suddenly come into friendly terms, and stand side by side when forced to face and fight a lion. Even the Church is coming to embrace a great multitude who "vigorously believing nothing, practice vigorously what they believe;" and it will be worse unless we redouble our fidelity to missions.

One of the highest incentives is found in the fact that missions thus *develop the life* that makes them possible. There never was a true mission born unless there was vitality enough to give it birth; but it is equally true that such child-bearing saves the very mother herself. The sacrifice is salvation. That word, Salvation, has a grander, fuller meaning than we often think. Justification may come to him who believes with the heart; but there is a full salvation only to him who confesses with the mouth, and witnesses to the world. To escape the penalty of sin is but the first step in salvation; to escape the power of sin, and the dominion of evil is the next step, sanctification. But he who advances not further and learns that service which delivers from the more subtle dominion of self, knows not the fullest meaning of salvation.

It ought to be motive enough that the Church's mission is to save the lost, and not simply to care for the saved. Solomon says, God hath set the world in man's heart—but the Hebrew term is *olam* —indefinite duration. There is a latent instinct of eternity in the human soul. Man knows that duration was before him and will be after him; and the believer is one in whose heart this latent instinct has been aroused to activity: his mission is to go forth and awaken that instinct in others and that is soulsaving!

VI.

New Incentives to Giving.

THE MODERN notions of giving are not only far below the Scripture level; they contradict Bible standards. An article in the "Nineteenth Century" told men how to live on seven hundred and fifty pounds a year: allowance was made for all needful outlay on food and clothing, house rent and house service; and a generous provision for culture and amusements. But not one penny was set aside for charity, which was not reckoned among necessities or even luxuries. An advertisement appears, offering a very large reward for a poodle, whose diamond-set collar was worth two hundred and fifty pounds sterling, and the silver chain, seven pounds more; but that is to be accounted among the reasonable indulgences, whether any provision is made for perishing millions or not!

The old doctrine will be unpopular in this degenerate day of a secularized Church, but it is still to be proclaimed, for the offence of the cross is not ceased. No setting apart of a tithe, or Lord's portion, will, in these days, suffice. It never did. The tithe was the Jews' minimum, not maximum; it represents what the poorest must give, not what the richest might use to buy off the right to keep the other nine-tenths! Instead of asking, How little can I spare for God and satisfy His claim and my conscience? we should invert the terms, and ask, How little can I expend upon myself and yet satisfy my actual needs, and how much can I thus spare for God?

The missionary age affords new opportunity and incentive for the culture of this supreme grace. Giving will bring its true blessing, its greater blessing, only when systematic and self-denying.

"Mammon" is simply another name for money, when, instead of a servant, it becomes a master, practically served—an idol worshipped. There is no difficulty in understanding how what is so grossly material as wealth came to be associated with divine attributes; for, as we have seen, its power to achieve great results suggests omnipotence; its power to represent the giver, wherever his gifts are bestowed and their blessings scattered, suggests omnipresence; and its power to perpetuate his influence when he is dead, suggests eternity. What a pity, what a crime, when such power is put in the fetters of selfishness, and locked up in the narrow cell of personal indulgence! when it achieves no result but to fatten and satiate the lust of greed, finds no sphere outside of a luxurious home, and perpetuates no influence but the example of the miser!

One of the foremost incentives to missions is found in the blessedness of giving. Christ spake a new beatitude, recorded and preserved by Paul, who said to the Ephesian elders: "Remember the words of the Lord Jesus, how He said, It is more blessed to give than to receive!" The full meaning and truth of that last beatitude is yet to be known, and can be known only as this work of missions is done as He meant it should be done.

This may be called a new motive, for its power is as yet unfelt. Our giving is not only imperfect and inadequate, it is radically defective; for its basis is, in a measure, wrong and unsound. The ministry of money is not understood, and stewardship is practically denied. That is a virtually effete notion, that all I have belongs to God; that it is not mine to do as I will with it, to hoard, or spend, to use in selfish indulgence or bestow in unselfish ministries; but that it is held in trust for God, and to be put to holy uses, so that even what I eat and drink and wear is to glorify Him. This may be treated with contemptuous scorn as an antiquated doctrine, but it will never be no longer binding while the word of God is our guide and a world waits to be saved.

This beatitude represents the crown of all beatitudes. There are three stages of experience: first, where joy is found only in getting; second, where joy is found in both getting and giving; third, where giving is the only real joy, and getting is valued only in order to giving. The first shows the purely worldly spirit; the next indexes the average disciple; the last marks the closest identity with the Lord. To this last only the few attain or even aspire. But to such it is the foretaste of heaven on earth. The curse even of our Churches is that *getting* is recognized as the one thing to be desired and sought; *giving* is at best recognized as a duty, not a privilege to be sought but an obligation to be accepted, and a thousand expedients are adopted to evade and avoid that *self-denial* which represents the very enrichment of giving. If money is to be raised, instead of counting it a blessing to give, and to give what costs self-sacrifice, the constant effort is to give what costs nothing; and resort is had to secular entertainments, concerts and exhibitions, tea-drinkings and picnics, bazaars and raffles, charades and tableaux, lantern shows and comic recitations—the whole alphabet of the world's amusements supplies the Church with easy expedients to gather a little money and escape self-denial; and modes, not only secular but unhallowed, are often adopted to secure funds for the most sacred cause of missions. The mistake is the more serious because it not only secularizes the Church, but it makes even our giving selfish; the cause of God must buy our support by some price paid to the eye, in the spectacular; to the ear, in the musical or the amusing; to the palate, in the delicate or the delicious.

Let us stop and once more ask *why and when it is more blessed* to give than to receive. Getting *without* giving is absolutely disastrous; even getting *with* giving is dangerous. And the only way to prevent the disaster and avert the danger is to give, constantly, systematically, abundantly, cheerfully, self-denyingly. Fire that has no vent, has soon no flame; if the flame cannot get out the fire goes out. A spring without outlet cannot have inlet; the water must give forth a stream, or it seeks a new channel underground. The Christian life is the fire of which giving is the vent; it is the spring of which active benevolence is the stream. He who hoards and withholds, cramps and crushes and cripples his own better nature.

But, as Lowell makes Christ to say, in the "Vision of Sir Launfal,"

> "He who gives himself with his alms, feeds three:
> Himself, his hungering neighbour, and Me."

The miser is an idolater and worships the golden calf. The law of all idolatry, twice thundered from the Psalms, is universal:

"They that make them are *like unto them*. So is every one that trusteth in them."

All idols make the maker and worshipper like themselves. If man worships a beast he becomes beastly and brutal; if it be a god of wood and stone, dumb and senseless like the image; if it be a clod of earth, earthy like the clod. He who worships gold—to whom the "almighty dollar," the "sovereign," the "Napoleon," is, as the names suggest, his practical monarch and master, becomes, as we have before hinted, a kind of coin himself. He gets to have a sort of metallic hardness and insensibility to impression, and a kind of metallic ring. His utterances, his preferences, his tastes, his actions have the sound of the brass trumpet, the silver cymbal, the gold-piece. And when he falls in death, it is not a man who has disappeared from among men—not some bright star suddenly fading into darkness, or some musical melody sinking into silence, or some fruitful tree tom up by the roots—only a sack of hoarded treasure falling upon the stony pavement of fate, and, as Death cuts the knot that has held its mouth closed, scattering its coins to be picked up by lawful heirs, or, more likely, by greedy lawyers! One who worships fashion becomes nothing but a tailor's dummy, a walking advertisement, a suit of clothes on legs, miscalled a man; or a wax-doll, trimmed with furs and feathers, and miscalled a woman. The worshippers of fast horses come to have the savour and flavour of the stall and the turf; they smell of the horse; life is to them a race for stakes, and their back is a saddle for jockeys.

The objection commonly raised against giving to foreign missions—that we shall never see the money again—the field is too far off to make returns—is itself an example of how a Scripture motive may be turned into a hindrance. Christ bids us, do good, hoping for nothing again—give to those from whom we can expect *no returns*. That alone *is giving*. If I invite to my supper those whom I expect to invite me again; or bestow a favour where I look for reciprocal favours, it is all selfish and breeds only selfishness. It is lending, not giving, for the loan is to be returned, perhaps with interest. To carry this principle into our benevolence makes benevolence impossible. If I put money into a savings bank, I have certainly given nothing to the bank. And if I put money into a Christian church or school, expecting returns in any form of self-gain, it may be a good investment, but is it true *giving?*

Our whole Christian life is in danger of being mammonized. The little boy who slipped his penny into the contribution box, and asked his mother what sort of sweets would drop out, whether caromels or lozenges, was a good representative of older people, who look on all so-called benevolent schemes as automatic sweetmeat machines, into which you drop your penny, or your shilling, your dollar or your pound, to get sooner or later some adequate returns.

Once more let it be learned by us that God's poorest ones need our gifts far less than we need the discipline of giving. To say "no" to my selfish greed and appetite, to curb my carnal self and give reins to my spiritual nature, to learn to give without thought of any returns—simply to confer good and impart blessing—ah! that is to be like unto God! The devil delights in returning evil for good; man is quite willing to return good for good; but God's joy is to give the best where is returned only the worst! Giving is God's corrective and antidote to selfishness, and, because the remotest field brings the slowest returns, and the most destitute objects leave the least hope of personal gains to tempt cupidity, missions to the heathen furnish the grandest opportunity we can enjoy for cultivating self-oblivion— pure, disinterested, unselfish, Christ-like ministry to want and woe.

In one sense, this is a new incentive, for there is a new appeal in the *changed conditions of Church life*. The primitive Church of the Acts was a poor Church, so poor that the few who had possessions felt constrained to dispose of their houses and lands and turn the proceeds into the common treasury. That was a simple, frugal age, in which there were no great monopolies and colossal fortunes as now. It was not, as this is, a materialistic age—when the very atmosphere was laden with the miasma of miserliness and incited to greed. We are living in a time when the rich are very rich and the poor very poor, and the gulf between them is becoming unbridgeable and hopeless alienation is the outcome. These are days when there is far greater risk of Christians' becoming electro-plated with fashionable avarice and hardened into a respectable insensibility to human sorrow and suffering; when it shall be easy to feed and fatten upon dainties, while Lazarus is left to the dogs; when it shall be common to be comfortable in luxury while a world is dying of poverty and in sin—than in any *previous age*. And hence the power of the new appeal. Because the very social life tends to dull our ears to human need, God permits the voice of the heathen's want and woe to be the louder and more clamorous and the more ceaseless. Intelligence is now so widespread that ignorance of the world's need is well-nigh impossible, and at least culpable; and, to know that a thousand millions of souls are starving for the bread of life, and that we can give it to them, and yet not to do it, implies an indifference, an apathy, whose crime and curse are proportioned to our greater information, ability and opportunity. In the days of the Apostles there were neither such chances of good, nor such risks of harm to the Church.

So important is this element of unselfishness in giving, that to avoid or evade it is to take away its vital principle. It is, then, the flower without the colour or odour—the gem without its radiance. As Mr. J. A. Froude says: "Sacrifice is the first element in religion, and resolves itself into the love of God. Let the thought of self intrude, let the painter but pause to consider how much reward his work will bring to him, and the cunning will forsake his hand and the power of genius will be gone. Excellence is proportioned to the oblivion of self." No doubt money may be raised for missions in ways that obviate self-sacrifice, but in proportion to our success is our failure—and the greater the success the worse the disaster. For this means that we have found a way to make the sacred ointment and leave out the perfume that, to God, gives it all its sweet savour.

And hence also it is that the more we succeed in making large gifts from the few supply the place of the many small offerings of the self-denying poor, the less practical power is there in our very gifts themselves. It is one of the mysteries of chemical galvanism that an increase of its power cannot be got by increasing the *dimensions* of the cells of the battery, but can be secured only by increasing the *number* of those cells. This peculiarity illustrates Christian service in giving. The cumulative energy of our gifts depends not on their amount, but on the sacrifice they involve, and so, the more the givers in whom this sacrifice is developed, the grander the spiritual force and impetus given by the aggregate of gifts. Hence, the highest Church power hangs on *all sharing in the giving*.

As Jeanie Deans said to the Queen: "It is not when we sleep soft and wake merrily ourselves that we think on other people's sufferings. Our hearts are waxed light within us then, and we are for righting our ain wrangs, and fighting our ain battles. But when the hour of trouble comes to the mind or to the body, and when the hour of death comes, that comes to high and low—long and late may it be yours O my leddy!—then it is na what we hae dune for oursells, but what we hae dune for others, that we think on maist pleasantly."

God has shown us, by nearly two millenniums of Church history, that missions have a vital relation to Christian life, and that their *reflex action* is so unspeakably precious that all the cost of money and men is far more than repaid in this returning tide of blessing. The vigorous pulsation which drives the blood to the ends of the body, invigorates the heart itself and strengthens its muscular walls. To nourish a missionary spirit is to enlarge, expand, ennoble our whole spiritual life. Take one example. Nothing is a greater perplexity and anxiety to true disciples than this—how to ensure a sanctified *family life*. It is lamentable that children of Christian parents so often grow up, not only strangers to God but open enemies and infidels. There seems to be some influence at work to annul and neutralize all the power of holy example. The fact is that nothing is so subtly fatal to all true symmetry of character as simple *selfishness*. There is a curious fact in botany. If you take out a scion from a tree, cut off the branch and set the scion downward, all others that grow out of that branch afterward, will grow downward—and hence, the ornamental gardener gets his drooping trees. The scions in our family tree get early set downward, and all future growths are earthward. There is as truly peril in a self-indulgent home as in a positively vicious one—let a child begin by being pampered, petted, indulged, taught to gratify whims and selfish impulses, and you have given a carnal tendency to the whole life. Now there is this precious fruit of very early training in the missionary spirit, that your boy or girl gets another centre of revolution *outside of self*. Others' wants and woes are thought of, and the penny that would be wasted on sweets, is saved for the missionary box. It seems a very small matter, but the scion gets an upward growth and all the future life, a tendency upward. Where missionary hymns are the lullaby sung at the cradle, and prayer for the heathen is taught to lisping lips at the mother's knee; where simple facts about the awful needs of pagan homes and hearts are fed to the child as food for the thought and tonic for self-denial, and the habit is thus early imparted of looking beyond personal comfort and pleasure, and feeling sympathy for lost souls—a new and strange *quality* is given to character. It is no strange thing, therefore, that in the homes where a true missionary atmosphere is habitually breathed we find children insensibly growing up to devote themselves and their substance to God.

And so in that larger family, the Church. Nothing so cripples even home work as neglect of the wider field. To withhold from the farthest is to cramp sympathy for the nearest. And so it comes to pass that what is often assigned as a *reason* or *cause* for a lack of missionary zeal and effort, is rather the *effect* of it. The Church that apologizes for doing nothing for missions abroad, because of its weakness and poverty, owes its feebleness and sickliness to turning all attention upon itself. If we but knew it, it is because we have such burdens to be borne in the home work, that we need the stimulus and strength imparted by active missionary effort for the most distant and destitute. As Bishop Brooks used to say, such excuses resemble the plea of a parricide who first kills his own father, and then pleads for the pity of the court, in remitting the penalty in view of his orphanhood!

No vice is more destructive of Christian character than greed. Avarice turns a man into a miser who has no thought beyond his hoarded gold, like that respectable manufacturer in Britain who spent every day for twenty years in counting his sovereigns that he might gloat over his treasures. And it works harm as much to the poor in his penury as to the rich in his affluence; as it led a wretched victim of avarice, in one of our American cities, to *split lucifer matches* so as to make one into four. On the other hand, he who learns the true uses of sanctified money understands how it can wield a power next to divine, spread the influence of a single life over a wide sphere, and perpetuate divine omnipotence in the power it may wield; omnipresence, in the wide sphere over which it spreads the influence of one life; and eternity, in the perpetuation of such influence long after death.

VII.

THE NEW APPEAL OF MAN.

WE TARRY to make more emphatic what has been already referred to—that *voice of human need* which constitutes a new incentive, for it has never been heard as now, and heard all round the horizon like a thunderpeal from all quarters at once. Never until now have we known what heathenism and paganism mean. The numbers which they represent, so great that in India alone it would take seventeen years to give each woman and girl a Bible, at the rate of 20,000 a day! And if the unevangelized passed day and night before us, one by one, the procession would be endless, for a new generation would have grown to majority before the present living host could march by! The need so awful and the woe so mournful that no words can do justice to it, and no figures illustrate it.

What increased knowledge of the wants and woes of heathendom! What a book might be written on the condition of mankind in pagan lands—especially of women and children; the curse of caste, of dishonoured labour, of human slavery and human torture; of the prostitution of virtue in the name of religion; of infanticide, parricide, suicide; and the countless, nameless enormities and cruelties that have made the places where paganism dwells, the habitations of demons. "In Darkest Heathendom" is a volume not yet written, but it needs to be written. The facts are not new, but the knowledge of them is new. The dark places of the earth were full of the habitations of cruelty in the prophetic and Apostolic ages, but the midnight had not then been penetrated, even by the explorer's transient lamp. Now we know the horrors and abominations of pagan, papal, heathen, and moslem lands—the awful superstitions and degrading rites that even "the Light of Asia" leaves undispelled.

Near Mauch Chunk, in Pennsylvania, is a burning mine at Summit Hill. For thirty-five years every effort made to quench it has failed, and at a thousand points steam and gas escape; vegetation is gone and the rocks are so hot as to blister the hand at the touch. That burning mountain is the awful symbol of heathenism. The unquenched fires have burned for ages. War has been the almost constant curse of a Christless paganism, and, as Henry the Fifth said: "War's three handmaidens are Blood, Fire, and Famine; and Famine, awful as it is, meekest of the three."

Nevertheless, there are great possibilities waiting for development, even in the heathen world. General Grant, after his circuit of the globe, pronounced Li-Hung-Chang one of the three greatest statesmen of the age, ranking him with Gladstone and Bismarck. Surely a country that can produce such a man ought to be permeated and penetrated by the gospel. Sir Bartle Frere witnessed to the indirect effect of Christian teaching, that it everywhere dignifies labour, sanctifies marriage and family life, and uplifts manhood; that, even where it does not convert and renew, it checks, refines, and reforms; and where it fails to sanctify, it, at least, subdues.

There is great need of new enterprise in the department of missions, and there is every encouragement for it. Christ still says: "Follow me, and let the dead bury their dead." Like Talleyrand, it behooves the Christian disciple to keep his watch ahead of the rest of mankind, and rather surpass than fall behind worldly men in enterprise for God. The time is coming when Christian disciples will look back to this age as radically deficient in energy and holy activity, just as we now look back to the age when William Carey sought to rouse England.

The men who are watching the times are oppressed with the incentives God gives us to immediate action. Hudson Taylor appeals for the evangelization of China within the present generation. Not one-hundredth part of the people have yet been reached. He has proposed that, within five years, a thousand more workers should be put into this special field; that two years should be allowed for the study of the native tongue, and three years given to direct labour; and he says that, estimating the population at about fifty millions of families, to reach fifty families a day, for one thousand days, by one thousand workers, would bring the first proclamation of the gospel to all.

We know also how *critical is the condition of the world field*, and an incentive to new diligence and greatly increased zeal and self-denial, is thus supplied. If ever in human history *delay* meant danger, nay, certain disaster, it is now. The seasons for sowing and reaping, planting and plucking, are fixed, and their limits are set by natural laws. A season is a fit time, and for all work there is but one fit time. The sower wastes his seed if he sows it after sowing time; and when the harvest is ripe the reaper must put in the sickle, or soon the harvest will not be worth the reaping, for ripeness borders on rottenness. *Immediate* is God's word: now or never. In all parts of the mission field it is either time to sow or time to reap; and in some cases the field invites both sower and reaper at once; for there are some who need the saving message, and others who have heard and are ready for further and fuller steps of teaching, training, ingathering, organizing. We must not think that, because the Church is more aroused than a century ago, it is safe to rest content with the present measure of interest and that we need only to maintain it. The Church of Christ has, thus far, not yet begun to deal in earnest with her duty to the human race. Four-fifths of the territory of heathenism and paganism yet remains to be occupied; and as to the Moslem millions, they are scarcely as yet approached! Even where civilization has gone, its contact with paganism has often been a curse rather than a blessing! Christian nations have been identified in India and China with opium traffic and licensed lust, and in Africa with firearms, slavery and whiskey! This century has known no document more pathetically significant than that first letter written in English by a Congo native, who thus addressed the Archbishop of Canterbury:

"Great and good chief of the tribe of Christ: Greeting: The humblest of your servants kisses the hem of your garment, and begs you to send to his , fellow servants more gospel and less rum. In the bonds of Christ—Ugalla."

There are other developments, besides those of time and tide, which "wait for no man." In the field given us to till, God's work cannot and will not wait. While we sleep Satan is busy. He will sow his seed if we do not sow God's. And his preoccupation will double the difficulty when we do undertake for God. Yes, if disciples do not sow the wide and open fields of the world, demons will. We must not sleep, for the devil never does.

In some cases heathenism is now a house without an occupant, "empty, swept, garnished;" people tired of idols and ignorance, fling away their false faiths and yearn for knowledge. When man is left without any religion, he is in greatest risk. Satan watches to take possession of the empty house, with sevenfold disaster to the soul. Apathy—neglect of opportunity—this is all that is needed on the part of disciples, and irreparable damage will ensue. While we are sending forth one out of five thousand Protestant Church members, to carry gospel tidings, and giving less than a tenth of one per cent, on our average income to keep them at work, the consecration of self and substance is so far behind that of the Apostolic Church that it hints an apostasy.

Watch Satan as he enters every open door, sending his agents everywhere, poisoning the minds of young Japanese and Hindus with Western scepticism before we have got our Christian books and tracts ready, flooding the Soudan and the Congo valley with the drink that drowns reason and conscience, before we have sent missionaries there!

Opportunity never lingers, and when, if ever, it returns, like the Sibyl its price is more costly and its precious treasures are less. The Emperor of Brazil accounted for the great inferiority of Brazil to the great Republic of the north, in one sentence. He said: "My countrymen always cry *manana*!— to-morrow, to-morrow; but the United States citizen says *to-day*!" Would to God the Church would stop all boasting of to-morrow and improve to-day.

VIII.

Harmony with God's Purpose.

To work with God and on God's plan is the only real bliss, and the only sure success. All else is disappointment and failure. President Lincoln was once taunted by an adversary with the temporary defeat of political measures which he had adopted in the interests of the eternal principles of right. His sublime reply was: "Defeat! If it were not one, but one hundred defeats, I should still pursue the same unchanging course." And, on another occasion, when, during the war for the Union, a timid man ventured to say: "I hope God will be on our side," his response was: "My only anxiety is to be on God's side." Audit was this man of an incarnate conscience whose heroic words were: "Let us believe that right makes might, and in that faith let us to the end dare to do our duty as we understand it." It is the same sentiment that Faber crystallized into verse:

> "He always wins who sides with God;
> With him no chance is lost."

It is, therefore, of immense importance to us to know *what God's plan* is and then to take *our place in it*. As to the purpose of God in this dispensation, Anthony Grant has, in his Bampton Lectures, given clear and brief statement: "That the gospel shall be preached in some places at all times, and in all places at some time." And beyond this we know very little. How large or rapid are to be the visible results in any one field is a matter never yet unveiled; it is one of the secret things that belong unto the Lord our God. But what is revealed is His will that we should go into all the world and preach the gospel to every creature.

Then if, as George Bowen told Dr. Norman McLeod of himself, thirty years are spent in India without one known convert, we can still *do our duty*—for in God's eyes that is success; all else, failure. In this doing of God's will on God's plan, the holiest aspiration finds satisfaction. A divine ambition engrosses the soul. This is the avenue to the purest, widest influence. One may, at God's bidding, go into comparative retirement and obscurity—as Bishop Butler, author of the famous "Analogy," into the little country parish of Stanhope, so that Archbishop Blackburne told Queen Caroline that he was "not dead, but buried"—but if it be at God's bidding it is no burial alive, except as a seed secreted for a crop. Butler, during that apparent burial, was writing that great work which revolutionized the thinking of that deistic age!

In great crises of Church history some word of God has become the rallying cry of His true followers. The motto of the Apostolic age was: "Christ died for our sins, and rose again, according to the Scriptures." During the Lutheran Reformation, the watchword was: "The just shall live by faith." And, for this age of missions, what is a more fitting battle-cry than that which has been spontaneously chosen by the Student Volunteers in their "New Crusade:"

The Evangelization of the World in This Generation!

This, now famous motto, has been traced to the writer of these pages, as its author, because he first gave it expression at the inauguration of this movement at Mount Hermon, Mass., eight years ago. But the fact is, he got this motto from the thirteenth chapter of the Acts, verses 22 and 36, where the Holy Spirit says of David, that, God in him found a man after His own heart, which should fulfil all His will, and that *he served his own generation by the will of God*. Let us write that divine motto on all our banners!

How much is included here! *Sovereignty*—a divine Master; *Service*—a world's evangelization; Sphere— our own generation; a *Secret* and *Signal*—the will of God.

A most expressive word is here rendered, "served" —it means to be an under-rower, and refers to the ancient galleys with their banks of oars, where every man who held an oar served under the control of the pilot. All God asks of us is to take the place which He assigns, and there do our work, watching His signal. When there is obedience to His will, there is sure to be co-operation with all other obedient souls, since they heed the same signal. The conception is magnificent. What a symphony of action! what a harmony of movement!—the oars rising and falling, dipping and dripping together, though the oarsmen see not each other, and plan no such co-operation; because one will sways all alike, and controls the synchronisms and coincidences of history by a unity of universal plan.

And what identity with God! His will is His personality. To serve under that will as the allcontrolling signal, is to be one with Him—to be about our Father's business. What authority! for all is done in the name of the one Master. What holy audacity! as when David approached Goliath: "I come to thee in the name of Jehovah, God of the armies of Israel, whom thou hast defied!" What security to him who does the will of God! "All things work together for good," in the orbit of obedience, which is a part of a universal system where God is Sun and Centre! And what success! Into the channel of our weak and wayward will is turned the very river of God—the mighty torrent of His omnipotence, to turn the wheels of our life and action, and insure uninterrupted power and ultimate accomplishment. And what is the natural *sphere* of every disciple's work and witness, if it be not his *own generation?* He cannot affect the past generations, and the best way to serve the future is by fidelity to the present. He may in a sense belong to the whole race of man, but he is especially related to the human family as living on earth at the same period with himself. Their claims on him are paramount, pressing, immediate, imperative.

If the Church would come into harmony with God's purpose, here is the secret:—He must be acknowledged as absolute Master, and His command must be the sole, sufficient authority. Service must be conceived as part of a full discipleship and even a complete salvation; and that service must be accepted as proclaiming the gospel to every human creature. The will of God must be the one all-commanding signal which we watch, study, and obey. And our own generation must be, to our constant thought and prayer, the great and present sphere for our energetic and consecrated activity.

God has given a banner to them that fear Him, that it may be displayed because of the truth. And let the Church lift that banner high and bear it in the very front of the ranks and the thick of the fight— with this motto emblazoned on it:

SERVING OUR OWN GENERATION BY THE WILL OF GOD.

IX.

The Blessed Hope.

ONE POWERFUL incentive, of which not only the Acts of the Apostles but the whole New Testament is full, is, we fear, far less prominent in the thoughts of the modern Church—we refer to the *blessed hope of our Lord's Return.*

This was, no doubt, the foremost of all motives, hopes and incentives, which moved early disciples to zeal and activity in missions; and to revive this hope —to make it practically the mighty motor to us that it was to them, is to provide a new impulse and impetus in the work of a world's evangelization. This motive, though so old, is an ever new incentive. Hope is the one impulse that never loses its youth, and above all, *this* hope. It never falls behind, but always goes before, onward, upward, finding in the goal of yesterday its starting point to-day, and in its goal of to-day only its starting point to-morrow.

The incentive, drawn from our Lord's promised Return, He Himself has forever connected with our duty to a lost world. He says, "*Occupy till I come.*" Mistaken notions, associated with His second advent, have so marred its visage as to make it even repulsive and distasteful to some disciples, so that, what to the Apostolic Church was the main help, has been spoken of as a hindrance, to missions. Out of the dust of neglect and contempt let us lift this standard of the mission host, and once more make it the banner which leads us on to victory!

Our Lord's Coming is represented as always imminent, and thus it *quickens our activity.* Imminence is the combination of certainty with uncertainty—certainty at *some* time, uncertainty at *what* time; and hence its perpetual warning: "Be ye always ready, for in such an hour as ye think not, the Son of Man cometh!"

The uniform teaching of the New Testament is that the Lord is ever at hand. "Behold the Judge standeth before the door," His hand on the latch! When He will open and enter, no man nor angel knoweth; but when He does, it will be suddenly, without knocking; and because we "know not when the time is," He bids us "Watch and pray." Such a sense of the imminence of His coming must inspire, quicken, stimulate, missionary activity.

As the Son of Man went into the far-off country to receive for Himself a kingdom, and to return, He committed to His servants, as stewards, the whole world as a mission field, saying: "Occupy till I come," giving no hint of the time of His return, that there may be constant alertness and watchfulness. And the natural consequence with every faithful servant is that he hastens to invest in trade what talents are left him in trust, that at his Master's Coming he may be found faithful and his gifts fruitful.

Such is the philosophy of this Hope. What is the fact? There are two immutable things in which it is impossible for history to lie, namely: first, the early Christians felt our Lord's Coming to be imminent; second, the early Church was conspicuous for missionary zeal. So vividly was the second advent at hand, to Thessalonian disciples, that they gave too little heed to those events which must first occur; and yet, when was any Church so permeated and penetrated with missionary enthusiasm! Paul sounds the keynote of their whole fidelity: serving the living God, and *waiting* for His Son from heaven!

Early Christians looked for the King's Return, at any time. He had entrusted them with a commission, and the King's business required haste. They tarried not, save for that enduement which was their equipment. Then to the bounds of Judea, Samaria, Galilee; to Antioch, Athens, Ephesus, Rome, they sped with the message. Peter went eastward to the elect dispersion; Paul swept, like a flame, westward, across Asia Minor, and into Europe, till he touched Italy, perhaps Spain and Britain. Within one generation, the Cross overtook the Roman Eagle, and the priests of false fanes feared lest their work was at an end. Such will ever be the power of this Hope over those who are by it held in constant expectancy of the Lord's advent.

On the contrary, so soon as we lose sight of its imminence and say, "My Lord delayeth His coming," we are tempted to indolence, self-indulgence, and controversy on minor matters. When disciples felt the time to be short and the duty to be urgent, they were "all at it and always at it;" self-denial was an easy yoke and petty jealousies were scorned as trifles. So soon and so long as that hope was dim, and Christ's Coming was pushed into the far-off future, the Church began leisurely working, then flippantly playing at missions, as though vast cycles of time lay before us in which to witness to the world. Revive this hope of the Lord's Coming and it begets hourly watching, ceaseless praying, tireless toiling, patient waiting.

Moreover this blessed hope is forever linked with the glorious *compensation for all service and sacrifice* for Christ. "Behold I come quickly, and my reward is with me, to give every man according as his work shall be."

His Coming then, not our death, opens the door to the wedding feast, and the "Joy of the Lord." Then the prize awaits the successful runner. Then the "crowns" are to be given—the "crown of life" to martyrs faithful unto death, the "crown of righteousness" to all who love His appearing, the "crown of glory" to shepherds who "feed the flock," the "crown of rejoicing" to those who win souls, the "crown incorruptible" to those who keep the body under and bring it into subjection.

Is it strange that the soldier of Christ endures hardness, fights the good fight of faith, carries the cross at all risks to plant it on Satan's strongholds, while he is looking daily for the coming of the Captain of his salvation, and knows not how soon he may lay down his warrior's armour for the crown of victory? Paul forgot all his losses in such gains—and counted all but refuse, for the sake of the resurrection hope. Fellowship with Christ in suffering brings fellowship in glory; and to die with Him as a malefactor is to be exalted with Him as a benefactor.

With many disciples, the eyes are yet blinded to this mystery of rewards, which is one of the open mysteries of the Word, and some cannot see how rewards can have any place in an economy of grace. But we must not confound salvation and recompense. It must be an imputed righteousness,—exceeding far that of the most proper Pharisee—whereby we *enter* the Kingdom of Heaven; but, having thus entered by *faith*, our *works* determine our relative rank, place, reward, in that Kingdom. Eternal life is God's gift to be had for the asking; but he who receives the gift, and does work, sowing and reaping for God, receiveth also wages and gathereth fruit unto life eternal. Gifts are bestowed; wages earned. Sinners become saved saints only by grace; but saints are rewarded for service. And so Paul warns Corinthian Christians that even he who is saved, may be saved as by fire and suffer loss in the burning up of his worthless work; or he may both be saved and have a reward in an abiding work.*

We shall never have Apostolic missions till this Apostolic Hope claims again its rightful place. Daily dying—so that in the body one bears the marks of the Lord Jesus—will be easy only to him who feels redemption drawing nigh; and who follows the Son of Man in His humiliation, as one who is to sit with Him on the Throne of His glory. His expected appearing is His saints' avenging and rewarding. It is the righting of the wrongs of the ages. Unrecompensed toil receives its wages, and long waiting martyrs reach their coronation. Then, however dark the discipline and dismal the failure of mission work, faithfulness and not success

---

* Cor. iii. 12-15.

will he the standard and measure of reward. We must have our work *always done*, ready for His scrutiny.

This hope *weans us from the world*, and by loosening the hold and lessening the worth of all present things makes stronger the powers of the age to come. The steward whose Master may at once come and call him to account, cannot hoard treasures of mammon or quaff pleasure's intoxicating cup. He cannot bury his "pounds" in houses and lands, costly plate and gems, stocks and stores; it must be turned into currency—current coin, passing from hand to hand, like streams that swell as they flow. The time is short, but eternity is long; and, therefore, there is nothing that is "worth while," but to push our lines of labour to the ends of earth, and keep our witness constant and clear to the end of time, that the eternal may sway us rather than the temporal.

Thus this blessed Hope both loosens the hold we have on this world and the hold this world has on us. A true belief in the testimony of our Lord that in such an hour as we think not He cometh, and that we must watch and pray because we know not when the time is—makes impossible all plans for a soft nest and an easy life of indulgence and indolence, for the end of all things is at hand, and the midnight cry may soon be heard. What have we to do with any pursuits or pleasures which His coming could interrupt or condemn, bring into contempt or bring to naught! If we are to build Heaven here, we may be justified in laying deep and firm foundations; but if all these things are to be dissolved, if all work not done for God is to be burned up as wood, hay, stubble, and the work done for God is to be tried by fire—then what folly to spend our faculty and vital force upon what is to be turned to ashes! Let us walk with God and work with God, and so prepare a structure of character and of service which shall survive the fiery ordeal.

Perhaps at no one point does the hope of our Lord's Return touch our need so closely and vitally as in this—that *it incites to unselfish service*. Missions appeal more than any other form of service to the unworldly and unselfish spirit, and find only in such spirit their support, nay their practical basis. Much that goes by the name of "Christian work" is leavened with self-love, is prosecuted in the energy of the flesh, and finds its real though unconscious incentive in the worldly hope of rich returns of temporal advantage. A railway corporation might, on commercial principles, help to build schools and churches along its lines, for these form a nucleus for population, and so for ultimate dividends to stockholders; much that men call benevolence is but the cloak that hides the shrewd Shylock, who has an eye to business.

The modern outcry that "missions do not pay," comes of this selfish, calculating spirit that demands prompt payments of interest on every investment. Cut to the core the apathy that exists as to work among the heathen, and you find simple selfishness. This work in the regions beyond, by its very nature forbids such returns: these distant, destitute souls cannot recompense us. The most passionate appeals for perishing millions along the Congo, beneath the shadows of the Himalayas or in the Corean valleys, will be unheeded by hearts electroplated with greed or petrified by selfishness. Of course missions "do not pay," if "pay" means any form of temporal recompense. Missions are not a mint for coining sovereigns, but a means of saving souls and witnessing to Christ.

To give money and send men and women to the ends of the earth to sacrifice themselves for cannibals and Hottentots, half brutal and half idiotic savages, "human baboons" and stupid barbarians, is putting money into a bag with holes and burying pearls in rubbish,—so say the worldly-minded. And we join no issue with such. Missions to the heathen yield slow returns, and seldom justify to human judgment the costly outlay. God, perhaps, does not mean they shall. He gives us this work as nearest in motive and spirit to that which brought Jesus to the cross, as the most unselfish work in which we can engage; and, because its essence lies in selfoblivion, the spirit of missions is the spirit of Christ. To be a true missionary we must be emptied of self— give to those from whom we cannot hope to receive, and bid to the feast those who are not likely to have any feast to invite us to; and so the miser dies when the missionary is born; the carnal is cast out if the spiritual is to come in; only he who loses himself can save others.

But just here the hope of the Lord's Coming supplies exactly what is needed. It gives us a loftier level than this world affords, from which to take our survey. Once let this conviction, this consciousness flood the soul of the believer, that the Risen Lord is himself coming back, and may at any time turn His promise into His presence—and this outpouring of consecrated gifts and devoted lives for the sake of the lost, becomes a breaking of the alabaster flask upon Jesus' feet, and there is "purpose" in this "waste." John may solve what to Judas is a mystery.

The blessed Hope, which our Lord would have us to restore to its former and deserved prominence, has a subtle influence in refining character of selfishness, and this makes it the very matrix and mould of missions. Its whole tendency is to turn our thoughts away from self to Him, to relax our hold upon all else, and remould us after the power of an endless life. It makes all time seem short and the whole world seem small, dwarfs the present age into insignificance, and lifts the age to come like a towering peak that leaves all else far below.

In those seven epistles to the Churches which open the Apocalypse, our Lord uses His imminent Coming as a perpetual hope, motive, incentive; and this is enough to make it a sin, if not a crime, to lose sight of it. It was because His

Coming was ever at hand when trials were to end and triumphs to begin, that the Ephesians must bear, have patience, and not faint; the Smyrnese endure the ten days of tribulation; the Pergamoans hold fast His name and not deny the faith; the Thyatirans resist Jezebel's seductions; the Sardians keep up their watch and keep white their garments; the Philadelphians keep the Word of His Patience, and the Laodiceans abandon lukewarmness for ardour and fervour.

This blessed Hope is the crown of all other hopes, and suggests to us an *expectation that will be realized.*

Much of the discouragement felt in connection with missions results from a mistaken notion as to what sis to be thsseir proper outcome; and it is so vital to both our true work and our true joy that we understand our Lord's plan, that it may be well for us to go back to the rudiments and begin anew, lest we have built into our missionary conceptions some elements not warranted by the Word.

There are many who understand by our Lord's parables of the mustard seed and leaven, a gradual growth and extension of the kingdom, during the present dispensation, until the world is transformed into one great believing brotherhood. In this view the gospel is a seed set in the soil of society, to take root and grow until the earth is filled with its far-reaching branches; or it is a leaven, hid in the three measures of meal—the world, the flesh and the devil! —to leaven the lump, modifying the evil it touches, until the world is changed into the Church, the flesh into the spirit, and the devil is driven out altogether, like the gases that escape from the fermenting dough.

Does the Scripture teaching justify us in looking for the "conversion of the world" during the present dispensation, or is this the period of the out-gathering of the Church from all nations? This is not a question of mere curiosity or speculation; it concerns the whole work of missions. For what are we to labour, and what is to be our rational scriptural hope? James bade the first council at Jerusalem hearken unto him as he reminded them of God's purpose as declared by Simeon, visiting the gentiles *"to take out of them a people* for His name."

That is not only uniformly declared to be the *exact purpose* of gospel witness during these times of the gentiles, but it has been the *actual result* of these nearly two thousand years of such witness. At this advanced age history is interpreting prophecy and expounding Scripture, if we will but hear it. We see good growths and rich harvests from the seed of the kingdom; but the tares are growing side by side with the wheat, and we are divinely told that they will so continue until the end of the age. Our highest "Christian civilization" is an amalgamation of the Church and the world; and the leaven of the world is as surely in the Church, as the influence of the Church is in the world. No doubt the world is more churchly, but there is as little doubt that the Church is more worldly. The dialect of Ashdod corrupts the language of Canaan. The strait gate is wider and the narrow way is broader than of old; and those who would come into the kingdom find an easy entrance and an attractive avenue, smooth-paved and bordered with flowers. How few even profess self denial in cross bearing! If the schools have found no royal road to learning, the Church has built one to Heaven.

The proofs are sadly at hand of that conformity to the world which is so positively forbidden. For ages the slime of the serpent has been upon certain worldly amusements which, whatever be their inherent quality, bear the stamp of Satan's ownership and use. And yet Church members sit till midnight over "progressive euchre," enter their thoroughbreds on the race-course, tipple over the wine cup, whirl through the giddy dance, sanction the theatre and use its flavour to give relish to church socials. Church life is honeycombed with worldliness, and practical separation is reduced to a minimum. The great body of disciples are only nominally such, either wholly worldly or worldly holy; at the door of frivolous gaiety they drop their Christian consistency, as an oriental guest shuffles off his sandals, and mix freely with the idolaters of folly and fashion. The Church is to-day in danger of the moral putrefaction that loses all godly savour, and the moral petrifaction that loses all godly sensibility. Apostolic piety scarcely survives in the Church at large. Disciples rarely keep themselves unspotted from the world; and, instead of the isolation and insulation necessary for receiving and conveying spiritual power, it is only here and there that we find a few who seem to be filled with the Spirit.

As to the condition of the world, even in this boasted nineteenth century, it is as far from "conversion," say the most sagacious students of history, as in the days of Augustus. When the glamour and halo of all this deceptive glory is penetrated, what do we find? An era of inventive genius and worldly enterprise, but God-denying and God-defying infidelity and anarchy. Giant sons of Anak go about breaking down faith in God and the Bible. Philosophy blooms into pantheism and materialism, rationalism and agnosticism. Some who have drawn their very life from Christianity now turn to curse the dam that nursed, and wound the breast that fed, them.

The ripeness of modern civilization borders on rottenness, and while men boast of society, its foundations sink; and the anarchy, which is the natural end of atheism, threatens all with wreck. Science itself has furnished the lawless with weapons which are equally mighty against ballot or bullet; and Germany and Russia, France and Britain, and the great Republic, are to-day at the mercy of the dynamite fiend!

Notwithstanding such signs of the times, there are some who regard the outlook as so hopeful that they think the recent "Parliament of Religions" was the inauguration of the millennium. What enviable sleight of mind that can turn everything into signs of progress! Popular education and swift locomotion answer to the prediction: "Many shall run to and fro in the earth, and knowledge shall be increased." In the triumphs of electric telegraph and telephone, the "lightning cometh from the east and shineth unto the west." Irrigation and agriculture make "glad the wilderness and solitary place, and make the desert to rejoice and blossom as the rose." The ocean cables and swift steamships have so joined the continents that there is "no more sea;" and in peace societies and courts of arbitration, nations "learn war no more." By wide dispersion of God's word and witnesses, the earth is "full of the knowledge of the Lord, as the waters cover the sea." In the sympathy and unity of believers our Lord's prayer is fulfilled, that they "all may be one." Rude and barbarous tribes are enlightened—"the cow and the bear feed;" and in converted cannibals, the lion eats "straw like the ox;" the savages, rapacious like the wolf, ferocious like the leopard, become, by civilization, the gentle lamb and harmless kid. Those who, with this singular ease, find fulfilment of prediction, have sometimes gone further, and suggested that in Britain we have the "lion," and in Russia the "bear," and in the young Republic beneath the setting sun, the "little child" that leads them! and that China may be the "red dragon," whose tail draws after it a third part of the race, yet in the contest with Christian England "prevailed not!"

From all such frivolous methods of dealing with the Scripture and with facts, we turn candidly to ask what does the New Testament encourage us to hope for as the outcome of our missionary work?

If we read aright, the teaching of our Lord is plain. God's present purpose is that the gospel shall everywhere be preached for a witness unto the nations and for the outgathering of the *Ecclesia*; and then shall the end come, and the Lord Himself return and possess the kingdom, and carry its triumphs to completion. It is true that, after nineteen centuries of Christian history, and at the close of this great missionary century, the gospel net encloses all sorts of fish, both good and bad—swordfish and toadfish, mansharks as well as blood-tinged salmon and delicious cod—devilfish as well as angelfish,—it is true that the tares still grow as vigorously as the wheat and defy uprooting. And yet this is exactly what the Lord foretold as the outcome of this dispensation; and to see this gives power to the faint and courage to the desponding. Instead of being dismayed at the parallel progress of good and evil, we expect it and are not disappointed. Hope is not crushed, for we have not attempted impossibilities. Signs of continued rejection of the message and abounding iniquity in the world, or of love waxing cold in the Church, do not overwhelm the true missionary with a sense of defeat. God is working out His plan just as He forecast it, notwithstanding. The devil's great wrath may only be due to the shortness of his time; and the ripeness of the tares may only hint the nearness of the harvest.

The prominence given to this blessed hope of our Lord's Return, in Scripture, justifies the prominence given to it in this treatment of the subject of missions, for it is vitally related to our courage and confidence in carrying on our work.

Hope defeated, or even deferred, makes the heart sick, and heart-sickness is fatal to successful service. There is a hope that banishes such a malady and in its place gives ever new vigour and strength for serving and suffering; and that is a hope founded on a distinct promise, and actually fulfilling before our eyes. If we are discouraged or despairing, our need and remedy is, perhaps, a laying hold of the hope set before us in the gospel. As the Scriptures warrant no expectation of the world's conversion in this age of witness, so far as we look for such result we *work on the wrong basis*, and will either be disappointed or deceived in the outcome.

The soldier who misconceives the object of a campaign, may falsely construe all the movements of the army. If he thinks the whole force of the foe is to be captured, the seizure of a few leading strongholds seems only next to absolute defeat. But, if he knows that this is exactly according to orders from headquarters, and that the plan of his great commander is thus carried out, seizing and holding certain strategic points, and waiting for him to arrive with reinforcements, what would otherwise have seemed defeat, now becomes success.

Does it matter nothing whether, in our work of missions, we are hoping for results which are moving on toward fruition or not? Let the disciple once get firmly planted upon this rock basis, that we are sent forth not to accomplish a world's conversion, but only its evangelization, and victory springs up out of defeat. Hope that had lost wings, plumes herself for a new flight, and over the grave of buried expectation rises with the song of a lark. Satan has gained no unforeseen advantage, and even his movements are all comprehended in God's wider plans. Every backward movement in history is like the receding wave, the preparation for a forward advance to a higher floodmark.

X.

THE NEW OUTLOOK.

THERE IS a promise and prophecy which all history is actually fulfilling. Watch the panorama of the ages as it unrolls; see each new scene in vivid colours fill out that shadowy outline pencilled by prophecy. Ever since Pentecost flamed with its tongues of fire, God has been visiting nation after nation, to take out of them a people for His name. At first the door of faith was opened to the Jew, and the proselytes, gathered from all nations, went back, like the Ethiopian eunuch, to witness to the peoples among whom they dwelt. Then the door was opened to the Samaritans, Syrians, people of Asia Minor and Greece; then to those of Italy, Gaul, Britain, Germany; till in our day God successively flings wide the portals of India and Burmah, Syria and Turkey, Siam and China, Africa, Japan, Corea and the Isles of the Sea; yes, even the papal strongholds, France, Italy and Spain.

And now Thibet, the shrine and throne of the Grand Lama, Buddhism's capital, seems compelled to open her two-leaved gates. God is doing with all these natives just as He said, and in some on a grand scale—"taking out of them a people for His name." Witness the Hawaiian Islands, now a Christian nation; the half million native converts in India; the scores of self-supporting churches along the Tigris and Euphrates; the Kho-thah-byu Memorial Hall, rallying and radiating centre for thirty thousand Christian Karens; the two thousand churches of Polynesia; New Japan, with its giant strides toward Christian civilization; McAll's hundred gospel *salles* and thousands of converts in atheistic France; Madagascar becoming to Africa what England is to Europe; and China turning converts into evangelists.

Starting from Jerusalem, over eighteen and a half centuries since, and moving westward, the flag of the cross has been unfurled successively in Antioch, Rome, Alexandria, and Constantinople; borne from the shores of Britain to a New World across the Atlantic; across that New World to the Pacific and the isles of the sea; over the Pacific to Japan and Corea and the various lands from the Chinese Sea to the Arabian Gulf and the Golden Horn; and thus, completing the circuit of the globe, we once more set up the standard in Jerusalem, the original place of the cross!

Meanwhile, this girdle of missions is widening into a zone, spreading northward toward the icebergs of Greenland and the snow castles of Siberia, and southward toward the Cape of Good Hope and the Land of Fire. We have only to lengthen our cords and strengthen our stakes, and every creature may yet be reached with the good tidings and hope may reap the fruition of Scripture promise. Then, when from gentile nations, the last convert shall have been gathered and incorporated into Christ's mystical body; when the *Ecclesia*—the "out-called" ones—shall be complete, and the Bride hath made herself ready, the Bridegroom shall return to claim His own. The fulness of the gentiles being come in, the blindness of Israel shall be removed; through eyes no longer veiled, and dimmed only by penitential tears, they shall look on Him whom they pierced and wounded in the house of His friends, and so all Israel shall be saved and the fallen and ruined Tabernacle of David be rebuilt. Then shall the residue of men and all the gentiles seek after the Lord, and see the salvation of God.

All these motives and incentives, old and new, unite to sweep over us a deep conviction and persuasion, like a mighty tidal wave beneath whose majestic movement all minor issues are buried. If we discern the signs of the times, there is a redness in the evening sky which hints the dawn of a glorious day. The present crisis of missions should compel us to forget all lesser interests and issues, and hasten to bear the good news unto earth's very ends. Labourers should be multiplied, gifts increased, and, with a new energy born in us of the Holy Spirit, this greatest enterprise of the ages should be undertaken.

This gospel of the kingdom must first be preached in all the world for a witness unto all nations; and then shall the end come.

There is a legitimate way of hastening toward, if not of hastening, that end: promptly to occupy every open door, and amply to sow every open field. While we pray, "Thy kingdom come," how far may we answer our own prayer! The whole creation groaneth and travaileth in pain together, waiting for an apathetic Church to do its duty. Within our generation a thousand millions of human beings will go down to the grave without faith or hope, life or even light; one hundred thousand die daily, while forty millions of Protestant believers, idle and unmoved, see this wholesale descent into the darkness beyond! And yet there are four hundred professed disciples in Protestant communions for every one of that hundred thousand that each day pass into the great unknown. How far-reaching and all-powerful might be the evangelism of these Protestant disciples, if once organized, economized and vitalized by the spirit of missions and the Spirit of God!

Since Jesus of Nazareth, through the rent veil of His flesh and the rent door of His tomb, opened to every believer the path of life, nearly nineteen centuries have fled, during which a vast number of souls, equal to twenty times the present population of the globe, have gone down to the grave, ignorant of Christ. And during all these centuries, He who is of purer eyes than to behold evil, has confronted the woe and want and wickedness of heathenism! Through all this time God has been preparing His Church to enter these new open doors, and the Messiah, who was cut off without generation, has been waiting to see of the travail of His soul and be satisfied, waiting for his bride to make herself ready and put on her beautiful attire.

During the last hundred years, since Carey led the way, a series of providential interpositions and gracious manifestations that deserve to rank with miracles, have set upon mission work the sanction and seal of God. Colossal obstacles have been removed and huge barriers subsided, long locked gates been burst, and grand triumphs won. Why do we hesitate! Let the hosts of the Lord rally to the onset. The great Leader of the host even now sounds His imperial clarion along the whole line of battle. Let us obey the signal, boldly pierce the very centre of the enemy's forces, turn their staggering wings, and in the confidence of faith, move forward, a united army, in one overwhelming charge!

Late one summer afternoon, now thirty years ago, a sudden rainpour fell in Virginia, Nevada. It was very unexpected, for those rainless summer skies seldom yield even a shower. After the rain ceased, a dense darkness drew its pall over the whole sky; and Mount Davidson's vast eastern slope that overlooks the city, was so enveloped in darkness that the mountain could scarcely be distinguished from the cloud masses that surrounded it.

A remarkable phenomenon drew all eyes toward the mountain peak. Upon the lofty summit a little tongue of golden flame moved strangely to and fro, like some supernatural signal. It was very small but bright, and the more conspicuous against the dense, dark background of storm cloud. Most strange of all, this fire neither waxed nor waned, but simply burned on.

It was at first a mystery; but, in fact, it was the nation's flag, planted on the mountain's peak, and waving in the wind. Through a narrow rift of cloud the rays of the setting sun had found their way; and that flag of the Republic lay just in the line of their direction, and so they touched it alone, resting upon it, glorifying, transfiguring it. For an hour that burning banner held the fixed, fascinated gaze of the multitude. And it afterwards proved that the setting sun, which thus gilded and glorified the star-spangled banner, had that same day looked down on the fall of Vicksburg and the victory at Gettysburg, which were the decisive turning points of the war for the Union.

Darkness overspreads the earth and gross darkness the people. But God's glory arises, and is seen in the work of missions. We have but to lift our eyes and look, and we may see that, on the very summits of heathendom and in the midst of the death-shade, the heroic soldiers of the Lord Jesus have planted the banner of the cross, and there it still waves, a trophy of coming triumphs. The glory of God rests upon all faithful testimony to His name, and makes it still a tongue of fire. While we set up the cross on the high places of the earth, and seem but solitary, God's great plan of battle comprehends both the world and the age, and takes in all fields of conflict and all faithful witnesses. We may not see it or know it, but elsewhere decisive battles are taking place, and strongholds of evil are giving way before the onset of God's hosts. In His eyes, which command the whole field and period of conflict, while we see only discouragement and defeat, the tide of battle may be turning!

The task on which we entered in the discussion of the great theme is now in a sense completed. No one could be more sensible than the writer of these pages, how little justice has been done to the marvels of this missionary century. But our eyes must be turned forward, rather than backward. What God has wrought, with a Church just waking from the sleep of fifteen hundred years, is but a prophetic hint of what He will do, if, thoroughly roused to holy action, His people meet the duty of the hour with the faith, the prayer, the sacrifice, the consecration, which the crisis demands.

The New Acts of the Apostles is, like the old, an unfinished book. Other chapters wait to be written. What shall they record! God grant that the unwritten history of the years before us may embrace far greater marvels than have ever been witnessed! New Pentecosts with floods of blessing, until, as Malachi says, there be "none left to pour out!" New Apostles, until God's chosen heralds leave no Regions Beyond unpenetrated, and no creature unreached! New visions and voices, until every divine lesson is learned, and the whole Church is in living accord with the Master! New converts and martyrs, until the Saviour's soul has found its full satisfaction for its travail! New signs and wonders, until even unbelievers confess the work to be of God! New hopes and incentives, if indeed, any be needful to inspire to ever-increasing fidelity, or possible to enhance the grandeur of existing motives!

But all this depends on the manifested Presence of the Redeemer, in the power of that Holy Spirit, whose holy ministries made luminous with glory the Acts of the Apostles!

INDEX

H

I

IDENTITY with God, 280.

Idolatry, Hatred of, 150.

Idols, Assimilation to, 269.

Ignatius, 97.

Ilala, 163.

Incarnation of Christ, 7, 15, 104.

Incentives, New, 232.

India, British Rule in, 219; Civilization of, 14; Converts in, 22; Education in, 17; Horrors, etc., removed in, 176; Famine in, 214-15; Intolerance in, 176-77; Missions in, 51, 58, 91, 174, 222, 235, 262; New Route to, 17.

Indians, N. A., 153.

Individual Rights, 23.

Individualism, 111.

Industry and Genius, 82.

Infanticide, 21, 172, 220, 236.

Inglis, Rev. Dr., Influence on Dr. Duff, 86.

Inglis, Dr. John, of Aneityum, 228.

Inouye, Count, 218.

"Inquiry," Carey's, etc., 49, 64.

Inquisition in Spain, 124.

Insane, Treatment of, 27.

Instincts, Universal, 122.

Intellect, Freedom of, 28.

Intelligence, 23.

Intercession of Christ, 241.

Inventions, Rapidity of, 27; Theology of, 12, 16, 26.

Isolation, 27.

J

JALNA, 159.

Jamaica, Slavery in, 31, 226; Emancipation in, 177; Missions in, 178.

James, King, 120.

Janes, Capt., at Higo, 192, 217.

Japan, 45, 76, 160, 204, 256; Missions in, 160, 216, 227; History of, 217.

Jericho, Fall of, 196, 204.

Jesuits, Order of, 72.

Jewett, Rev. Lyman, 11, 235.

Jews, Missions for, 245.

Joan of Arc, 84, 90.

Joel, Prophecy of, 8, 9.

John, Gospel of, iii: 8, 249.

John, Rev. Griffith, 244.

Johnson, W. A. B., 11, 58, 168, 233.

Jones, Mrs. Dorothy, 90.

Jonson, Ben., 120.

Judaism, Decay of, 14.

Judgment, Times of, 13; Miracles of, 105.

Judgments, The New, 213.

Judson, Rev. Adoniram, 11, 48, 68, 70, 90, 149, 229; Mrs. Emily C., 91; Mrs. Ann H., 91.

Juggemath, 21, 175, 235.

Juju-Rites, 225.

Justification by Faith, 14.

K

KAYARNAK, Conversion of, 142.

Kali, 220.

Kant, Emmanuel, 252.

Kanwealoha, 190.

Kapaio and Dr. Geddie, 207.

Kapiolani, 147.

Karens, 11, 72, 124, 148, 150, 207, 231, 290.

Keith-Falconer, 41.

N

O

Scripture Testimony Index

Carey, driven by his unwavering will and dedication to his mission, rose from humble beginnings to great success, impacting the lives of many others along the way. Similar to Wesley, he practiced self-denial, resisting personal gain to further the cause of God and mission work.

Robert Morrison, a missionary to China who learned the Chinese language through sheer determination and hard work, was dedicated to translating the Bible into Chinese. He faced challenges such as Chinese hostility and restrictions on preaching, but through his perseverance and collaboration with Richard Milne, he completed the translation of the entire Bible within fourteen years of arriving in China.

On Raratonga, Williams and the Aitutakian chiefs witnessed a remarkable transformation where plain natives destroyed idols, established a place of worship, and upheld Sabbath, leading to widespread conversion.

The significant contributions of numerous women in the mission field, such as Mary Moffat who worked alongside her husband among the Bechuanas and Maria Gobat who supported Samuel Gobat in Abyssinia and Malta is highlighted. These women, like Mary Williams and Anna Hinderer, displayed remarkable courage and dedication in their missionary endeavors, leaving a lasting impact through their selfless service.

Mary Chauner Williams was a devoted and selfless woman who dedicated her life to helping others in Raiatea, teaching women household skills and providing care for the neglected and elderly. Even in the face of tragedy, like the loss of her husband on Erromanga, she remained strong and steadfast, inspiring even the chief Malietoa with her resilience and compassion.

In 1843, when Mrs. Grant arrived in Persia, she found that girls' education was neglected, despite some progress in opening schools for boys. She dedicated herself to lifting Nestorian womanhood out of degradation by starting a girls' school, which eventually became a significant institution in Persia. Despite facing personal struggles and illness, her tireless efforts in promoting education and missionary work left a lasting impact both in Persia and back in Holyoke, Massachusetts.

Missionaries Matthew Stach, Frederick Boehnisch, and John Beck faced extreme hardships while trying to convert the Eskimos, who were resistant to Christianity and mocked their efforts. Despite being subjected to persecution, theft, and starvation by the Eskimos, the missionaries remained dedicated to their faith and persevered in their mission to bring Christianity to Greenland.

In 1738, as Beck was translating the gospels into an Eskimo Bible, Kayarnak, a Greenlander, was moved by the story of the cross and earnestly sought salvation. Guided by Beck and his Moravian teachers, Kayarnak, along with his family and companions, embraced Christianity and were baptized in 1739, marking the beginning of a new spiritual awakening among the Greenlanders.

Africaner, a feared Hottentot chief, was known for terrorizing the country in revenge for past wrongs by stealing cattle, enslaving captives, and waging relentless war against the Boers. However, missionary Robert Moffat succeeded in converting Africaner, transforming a notorious foe into a loyal friend who cared for Moffat in sickness and even risked his life to travel with him, demonstrating the power of grace to change even the hardest of hearts.

Kho-thah-byu, poor man and slave, who received Jesus and became an Evangelist to his people—the Karens, labouring tirelessly among them. "His preaching carried with it conviction, and compelled others to say, 'Truly this is the word of God.'"

Reverend James Evans tried to convert Maskepetoom and his warriors to Christianity, but Maskepetoom remained resistant to peace. However, Reverend George Macdougal's teaching on forgiveness ultimately led Maskepetoom to spare the life of the man who had betrayed and killed his son, demonstrating a profound act of forgiveness influenced by Christian teachings.

In Foochow, a man struggling with various vices and addiction to opium discovered hope through Rev. S. L. Binkley's preaching about Jesus' power to save, eventually finding freedom from his sins and addiction by putting his faith in Christ.

In Foochow, Ling-Ching-Ting, a former opium addict, found hope in Christianity through the missionary Rev. S. L. Binkley's preaching and experienced a miraculous transformation, breaking free from his addiction and spreading the message of salvation to others despite facing severe persecution.

Joseph Neesima, a Japanese man, became the first native evangelist of his race, preaching boldly and establishing the Doshisha college in Kyoto. Despite offers to join the government, he remained dedicated to his Christian mission, facing obstacles and gathering nine hundred pupils at his school. His perseverance mirrored that of Apostolic times, preaching Christianity under disguise and overcoming challenges to build the school.

One Bible and a prayer-book was all that was rescued when a bloody conflict broke out among the men of Pitcairn island. Through that Bible alone, John

Adams—a reckless, godless mutineer and the lone male survivor—not only became a Christian, but led many others to Jesus.

Christians are generous and hospitable 168
Acts 16:14-15 · Romans 12:13 · 1 Timothy 3:2 · Hebrews 13:2

William A. B. Johnson found liberated captives in Sierra Leone who had suffered greatly on slave ships, enduring terrible conditions and treatment. Despite facing hardships and resistance due to their history of mistreatment by white men, Johnson showed them compassion, taught them the gospel, and educated them, eventually winning their trust and spreading the message of Christianity.

Salvation transforms 178
2 Corinthians 5:16-17 · Galatians 6:15

One Bible and a prayer-book was all that was rescued when a bloody conflict broke out among the men of Pitcairn island. Through that Bible alone, John Adams—a reckless, godless mutineer and the lone male survivor—not only became a Christian, but led many others to Jesus.

Salvation transforms 179
2 Corinthians 5:16-17 · Galatians 6:15

Mr. Fuller, a missionary, confronted a chief over the practice of putting human heads on canoes, only for the chief to defend it based on his beliefs. Over time, the chief's sons rejected that practice, embraced Christianity, and even became preachers, leading to the abolition of such customs and the spread of the gospel among their tribe in Cameroons and even further in Africa.

There is salvation in no other name 181
Acts 4:12

When Mikani saw the charm he had complete trust in, fail to protect someone who had it from death, he finally realized that; the name of Jesus Christ, is only the only Name by which men must be saved.

Give to everyone who asks 185
Matthew 5:42 · Luke 6:30 · Acts 20:35 · 2 Corinthians 8:1-2 · 1 John 3:17

When Henry Richards—who was working among the poor and beggarly people of the Congo—came across Luke 6:37 which said to "give to the one who asks", he struggled to accept that it was to be taken literally. But after becoming convinced, he went on to not only preach, but to practice this command too and the impact this had in the life of the people was amazing.

Timely prayer for someone far away.. 206
Matthew 18:19 · John 4:53

In 1856, Rev. William C. Burns began an evangelization mission in South China and was arrested amid the chaos of the Tai-ping rebellion and brewing conflict between Britain and China. Despite the danger, he was safeguarded through the prayers of Mrs. Stewart Sandemann and her companions during his perilous journey under Chinese officials' guard, escaping potential death had he arrived later in Canton during Commissioner Yeh's turbulent reign.

Deliverance from enemies and circumstances............................207
Luke 1:71

When a Christian community was raided by a company of savage unbelievers, three children were taken captive. Taking to prayers, this community of believers—urged on by Dr. Bunker, sought God's divine intervention. And in the most remarkable way, he answered their prayers and all three captives were recovered.

Ask Me anything in My name 208
Matthew 18:19 · John 14:13-14 · John 16:23-24

In a remarkable and definite answer to the prayers of Hudson Taylor and a few other Christians aboard a ship, God sent a much needed and timely wind to help redirect their course; for a four-knot current had them drifting helplessly toward some sunken reefs—much to the dismay of the cannibals at shore—who were already lighting fires in anticipation of the preys they were soon to catch.

God answers prayer... 210
Luke 18:7 · John 15:7 · Acts 12:5 · James 5:15

A believer refused to contribute any money to a fund that was to be used for an idolatrous work aimed at protecting the houses on his street from an imminent fire disaster. He chose instead, to pray to God for deliverance and so it was for him; for even as the fires raged; consuming his next neighbour's, his house was miraculously spared by the God to whom he prayed!

God answers prayer... 211
Luke 18:7 · John 15:7 · Acts 12:5 · James 5:15

As the village of Nowar was being approached by an armed group of murderous savages, but as the people offered prayers to God in their panic-stricken state, He heard and sent help!

In what was a clear divine intervention, two Kings—who had finalized plans to banish Christian missionaries from their land and thus bring the work of God to ruin—died just before they could carry out their evil plans paving the way for more Christian-friendly successors.

When a famine struck China, God's people took the opportunity presented the same people who loathed them—the selflessness of the Christian Spirit and by so doing were enabled to win many souls to Christ.

Dr. Duff was skeptical about educating women in India, but today there are thousands of women being educated there. Christian women played a crucial role in unlocking the doors to Zenana, leading to a rapid and remarkable transformation in India that astonished even the most insightful observers.

During his time in Fiji from 1835 to 1885, James Calvert witnessed incredible transformation. Starting with the burial of victims of cannibalism, he eventually saw the same people partake in communion, celebrating their newfound faith. By the end of fifty years, there were 1,300 churches in Fiji and a significant majority of the population were regular churchgoers, showing a complete shift from their previous practices.

Johann Gerhard Oncken, a former servant who opened a bookshop in Hamburg, became a pastor after being baptized by Dr. Barnas Sears and played a key role in spreading the gospel, facing persecution and imprisonment but ultimately gaining the right to worship freely. Over 25 years, he established 65 churches with 750 stations and nearly 10,000 members, influencing millions with Bibles and tracts, illustrating the impact one person can have in sharing the message of Christianity.

Acts 26:16-18

John G. Paton spent three and a half years on Aniwa, transforming the society completely through his missionary work. His efforts turned the cannibal island into a civilized community with Christian values, overcoming enormous challenges and demonstrating the power of faith.

Acts 19:18-19

Despite initial resistance from the natives, when Thomas Powell left Elijah, a native evangelist, on Nanumaga island, the people's beliefs transformed significantly over two years. Initially worshiping multiple idol-gods, the entire population eventually gathered to worship Jehovah in a place of worship, and even the children were attending school, resulting in a complete shift in Nanumagan society's culture and values.

Mark 16:15 · Acts 1:8 · Acts 6:7 · Colossians 1:23

William Williams, alongside with Mrs. Williams, faced immense challenges in spreading Christianity, such as confronting idolatry, infanticide, and heathenism in places like Nanumaga, India, and Raiatea. Through their unwavering faith and dedication, they were able to convert thousands of idolaters, bringing civilization, religious conversion, and social progress to places like Raiatea and Samoa, without relying on government assistance.

Luke 11:5-10

In the fight for ending slavery in England and America, the efforts of God-fearing women in Boston, like the praying saints, played a significant role. Despite facing hostility and threats, they stayed committed to their cause, believing in the power of prayer to bring about change—a belief eventually confirmed when slavery was abolished for four million people.

Acts 1:14 · Acts 4:31

In "Revival Lectures," Charles G. Finney recounts the story of a poor, sick man in Western New York who prayed for the salvation of an unconverted merchant. The merchant was converted, leading to a great revival, demonstrating the man's impact on others through his steadfast prayers for churches and missionary stations. Despite his physical limitations, his prayers were heard by God, resulting in revivals in the exact order of his prayers, even reaching places like Ceylon.

Luke 11:5-10

During a time of despair in the mission to Tahiti, the London Missionary Society considered abandoning the mission due to lack of conversions, but some, like Dr. Haweis and Matthew Wilks, believed in the power of prayer and continued support for the missionaries. A miraculous event occurred when two ships unknowingly crossed paths in the ocean, one carrying letters of encouragement from London and the other carrying news of a mighty work of God in Tahiti, including the surrender of idols by the converted people, demonstrating the power of faith and prayer.

Luke 18:7 · John 15:7 · Acts 12:5 · James 5:15

In 1872, the Church Missionary Society prayed for more men to join their mission force. Over the next five years, they sent out 112 men in response to their prayers, doubling the number of missionaries they had previously sent out. Then, in 1880, the society asked for prayers for more money, and within months, they received enough donations to cover all their financial needs and even expand their work, inspiring many young university men to dedicate themselves to missionary work.

Walking Together Press is a non-profit publishing company devoted to supporting grassroots libraries in Africa through global book sales and through providing free library editions.

To read our story, to see our catalog, and to learn more about how you can help us in our mission, visit our website at:

walkingtogether.press